South-East Asian Social Science Monographs

Development Dilemmas in Rural Thailand

Development Dilemmas in Rural Thailand

Philip Hirsch

SINGAPORE
OXFORD UNIVERSITY PRESS
OXFORD NEW YORK
1990

Oxford University Press
Oxford New York Toronto
Delhi Bombay Calcutta Madras Karachi
Petaling Jaya Singapore Hong Kong Tokyo
Nairobi Dar es Salaam Cape Town
Melbourne Auckland
and associated companies in
Berlin Ibadan

Published in the United States by
Oxford University Press, Inc., New York

ISBN 0 19 588968 1

British Library Cataloguing in Publication Data

Hirsch, Philip, 1957–
Development dilemmas in rural Thailand – (South-East Asian social science monographs).
1. Thailand. Rural communities. Social change
I. Title II. Series
307.7209593

ISBN 0–19–588968–1

Library of Congress Cataloging-in-Publication Data

Hirsch, Philip, 1957–
Development dilemmas in rural Thailand/Philip Hirsch.
p. cm. — (South-East Asian social science monographs)
Includes bibliographical references.
ISBN 0–19–588968–1
1. Rural development—Thailand. 2. Rural development—Thailand—Case studies. I. Title. II. Series.
HN700.55.Z9C634 1990
307.1'412'09593–dc20
90–35056
CIP

Printed in Malaysia by Peter Chong Printers Sdn. Bhd.
Published by Oxford University Press Pte. Ltd.,
Unit 221, Ubi Avenue 4, Singapore 1440

To my father

Foreword

THE dilemmas, or contradictions, of development in rural Thailand are paradigmatic for much of the rest of the world. This study is set in a particular local context of agriculture in Lan Sak District of Uthaithani Province, west central Thailand, and yet it addresses the global issue of 'loss of local control over resources necessary for production entailed in an incorporative development strategy in which participation is invoked as a means of affording access to wider societal resources' (p. 224). The earnest official discourse of development stresses co-operation and participation in a supposed unitary strategy of development for all. In practice, this is contradicted fundamentally by processes of individualization, monetization and differentiation of social relations which the present study documents.

The problem, which is at the same time economic and philosophical, moral and political, is still basically that posed by the author's distinguished father, the late Fred Hirsch in his fine book, *Social Limits to Growth* (Routledge & Kegan Paul, 1977): 'the problem of translating individual economic improvement into overall economic improvement'. It is the paradox of economic growth, which is still the other name of development in most of its manifestations: even as it augments the well-being of an increasingly large minority and holds out an alluring but meretricious promise of distributive justice to come, it leads to social scarcity *for all* (viz., notably, environmental degradation) and an undermining of social solidarity.

This book has a special timeliness and should contribute to current debates about the government's role in rural development, the industrializing of Thailand, and perhaps, above all, the ecological debates about social control of the world's forests. A study of recently settled villages on the periphery of the central plains and at the edge of the forested mountain ranges which run north and south along the Thailand–Burma border, it is largely a history of the opening and closing of a frontier.

To a European used to the idea of 'village' connoting long settlement and pre-modern times, it comes as a surprise to learn that most of Thailand's 60,000 or so villages have been settled in the twentieth century. This rapid settlement has been a primary cause of deforestation, nowhere more so than in the province studied where the area under forest declined from 73 per cent to less than half that in the twenty-five years from 1961. The contradiction could hardly be starker: as a few accumulate, and poor farmers attempt to regain control over, land—the basic factor of production—by forest encroachment, there is a vicious circle of declining soil fertility, environmental degradation, poverty, migration, and yet more deforestation.

'Incorporative development', the state-led version of participation in a rural development strategy, as it is experienced by the poorer rural producer 'takes the form of increasing demands on his or her time, rising levels of debt, higher levels of uncertainty regarding means of livelihood, and decreased sanction over local leaders' (p. 230). It is not a form of participation which redresses inequalities of social power and increases popular control over livelihood. This study considers the prospects and possibilities for the latter definition coming to prevail in Thailand. In this, it draws from and develops the debate about participation to which in the 1980s the United Nations Research Institute for Social Development (UNRISD) notably contributed in its 'Popular Participation Programme'. The chapter on 'Co-operation and Development' argues, I would hope definitively, that on the one hand neither collectivism nor individualism is an inherently determined characteristic of either 'peasants' or Thai farmers, and on the other hand that both may be found in good measure, varying in locally and historically explicable ways.

This is not a book of predictions or prescriptions, but there is at the end a qualified optimism, somewhat against the grain, a discerning of spaces for legitimate action and a growing awareness of the rightness of the stronger sense of 'participation'. There is also a call for 'external developers', both NGO and government, to re-examine their status and function and consider taking on a more responsive and educative role in a rural development strategy undertaken by rural producers themselves, rather than by others for them in a hierarchical and domineering manner. If one of the many 'dilemmas of development' is the absence of a consensus as to what the rural development problem is, or what the problems are, this study argues persuasively for a problem firmly rooted in issues of social power and terms of control.

It is my hope that Phil Hirsch's book will be read as much for how it is done as for what it says. It is not just that its clarity and succinctness of exposition make it a valuable teaching text. He himself acknowledges the insights gained from a 'cross-disciplinary perspective', namely the combination of geography and social anthropology. For example, from one, we have approaches to spatial, environmental, and material resource issues; from the other, a concern with language and humour, with questions of local knowledge, local agency, and the subjective experience of villagers. In addition there is the concern to place the local and contemporary within a historical framework of the political economy of the region. And I know from a short visit to Lan Sak District with the author in 1985 of his excellent command of the Thai language and, over a long period of fieldwork, his readiness, as he puts it, 'to step as often as possible into the rubber flip-flops of a Lan Sak villager'.

Department of Anthropology ANDREW TURTON
School of Oriental and African Studies
University of London
April 1990

Preface and Acknowledgements

THIS book, like the thesis on which it is based, could not have been written without the help, hospitality, and insights of a more than usually large range of people. The people the book is principally about have been instrumental in shaping my ideas of what development is about, whom it is for, and where its hidden agendas lie. Some of these people are quite conscious of having helped to educate me in the range of big issues and little everyday goings on that are inherent to an understanding of the way in which development affects individuals and communities. Others have been more bemused at my presence, conversation, questions, interest in their lives, and intrusions on their time during and since the main period of fieldwork for this study.

I first arrived in Lan Sak in October 1983 on the back of a motor cycle, after a very bumpy last 40 km along what was then a gravel road. My main period of residence in the district was from February 1984 until July 1985. Acharn Sompong Suthiwong of the Nong Kha Yang Foundation for Rural Development was instrumental in getting me ensconced, but I am indebted to him for more than just the practicalities of helping select a site for fieldwork. Sompong also provided numerous and valuable insights, criticisms, and inspiration by example that kept me thinking and kept me going during what was occasionally—though not as often as I had expected—an isolated existence.

That my existence in Lan Sak was so rarely an isolated one is due to the immense hospitality of my village hosts. I stayed with a family in each of the villages of Bung Khiew and Ban Mai, and it is to Udorn, Somjai, Toedsak, Kitti, and Wilai Butsingh, and to Lamai, Lom, Kriangsak, Mali, and Man Wutikorn that I would like to offer my greatest thanks for extended hospitality. However, I am also grateful to numerous other village hosts in whose houses I slept, whose meals I shared, and whose time I encroached on. To all these village uncles and aunts I owe a great debt.

For the book's conceptual basis, Andrew Turton has been my key influence, in his written work on and commitment to the people of rural Thailand, and through practical and intellectual advice offered at the School of Oriental and African Studies (SOAS). Many other friends, colleagues, and teachers at SOAS and at Thai universities have provided stimulating discussion and criticism that have helped me to make sense of fieldwork data and to rework ideas.

I would also like to state my appreciation of the stimulating environment of the Geography Department at Sydney University, where I have been since February 1987. The thesis on which this book is based was started in a department of geography but written in a department of anthropology, while the substantial revision was done back in a geographical ethos. The insights gained and culs-de-sac avoided by a cross-disciplinary perspective have been invaluable. I would like to thank Kay Foster and Janette Brennan for helping reformat computer disks, and Richie Howitt in particular for helping reformat the cerebral disk back toward a human geographical mind-set—especially concerning the importance and richness of the relationship between global process and local response.

Soh's contribution has been the most valuable of all—a shared life where the work of each is supported by a common set of values, conversations, jokes, and by differences that serve to enrich rather than to divide. I look forward to her comments on this finished product.

Department of Geography PHILIP HIRSCH
University of Sydney
May 1989

Contents

Foreword vii
Preface and Acknowledgements ix
Tables xiii
Figures xiv
Plates xv
Abbreviations and Glossary xvi

1. Introduction 1
Development and Rural Thailand 1
Local Context of Study 3

2. Development and Developers 8
Rural Development 9
The Ethos of Development 10
Social Formation and Development in Rural Thailand 16
Participatory Development 28
Conclusion 30

3. The Dynamics of Forest Settlement 32
Extent and Pattern of Forest Settlement 33
Forest Settlement and Agricultural Expansion 39
Socio-political Aspects of Forest Settlement 47
Conclusion 53

4. Opening and Closing the Western Frontier 56
Settlement of Lan Sak 56
Cultivation in Lan Sak 63
Two Lan Sak Villages 67
Change in Frontier Communities 74
Development in Lan Sak 81
Conclusion 85

5. Production, Differentiation, Dearth 89
Production and Rural Differentiation 90
Control over Resources for Production 92
Production and Differentiation in Lan Sak 117
Response to Resource Shortage 139
Conclusion 143

6. Co-operation and Development 148
Collectivism and Individualism in Peasant Economy 149
Development and the Concept of *Klum* 158
Co-operative Development in Lan Sak 163

Potential for and Obstacles to Co-operation 176
Conclusion 180

7. Participation and Power in Development 183
Participation and Development 184
Revised Concepts of Participation 194
Issues of Control 201
Issues of Power 212
Participation and Rural Development in Perspective 219
Conclusion 221

8. Dilemmas of Participatory Development 224
A Participatory Development Dilemma 225
Obstacles to Participation 226
Spaces for Action 228
Implications of Participatory Development 229

Bibliography 232
Index 240

Tables

2.1 Relative Incomes in Thailand's Regions, 1960 and 1979 11
2.2 Distribution of Land by Size of Holding, 1978 26
3.1 Increase in Thai Cultivated Area, 1950–1978 42
3.2 Agricultural Investment, 1966 and 1974, and Productivity in Asia, 1969 and 1978 45
3.3 Expansion of the Thai Road Network, 1950–1980 50
5.1 Production Possibilities for Rice and Maize in Lan Sak 93
5.2 Tenant Characteristics in Ban Dong and Ban Mai 97
5.3 Access to Credit in Ban Dong and Ban Mai 100
5.4 Priority in Debt Repayment in Ban Dong and Ban Mai as Ranked by Twenty-four Debtors 104
5.5a Proportion of Cash Expenses Incurred at Each Stage of Cultivation for Various Crops: Ban Dong and Ban Mai 106
5.5b Proportion of Cash Expenses Incurred at Each Stage of Cultivation for Various Crops: Ban Dong 107
5.5c Proportion of Cash Expenses Incurred at Each Stage of Cultivation for Various Crops: Ban Mai 108
5.6a Proportion of Non-household Labour which is Hired or Reciprocal at Different Stages of Cultivation for Various Crops: Ban Dong and Ban Mai 112
5.6b Proportion of Non-household Labour which is Hired or Reciprocal at Different Stages of Cultivation for Various Crops: Ban Dong 113
5.6c Proportion of Non-household Labour which is Hired or Reciprocal at Different Stages of Cultivation for Various Crops: Ban Mai 113
5.7 Percentage of Households Using Only Own and Reciprocal Labour in Labour-intensive Stages of Production for Various Crops 114
5.8 Ban Dong Cropping 118
5.9 Ban Mai Cropping 127
5.10 Land Distribution in Ban Dong and Ban Mai 136
5.11 Control over Tillage in Ban Dong and Ban Mai 137
6.1 Permanent Groups in Ban Dong and Ban Mai 165
7.1 Crop Prices Received by Farmers in Lan Sak, 1984–1986 208

Figures

1.1 Location Map: Uthaithani and Places Referred to in the Text 4
2.1 Local Administration and Rural Development Structures in Thailand 17
4.1 Location Map: Lan Sak and Places Referred to in the Text 57
4.2 Communications in Uthaithani 58
4.3 Deforestation in Uthaithani and Lan Sak 61
4.4 Topography of Lan Sak, and Location of Ban Dong and Ban Mai 68
4.5 Ban Dong: Topography, Roads, and Settlement 69
4.6 Ban Mai: Topography, Roads, and Settlement 72

Plates

Between pages 110 and 111

1 Huai Kha Khaeng Sanctuary: Lan Sak's last remaining forest.
2 *Yaang* oil tapping.
3 Ban Dong Bridge destroyed by floods on the Tap Salao River.
4 Continued clearing in the hills behind Ban Mai.
5 Dry season fields near Ban Mai, cleared after 1978.
6 Ban Mai agriculture depends heavily on purchased inputs.
7 Farmers at Bank for Agriculture and Agricultural Co-operatives (BAAC).
8 Harvesting after drought in Bung Khiew.
9 *Ao raeng* (reciprocal) labour in Bung Khiew for rice harvest.
10 Measuring rice for milling.
11 Wealthier villager's house in Ban Mai.
12 Poorer villager's house in Ban Mai.
13 Isolated homestead in Bung Khiew.
14 Official symbolism of development in Ban Dong.
15 Ban Dong *kamnan* at village meeting.
16 Co-operation in Bung Khiew: Strengthening the bridge into the village.

Abbreviations and Glossary

ALRO	Agricultural Land Reform Office
ao raeng	reciprocal labour
BAAC	Bank for Agriculture and Agricultural Co-operatives
baht	unit of Thai currency (1 baht = US$0.04)
BDFA	Ban Dong Farmers' Association
CDD	Community Development Department
chanood	full freehold land title deed
chaobaan	villager
chaonaa	rice farmer/cultivator
chaorai	non-rice crop farmer/cultivator
CIDA	Canadian International Development Agency
CPT	Communist Party of Thailand
DAE	Department of Agricultural Extension
FAO	Food and Agriculture Organization (of the United Nations)
FFT	Farmers' Federation of Thailand
FMO	Farmers' Marketing Organization
HYV	High Yielding Variety
IBRD	International Bank for Reconstruction and Development
ISOC	Internal Security Operations Command
jaang	hire
ka	fixed payment rental
kamnan	subdistrict head
kanphathanaa	development
khaek	guest
khon to	traditional leader
klum	group
kwien	volume measure of rice (1 *kwien* = 2,000 litres)
LDAP	Local Development Assistance Programme
LDC	Less Developed Country
LDD	Land Development Department
LSAC	Lan Sak Agricultural Co-operative
NESDB	National Economic and Social Development Board
NGO	Non-governmental organization
NKYFRD	Nong Kha Yang Foundation for Rural Development
NS3	*Nangseu Samkhan* 3 (exploitation testimonial title deed)

NSO	National Statistical Office
paa	forest
phuu yai baan	village head
rai	measure of land area (1 *rai* = 0.16 hectare)
REGP	Rural Employment Generation Programme
RFD	Royal Forestry Department
RID	Royal Irrigation Department
tambon	subdistrict; cluster of villages
tang	volume measure of rice or maize (1 *tang* = 20 litres)
TC	*tambon* council
TPC	Thai Plywood Company
UNRISD	United Nations Research Institute for Social Development
UPRC	Uthaithani Pig Raisers' Co-operative
VC	village committee
WHO	World Health Organization
yaang	Dipterocarp tree tapped for its resin

1
Introduction

THE term 'development' covers a wide range of processes of change that impinge on every level of society. At one level, we speak of developing countries as if countries were independent agents, homogeneous entities determining a particular path of change for themselves. At another level, the processes subsumed by development have a direct impact on individual people. They also affect communities, regions, social classes, and other social and spatial groupings.

An important common feature of development is its incorporative nature, by which peripheral formations are drawn into the mainstream of a wider society, polity, and economy. There is a constant tension between development as a liberating force giving people more control over their own lives and access to a better standard of living, and development as a constraining influence in the sense that decisions affecting people's livelihoods are made at an ever more remote level. Thus development involves a shifting dialectic between local and central authority, between peripheral and central populations, and between the poles of all those other dichotomies included in the metaphor of under-developed and developed status.

Development at a local level is not therefore a simple microcosm of changes taking place on a higher plane. Rather, development of a local community reflects a changing relationship *with* (not just within) the macrocosm, since the latter is more than a sum of similar constituent parts. Changes taking place in the local arena are in turn shaped by this shifting relationship, and in consequence a number of dilemmas are created for development of rural communities. The present study is concerned with the experience of two communities in rural Thailand, not simply as a means of enhancing the detail of development experience that a local study affords, but also in order to highlight the communities' altered relationship with the wider system implied by development and the way in which this in turn impinges on intracommunity relations.

Development and Rural Thailand

Of all the countries commonly included in the developing world, Thailand has experienced one of the most spectacular rates of change in recent years. The economy has been substantially restructured as a result of increased involvement of capital in agriculture, nascent industrialization, and a rapid growth of the service sector. Rightly or wrongly, Thailand is often classed as the country next in line to join the select ranks of newly industrialized countries (NICs),[1] a status that has become almost synonymous with graduation from the developing to the developed world.

Despite its apparently advanced position on the development path, Thailand is still a largely rural country. Nearly four out of five Thais live in the countryside. Although agricultural production accounts for only one-sixth of the Gross National Product (GNP), the agricultural sector still employs two-thirds of the population. This is an indication both of the importance of rural production in the livelihoods of most Thais and of the inequalities that have arisen as a result of past and recent development strategies.

Historically, the land area that is now Thailand has been sparsely populated, and the population has been unevenly distributed. Large areas were until the twentieth century virtually uninhabited wilderness, including parts of the Central Plains that today form the country's heartland. An important process of development in Thailand has been the settlement of outlying regions and subsequent integration of these areas into the national polity and economy. At no time has this integration been pursued by the centre with such energy as during the period following 1960, when development became the principal national goal, and nor at any time has settlement of outlying areas been as rapid.

Rural development emerged as a concern in Thailand as a result of the uneven development of the national economy after the start of national development planning in 1961 (Saneh, 1983). While Bangkok and surrounding areas reaped the material fruits of rapid growth, peripheral parts of the country showed limited involvement in the national economy (IBRD, 1980: 36ff.). The imbalances that this created were behind some of the political changes of the 1970s, and the Fourth, Fifth, and Sixth National Economic and Social Development Plans have emphasized the need for rural development. A key element in the Fifth Plan (1982–6) was a poverty eradication programme which identified one-third of the country's districts as targets for special attention. All these districts are in peripheral areas, and most have been recently settled.

Rapid settlement of the Thai periphery and its subsequent integration as part of the national economic and political space is not only a fundamental part of processes of development in rural areas; it is also a primary cause of deforestation, and this has been especially so since the 1960s. The association between deforestation and development is more than incidental. Diversification of the agricultural economy and expansion of populations into peripheral areas has taken place largely at the expense of the country's forests. As a consequence, the social, economic, and political dilemmas thrown up by development have assumed another dimension, one that has been recognized belatedly world-wide as integral to problems of development—the ecological dimension. It is a dimension with profound implications for the fate of the poorest and most marginal groups in rural areas, who rely more directly on forest resources for their livelihoods than any other group (Khan, 1986), and yet whose access to these resources is diminished as a result of incorporation into a wider system.

The details and implications of this incorporative development for peripheral areas and their inhabitants are little recorded. Most local-level study has been of established communities in long-settled areas. Yet most Thai villages have been established during the present century as part of the process of settlement. They have subsequently been drawn into the wider society by a number of means. The experience of incorporation under the guise of rural development in peripheral rural communities forms the background to this study, whose objective is to provide insight into the dilemmas of development as experienced materially and subjectively at a local level.

Local Context of Study

In the 1960s, Lan Sak was a densely forested and sparsely settled outpost of Ban Rai District in western Thailand (see Figures 1.1 and 4.1). In terms of area, Ban Rai covered more than half of the province of Uthaithani, but it held only a few per cent of the provincial population. The provincial centre of Uthaithani was a remote three days away by cart from the isolated forest communities of Lan Sak. Uthaithani itself was an outlying province on the edges of the Central Plains and was still only accessible by means of a ferry across the Chaophraya River. Lan Sak was in every sense peripheral.

By the mid-1980s when the author arrived in Lan Sak, the area had been mainly cleared of forest. Lan Sak was an administrative district in its own right. An asphalt road linking Lan Sak with Uthaithani was completed in 1985. With a bridge linking Uthaithani with the Asia Highway, the journey from Lan Sak to Bangkok was reduced to five hours. In most senses of the term, Lan Sak had been 'developed'.

While implications of Lan Sak's development are the immediate subject of this study, the wider significance of Lan Sak's experience is manifold. It is a chapter in a process of settlement and linkage with the mainstream polity and economy that has occurred in various local and historical contexts. It is a story that reveals important linkages between ecological, social, economic, and political processes of change. Above all, it is a situation that reflects some of the dilemmas of development confronting previously peripheral areas and their inhabitants when they are incorporated into a wider system over which they have limited control.

In one respect, becoming part of a wider system is part and parcel of the objective of participation, a theme that has become a catchword in much recent development literature and in many development programmes. Yet participation is a theme with many different interpretations. An immediate contradiction, which poses itself as a dilemma underlying individual and community strategies for development in Lan Sak and much more widely, is participation on the one hand as a

Figure 1.1
Location Map: Uthaithani and Places Referred to in the Text

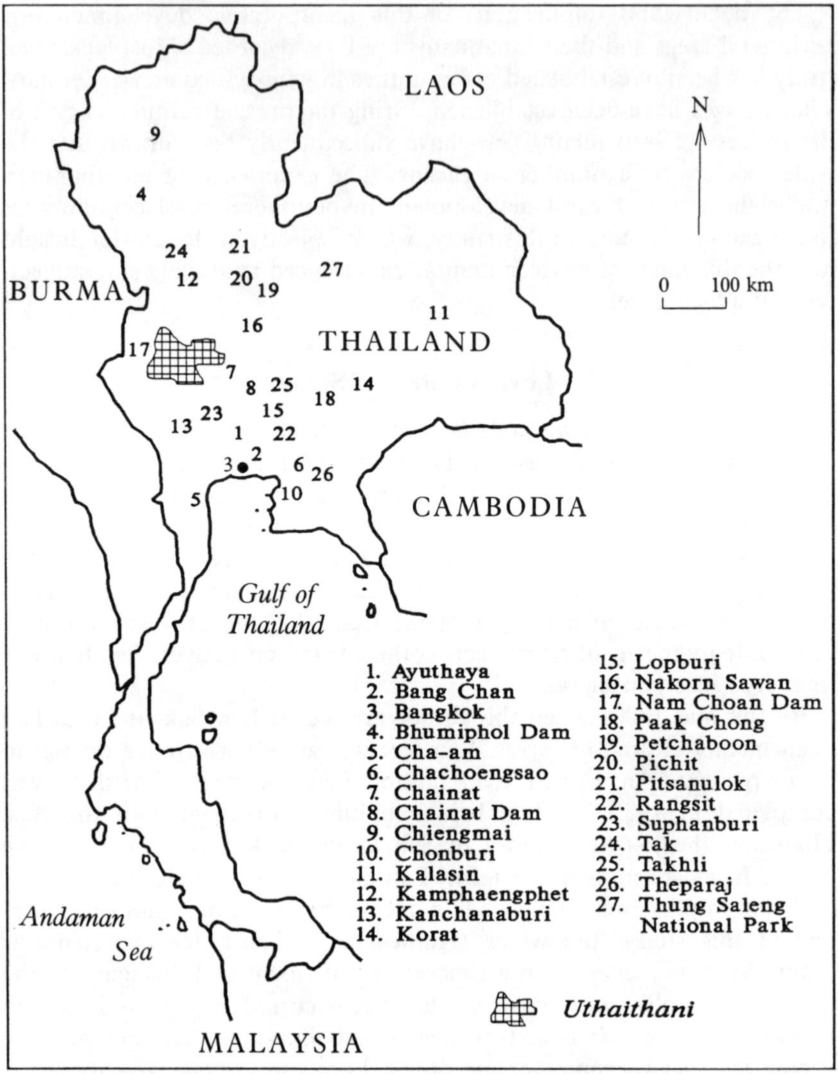

means of gaining access to and control over a wider system that is imposing itself on communities and the lives of individuals, and on the other hand as a means of maintaining or increasing self-reliance through a participatory rural development strategy.

A common but basic obstacle to recognition of this dilemma is treatment of communities as undifferentiated entities. The treatment of a territory, whether it be a community, district, or larger aggregation, as a unit for policy action fictitiously assumes a homogeneity of interest within that geographical area. Many strategies of development persist which hold that increasing the total monetary value of production in a defined area—be it nation, region, or village—necessarily increases the self-reliance of that area. By a similar token, treatment of the territorial community (village) as a unit equates community participation with incorporation into the wider system. Indicators of low gross regional product become indicators of low self-reliance; peripherality becomes the antithesis of participation. This is in manifest contradiction to the experience of most rural producers in the villages under study.

In contrast to many studies of development, neither a bird's-eye nor a worm's-eye view is taken in this book. Indeed, this is in many ways a false dichotomy that is compounded in the field of development by conflict between 'top-down' and 'bottom-up' approaches. Since the study is concerned primarily with the effects of integration into a larger formation on small communities and individuals within them, the interest is one of an outsider looking in, while the subject of interest is the insider looking out. Consequently the mode of description is omniscient (in the literary rather than epistemological sense!) and set in terms sometimes alien to modes of thought of the communities involved. Yet as far as possible, the perspective taken is that of villagers, peasants, rural producers, rural poor, or whatever term is applied to the women and men who make up the majority of most village populations and indeed of the population of Thailand and other developing countries. It is in an attempt to consider the experience of incorporative development in terms of what it means to such people in determining their own lives that the study opts to step as often as possible into the rubber flip-flops of a Lan Sak villager.[2]

Adoption of such a perspective has three main implications. First, the subjective experience of villagers and other actors is of inherent importance and is not merely an indicator of underlying processes. This means that local discourse is of key interest and is consequently drawn on frequently. Words, phrases, and longer statements made by local people often convey more than an outsider's abstract analysis of experiences, motivations or responses to change. Except for words or terms that carry a connotation specific to the local context, direct translation is made without a Thai gloss. Where meanings are specific to a certain interpretation, quotation marks are used.

Second, the life of a villager is not divided neatly into parcels that conform with academic disciplines, so the study does not limit itself to a well-defined aspect of village life (compare with Chambers, 1983: 22–3). The emphasis on production takes into account a distinguishing characteristic of peasant production, which is that it cannot readily be divorced from consumption or other aspects of livelihood.

Third, issues connected with rural development play an important but not a dominant role in villagers' daily lives. This means that care must be taken to see development issues as they fit into the broader schema of village life. It is necessary to recognize the ultimate indivisibility of a livelihood in which production, consumption, health, education, debt, and so on are intimately bound up.

The above notwithstanding, the local study is placed as much as possible in the context of broader development debates. Within these debates, there are two broad strains which run parallel but do not often enough intersect. The first is the discussion of development as a set of historical processes, structures, and interrelationships. The second sees development as a range of interventions, policy options, and programmes. The first debate covers opposing analyses of social, economic, and political change in the developing world. It is framed in terms of broad concepts such as modernization, dependency, modes of production, capitalist transformation, and class process. The second debate is essentially one of technique. It covers policy orientation, institutional design, bottom-up versus top-down, and so on.

At the risk of falling between two stools, this study attempts on the one hand to bring these together by relating the programme side of rural development to broader changes in the social formation, and on the other to suggest how an understanding of these changes provides insight into the directions new local-level initiatives can take, or are prevented from taking. The determinism that is sometimes a product of the first approach (Rostovian and Marxian economism alike) fails to allow for human agency, while the technocracy or introversion that is associated with the alternative shuts out broader forces that cannot be ignored (see Worsley, 1984). Rural development initiatives must be seen in terms of processes such as State formation, establishment of centralized control, capitalist development of agriculture, or alternatively of reaction or resistance to and negation of dominant processes. The aim of participatory development is, surely, for people as subjects to devise means to establish control over the way in which these broader forces affect their lives.

This book is a study of the development experience of two communities as they are incorporated into the mainstream Thai polity and economy. The organization of this book follows this concern with two scales of analysis, noting both the context of change in the wider system and the details of change at the local level. To this end, the following two chapters provide a conceptual and historical background to the development and settlement of outlying areas of Thailand. The fourth and fifth chapters turn to the case of Lan Sak, and the remainder of the book examines development dilemmas created as a consequence of the interaction of local and broader processes that have been discussed.

Chapter 2 begins with a consideration of rural development from a theoretical perspective. The place of development in wider processes of change is outlined, and an ethos of development is related to ideologies, discourse, and structures at the local level. Participation is considered as a dialectic between different groups of developers and those they set out to develop, and each of these is identified within the current social formation and rural development framework.

Chapter 3 sets the study in historical and geographical context. The processes, patterns, and significance of settlement in recently settled forest areas are considered, with special emphasis on the fringes of the

Central Plains. The importance of forest settlement in agricultural development in particular and rural development in general is discussed in historical and contemporary perspective.

The specific situation of settlement in one district of western Thailand is outlined in Chapter 4. Environmental considerations and their interaction with broader aspects of production are shown to be important. The villages of Ban Dong and Ban Mai are introduced, as are the local developers and those they seek to 'develop' in terms of the framework set out in Chapter 2. There is a preliminary exposition of state, non-governmental organization (NGO), and indigenous actors.

Chapter 5 provides a detailed analysis of production and control over resources in the two study villages. Changing production relations as part of incorporation into the wider spatial economy are associated with particular forms of differentiation among producers, and specific determinants of access to and control over resources for production are detailed in this changing situation. Responses to resource shortage are shown to have serious environmental consequences and to be increasingly oriented outside the local community.

The way in which rural development in its various forms applies to increasing control over livelihood by various actors is approached in Chapter 6 via the issue of co-operation. A contradiction between individualistic ethos and co-operative programmes is examined in light of broader debates on collectivism versus individualism in peasant society. The approach of various actors towards co-operation is used to show how it relates to the concept of control.

In a reconsideration of participation, Chapter 7 brings together the themes and data that have been covered. The two issues of control and power are shown to be fundamental in the conceptualization of participatory development. Specific aspects of these themes are discussed, drawing on preceding accounts of rural development and changing production relations. Specific local projects are reviewed in light of this new perspective.

The concluding chapter, Chapter 8, reiterates the dilemma of participatory development. Obstacles to participation are acknowledged, but spaces for action are also highlighted.

1. Newly industrialized countries: already included in this group are the four 'little tigers' of Asia—Hong Kong, Singapore, South Korea, and Taiwan. Also often included are Mexico and Brazil.

2. This is an appropriate position in which to stand for two reasons. First, flip-flops are the normal footwear of Lan Sak villagers. Second, as anyone with experience of village life can attest to, they are convenient above all in the ease with which they can be taken off and put back on when ascending and descending a house, and this ease of movement in and out of a villager's shoes is likewise useful for the perspective taken in this study.

2
Development and Developers

THE concept of development as something a country, a society, a people, or an economy does—or has done to it—is recent, but the processes behind it are not. The post-war emergence of development as an issue and a science was at once separate from pre-existing disciplines and yet initially based on the premise that the developing or underdeveloped societies must achieve certain transitions that had brought the developed world up to its high levels of productivity and consumption within integrated nation-states. As a result, development has served in one sense as a metaphor for underlying processes occurring at various levels of rapidly changing societies.

Most of these processes can be found in the history of what is called the developed world: state formation, national integration, growth, capitalist transformation, urbanization, industrialization, to name but a few prominent ones. Needless to say, this does not imply that such processes take the same form at present as they did in earlier developers (that is, countries, societies, or economies which developed earlier), to use the term retrospectively, given the very different historical specificities, different cultural and societal backgrounds, and new constraints imposed by the world system that are themselves a product of earlier transitions. The relevant point is rather that such processes are now subsumed under the generic term 'development', which has found its own niche in the ideology, discourse, and structures not only of international bureaucratic organizations and Western universities as is commonly supposed, but also within the domestic framework of developing countries themselves. The corollary of this extended 'rediscovery of the idea of progress under the name development' (Hainsworth, 1982: 83) is that a study of certain aspects of development within a national or even a local and highly specific context can reveal a great deal about some of the processes for which development serves as an intentional or unintentional front.

That Thailand, for example, is conceived of as a developing country is not just due to a place in the global division between less developed countries (LDCs) and (more) developed countries ((M)DCs), underdeveloped and (over)developed, poor and rich. It is as much to do with domestic pressures and a domestic awareness. Discourse centering on development has found its way into political, administrative, economic and everyday aspects of life in rural as well as urban areas (Demaine,

1986). Such a preoccupation shows little in itself about the intended nature or direction of development, but it does make the development issue a live and pervasive one. In its praxis and discourse, therefore, development reflects much about the current polity and social formation.

One common developmental theme, popular participation, is particularly important as it concerns the relationship of individuals and groups with the larger society and its resources. While the present objective is to show what participation means to different groups at different levels in Thailand, much of the analysis can be extended more generally. The theme has been applied particularly strongly in the Thai context (IBRD, 1980; Thawithong, 1984; Turton, 1984a), but a perusal of the international development literature reveals a heavy and growing emphasis on participation by analysts and practitioners alike (FAO, 1973, 1981; Pearse and Stiefel, 1979; Goulet, 1989).

Two facets of participation motivate the present study. The first is the wide variety of interpretations and applications of the term that makes it an important subject of study for understanding the motivations of the various actors on the Thai rural development stage. The second concerns the peripherality of the communities under study, since participation at any level implies involvement of individuals in a wider formation. Thus the relationship between participatory rural development and the incorporation of peripheral communities provides a key point of interest.

Rural Development

The process by which previously isolated agrarian communities become part of a wider society underlies much of what is now termed rural development. This process has both temporal and spatial dimensions. The temporal dimension is commonly referred to in terms such as 'modernization', 'movement from a backward to an advanced state', and even 'catching up'. The spatial dimension of this aspect of development is spoken of as 'integration', 'linkage' or 'incorporation'. More often, these dimensions are combined so that physical isolation implies backwardness, while proximity to the metropolitan core represents, for the community, an implicit modernity. Under such terms, a village develops both with changes in the system as a whole over time and by change in its position within the system.

Only by consideration of these two dimensions can the issue of development of a peripheral community in Thailand be understood. For more than a century, the principal dynamic in Thai agriculture and demography has been a steady expansion in the cultivated area facilitated by the establishment of new communities at forest fringes. Following settlement, these communities have seen a gradual integration within the wider spatial economy and polity, such that a majority of the approximately 60,000 villages now registered have undergone this type of transformation during the present century.

Such changes are very recent and thus highly visible in the villages of Ban Dong and Ban Mai. Both are in a recently settled forest area on the north-western periphery of the Central Plains (Figure 1.1). One is a lowland village whose economy is dominated by rice cultivation, the other an upland village whose economy is almost exclusively given over to cash cropping. One is a spontaneously settled community with limited state involvement, the other is a partially planned settlement affected by the state land reform programme. Both villages have experienced rapid transformation as a result of the collective incorporative processes subsumed under rural development.

An important aspect of this transformation is the way in which it has affected access to and control over resources. While rural development is often posited as a means for residents of small communities to participate in control over resources of the wider society, the access to village institutions and resources afforded to State, capital, and their local representatives by rural development at once diminishes control for the majority of villagers. These contradictory processes have both material and discursive aspects. The contradiction thus outlined is vital to understanding changes internal to the communities under study, so that rural development cannot be examined independently of an analysis of broader issues of control and the exercise of power.

The Ethos of Development

In Thailand, changes that are induced as part of the transformation of the economy and the extended role of the State have created an ethos of development with its own ideological bases, discourses, and structures. Since the First National Development Plan was formulated in 1961, development through economic growth within a context of national security has been a conscious national priority. To the extent that growth and development can be equated, moreover, the Thai national economy has fared well when compared with other developing economies. A cumulative Gross National Product (GNP) growth rate of 8.6 per cent was achieved between 1959 and 1969 (Ingram, 1971: 223), followed by a slightly lower rate of 7.5 per cent during the 1970s (NESDB, 1981). Despite a lull during the early 1980s, the Thai economy is once again one of the fastest growing in South-East Asia.

However, it has long been clear that growth alone is insufficient for even and sustained development as inequalities between rich and poor, centre and periphery, and urban (chiefly Bangkok) and rural areas increased, and as resource depletion and environmental deterioration became more apparent. In 1970, rural–urban income differentials in Thailand at 3 to 1 were among the highest in the world (Panayotou, 1983: 41). Between 1960 and 1979 per capita income disparities between Bangkok, Central, and North-eastern Thailand increased (Table 2.1). During the same period the agricultural land frontier was more or less closed and forest cover was reduced from 53 per cent to 34 per cent of total land area (Boonchana and Thongchai, 1983: 39). These imbalances took on a political significance during the 1970s that led the country's planners as well as students, academics, and other concerned groups to

TABLE 2.1
Relative Incomes in Thailand's Regions, 1960 and 1979

	Index of Per Capita Income	
Region	*1960*	*1979*
Bangkok	5.2	6.0
Central Region	2.4	3.5
North-east	1.0	1.0

Source: NESDB (1982: 338).

turn more specifically to rural development as a counterbalance to the policies that had failed to uplift the living standard of many of the four-fifths of the population who dwell in the countryside.

An ethos of development is thus well established in the sense of the awareness of change and concern about how to reorient that change. The current concern for rural development has sprung from the inequities of the past development strategy based primarily on economic growth and national security. The inequities have been posed as a development problem in a number of ways: politically, as a dangerous gap between aspirations and achievement; economically, as a failure to increase productivity and create a rural market; morally, as an unjust social distribution of the fruits of economic growth. How to ensure a trickle-down of these fruits to the rural poor has become the principal issue.

However, concealed within this broad concern lies a multitude of explanations as to how this unequal state of affairs has arisen and what strategies should be used to ensure a more balanced form of development. The ethos of rural development, far from being a monolithic set of values, assumptions, and approaches, is rather a heterogeneous milieu of tensions and contradictions obscured by an apparent consensus associated with this innocuous term. In the various manifestations of this ethos can be discerned some of the hidden struggles associated with the processes of change that are themselves the background to rural development.

Development Ideology

Behind state-led rural development, we have seen, lie more fundamental processes, primary among which are state formation and capitalist transformation. In the context of rural development, these processes involve penetration of the village by State and capital, effecting a reorientation of power structures and a change in agrarian production relations. Supporting these basic changes in turn lies an ideology that is expressed publicly as an ideology of development and that has acquired its own discourse. The objective of the state developer is to convey this ideology to the rural population as part of the legitimation process for state activity in rural areas. Meanwhile, alternative ideologies emerge from the actual experience of rural producers (Turton, 1984b: 62ff.) and from non-governmental approaches to development.

Apart from its anti-communist stance, the most clearly identifiable element of state development ideology is the need for modernization. In agriculture, this means a move away from subsistence-oriented production towards commercial crops, an increased role for capital through mechanization and use of inputs such as fertilizer and pesticides, supported by increased rural credit in pursuit of higher yields. It is a capitalist ideology that promotes individual accumulation of wealth and monetized production relations, one that promises material prosperity. Meanwhile, Buddhism as the national religion is invoked along with associated moral values such as honesty, hard work, and punctuality.[1] This is part also of the broader nationalist ideology of nation–religion–monarchy and associated ideals of unity, order, and respect for national institutions. Also present is a statist ideology of unity through integration of national institutions in the name of democratization. In short, state rural development ideology is one that promotes capitalist transformation and state penetration as a path from poverty to prosperity, from isolation to integration, from backwardness to civilization.

An important part of village-level rural development activity by the State is devoted to imparting this ideology, as is evident from the emphasis on training programmes whose content is largely ideological. One government training manual, for example, stresses the importance of ideology, whose importance is as 'a system of ideas with a plan to inspire actions, or abstinence from certain actions, in order to achieve the best conditions possible at a given time'. Ideology is to be created by exemplary behaviour, symbols, songs, slogans, and institutionalized training (National Primary Education Office, n.d.: 1–2). Most of the songs and slogans in the manual concern respect for national institutions, unity, and individual morality.

Non-governmental approaches to development are varied and cannot be identified with a clear alternative ideology. The principal oppositionist ideology until the early 1980s, that of the Communist Party of Thailand (CPT), has long been illegal and in direct challenge to the State. As a result, it cannot be propounded by those working in the field of rural development, although many state rural development activities were conceived at least in part as pre-emptive measures to the taking hold of this opposition ideology. Many NGOs do, however, have a populist anti-capitalist ideology and emphasize subsistence before commercial production, self-reliance, the bargaining position of the poor, and traditional (as opposed to state) Buddhist values.[2] Meanwhile, as a result of a process of what Turton (1984b) calls 'negation', elements of a popular ideology that differs from the dominant state ideology can begin to be identified.

Development Discourse

As a tool for analysis, language is a two-edged sword. On the one hand, use of language is revealing of subjects' values, motives, perspectives or other abstract variables that cannot be measured or determined in any other way, but which nevertheless influence and help explain actions. On the other hand, language can just as easily be used by subjects to obscure intentions and cannot be taken at face value. However, this latter aspect of language is not entirely a negative influence on its interest as an item for study, for ambiguity itself contains significant meanings that can be interpreted where the context is clear. Ambiguity may be a deliberate technique to disguise intentions or paper over contradictions, or it may (as is probably more often the case in the present context) be a logical result of contradictions inherent in a particular process.

Language also has intrinsic interest in that it represents communication and hence interaction between subjects under study (see *New Internationalist*, January 1989). Language is an important part of the discourse of change—the non-material expression of transformed relations of power. Although in this broad sense discourse refers to that which conveys meaning, the term is used in a narrower sense here to refer to language in context. As a discrete entity, *a* discourse refers to language used or found in a particular context, and that context can be defined either by the user of the language or by the situation in which it is used. The most specific discourses, therefore, are those used by specified groups of people in specified situations. At one level, the linguistic aspect of discourse appears as mere jargon; at another, it is part of a dynamic engagement of conflicting praxis. In Parkin's (1982) analogy, we need not only to interpret fixed orders, but also to interpret interpretations internal to those orders. Without discourse, ideology and non-material influences on the formation of the social subject are devoid of means of transmission. Therefore, while at one level we must be wary of literal interpretations, at another we can treat discourse as an expression of the dialectic between groups under study. In the present context, the discourse of the developers and the counter-discourse of their targets, the developed, both give insight into the ethos of rural development in Thailand.

Thai rural development programmes have acquired a vocabulary of their own, and this set of lexical items is a reflection of the priorities associated with such programmes. Development is often equated with 'prosperity', or 'civilization'. An expression of underdevelopment is that a village is far from prosperity or civilization. Prosperity and civilization in this case take on urban, material forms of fences, streets, consumer goods, order and tidiness, and reflect the urban orientation of development strategy whereby villages and villagers are to develop by catching up. Other concepts that reflect this orientation include 'convenience' associated with roads and electricity, and the contraposition of rurality as expressed in the word for forest, *paa*, as backward, wild, dangerous, with civilization as secure, a measure of achievement.

Discourse associated with development training programmes emphasizes individual action. Much is made of the need to develop people by effecting moral and spiritual development. This is further refined in terms of the need to impart values such as diligence, punctuality, and honesty among other civic virtues. The implication is that underdevelopment comes from a lack of these virtues in individual villagers, and lectures, songs, and exhortations stress this implicit failing. A village is seen as 'ready' for development according to the moral fibre of its citizenry as defined by outside developers according to these values. Programmes such as the national-level *Phaen din tham—Phaen din tho'ng* (literally, land of [Buddhist] virtue, land of gold) programme emphasize giving up alcohol, gambling, and other pursuits deemed as representing obstacles to development.

Another important aspect of state-led rural development at the village level concerns 'security'. A number of specific programmes are justified in terms of villagers' security, or as a means of ensuring 'ease of administration'. More ambiguously, intrusion of state structures into the village are sometimes justified as to ensure 'comprehensive coverage'. However, this implies not only paternalistic 'watching over', but also potentially repressive 'keeping an eye on'. This control and access by the State represent another key element of its rural development strategy as reflected in its (albeit ambiguous) discourse.

The most recent strand of discourse in the various programmes involves an attempt to move away from the traditional welfare role of state aid to rural areas. It also reflects the influence, some would say the co-opting, of alternative discourses. Participation, expressed literally as 'to come in and take part', is an exhortation for villagers to become involved in programmes. Self-help is an ideal of reducing the dependence of villagers on the State for various services. However, closer examination of these concepts as applied reveals an emphasis on the doing rather than the initiating or deciding, and participation or self-help is very much on the terms set by outsiders. At its extreme, this form of participation represents a new type of corvée!

The discourse that emphasizes urban-style prosperity and security as objectives for rural development suggests continuity rather than a break with previous development strategy. At the same time, it is an ambiguous form of discourse in the sense that not all groups stand to gain equally from this prosperity and security. Rural differentiation and emerging rural power structures mean that the prosperity favours those with access to capital and transport, while security is a potentially repressive development within the village. Emphasis on the individual takes the focus off underlying structures, while participation and self-help are based on the (unstated) premise that, first and foremost, villagers require training in order to be willing (in the case of participation) and able (in the case of self-help) to take on externally defined development tasks without having to rely on the paternalism of the State.

There is a more general ambiguity that lies behind the inherent contradictions of a strategy of rural development through national integration. The discourse of rural development contains much that deals with villagers' increasing their rights, duties, and responsibilities as citizens, and the unity of the Thai people. Implied is a sense of belonging, of the village as an integral part of the State, of villagers as subjects rather than objects of state policy, of farmers as the 'backbone' of the nation. Yet by the same token, the official discourse of nation, religion, and monarchy is reinforced by physical and institutional accessibility afforded by schemes falling under the aegis of rural development to establish an increasing monopoly in terms of legitimacy of state institutions and procedures affecting the everyday social and economic life of village and villagers.

To some extent, the ambiguous implications of official discourse succeed in obscuring some contradictions inherent in the rural development strategy, and to this extent such discourse serves a useful function for the State in its ideological training programmes. Nevertheless, certain aspects of peasant discourse in reaction to the programmes with which the dominant discourse is associated show that contradictions are not wholly submerged. Feelings of being continually 'pestered' by rural development programmes, various development tasks, and so on are commonly expressed. Many feel 'forced' into activities. Individual programmes are punned—for example, '*Phaen din tham—Phaen din tho'ng*' becomes '*Phaen din tho'—Phaen din thae*', or 'land of desperation', in the words of some villagers.

It must be stressed that this discourse and counter-discourse is not exchanged in neutral dialogue. Development discourse is to be understood in terms of power structures within as well as outside the village. Meanwhile, counter-discourse is a dialectical response to the dominant discourse, but at the same time it is contained in what James Scott calls the 'hidden transcript' of the powerless (Scott, 1985). That is to say, those against whom development as reflected in the dominant discourse is objectively or subjectively biased refrain from presenting their counter-discourse in front of its articulators.

An enigmatic aspect of the dominant discourse is what may be termed an implicit dialectic in key terms. 'Democracy' implies (negatively associated) communism as the alternative to state ideology. Espousal of virtues such as discipline and diligence evokes a disorderly and lazy impression of undeveloped village life, though this is never made explicit. The unstated alternative of security implies danger in opposing coercive elements of state policy at the local level. Civilization, prosperity, and order as key objectives within development discourse imply a cultural as well as physical underdevelopment represented in the backwardness, poverty, and lack of regimentation in village life.

A last point on development discourse is that it would be wrong to give the impression that the dominant (statist) discourse and the counter-discourse represent exhaustive categories. Significant also are non-governmental organizations, whose perspective and ideology tend to be distinctly non-statist. Foremost in the NGO discourse are concepts of dignity, self-reliance, decision-making power, bargaining power, and others reflecting an alternative conceptualization of rural development. Of equal interest is the element of common discourse, whereby participation and spiritual development, for example, are basic principles of NGO approaches to a bottom-up, non-materialist development strategy. Connotations are defined by context, however, and a study that traced the connotative transmutations as items of discourse pass from one user to the next would reveal the necessity of interpretation. In each case, 'we should identify as far as possible the circumstances by which the apparently chance event becomes an interpretative inspiration' (Parkin, 1982: xlvii).

Development Structures

The broad range of activities carried out by the Thai state bureaucracy at the local level are generally labelled as rural development (Figure 2.1). State programmes consist of a purportedly benign transformation or initiation of legal and administrative institutions and implementation of specific schemes directed at local people's welfare and increasing agricultural production.

The principal local administrative arm of the State is the district administration, in the form of departments of the four principal ministries with statutory functions at the district level. These are not necessarily co-ordinated in a common development strategy, but in local training programmes they come together as the direct representatives of the State. Other state structures support these activities, such as the military, various departments providing occasional services (public works, land development), and the Bank for Agriculture and Agricultural Co-operatives (BAAC), the principal formal agricultural credit institution.

Government controlled co-operatives have been in operation in Thailand for over sixty years, but these are usually little more than agricultural credit institutions, mainly catering to the better-off farmers. Farmers' associations at the *tambon* (subdistrict) level serve a similar function. Limited attempts at agricultural marketing and supplying in collaboration with the state-run Farmers' Marketing Organization (FMO) have come to little.

At the *tambon* and village levels, *tambon* councils and village development committees are now integrated into the rural development framework and play a part in administration of rural development programmes. These bodies are dominated by the *kamnan* (subdistrict head) and village heads respectively, and their position as agents of the State in the village is often further enhanced by their rural development roles.

Non-governmental organizations have projects in many districts. Most NGOs undertake village-level co-operative activities and training, and they often involve informal leaders from among the poorer sections of the community. The role of NGOs is further discussed below.

Social Formation and Development in Rural Thailand

So long as the motivation behind rural development arose as a result of the inequities of past development strategy, development could be posited as a corrective to urban bias, neglect of agriculture, and lack of attention to rural areas in general. The rural development problem was one of making good these deficiencies. In conventional planning terms, it was time some of the benefits started to trickle down. Rural development was in effect a problem of how to direct national resources to rural areas and thereby increase the prosperity and productivity of these areas.

Figure 2.1
Local Administration and Rural Development Structures in Thailand

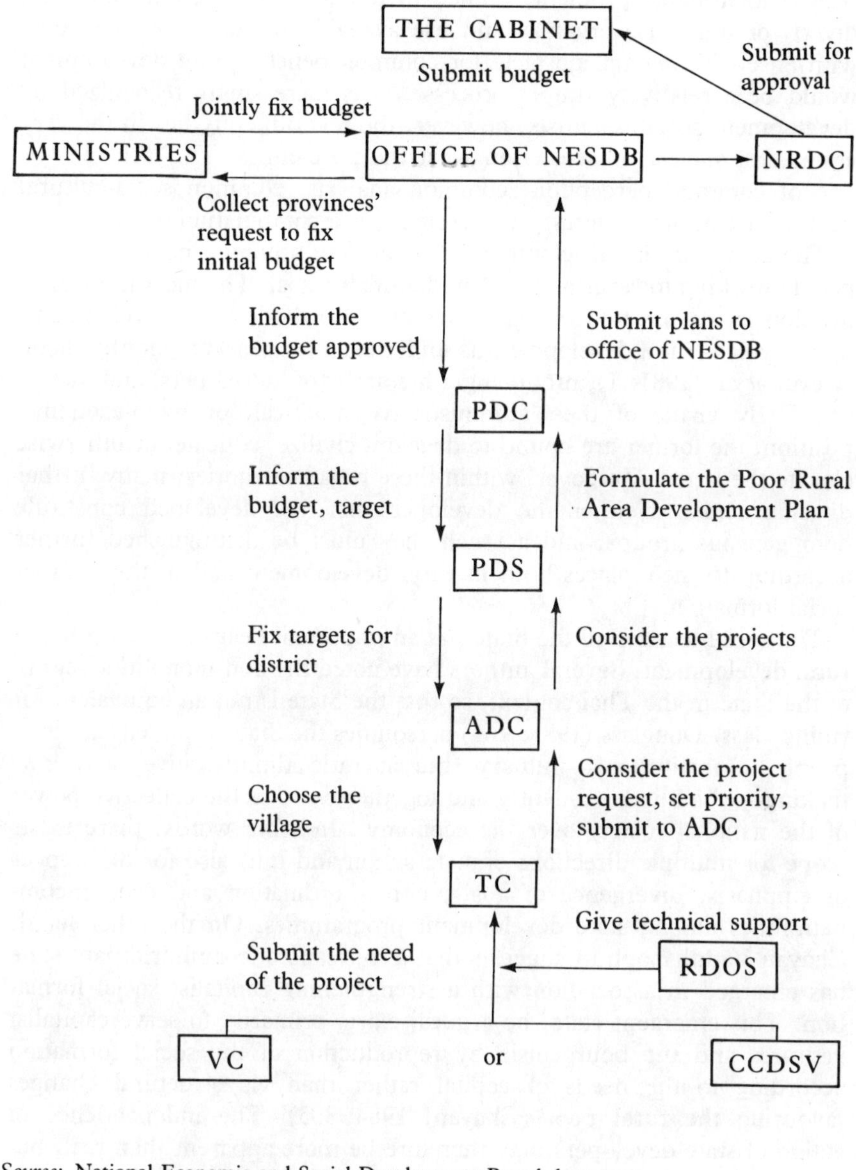

Source: National Economic and Social Development Board document.
Note: NRDC = National Rural Development Committee
NESDB = National Economic and Social Development Board
PDC = Provincial Development Committee
PDS = Provincial Development Scheme
ADC = *Amphoe* Development Committee
TC = *Tambon* Council
VC = Village Committee
CCDSV = Central Committee of the Development and Self-defence Village
RDOS = Rural Development Operational Support

Such a one-dimensional approach does little to illuminate and much to obscure the rural development 'problem', or the underlying processes that are a part of rural development strategy. Were there to be such a readily identifiable problem, framed in terms of how best to mobilize, divert, or otherwise organize and use available resources so as to deal with an environmental obstacle for common benefit, rural development would be a relatively simple process. As is increasingly recognized by development social scientists, however, the real difficulty lies in the very absence of such a consensus on what the problem is. The lack may be one of common perception, common analysis, common socio-cultural values, or common interest; more often it is a combination of these.

The actors on the development stage are not a homogeneous group of people working towards a common identifiable goal. The most immediate division is that created by the conventional orthodoxy of development, under which 'rural development is undertaken for peasants, not by them' (Heyer *et al.*, 1981: 1), producing a hierarchy of 'developers' and 'developed'. By virtue of their administrative, political, or socio-economic position, the former are bound to develop, civilize, educate, or otherwise elevate the latter. Moreover, within these broad categories, many further divisions exist. Neither the developers nor the developed constitute homogeneous groups, and as such they must be distinguished further according to their places both in rural development and in the broader social formation.

The social location of the State has an important bearing on its place in rural development. Several authors have noted the non-monolithic nature of the State in the Thai context, so that the State is not an equivalent for ruling class. Douglass (1983: 164) personifies the State as an 'ensemble of people in institutions—military, bureaucratic/administrative, and law-making—which independently and together exercise the collective power of the national society over the economy'. In other words, there exists scope for multiple directions of state action and thus also for differences of emphasis, divergence of goals, non-co-ordination and even incompatibilities among state development programmes. On the other hand, Chayan Vaddhanaphuti suggests that a 'bureaucratic–authoritarian' state has emerged in association with a strengthening capitalist social formation. This emergent state, he argues, exists primarily to serve capitalist ventures and the bourgeoisie by reproduction of the social formation according to the needs of capital rather than via structural changes favouring the rural poor (Chayan, 1984: 305). The independence of action of state developers may therefore be more apparent than real, but it would nevertheless be an error to treat the State as a monolith.[3]

Divisions in Rural Society

Characterization of Thai social formation in terms of Marxist or other Western categories is problematic (see Reynolds and Hong, 1983). Despite the considerable inroads made by capitalism and consequent changes in production relations, class structure still does not approximate that of more industrialized societies. This is partly due to the rurality of Thai society, with some four-fifths of the population still living in the countryside and much of the urban population being first- or second-generation urbanites. Moreover, the pace of change in Thai society is such that a static view of class divisions carries little meaning. A brief outline of traditional divisions in Thai society will be helpful in setting the scene for understanding present-day cleavages.

Excluding the King at the apex, Thai society has been characterized historically by a two-class division into nobles and commoners (*naai* and *phrai*). The former were princes and lesser nobles, who were given ranking expressed in terms of rice-lands (*sakdina*) but whose real power depended on control over labour. This ranking was obtained initially by royal patronage, and by hereditary process it declined with each succeeding generation. The commoners consisted of serfs who had to pay labour services either directly to the King or to a local noble, and of slaves who had sold themselves into debt-bondage and comprised one-third of the population during the mid-nineteenth century. Only the Chinese remained outside this system, and in so doing they assumed an increasingly important role as entrepreneurs and free, mobile labour (Akin, 1969; Girling, 1981).

The modernizing reforms during the reign of King Chulalongkorn transformed this system, which had lasted through the Ayuthaya and Thonburi periods and the first century of the Bangkok era (after 1782). In abolishing slavery and doing away with corvée labour, the reforms released Thai labour for the first time. In introducing an administrative system based on European principles of functional ministries, a bureaucracy was established, which until 1932 was accountable to the King. Former serfs and slaves constituted a peasantry that was at once increasingly mobile and commercialized, while bureaucratic positions went to the ruling class—that is, the former nobles. Meanwhile, secularization of education and the beginnings of meritocratic ideas provided alternative ways into the bureaucracy. As such, the two-class system was maintained, but it was one in which a certain degree of mobility was possible. The bureaucracy, in particular the military arm, was strengthened by the abolition of the absolute monarchy after the 1932 coup against the palace (Girling, 1981: Ch. 3; Morell and Chai-anan, 1981: 50–64). As society was increasingly urbanized and Westernized, the élite or upper class was referred to less frequently in terms of its landed status (*naai*, *sakdina*) and more often in terms of social attributes as contained in the terms *phuudii* (approximating to 'gentlefolk') and *panyaachon* (literally, 'intellectual', but in fact referring to a broad section of society regarded as educated).

The two-class structure of traditional Thai society is still evident in village discourse. For most rural dwellers there are two classes of Thai: villager (*chaobaan*) and official (*khaaraachakaan*—literally, 'royal servant'). Traders, the other main group with whom villagers come into contact, are mostly of Chinese descent and called *jek*, often just descriptively but sometimes pejoratively. Officials and others of higher status are often addressed as *naai*, reflecting the persistence of traditional categories in social discourse. Senior local officials are addressed and referred to publicly in the third person as *than*, a respectful indication of higher status that is also used for royalty and clergy. The status and security associated with official position is such that villagers place high priority on attaining posts for their children as an objective of investment in their education, sometimes expressly in order to 'have them be lords and bosses over others'.

The simplicity of the traditional two-class structure is based on a relative homogeneity of the rural population in the absence of caste, and on the historically limited differentiation of economic status in production. However, this simplicity breaks down with the increasing influence of capitalist relations of production in rural areas, and divisions multiply within rural groups as specialization increases not only at the regional level but also within villages. Increasingly common are village élites consisting typically of some 5 per cent of the population who, while retaining the status of villager, cease to be included by poorer villagers as 'us lot' and are sometimes referred to instead as 'village society' (Turton, 1984b: 30–1). As these élites develop connections with local officials, their social and political position often becomes ambiguous.

In terms of rural development, the principal division between developer and developed is still a key one, with important implications for participatory development. For many purposes, this division follows closely the official–villager, outsider–insider cleavage described above. However, it is increasingly necessary to look beyond the simple dualism in order both to understand more fully the variety of currents subsumed under development and personified in the various groups of developers and to take into account the differentiation of village society.

The Developers

Our main concern here is the range of development activities at the local level. However, the role of policy decided at a non-local level should first be emphasized. For the villager, rural development impinges most visibly on the persons of local development personnel, but the centralized nature of the bureaucracy and the increased links between local and national-level polity and economy mean that decisions made at supralocal levels are an important influence on rural development. Of particular influence are pricing and fiscal policy for rice and other crops, large-scale infrastructural programmes, forest reserve and land title policy, and agricultural credit programmes. More general in terms of policy but specifically geared to rural development is the National Economic and Social Development Board (NESDB), which is responsible for development planning but carries no regulatory power. Decisions are made by technocratic government agencies with only limited reference to Parliament, the one forum where nominal representatives of villagers have any influence at the national level. Thus to a large extent, important aspects of rural change are entirely removed from local direction.

The above notwithstanding, the 1980s have seen a mushrooming of development activities at the local level, and with this has come a plethora of developers. The main, commonly recognized distinction between these developers is that between state and non-governmental (NGO) workers, but within each of these groups further differences arise. Common interests and characteristics of each of these two major groups are offset by cleavages within each sector.

State-led rural development has been an issue on the national agenda for over two decades. During the 1960s, programmes concentrated on potential trouble spots for the government, mainly in the North-east under the United States-backed Accelerated Rural Development scheme. Emphasis was placed on building roads into sensitive areas, and a close link was thus established between rural development and counter-insurgency and more general aspects of 'national security'. This link was maintained through the 1970s and re-emphasized during the 1980s with the political element of counter-insurgency contained in the important 66/2523 policy, which emphasized rural development in remote areas. Returnees from the forest (that is, from joining forces with the Communist Party of Thailand) are officially termed 'national development participants', and the Community Development Department (CDD) under the Ministry of the Interior continues to serve the dual purpose of welfare and surveillance at the *tambon* level.

Another aspect of State-led rural development is the emphasis on increasing the place of the rural sector in the commercial economy. This is effected by agricultural extension that emphasizes cash cropping and new inputs and varieties that are intended to increase output and thus agricultural surplus. It is reinforced, as is the security emphasis, by increased accessibility afforded by construction of roads. State agricultural credit has also been in support of high-input agriculture since 1966, channelled directly or indirectly (via co-operatives and farmers' associations) through the Bank for Agriculture and Agricultural Co-operatives (BAAC). The BAAC programme has been expanded greatly since the mid-1970s as commercial banks use it to fulfil their requirements to place at least 13 per cent of investments in the agricultural sector.

The two principal concerns for rural development—national security and growth—still obtain, but the measures taken during the 1970s and followed by the Fifth Plan (1982–6) reveal a broadening of concerns. Following pressure from the Peasant Federation of Thailand in 1974, the Government passed legislation—including the Land Reform Act that established the Agricultural Land Reform Office (ALRO)—which was charged with reallocating illegally settled public lands and carrying out reform on private lands in areas of high tenancy. Prime Minister Kukrit's revolving fund scheme was intended to increase rural employment and provide basic infrastructure, and this has been followed up with the Rural Employment Generation Programme (REGP), in which *tambon*-level decision making is emphasized. Meanwhile, the Fifth Plan was the first to address past failures in development strategy and make limited suggestions for a reorientation in favour of rural areas. However, no fundamental restructuring of the bureaucracy is evident. Rather, emphasis is given to the area approach, whereby selected target districts are given special attention by the existing local administration in the form of extra assistance under 33 separate programmes, with a total budget of 8,593 million baht over a five-year period. Using the 1980 figure as a base, this amounts to approximately 0.25 per cent of Gross Domestic Product (GDP).

The broadened state interest in rural development can be attributed to a number of concerns. First, there is a recognition among many government departments that two decades of rapid growth failed to improve the lot of the rural poor. NESDB in particular fears the increase in income disparities and notes that, if measures are not taken, the decline in rural poverty may be reversed with the disappearance of the agricultural land frontier as an outlet for the landless (NESDB, 1981: 278). Second, an awareness of low productivity in rural areas as reflected in low incomes, low level of technology and other inputs, and low yields leads to a sense that Thai agriculture has fallen behind that of other Asian countries. Third, conflict in rural areas during the 1970s resulted in an increased sense of urgency regarding the disparities in living conditions and the social gap between villagers and officials. Fourth, there is a recognition that industrialization and economic growth depends on the establishment of a national market, and this means raising incomes in rural areas (IBRD, 1983). In sum, therefore, the emphasis is still on economic growth and national security, but awareness of the importance of rural areas in achieving these ends has led to increased state activity in the countryside.

The foregoing discussion has focused on state developers as an ensemble; the following considers the state-led rural development apparatus as a differentiated entity. Although the departments of the four ministries at the district level are supposed to act in concert, accountability and promotion are still largely internal to each department. Vertical rather than horizontal communication is the result, since bureaucratic relationships are still largely based on patronage, and local-level officials gain merit points by following orders from the next rung up the administrative ladder rather than by knowledge of or skill in dealing with local affairs (Withaya, 1984: 157). Frequent transfers ordered centrally, ostensibly to avoid local officials establishing a power base, further inhibit local orientation. Centralization is reinforced by promotion structure and the status accorded to transfer from district to provincial level and from provincial level to Bangkok. Figure 2.1 shows the vertical nature of decision making within the development bureaucracy.

The effect of this entrenchment of vertical linkages at the expense of horizontal linkages is to inhibit co-ordination between the State's local-level developers. Each department within each ministry runs its own projects with its own budget, and duplication is rife. Furthermore, it is in each department's interest to expand its role at the expense of others in order to secure larger budget allocations. While the interdepartmental infighting related to budget allocations is largely at the national level, it does little, given the nature of linkages described above, to secure co-operation or co-ordination between departments in the implementation of local programmes. Prominent political scientist Chai-anan Samudavanija compares the Thai bureaucracy to a bamboo thicket, in which the leaves at the top intermingle while the inflexible stalks at the bottom remain isolated from one another.

Other state agencies have self-appointed roles in rural development. BAAC works independently of the rest of the state apparatus. The military operates numerous programmes that are labelled as developmental, and other enforcement agencies have followed in this mould, notably the police and the Internal Security Operations Command (ISOC).[4]

The multiplicity of state developers at the local level commonly leads to duplication and competition. Sometimes it goes further and leads to conflicts of interest. These may be personal, involving competing attempts to control a particularly lucrative source of pay-offs, notably forestry. Alternatively, they may revolve around issues where, for example, the Forestry Department's desire to preserve forest reserve status may be undermined by the Department of Local Administration's desire to maintain control by registration (and therefore legitimization) of new settlement and the Primary Education Department's concern to build new schools to serve such areas.

NGO developers start from a different perspective to that of their state counterparts. This can best be understood in light of a brief history of NGOs in Thailand. Non-governmental approaches to development have been in existence for some time, despite periods of suspicion and harassment of independent initiatives by an absolutist state bureaucracy. The Thai Rural Reconstruction Movement was set up at Chainat in 1969 by Puey Ungpakorn and others. It was based on the principle of working directly with the people and learning from farmers, based on James C. Yen's experience and ideas in pre-revolutionary China and the Philippines. At the same time that state interest in alleviation of rural problems increased during the liberal period between the 14 October 1973 student uprising and the 6 October 1976 coup, there was a realization—particularly among students—that potential existed for effecting rural change outside state structures. The largest scheme to be set up at this time was the Maeklong Integrated Rural Development Programme, which involved co-operation between three universities (Akin, 1980: 9). In addition, a large number of students gained first-hand experience of rural problems during this period by means of student work-camps, many of which included political 'consciousness raising'. This brought students and villagers under suspicion and sometimes into conflict with state authorities, which further increased scepticism regarding state development programmes. Following the 1976 coup and military clamp-down, non-governmental development work in rural areas was proscribed. Many who had previously worked for change within the system fled to the forests to join the CPT, since non-state activity at this time was regarded as oppositionist and those involved were placed in jeopardy. However, following the 1977 coup and limited liberalization that followed, particularly after 1980, the NGO movement flourished. By the late 1980s, more than one hundred NGOs were working in rural development in a large number of districts (Thai Volunteer Service, 1987).

The extent to which NGO developers are alternative and the extent to which they are supplementary to state programmes is not well defined and depends in part on the NGO developers in question. Many of those working with small-scale organizations were involved in student activities during the 1970s, and their perspective differs significantly from that of state developers. There is an emphasis on increasing the bargaining power of villagers, often *vis-à-vis* the bureaucracy. Approaches to working with farmers differ from those of most state developers, being more cadre-oriented and less technocratic in order to reduce status differences since, like their state counterparts, NGO developers generally come from educated, middle-class backgrounds. Most NGOs rely on funding from abroad, and the sponsoring organizations are themselves often keen to see alternative approaches to what are generally perceived of as unsuccessful bureaucratic methods. The result of this has been for NGO developers to stress issues such as participation, spiritual development, self-sufficiency, and working specifically with the poorer groups, rather than technocratic, materially oriented projects, and commercial cropping on an area basis.

On the other hand, liberalization by state authorities and recognition on the part of NGOs of the necessity of working within the existing framework have led to an increasing degree of co-ordination between state and NGO activity. While differences in approaches and suspicions persist, many NGOs work directly with state officials such as teachers and health workers. In a move that at once makes NGO activity less precarious but also raised the suspicions of many NGO developers, the Government indicated a desire for much closer co-operation between the State and NGO sectors in the Sixth Plan (1987–91).

Within the NGO movement, a number of different approaches is evident. One approach, which may be characterized as avoidance, is to emphasize traditional cultural values and preserve existing relationships against the dislocations of capitalist development by 'going against the current'. The alternative engagement involves increasing bargaining power and ability to operate within the system, accepting that capitalist and other outside forces already affect village society. Other NGOs take a specifically Buddhist approach, emphasizing particular values within a locally bound situation and not regarding themselves as part of a wider process. This classification is neither exhaustive nor mutually exclusive, but it highlights the heterogeneity of approach among non-governmental developers, which itself leads to a running debate at numerous seminars that covers the dilemmas faced by independent developers as a result of certain contradictions that are brought out in the following chapters.

It is clear from this account that the task of rural development has been taken on in a number of ways by various bodies at different times. Each developer maintains a role in the social formation and objectives that vary with historical specificities of the contemporary situation. State structures and priorities vary not only over time but also between and within government departments or organizations. NGO activity varies not only according to limitations set by the State, but also with the range and diversity of developmental philosophies.

The Developed

The most straightforward description of the target of developers is *chaobaan* (villager). However, this term fails to take into account the increasingly differentiated nature of rural Thai society as a result of changes in production relations. Differentiation is considered in more detail in Chapter 5, so for the time being the discussion is limited to a review of the principal divisions among village populations.

The criterion employed by the National Statistical Office for calculating rural poverty in 1976 was a cash income below 150 baht per month (IBRD, 1980: 62). If cash income is taken as a measure, the rural population shows great inequalities. In 1970, the top quintile received 51.0 per cent of income, as compared to 5.5 per cent for the bottom quintile. Moreover, this represents a deterioration over the situation in 1962, implying a sharpening of inequalities (Panayotou, 1983: 39). However, such a measure is inadequate for a number of reasons. An important proportion of rural production and consumption is outside the cash economy. Calculation of income is of limited significance when household labour is used for home production. In any one year, outlays in capitalized farm operations may exceed proceeds. Quite apart from this, no adequate system of income measurement has been established. Of greater significance, therefore, are differences based on production potential, measured in terms of access to basic means of production.

Land tenure in rural Thailand varies from region to region, but overall the situation has not traditionally involved a high degree of landlessness. This is partly due to the availability until recently of uncleared land suited to agriculture, which has enabled dispossessed farmers to clear new areas. Nevertheless, substantial inequalities remain, both in quantity and quality of land owned. Land tenure is most even in North-east Thailand, where land is of lowest quality. The areas of highest tenancy and landlessness are in the fertile and well-irrigated Central Plains and valleys of the North. Table 2.2 shows the situation of land ownership in the regions, along with the concentration of ownership. The increasing importance of capital in agriculture has led to concentration at the village level, producing a growing landless class who are dependent partly or wholly on wage labour in the village and elsewhere. A concomitant trend is the emergence of a locally based landowning minority who use a combination of externally raised capital and local labour to farm their land. In a study of nine Central Plains provinces, it was found that 18 per cent of farmers possessed little or no land, while 45 per cent of rural households in upper northern Thailand were found in a subsequent survey to be landless or near landless (Suthiporn and Worawate, 1981; ALRO, n.d.). The problem of landlessness is expected to increase rapidly as vacant frontier land is more or less fully occupied.

Inequality of land ownership is reinforced by unequal access to capital

TABLE 2.2
Distribution of Land by Size of Holding, 1978

	Whole Kingdom		*Centre*		*North-east*		*North*		*South*	
Gini Coefficient	*0.45*		*0.47*		*0.40*		*0.49*		*0.44*	
Size of Holding (Rai)	*Percentage of Holders*	*Percentage of Land*	*Percentage of Holders*	*Percentage of Land*	*Percentage of Holders*	*Percentage of Land*	*Percentage of Holders*	*Percentage of Land*	*Percentage of Holders*	*Percentage of Land*
<2	1.6	.02	3.0	0.03	1.0	0.01	2.8	0.03	0.8	0.01
2–6	14.3	2.3	12.8	1.7	9.2	1.4	22.5	4.1	16.8	3.2
6–15	27.4	11.4	21.6	7.5	26.3	10.6	30.5	14.3	33.4	16.4
15–30	29.0	25.7	27.2	20.3	33.4	28.4	22.6	23.3	29.7	31.0
30–50	17.3	27.1	19.8	25.9	19.8	29.6	13.5	24.6	13.3	24.6
50–100	9.0	24.3	12.8	29.0	9.1	23.4	7.8	24.9	5.3	16.9
>100	1.4	9.3	2.7	15.5	1.2	6.5	1.3	8.7	0.8	7.8

Source: Adapted from NSO Statistical Report of Thailand, 1981–1984.

Notes: These figures omit households with no land at all.

Inequality of land ownership in Thailand is still lower than in many other Asian countries if measured by the Gini Coefficient of 0.45. While South Korea and Taiwan show the lowest degree of concentration (coefficient of 0.32 in 1973 for the former), India, Pakistan, Malaysia, and the Philippines all show a higher land concentration, with figures of 0.63, 0.60, 0.54, and 0.51 respectively (Douglass, 1983: 196).

in an agricultural economy increasingly oriented to high-input agriculture. In part this inequality is a product of skewed land ownership, for access to formal credit depends to some extent on collateral in land. Agricultural credit from the principal formal source, BAAC, is biased in favour of larger farmers, so that 81 per cent of BAAC clients possess more than the median amount of land for their province (Lightfoot, 1985: 13). Meanwhile, mechanization involving lumpy investments amidst a general shortage of capital has enabled wealthier villagers to profit from possession of tractors and other items of machinery. Informal borrowing at high rates of interest is not new to rural Thailand, but such borrowing is on an increasing scale and more and more frequently involves fellow villagers rather than outside middlemen. There is no evidence to show that institutional credit replaces rather than adds to non-institutional debt.

It is evident that the developed are an increasingly differentiated group whose interests not only vary but may be in direct conflict. Nevertheless, attempts to characterize the rural population in simple class terms or other categories are problematic. Not only is the process of differentiation incomplete, with a majority of rural producers retaining control over what is at least perceived as the basic factor of production, namely land, but class consciousness has not kept up with the material realities of changing production relations. There is a need for concrete historical analysis in examining the development of class relations and a recognition of the difficulty of generalizing the rural social formation in crude class terms. Such generalization fails to take into account two basic disjunctures—that between material realities as perceived by an outside observer and as felt by villagers themselves, and that between the situation in different villages depending on specific local and historical experience. This latter point is evident in the present study of villages only 10 kilometres apart but with very different experiences of differentiation. Two Thai studies bear out these points more generally.

Anan Ganjanapan writes of 'classes and groups of rural producers' and uses a production approach to stress the contradictions internal to the northern Thai village where he was working, particularly those contradictions between wealthy landowners and their tenants and wage labour (Anan, 1984: 1–3). Households fall into five groups: landless labourers; poor, middle, and rich peasants; and an emerging class of capitalist farmers. This classification was initially based on size of land holdings but modified in light of additional information regarding production and employment. Anan notes the increasing tendency among villagers themselves to differentiate according to cash as well as land holdings (Anan, 1984: 10, 409–11).

Siwarak also notes the need to take into account more than one factor of production in determining class position (Siwarak, 1985: 2). She stresses labour as the principal indicator, both direct wage labour and labour secured indirectly by way of tenancy. Use of abstract categories such as landlord, rich, middle, and poor peasants, and landless labourers is criticized and traced to Maoist influence.

Both Anan and Siwarak stress the need for a historical approach involving the concrete realities of class differentiation by examining changes in production relations, and Siwarak notes the slow development in class differentiation due to the abundance of land (Siwarak, 1985: 17). In a case study of a central Thai village, she identifies five classes: capitalist landlords, independent farmers (that is, those farming their own land), sharecroppers of creditors, tenants, and landless labourers. Villagers use the term 'group' rather than 'class'. Persistence of the patronage system and the effectiveness of state domination lead to a lag in emergence of class consciousness behind material relations of production.

While a strict categorization of the rural population into rigidly defined socio-economic groups is to be avoided, more fluid but no less pronounced divisions are important. The emphasis is on the coincidence of economic status that is based on a combination of control over production and trade, with the assumption of political position within the village at a time when such position is increasingly ambiguous *vis-à-vis* representation of interests. This coincidence is much more readily recognizable in local discourse than are more formal class identifications, with categories such as 'village bosses', 'the rich', or 'tractor owners' commonly identified as exploiters who also control and benefit from externally oriented village institutions. Through *tambon* councils and village committees (discussed in Chapter 7), these formal village leaders are taking on more and more official duties, and many of these are in the name of development. This involves channelling state development resources in such a way that a blurring of the margin between official and villager is paralleled by an increasingly fuzzy distinction between developer and developed. At a development training session in Lan Sak in 1985, *kamnan* and village heads were repeatedly addressed by officials as 'fellow developers'.

It is at this point that the social roles of developer and developed need to be called into question. For if rural development is to respond to the situation of rural producers in other than a paternalistic way, then these actors must take on the role of subjects who participate in making decisions affecting their own lives. However, if participation in decision making is limited to key individuals in structural contradiction to the majority at the village level, then there is less a decentralization of power than a process of co-optation. In the consideration of participation that follows, the issues of control and power are brought to the fore.

Participatory Development

Concern for rural development has clearly arisen due to imbalances created by an urban-oriented growth strategy. Consequently, rural development has been put forward as a means of allowing the rural poor to participate in this growth, both by consumption of the fruits of growth that result from a channelling of state resources to the rural sector, and by production within the wider system by reorienting agriculture to national and international markets using non-local inputs. A more recent interpretation has been to move away from a paternal welfare approach of providing services in rural areas towards encouraging villagers to participate in many of the construction projects, training programmes, and other concrete aspects of rural development. Meanwhile, small-scale non-governmental development organizations emphasize participation in planning, carrying out, and following up projects.

Thus it appears that as an item of development discourse, participation is ambiguous in its implications for the role of villagers in change at the village level. Is participation merely a redistributive measure to include villagers in what they have previously been left out of? Indeed, is participation on these terms necessarily redistributive? Is participation effected by persuading or forcing villagers to join in new programmes, or by making villagers more amenable to change desired by outside developers? Or does participation arise from facilitating adjustment of local power relationships to benefit those who suffer most under existing arrangements? The answer to these questions clearly lies in our definition of participation.

The most elementary formulation of participation is a moral position that holds that, in a society producing an ever larger cake, the slices should be shared more evenly than hitherto—in other words, that all should have a right to participate in the consumption of Society's produce. This redistributive approach to participation does not address the questions of the method by which the cake is produced or of who takes part in producing it. These questions are raised to some extent by those who regard participation as an opportunity to produce within the broader capitalist economy.[5] Under this interpretation, participation implies production within the formal cash economy, just as participation rates in Western economic jargon measure the number of people in formal paid and taxed employment positions. So-called informal sectors, subsistence agricultural production, or non-economic pursuits become the antithesis of participation.

The common factor in the above interpretations of participation is the conception of state and capitalist economy as being on the 'inside', while village institutions that are non-statist or non-capitalist in function are so by definition on the 'outside'. Participation means moving 'in' from the 'outside' and development is thereby spread to include all. This is, although it may seem a contradiction in terms, a top-downward view of participation.

A polar opposite perspective is to set participation entirely in terms of village society. In Thailand, certain populist development workers and academics maintaining this perspective are known as culturalists. A leading culturalist suggests that it is wrong to regard the village as a micro-level unit within the larger macro-level system. In terms of villagers' lives and experience, the village is the macro-level unit, while outside (higher) influences are only secondary, or micro-level according to the villagers' frame of reference (Apichaat, 1984: 21).

Although they represent polar opposites, these approaches share the assumption that village and supravillage (the latter pertaining specifically to outside capital and the State) are institutionally separate and that development can only be achieved by subjugation of one by the other. As has been suggested, however, this contradistinction is no longer appropriate, and participation must hence rather be seen as a means of adjusting the terms of individual and community relations within the larger society. Moreover, divisions internal to the village involve a divergence of interests among villagers and a partial convergence of interests between village élites and state developers. Participation becomes an issue of power, and participatory development a dialectic between different groups over the nature of change.

Participation in its broadest sense refers not just to what individuals get from the larger society or how they get into it, nor to a denial of the existence or importance of influences that the larger society has over village life. Rather, it refers to terms of control. The following chapters show how these terms have changed with incorporation into the wider system, and in Chapter 7 the participation debate is reviewed in these terms.

For the time being, we can see participation under current development strategy as illusory due to a basic contradiction. On the one hand, integration of village institutions into supravillage structures gives villagers potential access to supralocal resources and influence over decisions affecting them that are made at a higher level. On the other hand, the penetration of State and capital into the village that is a concomitant part of this process transforms village institutions in such a way that they take on state functions or are reduced to monetized relationships within the larger economic system. This *reduces* villager control over local resources and decisions in deference to state power, which itself falls into the hands of powerful individuals within the village. Meanwhile, differentiation means that access to the wider resources lies in the hands of a village élite, who themselves take on state roles as mentioned above. This means that any programme of change under rural development represents not so much a changing relationship between homogeneous village and separate state, as in the community development ideal, as a readjustment of arrangements internal to village polity and economy.

Conclusion

Through the example of rural Thailand, we have seen that the sense of positive change implied by the term 'rural development' serves as an ideological tool for influencing the direction of change in rural areas. It also serves to cover over some of the contradictions inherent in rural development strategy *vis-à-vis* popular participation and the tensions that result. In the same way that discourse is of general interest both in what it tells us about its separate articulators and in its role in the interaction between them, so too an examination of rural development can be expected to shed light both on the underlying contradictory processes within it and on the role of the actual concept in obscuring the contradictions to the actors themselves. An understanding of participatory development requires first and foremost a demystification of the supposed unitary path to development, and a dialectical unravelling of contradictions. As suggested at the beginning of this chapter, such a task can be approached by a study of development in a local and specific context, and it is to this context that we now turn.

1. Turton (1984b: 39–40) provides an interesting discussion of the ideology of clock time in a similar context. For a discussion of the close relationship between the Buddhist *sangha* and the Thai State, see Somboon (1982) and Ishii (1986).

2. Some of these values are espoused in Schumacher's (1973) chapter on Buddhist Economics. It is interesting to contrast this use of Buddhism with that of state developers.

3. For detailed analysis of the Thai state apparatus, its structures, values, and motivations, see Wilson (1962), Riggs (1966), and Morell and Chai-anan (1981).

4. For analysis of the role of the Thai military in rural areas, see Hirsch (1987). Suchit (1987: 53–8) also gives an interesting account of military programmes in the Thai countryside.

5. See, for example, IBRD (1980); see also Gould (1981: 56) for general and Anan (1984: 365) for specific critiques of this position.

3
The Dynamics of Forest Settlement

SETTLEMENT of forest land has been the principal dynamic of Thai agricultural expansion for more than a century. In the mid-nineteenth century, Siam was still lightly populated in relation to its agricultural potential. As late as 1931, outlying areas were seen to be in need of settlement, while no serious possibility of over-population was in sight. In his rural economic survey, Zimmerman (1931: 311) noted that every district was still within 50 kilometres of an underpopulated area, with all the outlying districts needing more people. Yet by the 1980s, demographic and agricultural expansion has made deforestation and shortage of agricultural land a serious concern. A number of factors lead to continuing pressure on the seriously diminished supply of forest land suited to agriculture. These include a momentum established by social and legal structures, as well as associated expectations that have developed with past experience of land settlement.

To understand the place of forest settlement in the incorporative process of rural development, it is necessary to look beyond the common historical image of an inexorable migratory response to demographic pressures, of which the current situation is the tail end. The steady expansion of cultivated area at the expense of forest land in Thailand over the past century has taken place at the same time as major internal and external structural changes in the Thai political economy. The background to these changes is found both in the expansion of the bureaucratic state apparatus and in the partial integration of the Thai economy into the international capitalist system that have taken place since the late nineteenth century (Wilson, 1962; Morell and Chai-anan, 1981; Chatthip and Suthy, 1981; Chatthip *et al.*, 1981; Anan, 1984). It was the latter that led to rapid expansion of the rice economy (Johnston, 1975) and later to demand for upland crops such as maize, cassava, and sugar-cane (Uhlig, 1984). In turn, the pattern of structural change has been influenced both by the persistence of a habitable periphery outside centralized control, and by a resource endowment which allows agricultural expansion by encroachment on the forests. One outcome of this is a state rural development strategy that is oriented to communities 'catching up' with longer-settled areas, their transformation from 'forest' to 'civilized' status, and above all integration of peripheral areas into the national economy and polity.

Extent and Pattern of Forest Settlement

It is easy to forget how recent is general concern for preservation of tropical forests. In Thailand, forest settlement for agriculture and associated timber operations has been responsible for a large measure of the country's deforestation. Until recently, the rate of settlement has been such that depletion would leave little land under forest by the end of the century were recent trends to continue (Nart, 1984: 86). Yet for most of the past century, forest settlement by expansion of broad frontiers, movement into forest land that previously surrounded isolated villages, and settlement deep in forest reserve areas have been supported by institutional, economic, and infrastructural measures by government and also by agents of capital. Despite notional recognition of the need for conservation of remaining forest areas, many current programmes and policies support continued forest depletion.

History of Settlement

It has been estimated that the cultivated area in Thailand increased sixfold from 1850 to 1950, representing a 1.8 per cent annual increase, while the period 1950 to 1970 saw an acceleration to 2.7 per cent (Marzouk, 1972: 17). Over the period, growth in cultivated area has outstripped population increase (Feeny, 1984: 50). Except in the delta grasslands, most of this expansion has been by clearance of forest areas. It has been compared to the period of medieval forest clearance (Mittelalterliche Rodungsperiode) in Europe (Uhlig, 1984: 9). The scale of deforestation is difficult to determine precisely, but it is likely that from the beginning of the twentieth century the forest area has declined from over three-quarters to less than one-quarter of the national area (Feeny, 1984: 53–4).

Until the mid-nineteenth century, settlement had mainly been along river banks and coastal areas in the Central Plains (Sharp and Hanks, 1978: 36), in isolated pockets of alluvial land near water courses in the North-east, and in intermontane valleys and plains in the North. Expansion of cultivation commenced in earnest with demands for rice exports after the signing of the Bowring Treaty in 1855, although Tanabe (1978: 53–4) notes that the expansion was a far from smooth progression. Initially, settlement involved clearance of new areas in the Central Plains, but expansion of the commercial economy together with the need for new rice-land for subsistence needs later also affected the North and North-east. The depression in the rice economy early in the twentieth century was only a temporary interruption, and settlement continued apace. Following the Second World War, the agricultural economy diversified, and settlement of upland areas unsuited to wet rice became the main feature of agricultural expansion.

At each stage, infrastructural development by the State has been an important stimulus to settlement. In the latter part of the nineteenth century and early on in the twentieth, construction of canals played an essential part in expansion of rice cultivation (Tanabe, 1978: 52ff.; 1981:

222–6; Takaya, 1987: Ch. 4). The railways constructed early in the twentieth century linked the North-east, North, and South with Bangkok, opening up those regions for commercialization. More recently, especially since 1950, road construction has increased accessibility immeasurably, and this has played an important part in the settlement of new areas. Table 3.3 shows the rapid expansion of communications in the post-War period.

Settlement has also to be understood in terms of changing institutional arrangements concerning labour and land (see Feeny, 1982: Ch. 6). Following abolition of slavery and later of the corvée labour tribute under Chulalongkorn's reforms, the peasantry became at once more mobile and free to settle new land. However, there is evidence to suggest that land settlement was facilitated for some families by access to slave labour. Ananya (1985: 88) describes how slaves helped in early clearance of land in Theparaj and how, once freed, they went on to clear their own land. Johnston (1975: 24–5) recognizes the ambiguous effect of abolition of slavery on new settlement in at once freeing labour, but at the same time both depriving potential large-scale cultivators of labour and depriving small-scale cultivators of their only mortgagable security, the promise of bonded service with which to raise the finance for expansion of cultivation. Decline of the corvée unambiguously favoured increased settlement, as did its replacement by head taxes which required expansion of cultivation for production of a marketable surplus. Introduction of wage labour was an important step in allowing for entrepreneurial settlement. Meanwhile, reform of the system of land tenure in 1902 increased the incentive for land settlement and improvement. Issuing of land titles or expectation of such led to an increasingly speculative element in the motivation for land settlement.

The settlement has been in response not only to demographic pressures, but also to demands of the market and changing physical and institutional structures. The State has played a role in establishing the infrastructure facilitating or encouraging settlement, and this it uses as a means of increasing its control over the area within national boundaries.

Regional Patterns of Settlement

Settlement of forest areas is a response to a number of pressures and incentives which vary over time and space. Moreover, patterns of settlement are both ecologically and culturally determined. As a result, these patterns vary considerably from region to region. In Thailand, three broad regional patterns of settlement are usually drawn.

In North-eastern Thailand, an egalitarian village structure has traditionally precluded acquisition of new land from poorer neighbours. This has meant that migration for clearance of forest land is the only alternative to subdivision of holdings, and new villages have traditionally been established 3–5 kilometres away from the original village in a 'leap-frog' process that leads to a 'leopard spot' pattern of settlement (Ng, 1978: 42). However, longer distances are also covered in search of better land than that normally found in the dry, infertile North-east, and distances of 100 kilometres or more may be covered as a group of villagers moves *en masse*. Ng (1978: 42) cites the case of relocation of part of a village in Kalasin Province to Pichit in the upper Central Plains.

In Northern Thailand, where much of the older settlement is in intermontane valleys, new land settlement is patterned accordingly. Incremental settlement usually takes place on higher land adjacent to the village, requiring terracing and usually involving a move to lower quality land. Alternatively, new communities are established higher up the valley, often commencing with cultivation of *miang* (Northern Thai tea, the leaf of which is fermented and chewed; see Chayan, 1984: 187ff.). With the move into the uplands for cash cropping, the constraints on valley settlement are removed, and this has led to the rapid clearance of upper slopes for planting of maize and other crops. Meanwhile, minority groups such as the Hmong, Karen, Lisu, Yao, and Lahu have been extending their shifting cultivation with population growth and engagement in commercial cropping, and this has led to conflict amongst these groups and between these groups and lowland Thais. Turton (1975: 356–62) describes Thai encroachment on Karen settlements as land is terraced at higher elevations. Minority groups and lowland Thais are also in conflict with the State, since much of the land involved is officially classed as forest reserve.

In Central Thailand, settlement of forest lands has followed a more conventional frontier-type of settlement. This has involved a steady movement outward from the older core areas of settlement, particularly the Chaophraya Delta area around Ayuthaya and Bangkok. Several fronts of settlement are apparent at any one time, and these emerge as a result of several influences: availability of land; popular knowledge of such availability; suitability of the land for cultivation of a crop currently in demand; provision of infrastructure such as roads and processing facilities; marketing structures; and provision of finance by entrepreneurs who encourage settlement (Uhlig, 1984: 126; see also Rigg, 1986).

Settlement along the frontier in Central Thailand takes a number of forms. Uhlig, author of the most comprehensive study to date of the under-researched subject of spontaneous land settlement in Thailand, identifies three types of settler. First, there is the incremental type of settler who opens up land close to the existing community, supplementing existing cultivation. Second is the permanent long-distance settler, who leaves behind the old area of settlement. Third is what is termed the 'commuting' farmer, who maintains the original residence but expands cultivation at some distance—up to 100 kilometres—from the home village. Over time, the composition of a settlement may change: Moerman's (1968) Ban Ping study shows evidence of a move in dominance from the third to the second type, while the case of Ban Mai in the present study shows evidence of a move from the first to the second type.

Social Patterns of Settlement

Those who engage in forest settlement are not necessarily those who benefit most from it. Early settlement sometimes involved those displaced when their land was seized by the army or railway authorities (see Sharp and Hanks, 1978: 89). Alternatively, prisoners of war were settled in areas that the central authorities wanted developed (Sharp and Hanks, 1978: 40–2). More recently, settlement has often been promoted and financed by wealthy timber traders, maize and cassava merchants, or sugar millers (Uhlig, 1984: 41). Thus settlers differ from pioneers in the popularized American mould, making do with harsh conditions rather than seeing themselves as on an entrepreneurial mission of transforming a wilderness (Sharp and Hanks, 1978: 57–8).

Settlers have usually faced some sort of displacement. This may be due to population growth accompanied by a reluctance to subdivide land, at which point elder sons and their young families move to clear new land, at some distance if necessary. Alternatively, displacement may be more purely economic, due to debt foreclosure, loss of tenancy rights, or insufficient capital to purchase land on the part of young families. Displacement may be caused by infrastructural schemes, notably dam construction and associated reservoirs, in which case resettlement is usually planned and state directed. Environmental problems may lead to large-scale migration in search of better land, particularly in the case of sustained drought in the North-east. Problems of drought, flooding, and siltation that arise from deforestation have led to displacement in the piedmont areas on the edges of the Central Plains. A cycle of migration, forest clearance, environmental deterioration, poverty, and further migration in a leap-frogging pattern is evident.

Several authors have commented on social attributes that encourage migration for settlement of new lands. Uhlig (1984: 125) suggests that Thai farmers are not tied to the village community (see also Kemp, 1987). Established mechanisms for settlement are embodied in various social practices. Matrifocal residence encourages forest settlement, as sons-in-law are encouraged by parents-in-law with limited land to seek out new areas. The movement *en masse* from North-eastern villages is supported by return visits to the home village during the annual *Phaya paa baa* ceremony (at which merit is made with offerings to a Buddhist temple often at some distance), during which friends and relatives may be told of opportunities in the new area of settlement and encouraged to follow (Ng, 1978: 42–3). Alternatively, residents of villages on the edge of forest areas may encounter areas of settlement or land suited to settlement when on recreational hunting trips during the dry season, and this may lead to a permanent move at a later date.

The social characteristics of new communities vary, but those communities on the edges of the Central Plains are popularly renowned for their individualism and violence. Individualism is attributed to a number of factors. The very move to clear new land is seen as an individualistic venture. The staking out of land is assumed to be more concerned with establishing boundaries and therefore distance between neighbours than in establishing co-operation between settlers. This is reinforced by the well-known multiplicity of origins of settlers in many areas, reducing the potential bond of previous ties that might otherwise be maintained.

Violence is presumed to result partly as a natural consequence of individualism. Other factors often mentioned are the shortages of state law enforcement personnel and the use of such areas as hideaways by fugitives from the law.

There is some basis for these common perceptions. Land disputes feature prominently in the high rate of murder that characterizes many new areas of settlement, since land title is non-existent and claims to land can only be supported with authority backed by force. This situation is exacerbated by the fact that, during initial settlement, land is plentiful and carries little value, resulting in boundaries being poorly defined, if at all, by marks placed on trees. Following migration on a larger scale, land rapidly increases in value while the boundary markers have often disappeared, at which time disputes arise. This is comparable to the situation described by Johnston (1975: 125), in which the initial low value of land along the Prawetburirom Canal led to its original owners leaving the land fallow for several years following clearance. Such land would then be settled and cultivated by new claimants, resulting in subsequent disputes as the land increased in value.

Nevertheless, the individualism of frontier society can be overstressed. As we saw in the previous section, migration is commonly a joint enterprise involving substantial sections of whole villages. Even where it is more incremental, it often involves movement to areas where kin or other acquaintances have already settled. The initial process of 'staking out' is normally the prerogative of influential individuals rather than of the majority of poorer settlers. Where disputes develop among the latter group, it is usually because they have been sold, or otherwise allocated in return for services rendered, plots of land that overlap with those sold or allocated to others. The issue of state enforcement personnel is not clear-cut. In early stages of settlement, there is usually little violence and community mechanisms are utilized for resolving disputes in the absence of state authorities. It is during the later stages of settlement, which usually coincide with the construction of roads, district offices, and other aspects of state infrastructure, that violence abounds. Police and rangers often use a policy of getting rid of undesirables—ruthless men of violence referred to as *seua* ('tigers')—by a policy of extrajuridical killing. Only when state authorities are well established and land titles issued does the violence decline somewhat, but even then there is little evidence that this is due to an increased police presence. On a historical note, Johnston (1975: 186ff.) gives an account of the spread of police authority into rural areas. This appears to have led more to a general sense of security rather than a demonstrable decrease in crime, as law enforcement was regularized in place of the *ad hoc* military suppression campaigns that had previously dealt with rural banditry. It is also suggested that banditry in frontier areas was partly a result of suppression in more accessible areas of older settlement, suggesting that enforcement displaces rather than eliminates banditry.

The distinction between an individualistic and a communal spirit of settlement is sometimes assumed by outsiders to be evident in spatial patterns of settlement. The two types commonly recognized are clustered and scattered settlement, or 'village' and 'line' patterns (Uhlig, 1984: 35). Uhlig (1984: 140) suggests that the latter pattern is evidence of individualism in the process of settlement, since 'during this stage, the relationship between neighbours is more characterized by the staking out of personal property than by joining it together'. However, he fails to mention that this pattern of settlement follows widespread and longstanding Central Plains preferences for residence near the fields, precluding clustered settlement. Furthermore, this is not incompatible with co-operative working practices. In the following chapter, the history of settlement in the villages under study illustrates the general danger of utilizing form to interpret function, more specifically in drawing conclusions about the nature of frontier society from patterns of residence.

It is important to underscore the pace of change that is a feature of frontier society, particularly in the areas with which we are most concerned, the fringes of the Central Plains. Early settlement is usually for subsistence agriculture on newly cleared plots, using family labour. In upland areas, this rapidly gives over to commercial cropping, which leads to a relatively rapid process of social differentiation. Processes of differentiation are intimately related to the transformation of the environment. In early swidden plots, family labour and local inputs are used in all stages of production. The importance of family labour in early settlement cannot be over-emphasized. Prior to cultivation, labour is needed to clear land, and at an even earlier stage to lay claim to it. In the settlement of one Central Plains community in the late nineteenth century, 'The provision of labour, not of material resources, was the problem; and it is no wonder that an enduring tradition developed that material wealth in Bang Chan should be measured not in material possessions but in the number of productive workers included in a household over the long term' (Sharp and Hanks, 1978: 45). In more recent settlements, this overriding importance of family labour typically lasts for three years, after which a tractor is used to plough the land. At this stage, money is borrowed from traders for the first time, leading eventually to a high rate of indebtedness and the start of the process of differentiation (Uhlig, 1984: 165–7).

A final point to note concerning social patterns of settlement in forest areas is the role of influential backers. Historically, settlement was directed by the élite. The Saen Saeb Canal area east of Bangkok was settled by prisoners of war under royal direction. Ministers with distinguished service were given lands in newly cleared areas, as well as prisoners of war to develop them (Sharp and Hanks, 1978: 40–2). These prisoners later became tenants or cleared new lands for themselves. Ananya (1985: 88) notes the importance of slaves in early clearance of lands near Paedriw (Chachoengsao). Once freed, these slaves would go on to clear their own land, to which many ultimately gained control. More recently, cassava and maize traders have often financed settlement, for example, on either side of the Lom Sak–Pitsanulok Road in Thung Saleng National Park (Uhlig, 1984: 47). Traders in forest products collected by subsistence cultivators encourage and finance expansion of cultivation such as that of maize. In the case of clearance for sugar-cane planting, control by the influential persons involved is more direct. Contract farmers (*pa boei*) are hired to clear new land for planting. Once the land is developed, the *pa boei* move on to clear new land, while the sugar-cane planters (*long juu*) arrange a contract for production with nominal owners of the land, poor farmers to whom the land had been sold (*luuk rai*). This makes it difficult for the authorities to suppress incursion on forest reserves, since the cultivators are numerous and can easily be bailed out by their patron. In this way the 'sugar-cane front' in Chonburi has progressed 35 kilometres in fifteen years. Typically, 10 kilometres ahead of this front are subsistence cultivators in isolated clearings, who are moved on by the *long juu* using their *pa boei* clients in sometimes violent confrontations (Uhlig, 1984: 212–20).

A similar process goes on in other areas, including that which is the focus of this study. In this case, the influential persons behind settlement are illegal timber traders, who promise poor, often landless farmers a piece of land in exchange for help in timber operations. In this case too, it is the small farmers who take the risks of arrest, and the backers take advantage of this fact either by bailing out those who are arrested or by assuring their clients that in such a politically sensitive area,[1] the Government would not dare risk alienating them by arrest.

Forest Settlement and Agricultural Expansion

Agricultural growth has been via expansion of the cultivated area, and this expansion has been achieved largely at the expense of forest land. Although forest exploitation has often initially been for other purposes (notably timber felling), farming is the end-use of forest land when it is sustainable in the long term. Since the economy and people of Thailand have been oriented overwhelmingly to agriculture as a way of life and means of sustenance, this expansion is of primary importance in the development of the present-day economy and, by extension, of the national polity. The connection between forest settlement and expansion of the agricultural economy can be traced first to expanded rice cultivation, then to diversification into upland crops. It is also related to development of the wider political economy.

Expansion of Rice Agriculture

The seventy-five years following the Bowring Treaty of 1855 saw a twenty-fivefold increase in rice exports. Over the same period, the Thai population doubled to about 12 million (Ingram, 1971: 37–40). Meanwhile, productivity of rice-land fell substantially, from 1 883 kilograms of paddy per hectare in 1906 to 1 294 kilograms in 1940 (Feeny, 1984: 58). Since rice was and remains the staple food crop, the only way the surplus required for exports could be achieved—especially when domestic demand had increased—was by a rapid increase in the area under rice, from less than 6 million *rai* (1 *rai* = 0.16 hectare) in 1850 to more than 9 million *rai* in 1905 and 35 million *rai* by 1950.[2] Half the increase in area was in the Central Plains region, and this accounted for the bulk of exports (Ingram, 1971: 43). This expansion required large-scale clearance of forest areas.

Johnston (1975) has studied this expansion in detail, covering the years 1880 to 1930. He shows that much of the early expansion was facilitated by canal construction in the Delta area. Among the earliest waterways to be constructed, Phasijaroen and Damnoensaduak Canals to the west of Bangkok were a product of initiatives by high-ranking officials using government revenues under their jurisdiction. These officials had a personal stake in trade and development of new land following the opening up of the economy after 1885. Initially, cultivation and transport of sugar-cane provided the main source of revenue, but rapid expansion of the rice economy from the 1880s and the boom of the 1890s created a seemingly insatiable demand for rice and so also for new rice-land (Tanabe, 1978: 58–67). Some of the early expansion was not at the expense of forest. The Prawetburirom Canal to the east of Bangkok was dug by the Government in order to open up grasslands for cultivation, and land settlement was both encouraged (by exemption from land tax for the initial period of cultivation) and regulated (by registration of land). Establishment of the Siam Lands, Canals, and Irrigation Company in 1888 by royal and Chinese capital resulted in a virtual monopoly over canal building, and thus control over land settlement by this one company. The Rangsit network of canals north-east of Bangkok was the most comprehensive result, accommodating 100,000 new settlers on up to 1.5 million *rai* of land by 1905, accounting for one-quarter of rice-land in the Central Plains.

Following this period of rapid expansion, there followed a sharp but temporary reversal of fortunes in the rice economy during the period 1905 to 1912, particularly in the newly settled areas. This resulted from a combination of adverse weather conditions, disease, siltation of canals, a rise in land taxes, labour shortage, and a fall in the domestic price of paddy brought about by appreciation of the baht by approximately one-third its previous value. The population of the Rangsit area fell by as much as 35 per cent during this period due to emigration and tenants' abandonment of rice-land. Although this slowdown and localized reversal in settlement of forest lands for rice cultivation was short-lived, it was significant in marking a watershed between boom conditions and the more gradual expansion that followed. Whereas rice exports had increased more than fourfold between 1880 and 1884, and between 1905 and 1909 (taking five-year means), exports did not even double in the period from 1905 to 1929. This more gradual rate of growth was largely due to shortages of the labour and capital necessary for the opening of new lands, both of which had to be found domestically unlike the situation in Siam's colonial neighbours. Johnston (1975: Ch. 9) suggests that the slower rate of expansion in Thailand as compared with Burma, for example, resulted in sufficient 'slack' in the economy which enabled the

Thai peasantry to adapt to depression in the 1930s by reversion to subsistence production of many goods. Farmers responded to the fall in rice prices of 40 per cent between the 1920s and 1934 by *increasing* their production. This was effected by continued land clearance in order to maintain cash incomes, while cash outlay was minimized by further extensification of production and utilizing leisure time for home production of goods in place of cash purchases.[3]

Disruption of trade during the Second World War led to a sharp decline in rice production, but this was soon reversed following the end of the War. In the 1950s and 1960s, a number of factors led to a reduction in the rate of increase of area of rice-land. One was the growing shortage of land suited to rice cultivation, as clearance took farmers onto more marginal land. This was concurrent with the first major steps toward intensification in rice cultivation on existing land, with the construction of large-scale irrigation works associated with the Chaophraya Dam at Chainat and smaller schemes in the North-east. This also followed limited development of new seed varieties and use of inputs such as fertilizers and pesticides, but these latter had limited overall impact on yields. Of greater significance was the expansion of opportunities in non-rice agriculture, opening up large areas hitherto unexploited due to their unsuitability for cultivation of the subsistence crop.

Expansion of Upland Agriculture

Until approximately 1950, rice cultivation accounted for a stable proportion of all annual cropping in Thailand—approximately 90 per cent. As can be seen from Table 3.1, however, the period following 1950 saw a rapid increase in the importance of other crops, notably maize, sugarcane, and cassava. It should be noted that the area under rice has continued to expand, and that it is only in relative terms that rice cultivation has diminished in importance.

While the diversification away from rice in favour of upland crops has been commented on widely (for example, Ingram, 1971: 237, 261; IBRD, 1980: 10; Girling, 1981: 65–6), the close relationship between this process and that of forest clearance is relatively unexplored. With the notable exception of Uhlig's 1984 study, social aspects of the relationship are even less often touched upon.

Despite the fact that the traditional occupation of the Thai farmer has been rice-growing, more recent agricultural expansion has been in cash crops that are for export or to meet other non-local needs: 'The modern clearance settlement, . . . following a new socio-economic development, has abandoned the traditional wet-rice cultivation in favour of marketable crops of dry field cultivation' (Uhlig, 1984: 27). The reasons for this switch are complex, relating to pricing policies, marketing structures, ecological imperatives, and more general social and economic developments. The rice premium[4] as a disincentive to commercial rice-cropping is often quoted as a key element in encouraging a switch to other crops, but there are a number of problems with too simplistic an analysis. At the

TABLE 3.1
Increase in Thai Cultivated Area, 1950–1978

	Total Cultivated Area		*Rice-land*			*Dry Land/Perennials*					
Year	*'000 ha*	*Index*[a]	*'000 ha*	*Index*[a]	*Percentage of Total*	*'000 ha*	*Index*[a]	*Percentage of Total*	*Cassava*[b] *'000 ha*	*Maize*[b] *'000 ha*	*Sugar-cane*[b] *'000 ha*
1950	6 271	100	5 540	100	88	731	100	12	14	36	54
1960	7 717	123	5 921	107	77	1 796	246	23	72	286	158
1970	10 867	173	7 494	135	69	3 373	461	31	225	829	138
1978	15 197	242	9 346	169	61	5 251	800	39	1 323	1 356	510

Source: Adapted from Uhlig, 1984: 123, 124.
Notes: [a]Index is taken as 100 in 1950.
[b]These are the main 'upland' crops grown on the western fringes of the Central Plains, including the area under study.

level of production, a subsistence crop such as rice, whose cultivation chiefly involves family labour and non-cash inputs, is not strictly comparable with upland crops, which require cash inputs and entail the extra cost of land clearance. The reality of choices for most farmers does not involve straightforward trade-offs between crops on a particular piece of land. Thus the diversification that has taken place at the national level is not based on a fundamental change in the pattern of agriculture in older rain-fed rice areas; as Uhlig (1984: 125) puts it: 'the increase in agricultural production and the diversification of crops were not so much the result of successful intensification and crop diversification in the rice areas, but were mainly due to the rapid development in the areas of spontaneous land clearing'. This was facilitated by world market demand for the crops suited to newly cleared upland areas (Girling, 1981: 66n), a demand which was timely given the unsuitability of most of these areas to rice cultivation.

Three crops are pre-eminent in the expansion of field-cropping on the fringes of the Central Plains area.

Maize was the earliest field crop to obtain widespread popularity, especially after the introduction of Guatemalan hard maize during the 1950s. Its cultivation is spread over a diverse range of areas, but it is the Upper Central Plains area (administratively classified as the Lower North) that is commonly termed 'Thailand's corn belt'. Approximately 90 per cent of maize cultivation is for export, mainly to supply the livestock feed industries of Japan and Taiwan.

Cassava became popular in the 1960s with increasing demand for alternative feeds by the European Economic Community (EEC). Although the bulk of its cultivation is now in the North-east, where it has provided an alternative to kenaf,[5] it has also remained popular in the South-east and become so in other Central Plains fringe areas. Demand reached a peak during the 1970s when alternatives to grain were in high demand, but it has since tailed off and the EEC has set strict quotas for import of tapioca products. Nevertheless, the hardiness, flexibility, and limited labour demands of cassava make it a popular crop, leading to overproduction.

Sugar-cane has a long history in Thailand, and indeed rice specialization in the late nineteenth century coincided with a decline in the sugar industry (Johnston, 1975: 26–31) that was only revived under government encouragement during the 1950s and 1960s. The 1970s saw buoyant prices for sugar, and large areas on the eastern and western fringes of the Central Plains in Chonburi and Kanchanaburi Provinces respectively were turned over to this crop. Unlike maize and cassava, sugar enjoys a substantial domestic market, but more than half is still exported and the price received by producers is dependent on world market fluctuations.

Although the pattern of settlement for upland cropping is that of farmers geared to permanent agriculture, some doubts arise as to the long-term viability of current agricultural practice in many areas. Many of the newly settled areas are of low natural fertility, and yields in the early years following clearance are only obtainable due to a residual humic content of the soil that quickly dissipates with removal of the forest cover. Repeated monocropping of such soils can lead to rapid loss of soil nutrients, and problems of soil exhaustion, soil erosion, and invasion of weeds (notably *Imperata cylindrica* and *Pennisetum polystachyon*) are visibly evident in many areas. Certain soils are suited to long-term monocropping of upland crops given proper management and inputs, notably those associated with limestone formations, but these cover a small proportion of the areas cleared. Thai lowlanders who settle upland areas do not practise shifting cultivation in the same way as, for example, the Lua (Stott, 1978: 11–12), and there is an increasing tendency for soils to be 'mined' until they are taken over by *Imperata*, at which time farmers move on to clear new areas. In Conklin's now standard terminology, they are 'partial' shifting cultivators.[6] Uhlig (1984: 20–1) notes the irony of the current policy of trying to settle ethnic minorities who, in their 'integral' shifting cultivation practice, may have developed the only ecologically sustainable use of the forest (see also Chin, 1977: 110; Stott, 1978: 9), while at the same time lowlanders are moving into what inadvertently turns out to be temporary swidden agriculture.

Thus the settlement of upland areas contains the paradox of opportunistic adaptation to world market demand that results over the long term in impoverishment of many of those involved in settlement and the environment in which they have settled. This helps to explain why such areas are home to some of the poorest of Thailand's poor, while at the same time they are represented as the 'most dynamic, wealthiest, and innovation-receptive agrarian regions' (Uhlig, 1984: 43). Incorporation and differentiation, we will see, go hand in hand.

The Political Economy of Agricultural Expansion

Thailand is the world's largest exporter of rice and tapioca and an important exporter of maize and sugar. Yet area yields of all of these products, particularly of rice, are extremely low by world standards (Table 3.2). An important factor in this low productivity has been the reliance on extensification of agriculture by continuous land settlement rather than intensification on existing lands. Recently, yields in both new areas of settlement and in some older areas have shown downward trends. This is because deforestation associated with land settlement has resulted in environmental deterioration affecting agriculture both locally and in older areas. The extensive pattern of agricultural growth is a result of conscious choices of those in power.

Feeny (1977, 1982) analyses trends in rice productivity during the period prior to the Second World War to show that the decline in yields was due to a divergence between the social rate of return from investment in agriculture (particularly irrigation) and the return accruing to the élite who made the decisions to invest otherwise (notably in railway construction). The area under paddy increased by 3.14 per cent annually between 1911 and 1941, while the annual increase in output was only 1.91 per cent (Feeny, 1982: 24). In 1941, paddy yields in the Central Plains were

TABLE 3.2
Agricultural Investment, 1966 and 1974, and Productivity in Asia, 1969 and 1978

	Agriculture as Percentage of Total Government Investment		*Cultivated Area Per Capita (ha)*	*Paddy Yields (kg/ha)*	
Country	*1966*	*1974*	*1976*	*1969*	*1978*
South Korea	17.0	28.0	0.06	4 661	6 385
India	15.0	12.0	0.29	1 609	1 963
Malaysia	23.0	20.0	0.49	2 315	2 502
Pakistan	17.0	11.0	0.34	2 220	2 466
Philippines	14.0	36.0	0.20	1 681	1 972
Sri Lanka	16.0	16.0	0.17	2 565	2 895
Taiwan	n.a.	n.a.	0.01	3 867	4 468
Thailand	12.0	10.0	0.41	1 934	1 875

Source: Douglass, 1983: 196.
Note: Paddy yields are given for 3–4 years following investment figures, since a lag is to be expected between investment and returns seen in higher productivity.
n.a. = Not available.

only at 82.2 per cent of their level twenty years earlier (Feeny, 1982: 45). By the 1970s, rice yields had recovered to their early twentieth-century levels, but productivity could hardly be seen to have shown a dramatic improvement.

Part of the explanation for declining yields certainly lay in the diminishing quality of land being settled for cultivation, and much of the rest of the explanation lies with declining factor inputs per unit area that are themselves associated with extensification. Feeny argues that the main reason for lack of intensification at a time of increasing demand for rice both domestically and on the international market was failure to implement the large-scale irrigation scheme proposed by Van der Heide in 1902.[7] Pelzer (1945: 60) suggests that the failure to implement the former scheme was a direct result of political pressures brought to bear by landlords in the Rangsit area, who feared the loss of tenants that would result if large new areas of potential rice-land were made available in Suphanburi and elsewhere. Feeny (1982) analyses the politics of the non-implementation of Van der Heide's proposal in more depth, showing that the Rangsit landlords were influential in palace circles. He establishes a direct connection between failure to invest in irrigation and the decision to invest in railway connection of the North, North-east, and South as an alternative use of limited funds (see also Johnston, 1975: 93ff.; Takaya, 1987: 225). Feeny shows that irrigation would have produced a minimum return of 19 per cent per annum, as compared with less than 1 per cent for the railways. However, the return on increased agricultural productivity would have been difficult to recapture, particularly in light of the limit imposed on land taxes under the terms of the Bowring Treaty. In general terms, as Feeny (1982: 9) puts it:

While the demand for institutional change will respond to changes in potential profits for economic units (such as farm producers) associated with some change in institutions or policy, the supply will respond to changes in the potential profits for the elite decision makers. This difference represents a potential source of a divergence in the expected rate of return on a change for the economic units and the elite. In the Thai case this divergence was, in fact, quite important.

Railways were seen by the élite as necessary for national security purposes, specifically in extending central control from Bangkok over the outlying regions, given European expansionism in surrounding territories (Feeny, 1982: 80–4) and given provincial rebellions (Johnston, 1975: 93).

Although the post-War period has seen increased state attention to increasing agricultural productivity, agricultural pricing and export strategies have played a part in the continued importance of forest settlement in agricultural expansion. Following the Second World War, intensification of rice agriculture was further stunted by imposition of the rice premium, which was initially an important source of state revenue (see footnote 4). Later, the premium became more useful as a means of depressing the price of rice for urban consumers, which in turn has allowed urban wages to remain low as part of the Government's emphasis on industrial expansion. Meanwhile, the desire to increase exports and to diversify agricultural production away from rice led to a set of policies that combined with favourable world market conditions to promote the cultivation of upland crops as outlined in the previous section. As we have seen, this expansion was at the expense of forest areas rather than rice-land, and the period since 1960 has seen a decline in forest area from over 50 per cent of the national land area to under 20 per cent by 1989.[8] By the late 1980s, the most peripheral areas were producing crops for urban and export markets.

It would certainly be wrong to write off state programmes in support of agriculture in recent years. Construction of the Chainat Dam in the 1950s followed Van der Heide's plans more than half a century after they were drawn up. Research into improved rice seed, pesticides, mechanization, and other aspects of cultivation technology has increased following its extremely limited pre-War results. Agricultural extension work has aimed at increasing yields through application of new technology. Yet the fact remains that proportional investment in the agricultural sector remains extremely low compared with other Asian countries, and yields remain low while continued forest settlement maintains extensification. This extensification has been facilitated not only by neglect of agricultural investment, but also by other aspects of state spending in rural areas, notably on roads. Despite important changes in Thailand's polity and economic structure, agricultural development—as an opening up of new areas through improved communications rather than increasing productivity in existing areas—provides a continuity in the political economy of agricultural expansion up to the present day.

Socio-political Aspects of Forest Settlement

The foregoing discussion suggests that agricultural expansion, and therefore forest settlement, is an expression of particular aspects of the Thai political economy. However, expansion into forest areas must be seen also in the light of social and political concerns that are not in themselves part of the agricultural economy. An understanding of the cultural background to forest settlement provides the basis for an appraisal of the interplay between central and peripheral forces in the process of settlement.

Ideas about the Forest

Thai conceptions of the forest are varied, influenced as they are by elements of animism, Buddhism in its various forms, and Western ideas alternatively of 'progress' and 'conservation'. Popular discourse contains much that reflects the lawlessness, backwardness, and danger associated with the forest. The phrase *paa theuan*, or 'illicit forest',[9] is used to describe an area that is far from the centres of power, whether or not there is anything illegal going on and whether or not there is actually any forest remaining in the areas. *Khon paa* ('forest people') is a pejorative term for the backward, uncivilized, wild, as opposed to *khon meuang* ('town people'), a term which includes Northern Thai villagers who are not *khon paa*. Villages that are some distance from provincial towns are said to be 'in the forest' to indicate their peripherality. The 'law of the forest remaining in the areas. *Khon paa* ('forest people') is a pejorative state law. *Paa* as a suffix denotes 'wild' as opposed to the urban(e), civilized *baan* (house); wild and domestic cats, for example, are *maewpaa* and *maewbaan*.

The contradistinction between forest and authority, urbanity, civilization, safety, metropolis is contained in numerous such expressions and in other forms. One of the most interesting is a song that has been a radical 'Songs for Life',[10] a revolutionary song, and more recently a 'song for development' used in one of the Government's ideological training programmes:

> History may have many aspects
> But never has the worker been mentioned
> Bearer of burdens, wader through water and mud,
> Creator of the city from the forest
> The magnificent walled city
> With the blood and muscle of the road builder
> The way is cleared
> For others to follow.
>
> From one lonely forest to another
> As a wanderer, only the ground to call 'home'
> However cold, painful, dangerous
> Never a flinch of fear
> Hurrying forth to clear
> For others to follow

Their every footstep like fading shadows
Their names and bodies buried within the land.
(Author's translation)

Progress as the laudable product of forgotten heroes is set in terms of transformation of the wild forest into a habitable domain.

Traditional ideas about the forest are reflected in local cultural practices. In North-east Thailand, villages maintain a resting place, called a *paa chaa*, for the remains of the dead. This consists of a small area of sacred woodland. In addition, near some villages is an area of forest that belongs to the spirit of the male ancestors. Trees in this area cannot be cut for fear of offending these spirits. Elsewhere, non-affinal spirits are believed to hold influence over areas of forest, and it is believed that anyone who cuts wood from such an area will soon meet a violent death. In Chonburi, *takien* trees are protected by a malevolent female spirit (Stott, 1978: 16). In the Tai autonomous region of Xishuangbanna in southern China, forests in near pristine condition on some 400 'holy hills' are preserved as the gods' gardens and account for between 1.5 and 2.5 per cent of the total land area (Pei, 1985). Stott (1978: 17) mentions the significance of the Buddhist ascetic tradition of 'forest dhamma' which requires the forest as a place of retreat and tranquillity.

Thus forest and civilization have been seen as opposites, but with certain forces to be considered before the forest is destroyed. Traditional beliefs provide an indigenous mode of conservation, and local development workers have noted the 'mini-forest reserves' of the North-east. Conservation strategy as pursued by the Government has, on the other hand, adopted a Western approach and does not take into account uniquely Thai or other local cultural approaches to conservation (Stott, 1978: 18). Indeed, colonial legacy in forest policy as a result of Britain's influence in the structure and ideology of the Royal Forestry Department (RFD) may have positively hindered effective conservation. In the 1980s, a number of environmental issues achieved national political prominence, supported by public awareness of the problems of deforestation through extensive coverage in the media. The controversy that arose over proposed construction of the Nam Choan Dam in Kanchanaburi is an example of increased and effective public participation in forest conservation (Nart, 1984: 91; see also Hirsch and Lohmann, 1989), and cancellation of logging concessions in 1989 showed a responsiveness to public mood.

Settling and Connecting the Periphery

The centralized nature of power in the Thai context has traditionally meant that control radiated out from the centre and diminished with distance. The concept of fixed frontiers at the periphery is a new one (Withaya, 1984: 150–1; Thongchai, 1988). As a result, central authority has normally been established by strengthening administrative and physical links between outlying areas and the centre, which for over two centuries has been in Bangkok.[11]

In the nineteenth century, the release of previously tied serfs and slaves resulted in central authorities' being anxious to maintain control (Sharp and Hanks, 1978: 88):

> Such a large group could not be permitted to run the risk of vanishing or of abandoning society. So they were carefully settled on virgin or other lands by newly appointed commune chiefs, registered at newly built district offices managed by officers newly trained in the recently established civil service, and supervised by the newly organized police.

Soon after the signing of the Bowring Treaty, cultivation had been encouraged by lifting of taxes on newly cleared land. During the reign of Rama V (1864–1910), land settlement was encouraged by construction of canals. Even earlier than that, canal construction had also had a strategic aspect, notably in the case of the Saen Saeb Canal during the reign of Rama III (Sharp and Hanks, 1978: 39; Johnston, 1975: 42–3). Early in the twentieth century, railways were constructed to link peripheral regions even further afield.

Initially, promotion of settlement and linking of outlying regions was achieved mainly by provision of administrative and physical infrastructure, together with a range of incentives, as well as institutional reforms, notably in the area of property rights. However, since 1940 the Government has been involved more directly in land settlement, in particular through the Land Settlement Division of the Public Welfare Department under the Ministry of the Interior, and through the Self-help Land Settlement Schemes of the Ministry of Agriculture and Co-operatives. Uhlig (1984: 32–3) notes six other government departments also involved in land settlement, while others have counted a total of fourteen and commented on problems of duplication and lack of co-ordination (see Demaine, 1984). These departments include the Agricultural Land Reform Office (ALRO), set up following the 1975 Land Reform Act. Ostensibly established to deal with growing problems of landlessness, particularly in the Central Plains and parts of the Upper North, ALRO has tended to locate projects in recently settled areas in order to legitimize control over land that would otherwise be occupied by forest squatters. In some cases, forest land has been cleared specifically to make way for a 'land reform' settlement.[12] In all settlement schemes since 1940, some 230,000 families have been settled on 700,000 hectares of land. To put these figures in perspective, however, there are estimated to be at least 1,000,000 squatter families farming 5,000,000 hectares of forest reserve (Feder, 1987: 37–9).

Since the 1960s, the largest part of government investment in rural areas has been in road construction (Table 3.3). Concentration in 'sensitive' areas, such as the North-east, and the co-operation of the United States Operations Mission (USOM) show the security orientation of this investment in roads and the emphasis on maintaining or increasing central control over peripheral areas. Feeder road construction has received a boost since the 1970s with the various *tambon* schemes, and major strategic road construction has been under way since the early 1980s to make accessible peripheral areas that had previously been under

TABLE 3.3
Expansion of the Thai Road Network, 1950–1980

	State Highways		*Provincial Roads*		*Total Length*
Year	*Paved*	*Unpaved*	*Paved*	*Unpaved*	*(km)*
1950	809	5 022		5 831	
1955	1 815	5 299		7 114	
1960	2 972	5 474	151	1 967	10 565
1965	5 046	4 436	405	2 388	12 275
1970	8 620	1 781	1 478	4 413	16 292
1975	11 840	818	3 398	4 043	20 099
1980	13 733	160	8 670	5 587	28 151

Source: Uhlig, 1984: 126.
Note: These figures do not include the network of approximately 43 000 kilometres of rural roads.

the influence of the Communist Party of Thailand. The vast majority of villages are today accessible by four-wheeled motor vehicles. This opens up large areas for commercial cropping, and it has been noted that apart from security considerations, road construction is also concentrated in areas suited to cultivation of export crops (Uhlig, 1984: 126).[13] Roads linking maize-producing areas with Bangkok have been shown to reduce marketing costs by 20 per cent (Goldberg, 1979: 359), while local feeder roads are vital in making cash cropping feasible. Even improved bus communications promote land settlement by increasing the contact between new settlers and potential settlers in home villages, and by increasing the possibilities for 'commuter' farming.

Other than provision of infrastructure, the Government has taken a number of other measures which directly or indirectly promote land settlement. In particular, sugar-cane planting was promoted as part of the import substitution and export promotion policies of the 1960s and 1970s. Initially, sugar actually had to be imported to feed the mills, but expansion in peripheral areas soon made up the shortfall, and there was a rapid expansion onto forest lands during the sugar boom of the early 1970s. Cultivation of maize and cassava was also supported by government export promotion, and this cultivation too has normally been on previously forested lands.

An important part of increasing control over peripheral areas is the establishment of administrative structures. Uhlig (1984: 140) characterizes the formation of new administrative units in newly settled areas as a type of 'successive cell division'. This is the process by which a *tambon* (cluster of villages) becomes a temporary branch district with limited administrative functions, and usually within three to five years it becomes a district with the full range of functions. The new district is made up of several *tambon*, which may themselves eventually be 'promoted' to district status. Johnston (1975: 36–8) suggests that the creation of administrative units called *khwaeng* (equivalent to a present-day district) is the best evidence we have for early population growth and expansion of cultivation in Ayuthaya Province.

The process of establishing state control over peripheral areas by increasing administrative and physical links is one fraught with conflict. Part of the conflict is internal to the bureaucracy. Conflicts of interest arise between departmental objectives, such as the protection of forest reserve by Forestry Department officials, as against the desire for registration of villages and provision of schools by the Interior and Education Ministries respectively. Such conflict does not only revolve around issues of departmental function; it also arises due to the desire for various departments to expand their range and scale of activities (Morell and Chai-anan, 1981: 49), resulting in a competitive duplication of function that may take on a territorial dimension[14] most clearly evident in the staking out of new areas for land settlement programmes. Other areas of conflict surrounding land settlement are between settlers and the State. Settlers on forest reserve land are mistrustful of state intentions in projects such as land reform, while state officials are keen to gain administrative control over scattered outlying settlements. Resettlement or even physical removal of whole villages may result, while villagers may in turn devise means to evade such control.

The Forest Haven

Despite the dangers associated with the forest, the shelter, resources, lands, and protection afforded by it have historically made this peripheral environment a source of security for individuals. Onerous corvée and military service up until the nineteenth century frequently caused people to take to the forests (Akin, 1969: 87; Chayan, 1984: 187–8; Withaya, 1984: 154), leading to the tattooing of bonded men. Early settlement of Bang Chan (now almost a suburb of Bangkok) was effected by those escaping corvée obligations, since until the 1890s, 'Bang Chan lay beyond the orbit of government, its inhabitants having "headed for the woods (*pai paa*)" as effectively as an escaped slave' (Sharp and Hanks, 1978: 65).

While the corvée was still in operation, the option of fleeing to the forests gave serfs some sanction over the demands of their masters, since excessive exploitation would lead to an escape to the forests (Sharp and Hanks, 1978: 82), at a time when control over labour was more important than control over land (see Feeny, 1982: Ch. 6). However, the forest offered a different source of security, once slavery and the corvée had been abolished ... '[O]nce the wilderness had been a retreat for the disaffected few. In the new social order the many more without a place in the productive scheme had to fend for themselves, and the wilderness offered them a haven' (Sharp and Hanks, 1978: 88). Thus forest settlement to avoid control by higher authorities was partly replaced by migration in the search for means of subsistence after displacements caused by institutional changes at the centre.

During the twentieth century, the forests have continued to offer both a political haven and an economic alternative. Disaffected groups took to the hills and forests following the outbreak of armed hostilities between government forces and the Communist Party of Thailand in August 1965. By the mid-1970s, bases had been established in forest areas of most provinces, and these served to receive those fleeing political repression following the massacre at Thammasat University on 6 October 1976. The action of escape was referred to most commonly as 'going into the forest'.

As an economic haven, forests over the past century have yielded sustenance mainly in the form of land to millions of new settlers. Although population pressure has been partly responsible for this displacement, social and economic displacement has also arisen as a result of structural changes. It is estimated that at least 1,000,000 rural households are tenants and 500,000 are landless labourers, and the 30 per cent of farm households that this represents may choose to seek security in further forest settlement.

A final aspect of the forest haven is the aesthetic one. The forest as Buddhist retreat has already been mentioned, and some forest monks have attracted large urban lay followings in recent years. This can lead to construction of permanent roads, buildings, and other infrastructure, resulting in occasional conflicts between certain sects and local authorities. In other cases, monks have been instrumental in helping villagers to preserve forest on upland watersheds whose destruction has been threatened by development projects. A more Western type of aestheticism is manifested in the establishment of more than fifty national parks and wildlife reserves, but here too there is a conflict between preservation of the forest and its opening up as a retreat for urban dwellers.

Forest Settlement and Rural Development

This chapter has reviewed the process of forest settlement, its place in overall agricultural expansion since the opening up of the Thai economy, and the social, administrative, and political contexts of forest settlement. So far, the pattern of settlement has appeared as a set of interactions between central authorities and peripheral populations. These interactions are an outcome of struggles for control by the groups involved. On the part of the State, the objects of control have been people, territory, and economic surplus generated in peripheral regions. On the part of peripheral populations, the concern has been to maintain control over their own labour, physical safety, and means of sustenance. The most recent arena for interaction in this dialectic is that of rural development.

Rural development as directed change in rural areas is naturally concentrated in those areas in which the developers are most concerned with the need and potential for change. In the case of state developers, a number of considerations are taken into account. There is a close link between development and 'security' considerations—that is, the maintenance of centralized control over the polity. Other considerations concern reduction of regional income disparities and increasing efficiency of resource use. These considerations combine to place the emphasis on peripheral areas, many of which are also areas of recent settlement.

During the Fifth Plan, 276 districts were first earmarked for special attention. As the NESDB (1981: 281) explains it, most of these 'poverty concentration districts' are peripheral to the older areas of settlement, since:

> In the selection [of the districts], the principal criterion will be the actual physical areas, and not the income level. There are two reasons for this. Firstly, the concept using spatial distinction will assist in grappling with important causes of poverty concentration problems. Secondly, it is necessary to solve poverty problems in the areas from where the problems originate. If the people are not urgently assisted they have to find ways and means of living. The result has been the destruction of natural resources and migration, both temporarily and permanently.

The rural development measures undertaken in these areas are nominally concerned with improving the welfare of the majority of Thailand's rural poor who live in the target districts. While there is no doubt that many of the programmes are sincerely intended to fulfil just this purpose, this study suggests that welfare improvement is only one aspect of rural development as practised by state authorities, that it is an aspect that achieves only limited success, that certain measures are positively detrimental to welfare improvement even in terms set out by the developers and, most importantly for the present discussion, that rural development represents in an important way a continuity with past attempts to gain control in the power struggles between the centralized State and peripheral populations.

Most NGO projects are also located in peripheral areas. This is due partly to the poverty of such areas, but it is also considered more practicable to set up community schemes in villages less affected by urban influences. As discussed in the previous chapter, NGO activities are often oriented to increasing the bargaining power of the rural poor. While the Government on the one hand welcomes the input of resources that NGO schemes provide for such areas, it is at the same time often suspicious of alternative approaches in areas considered politically sensitive, and this has produced another axis in the dialectic of control and power in peripheral areas.

Conclusion

The issues addressed in this chapter suggest a new perspective in looking at the Thai periphery, which has been roughly equated with areas of existing or recently cleared forest. Rural development in such areas is to some extent a continuation of processes of agricultural expansion and socio-political change discernible for more than a century. Nevertheless, there is a shortage of information on the process of incorporation, of which rural development is the latest manifestation, and the need for detailed case studies has been noted (Uhlig, 1984: 10). The recent experience of two communities in a peripheral area of the Central Plains illustrates the way in which processes described above have worked themselves out at a local level.

1. Many recently settled forest areas are politically sensitive ('pink') due to their proximity to zones of recent Communist Party of Thailand (CPT) influence. They are distinguished from CPT-held areas ('red areas') and are alternatively known as 'infiltration zones'. Parts of Lan Sak were classified as such in the late 1970s.

2. Declining productivity of rice-land was in turn related to the expansion into more and more marginal lands (see Uhlig, 1984: 13) and to declining factor inputs (Feeny, 1982: 49ff.).

3. Such a response is a classic Chayanovian response by the peasantry to hard times. Rather than cutting back on production with a fall in prices, leisure time was sacrificed in order to maintain acceptable subsistence levels. This is evidence in favour of a strong subsistence orientation even among the relatively commercialized Central Plains population at this time, and such an orientation is supported by accounts given by elderly villagers in Lan Sak of the revival of crafts such as weaving in times of shortage during the Depression and War years. The response was no doubt facilitated by the considerable scope remaining for expansion of rice-land in parts of Thanyaburi and on the west bank of the Chaophraya, despite more congested conditions in some older areas of settlement. This contrasts with the contemporary situation in Burma (see Johnston, 1975: Ch. 9).

4. The Rice Premium is an effective tax on rice that was first instituted in 1955. Between 1955 and 1976, the premium provided the Government with between 1 per cent and 17 per cent of its revenues. The chief benefit of the premium for the Government has been the holding down of domestic rice prices, and thus also urban wages. Various estimates show that, were the premium to be removed, farmers would receive farm gate prices for paddy higher by anything from 23 to 85 per cent, and there is widespread agreement among economists that the premium serves to discourage intensification of rice production and distorts agricultural incentives. The principal beneficiaries are state revenues and urban consumers, and as such the rice premium represents a regressive resource transfer from rural to urban populations. Between 1953 and 1963, for example, the rice premium represented 60 per cent of the net flow of resources from the agricultural to the non-agricultural sector (Feeny, 1982: 113–14, 116; Girling, 1981: 63; see also in particular Ingram, 1971: 243–61 for arguments for and against the rice premium and its effects *vis-à-vis* broader development strategy).

5. The fibre crop kenaf, an inferior substitute for jute, is used mainly in making gunny sacks for rice and other grains. It was promoted in the North-east in support of a policy of industrialization from the 1950s onward (see Silcock, 1970: 77–8).

6. Chin (1977) discusses several classifications of shifting cultivation. Many of these are evolutionary in orientation or distinguish systems according to levels of technology. However, the most significant distinction is that between what Conklin (1957) has called 'partial' and 'integral' systems. Integral systems are those that have developed over a long period of time and involve cultural and ecological adaptation of the shifting cultivators to their environment in a non-destructive use of tropical forest land. Partial systems, on the other hand, involve cultivators familiar with permanent field cultivation and monocropping, who use soils more destructively.

7. Without water control, rice agriculture in the Central Plains is at the mercy of the elements (see Takaya, 1987). Whereas 1 800 millimetres of rainfall are needed for ideal cultivation, only 1 000–1 500 millimetres can be expected in the Central Plains (Johnston, 1975: 4). Dependence on annual flooding by the Chaophraya River before construction of the Chainat Dam was risky: of the 99 years to 1945, only 32 had satisfactory water levels; in 30 years, levels were too low; in 22 years, they were barely sufficient; and in 15 years, there were floods (Pelzer, 1945: 60). Variations in flood levels have to some extent been evened out by the Bhumiphol and Chainat Dams (Donner, 1978: 223–5).

8. It should be noted that official figures for forested area are open to interpretation, depending on the criteria used in delimiting natural forest. It is clear, for example, that for some time rubber plantations were included in the figures reported by the RFD, and the official forested area was revised downward from 29 per cent in 1985 to 19 per cent in 1989.

9. The Khmer word *theuan* (illicit) itself originally meant 'forest', 'jungle', or 'wilderness' (MacFarland, 1944). Modern usage and more recent dictionary definitions refer almost exclusively to the metaphoric sense of the word.

10. 'Songs for Life' were popular among students and other radical groups during the period 1973 to 1976. Following the coup of 6 October 1976, many of these songs were banned and thus became associated with opposition to the Government. Several of these have latterly been taken up by state developers and their connotations have been transformed by their new context. Others remain popular with students in a period characterized both by a more liberal regime and less radical student population.

11. Takaya (1987: 200) shows that, early in the Bangkok era, forest products from outlying areas were the main source of state revenues. This provided fiscal reasons for strengthening physical links with the periphery.

12. The first discussions of land reform in Thailand, in 1906, placed an emphasis on land colonization rather than redistribution (Johnston, 1975: 379n).

13. The ambiguity of purpose in road construction is matched historically by early canal development. Johnston (1975: 43n) notes the difficulty of differentiating between political and economic motivations of Government in such development.

14. Until Chulalongkorn's administrative reforms of 1874, organization of government ministries was partly on a territorial rather than a functional basis (see, for example, Johnston, 1975: 6). The names of some ministries still reflect this organization. For example, *Kaalahoom* (or Defence) was responsible for the southern region, and *Mahaad Thai* (or Interior) for the northern region (Akin, 1969: 66). Girling (1981: 30) (after Tambiah) relates this to the traditional 'cosmological design' of authority and administration, which involved a 'totalizing' of religious and secular, civil and military, as well as territorial and functional. He shows how such attitudes have persisted up to the present despite structural reforms. Morell and Chai-anan (1981: 42ff.) characterize operations of the Thai bureaucracy as a type of 'internal colonialism'.

4
Opening and Closing the Western Frontier

In the thirty years that have seen the opening and closing of a frontier, the western Thai district of Lan Sak in Uthaithani Province has undergone a dramatic transformation. The forest has almost completely disappeared. Isolated forest communities have become accessible cash-cropping villages. Local autonomy enforced by isolation has given way to political and economic integration into a wider system, enforced by accessibility, but prompted in particular by the local context of rural development.

Settlement of Lan Sak

Although included in the Lower North Region administratively, Uthaithani Province is geographically part of the north-west fringe of the Central Plains. Bordering the Chaophraya River in the east, just below its emergence as the confluence of the Ping, Wang, Yom, and Nan Rivers that drain much of northern Thailand, Uthaithani rises westward into the mountains that extend through Kanchanaburi and Tak Provinces into Burma (Figure 4.1). Until 1961, 73 per cent of Uthaithani Province was covered by forest. By 1985, forest cover was less than 41 per cent (RFD, 1987), and deforestation continues apace. For many years, Uthaithani was known in surrounding provinces and further afield as a province of opportunity, where land was to be had virtually for the taking. It also became known as a wild frontier area, where hazards to life and limb included malaria, wild animals, and later on murderous land disputes. Land pressures in neighbouring areas, however, ensure that settlement has continued unabated. Settlement was facilitated in no small part by the clearance of large areas of forest under concession to the state-run Thai Plywood Company (TPC). Construction of roads has also been crucial. As recently as 1966, Uthaithani had no hard-surfaced road outside the provincial town and only 40 kilometres of all-weather light surfaced road, and until 1978 the province could only be reached by road via a ferry across the Chaophraya River at Manorom. Now a bridge connects the Asia Highway (the main Bangkok–Chiengmai road) with approximately 200 kilometres of hard-surfaced road and hundreds of

Figure 4.1
Location Map: Lan Sak and Places Referred to in the Text

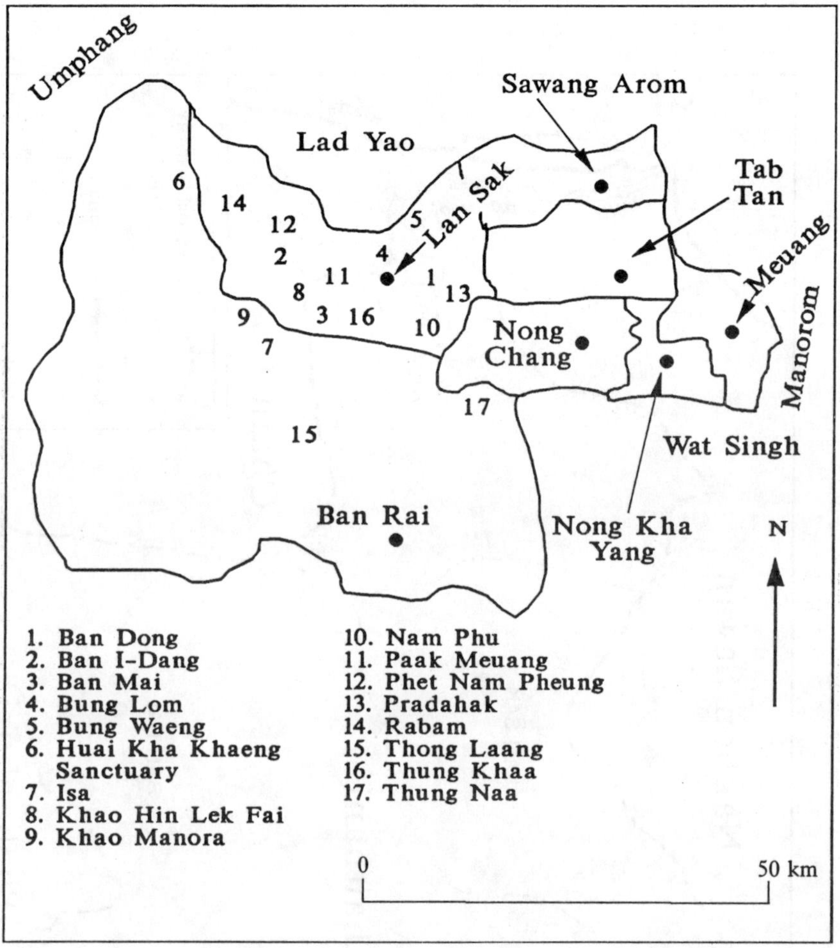

kilometres of all-weather gravel roads in the province (Figure 4.2).

The earliest historic inhabitants of western Uthaithani[1] were Karen upland subsistence cultivators. Lao[2] settlers were the earliest lowland people to move into the area. The oldest Lao residents report that settlement in Ban Rai dates from the forced migration of prisoners of war associated with the defeat of Laos during the reign of Rama III in the early nineteenth century; the oldest Lao resident reports that his great-grandmother had come from Vientiane at this time. Early communities were only semi-permanent. When someone died of sickness, the small community might move on to another part of the forest, taking only what they could carry across their shoulders on a pole. The first Lao community in what is now Lan Sak District dates from the second decade of the twentieth century, and until the 1950s it consisted mainly of thirteen families, settled at the site of what is now Ban Dong. Lao and Karen

Figure 4.2
Communications in Uthaithani

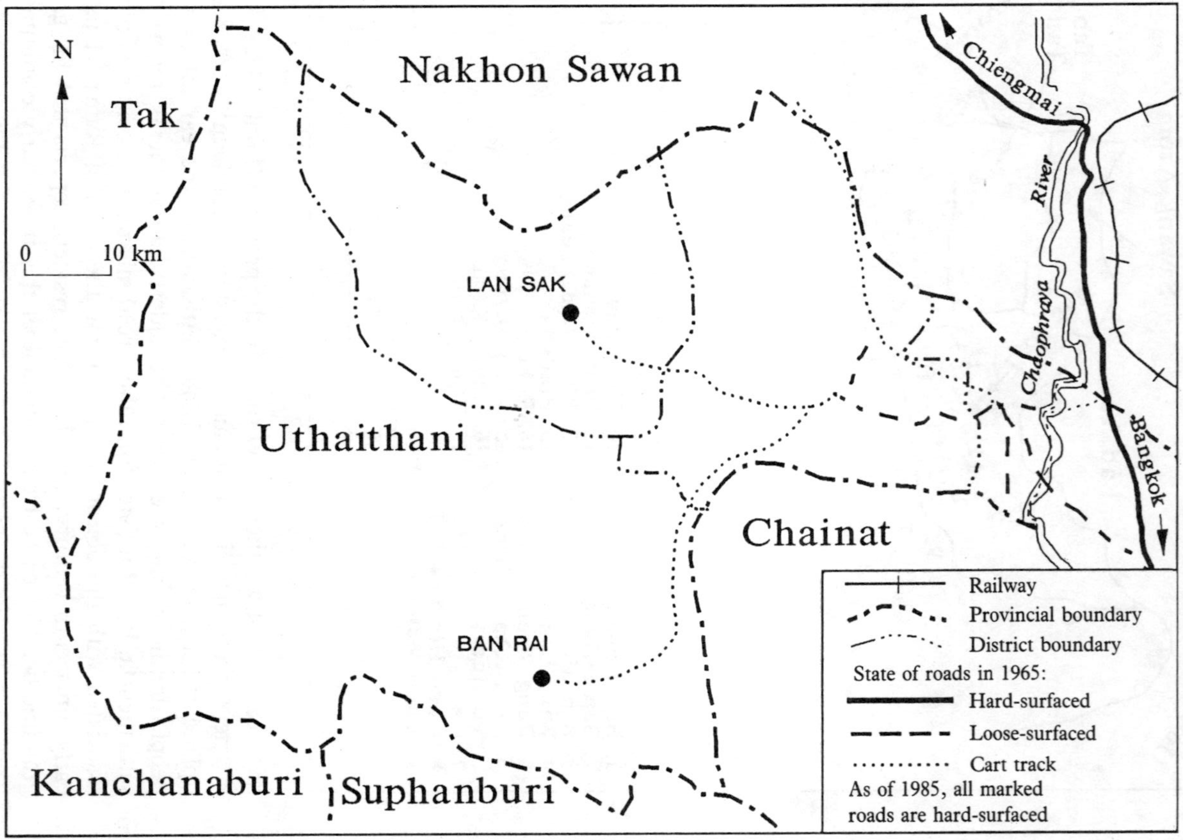

coexisted mainly in separate communities, but in the case of one settlement, Ban I-Dang, there was intermarriage between the two groups.

Being Lao implies an ethnicity distinct from the Thai (lowlanders) or Karen (upland shifting cultivators). In the local context, the Lao occupy an intermediate position, in having for several generations lived an isolated existence in forest communities, despite having roots in a lowland rice culture. Apart from linguistic and other cultural distinctions, Lao settlers appear to have developed a relative immunity to malaria. This and their ability to cope with other rigours of forest life helped to maintain their isolation from lowland Thais, whose fear of the forest was a factor inhibiting large-scale migration in the absence of great land pressures. Lao settlers planted rice, chillies, and other subsistence crops in small forest clearings. Land rights were according to usufruct and had no legal basis, and for many years after settlement land had no exchange value. The same held true for timber, whose abundance and lack of exchange value prevented competitive exploitation. Communications were by foot or cart track, and trade was limited to sale of forest products such as *yaang* resin[3] and skins in exchange for salt and a limited number of other non-local goods. Trade was effected by buffalo cart and carried out with lowland Thais. Clothes were made of cloth woven from home-spun, home-grown cotton. Rice was husked by foot pounding. Wildlife was abundant, and the Tap Salao River teemed with fish, so that there was no need to rear livestock other than chickens for meat. The village leader had only occasional contact with the outside world, since to get to the district administration at Ban Rai involved a full week's round trip. Decisions and rules were internal to the community.

In the 1950s, the first Thai settlement was established at Thung Khaa by enterprising settlers who came to make a living off trade in *yaang* oil, whilst maintaining subsistence plots similar to those of the Lao communities. One of the earliest settlers became the *de facto* leader of the community, referred to as the *khon to* ('big man'), and he took in new settlers who in his words 'had not received justice (that is, entitlement to land) from their parents'. The locality had previously been unoccupied apart from a few Lao and a small number of Karen, most of whom moved away into the hills with the influx of the Thais. This community of about twenty families was also relatively isolated: a trip to the nearest market town, Nong Chang, took two to three days.

Pressures of land and increasing problems with lowland agriculture led to a growing stream of Thai settlers from neighbouring districts and provinces in the 1960s. Settlers were mainly landless or near-landless farmers, or those whose land was insufficient in size or productivity for their children to make a living on. With this influx, land sales commenced, albeit at negligible prices. Foresight had led some Lao residents to claim areas of forest land which they later divided among the Thai settlers. Likewise, certain residents in Thung Khaa claimed areas of *yaang* forest land that they had worked (measured by number of trees rather than by land area) and retained these for later sale to new migrants. As land took on value, a claim to a tract depended increasingly on ability to control it, and this meant wielding a certain amount of authority. In order to do so, in one villager's words, 'You must have a following, or group of mates.'

Nevertheless, despite increasing pressures for new settlement and staking out of large tracts by influential individuals, the pace of settlement remained gradual. Many older Lao residents complain now of their lack of foresight in not staking out land, or in giving away land to early Thai settlers. Few imagined that, within a short space of time, land would take on such value, or that the landscape of their community would be transformed from a clearing in the forest to a cluster of planted fruit and coconut trees, amid an otherwise virtually treeless landscape dotted by scattered homesteads with their own clusters of young trees.

The significant change came with the granting of a concession to the TPC in 1970. This led both to a legal clearance of large areas of hardwood forest for timber, and to a lucrative illegal timber trade arising from abuse by subcontractors to the concessionaires and from the surreptitious trade in non-concession areas that was now facilitated by the new timber roads. Where timber previously had no monetary value (many villagers say they could cry when they think of the timber they burnt in clearing subsistence plots), it soon acquired a value far in excess of the land it was standing on. Quick profits were made by employing landless settlers to extract the wood in exchange for promises of free land or land at token prices.[4] Clearance of forest by concessionaires and others removed a major constraint to settlement—the hostile forest environment. This coincided with a time when crop diversification was encouraged and prices for maize and other field crops[5] were buoyant, and when land shortages in the Central Plains and elsewhere were increasing. Moreover, deforestation in the west of Uthaithani Province had started to cause problems of flooding[6] and erratic stream flow in the lowland eastern part of the province, reducing the productivity of rice agriculture in Nong Kha Yang, Meuang, Tap Tan, and Nong Chang Districts. This started a vicious circle of environmental degradation, poverty, migration, and further deforestation that continues to the present. With all these contributing factors, it is hardly surprising that such a spectacular rate of deforestation has occurred. If available, the figures for Lan Sak would be even more dramatic than those for Uthaithani, but the extent of deforestation can be gauged from Figure 4.3.

The period of heaviest immigration was the second half of the 1970s. The year 1975–6 in Lan Sak saw a 37 per cent population increase from 13,565 to 18,580, followed by a 34 per cent rise the following year to 24,883. By 1979, the population stood at 32,505 (NSO, 1980: 8–9), 38,533 by 1981 (Ministry of the Interior, 1982), and 46,927 by 1987. Many of the settlers came from Nong Chang, Nong Kha Yang, and Tap Tan Districts in the same province, while others came from neighbouring provinces or from further afield—in particular, the North-east. The vast majority came in pursuit of land. A combination of land alienation arising from commercialization of agriculture and debt foreclosure, environmental degradation leading to drought and flooding, and population growth had forced many to uproot. Often, settlers came in groups, and

Figure 4.3
Deforestation in Uthaithani and Lan Sak

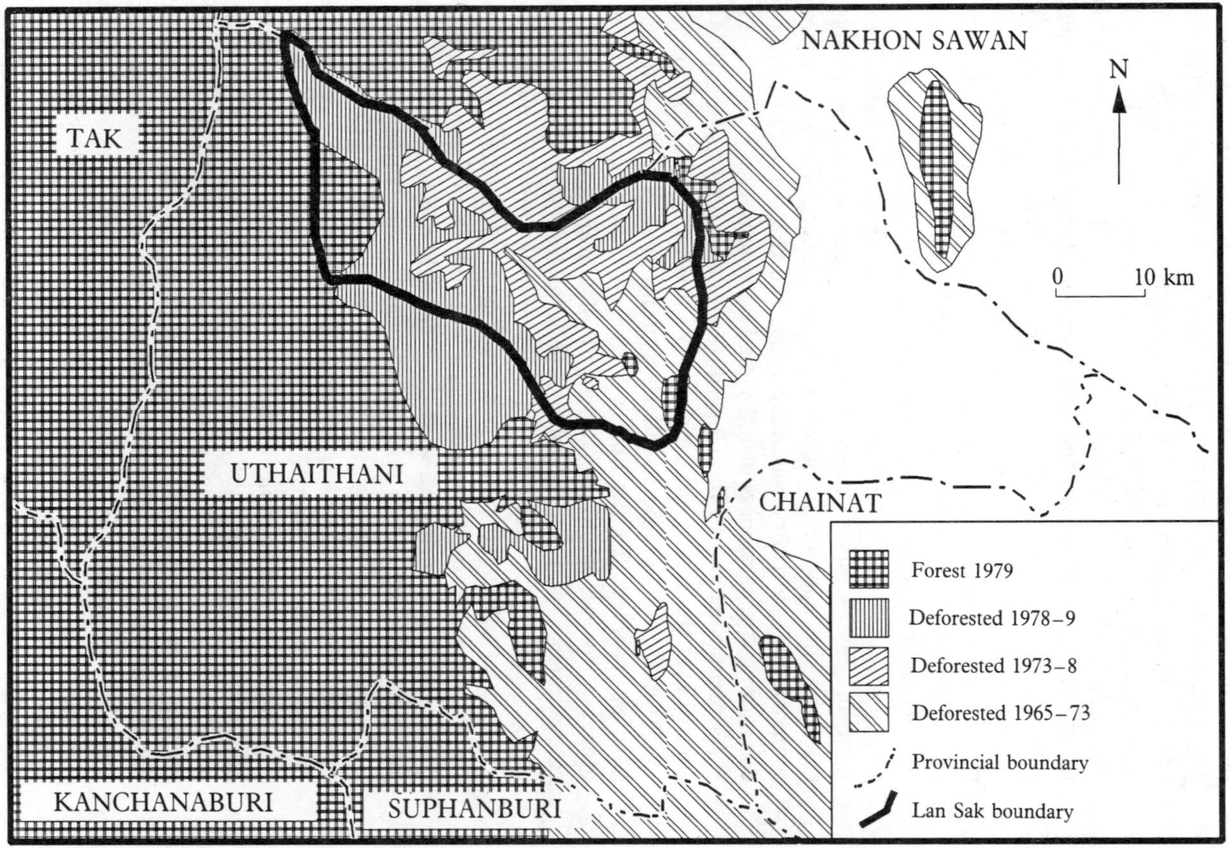

Source: Royal Forestry Department, Uthaithani.

on occasion whole villages or sections of villages transplanted themselves from Petchaboon and north-eastern provinces.

The period of rapid immigration during the mid-1970s was one of violent land disputes. Villagers speak of a single month during this period in which there were thirty murders in Lan Sak, out of a total population of less than 20,000. Even official statistics show 128 cases of murder being brought to Uthaithani courts in 1976, mostly in the two western districts, and this represents only a fraction of the actual total (Uthaithani Provincial Administration, 1977). Disputes arose over the indistinct land boundaries that had been established when land had little value, but which assumed importance once demand for land and the timber on it pushed up the price of both. In this province, authority is the key to control over land: land boundaries were sometimes demarcated by the sound of a gun fired from a central point in the forest, signifying that whoever was within earshot was on that claimant's territory. The area also served as a hideaway from the law, since state authorities were more or less excluded access to many villages. Influential people who ruled by the gun were known as 'tigers' (*seua*). To be a stranger in someone else's territory was dangerous, and this served to reinforce the cohesion and separateness of individual communities.[7]

As mentioned above, the Government at this time had relatively little control over the area. Lan Sak was still a *tambon* of Ban Rai District until 1975, and only became a full district in 1981. As the Thung Khaa *kamnan* observed, 'By the time a death had been reported at the district office, a corpse would be rotten.' Police were hardly seen in most communities, and until the late 1970s schooling only extended to a few villages. Rules were made and enforced by the community itself, generally through an influential person who may or may not have been formally elected village head or *kamnan*. Early on, settlers practised a subsistence economy, usually bringing with them enough rice to tide them over the first year and sometimes enough to exchange in barter for a parcel of land. Upland rice was planted initially, along with field crops. Wildlife remained abundant until large-scale forest clearance destroyed the natural habitat of the larger animals.

Commercialization came both with the construction of roads by the Highways Department, the Agricultural Land Reform Office (ALRO), and the TPC, and later by villagers themselves, and with the establishment of a market at Paak Meuang in 1980 by an influential, Uthaithani-based Chinese trader. Meanwhile, this same trader (later shot dead by a business rival in Lan Sak) provided land for establishment of the district administrative headquarters a few kilometres east of Paak Meuang, near to which a police barracks was built. At this time, Lan Sak was classified as a (Communist) 'infiltration zone', which gave the Government an added interest in establishing state control.

Settlement patterns were varied. The traditional Lao settlement is similar to that generally found in North-east Thailand—a cluster of houses with animals and implements kept under the house, and many of the fields located at some distance. Initially, many of the new Thai settlements followed this clustered pattern for reasons of security and convenience in the common task of clearing areas of forest for subsistence cultivation. However, with more complete clearance of forest, enlargement of agricultural holdings, reduced concerns about security, and anxiety over fire in the clustered settlement, houses were moved closer to the owners' fields in conformity with the traditional pattern of settlement in lowland Uthaithani and elsewhere in the outer Central Plains. Small clusters of settlement can often still be noticed, but these tend to be extended family units or small groups of settlers from the same area rather than the entire village or community with which the settlers identify. Latterly, this tendency toward dispersal has been checked in some cases by a government policy of grouping houses together. (This is discussed in greater detail below.)

By the late 1980s, virtually all but the steepest land of Lan Sak was under cultivation. Forest still stands on the steeper mountainsides, and in the TPC reforestation project at Rabam, and in the portion of the Huai Kha Khaeng wildlife reserve lying within Lan Sak.[8] A stand of teak trees near Paak Meuang remains isolated, having been pronounced sacred by a widely respected monk in Uthaithani,[9] a reminder of the forest that covered much of the area until as late as the mid-1970s. Environmental degradation is evidenced in reduced rainfall,[10] periodic flooding such as that in 1983 which caused loss of life and severe damage in Lan Sak and in the rice-lands of lowland eastern Uthaithani, in soil erosion and gullying, siltation of irrigation channels, and poisoning of water sources by pesticides.

Cultivation in Lan Sak

There are both spatial and temporal determinants of agricultural production in a recently settled forest environment such as Lan Sak. Spatially, cultivation is influenced by gradient, soil, access to markets, water supply, and patterns of land tenure. However, these influences change over time as land is improved or, alternatively, as soil erosion and other forms of degradation occur, access increases, water control improves or deteriorates, as land tenure changes, and commodity prices fluctuate. This pattern and the factors affecting it can best be illustrated with reference to specific crops and parameters which have a bearing on their distribution.

Rice

Rice holds a unique place in Thai agriculture as the principal subsistence crop. It is the crop that farmers are most adept at cultivating, and is generally the preferred crop. However, rice is demanding in terms of water requirements and level land, as a result of which it is grown on only one-sixth of the total cultivated area of the upland district of Lan Sak.[11]

Rice is grown primarily on the level, low-lying land near the Tap Salao

River in the eastern part of the district. Here a limited area of land is irrigated by water diverted from the river and small streams by locally constructed and managed irrigation channels. However, most rice-land is entirely rain-fed, lying at elevations too high for diversion of irrigation water. Meanwhile, the desire to grow rice at least sufficient for their own consumption—a desire born from an aversion to relying on an uncertain cash income for purchase of such a basic element of subsistence—leads many upland farmers to cultivate plots which are often tiny and which are amenable to rice by virtue of micro-environmental suitability. These include gullies, shallow depressions, or level land adjacent to a water source from which water can be pumped.

Nevertheless, Lan Sak is a marginal environment for rice. Irrigated areas are low-lying and increasingly prone to flooding such as that which ruined a large portion of the crop in late 1983. Rain-fed areas suffer periodic drought—as, for example, in 1984 and 1987. The topography and pattern of land holding is such that, for most farmers, risks cannot be minimized easily by the strategy, common elsewhere, of dividing a household's planting between flood-prone and drought-prone areas. This is because of the gradual rise of land away from the Tap Salao River, which means that only a minority of farmers have land that straddles the boundary between flood-prone and drought-prone conditions. Those who do vary rice strains accordingly (see Ng, 1978: 40).

Rice cultivation in Lan Sak requires few inputs. Ploughing is generally carried out using buffalo, although power tillers are becoming popular since they are labour-saving and less susceptible to theft. Planting and harvesting are carried out by hand, planting involving the use of nursery beds and transplanting (except on poorly watered land where broadcasting is sometimes used), and harvesting being by sickle. Chemical fertilizer use is minimal, buffalo manure replenishing the soil. Seed is kept over from the previous harvest or obtained at the Department of Agricultural Extension (DAE) office in straight exchange for old grain. Various rice varieties are used, depending principally on irrigability and susceptibility to flooding, since new varieties are short and cannot survive inundation as well as traditional varieties.

Rice-land is classified locally into three types: low-lying, middle, and elevated. Rice is classified first and foremost by its growing period as 'heavy' rice, with a lengthy growing period of approximately six months, 'medium' rice, with a moderate growing period of approximately five months, and 'light' rice, with a short growing period of approximately four months. The heights and ability to grow quickly if inundated increase with their 'weight' or length of growing period. Thus 'heavy', 'medium', and 'light' rice tend to be grown on low-lying, middle, and elevated land respectively, although this is an over-simplified portrayal. In a high-risk environment such as this, and without adequate water control, little difference in yield between varieties is apparent; where new varieties are used, it is primarily for their short growing period. Intensive, high-input rice farming is practised only in the few fields where a reliable second rice crop can be grown.

Although rice production is primarily for subsistence, it is also the principal source of cash income for many farmers. Traders come from the market towns of Uthaithani and Nong Chang to purchase rice at prices comparable to those found elsewhere in the province. Rice grown for home consumption is milled mechanically, and for many farmers this involves having to transport rice to the mill at Paak Meuang. Increasingly, however, small mills are being constructed at the village level. The terms of milling are standard: rice is milled in exchange for the bran, broken rice, and husks. The husks are used in some cases to power the mill, while the bran and broken rice are either sold or used by the mill owner for pig rearing.

Since the early 1980s, many rice farmers have used their rice-land for cultivation of mung beans as a second crop between January and March. Other than providing a small subsidiary income, cultivation of this leguminous crop is recognized as being beneficial for soil fertility (by fixing nitrogen). Mung beans are a demanding crop in terms of water requirements, even though total rainfall needed is low. In 1984, many Lan Sak farmers recorded a loss due to a complete absence of rainfall, while in January 1985 an unseasonal downpour ruined the crop of those with low-lying land. Caterpillars have rapidly become a hazard, and even the expensive insecticides are proving ineffective as the pests appear to build up a resistance.

Field Crops

Most of the cultivated area of Lan Sak is given over to field-cropping. Although diversification away from rice in the form of field crops has been the principal feature of change in cropping patterns in Thailand over the past quarter of a century, this has been a national strategy supported by land settlement patterns rather than a deliberate household strategy adopted by the majority of farmers (see Uhlig, 1984: 37). This is particularly the case in the Central Plains and on its fringes. That is to say, it is mainly out of necessity rather than farmer preference that the agricultural growth afforded by settlement of new land has involved non-ice annuals, since the rice-land frontier had largely been occupied by the 960s. Thus it is important not to over-emphasize, as has sometimes been done (for example, IBRD, 1980: ii), the enthusiasm with which farmers have 'diversified'. Comparison of upland cropping and rice farming is in any case problematic, given the very different cost considerations between commercialized and subsistence production (Uhlig, 1984: 164).

For a period, though, settlers in Lan Sak did appear to be facing conditions favourable to a switch away from the rice farming that most would have been accustomed to. Moreover, in some cases, albeit a minority, the prime motivation for settlement in Lan Sak was indeed the belief that commercial field-cropping would be a quick route to riches, unlike the modest albeit stable income that was possible under rice cultivation. Yet others did in fact make a conscious diversification decision, either by settling land amenable both to rice and to field crops, or by maintaining links with lowland rice farming through kinship ties. The majority, however, had little choice but to cultivate according to the dictates of the micro-environment, and this meant field-cropping for the most part.

Field-cropping on newly settled forest land produces highest yields for lowest inputs soon after clearing, and thereafter it involves a progressive deterioration. This has been accompanied in Lan Sak by unstable and generally falling prices for the major field crops (following world market trends) after the earlier buoyancy, as a result of which certain of these have become progressively less economic. Even many of the farmers who originally came to Lan Sak specifically in the hope of moving out of rice farming into field-cropping say they would prefer to switch back to rice. This is reflected in the premium placed on rice-land and by the pattern of land use.[12]

Maize is the main field crop grown in Lan Sak. Cultivation of the main crop is normally from May to August. Production is almost entirely for the market.[13] Ploughing is mainly by tractor. The dominant seed is the commercially developed Suwan 1. Planting is done by hand, in teams of hoers and sowers. Rodenticides and herbicides are necessary inputs, although in some cases weeding is carried out by hand to decrease dependence on the latter. Until 1985, fertilizer use was minimal. Harvesting is also manual, and husking is done largely by machine.

Latterly, maize yields have declined significantly. This is attributed in many cases either to disease or to poor seed, termed by farmers 'sterile' or 'transvestite'. Soil exhaustion is clearly a major factor, and this is acknowledged to varying degrees by maize farmers. As a result of declining yields, many farmers have gone into debt from maize cultivation. Yields vary according to soil type, rainfall, and intensity of cultivation, but overall the DAE office reports an average of 19 *tang* per *rai* for 1984, which at going prices of 35 baht per *tang* is not even enough to cover inputs estimated by the DAE to be 750 baht per *rai*. This is not to mention imputed labour costs and interest on loans for inputs.

Following the maize harvest, a second crop is usually planted. Although some plant a second maize crop, most favour other crops. Mung beans, sorghum, and soya beans are the most popular second crops. All these are also relatively high-input crops, mung and soya beans more so and sorghum to a lesser degree. Cultivation and milling of these second crops can last until January or February, with little time remaining before field preparation in March or April for the following season. As a result, some have turned to less intensive crops such as cassava,[14] which is left in the ground for nearly a year with little attention. This allows farmers to seek waged employment for extended periods. Alternatively, larger farmers may opt for this extensive form of cultivation on rented land to minimize labour and supervision necessary for other crops.

A third stage in extensification of cultivation is apparent with the expansion of sugar-cane production. Sugar-cane is a crop limited to those with considerable long-term capital, and it has been planted by a few large owners who gain control over land either by purchase or by rental from debtors who can less and less afford to cultivate their own land. In one Lan Sak village in particular, there is a visibly expanding green carpet of sugar-cane engulfing surrounding fields. This is a progression that parallels that which has occurred in other recently settled forest areas of western Thailand, notably in Kanchanaburi Province to the south of Uthaithani. Its future is uncertain with the instability in world sugar prices, but other forms of large-scale agriculture are becoming increasingly popular in Lan Sak and elsewhere, notably cattle ranching.[15]

Two Lan Sak Villages

Two of the thirty-three administrative villages in Lan Sak District were selected for detailed study (Figure 4.4).[16] One is an extension of the early Lao settlement at Ban Dong, while the other is an extension of the first Thai settlement at Thung Khaa. The first represents a lowland settlement based primarily on wet rice agriculture, with field crops important but secondary to the village economy. The second represents an upland settlement whose agricultural production is dominated by field-cropping and with few areas suited to wet rice. Other notable differences include the nature of government involvement in the two communities, their age, the degree and nature of NGO activity, degree of differentiation, relative importance of land and capital as factors of production, and relative significance of off-farm employment. Similarities include problems of leadership, factionalism and fragmentation, and multiplicity of origins of the inhabitants. An examination of how these two villages have emerged, changed, and ultimately been subject to 'rural development' sheds light on the place of development in marginal areas more generally.

Ban Dong

Ban Dong is an administrative village of approximately 300 houses located on the north bank of the Tap Salao River (Figure 4.5). It consists of a core settlement of mainly Lao families, whose residence dates from the original settlement which was located on the opposite bank of the river, and several scattered communities of more recent Thai settlers. These Thai settlers maintain their own separate cohesion but nevertheless identify themselves with Ban Dong by virtue of its temple, its school, and its administrative function as well as certain other functions. However, this identification decreases somewhat with distance and proximity to other administrative villages.

Much of Ban Dong is level, at an altitude of approximately 100 metres above sea-level. A granite outcrop forms the core of a ridge and associated higher ground west of the village, and fields rise gradually northward in a way that affects the irrigability of the rice-fields.

Until the early 1970s, settlement was mostly near the Tap Salao River. A dry-season cart track made this one of the first points of contact for lowland traders, but the Lao villagers were virtually self-sufficient in food, clothing, building materials, and other basic necessities. Around

Figure 4.4
Topography of Lan Sak, and Location of Ban Dong and Ban Mai

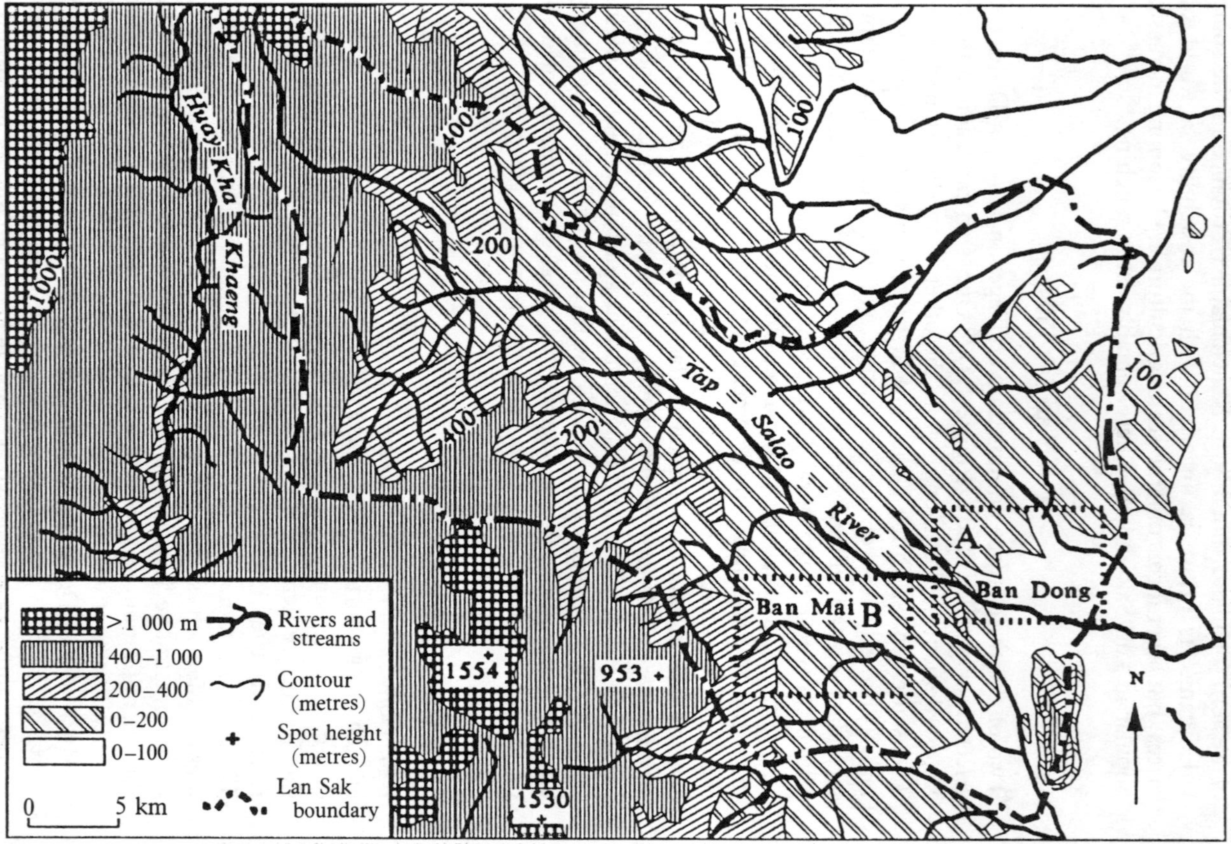

Figure 4.5
Ban Dong: Topography, Roads, and Settlement

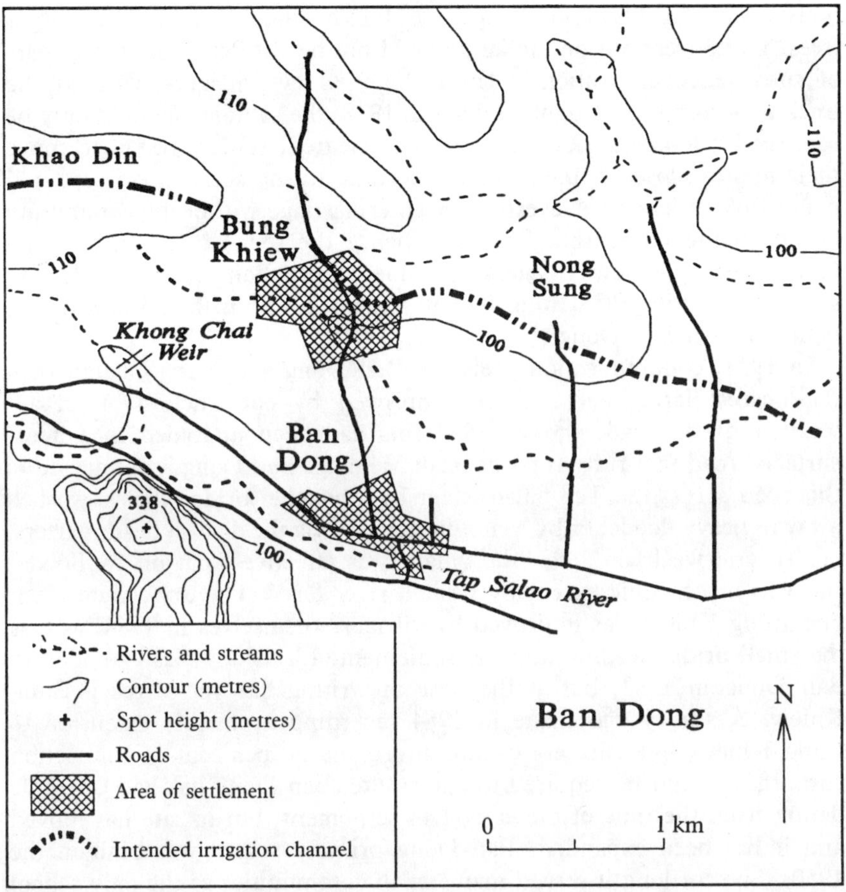

this time, settlers mainly from neighbouring Nong Chang District had begun to arrive and to purchase land from the earlier settlers who had laid claim to large tracts. Initially, these new settlers were preoccupied with clearing sufficient land for subsistence and surviving the hazards of forest life. Wild elephants were feared in particular, and fires had to be kept burning at night to keep animals at bay. The task of clearing land was done communally. For these reasons, early settlers clustered their houses together, even though this placed some at a considerable distance from the land that they had purchased, staked out, or been given.

An example of one such cluster that was later to become a community in its own right is Bung Khiew. This now scattered settlement of approximately forty houses is located 3 kilometres north of Ban Dong temple. The earliest settlers arrived here during the 1960s from Wat Singh District in neighbouring Chainat Province, and from Nong Chang District in Uthaithani. Later, they were followed mainly by Nong Chang settlers. Most of the settlers had received little or no land from their parents, and some had previously been renting rice-land, paying half their crop in rent. Typically they would pay 100 to 200 baht per *rai* for forest land. Timber remaining on the land would be used to construct a house, the Thai Plywood Company (TPC) having cut most of the larger trees. Large trees left on the land would not be cut for the first few years of subsistence cultivation.[17] Until Bung Khiew villagers widened the track to accommodate light vehicles in 1978, the settlement could only be reached by footpath. As the forest was cleared, settlers began to move their houses closer to their fields according to the accustomed scattered pattern of settlement. Nevertheless, intermarriage within the community has strengthened kinship links and hence the social cohesion of Bung Khiew. Bung Khiew villagers continue to use Ban Dong temple and school, and until 1988 Bung Khiew remained within the administrative boundaries of Ban Dong.[18]

In 1973, communications between Ban Dong and Nong Chang, then the nearest large market, were improved by construction of an all-weather gravel road, and by 1985 this had been upgraded to a hard-surfaced road that runs as far as Paak Meuang. Ban Dong is connected to this road across the Tap Salao River by a wooden bridge that is washed away in heavy floods, or by a circuitous route via the district headquarters. For several weeks in 1983, the village was effectively cut off by floods, and was inaccessible except by a small river ferry. The dry-season track into Bung Khiew was improved by villagers themselves in 1984, as was the small bridge leading into the settlement. Electricity was extended to Ban Dong in 1982, but at the time of writing has yet to reach Bung Khiew. A survey was made in 1984 regarding a possible extension to Bung Khiew, but villagers cannot afford the 30 per cent of connection costs they would be required to contribute. Ban Dong has had a temple dating from the time of the early Lao settlement, but its site has moved and it has been expanded. Ban Dong primary school was built in the 1950s, and for long it served many small communities as the only school in Lan Sak.

Ban Dong was originally located in what was 'preparatory forest reserve'. This meant that land was officially state owned, but a traditional feature of land ownership in rural Thailand is that ownership is by usufruct or by staked claim. This is reinforced by the collection of tax by the Land Department, often to the annoyance of the Forestry Department whose forest reserve policy is undermined, since tax receipts are treated as official land title by the holders. In Ban Dong, land title has more recently been upgraded to NS3, or 'exploitation testimonial', which gives the holder right of transfer and therefore permits use of land title deeds as collateral for loans. In 1985, the first *chanood* (full title deed) was granted in some parts of the village. Land ownership is uneven, and landless labourers, partial tenants, and full tenants comprise approximately 20 per cent of the households. Average land ownership is 25 *rai*.

Wet rice agriculture is the mainstay of the village economy, with subsidiary income from maize, millet, mung beans, cassava, and other field crops. A portion of the village is irrigated by a channel dug by early settlers. This directs water from Paak Meuang weir, which is constructed of logs and woven timber panels. A water committee maintains the weir and administers water distribution in exchange for a fee based on area irrigated and paid in rice.[19] A few households obtain a dry-season rice crop. However, most manage only a single rice crop, some with a secondary crop of mung beans, and the majority depend entirely on rainfall for watering their fields. The whole of Bung Khiew is in this position, despite several efforts to divert irrigation water. Higher land is used solely for field crops. Buffalo are still used for ploughing, although two-wheeled power tillers (also known figuratively as 'iron buffalo' or onomatopoeically as *rot itaek*), and even four-wheeled tractors are increasingly in use. Threshing is mostly by hand or by using buffalo, although threshing machines are also becoming popular. In recent years, buffalo raising has become a popular source of income.

Apart from agriculture, employment within the village is limited. Only a few traders, artisans, or civil servants depend entirely on non-agricultural incomes. On the other hand, many families earn a subsidiary income from occasional activities within the village, ranging from hairdressing to selling home-made sweets. Off-farm employment outside the village is still at a low level and involves younger males for the most part. However, this is increasing not only due to the opportunities for construction work in Bangkok and certain provincial towns, but also due to the declining opportunities for productive dry-season activity with local resource depletion. Another increasing employment trend is wage labouring in surrounding villages, mainly on larger farms and in some cases on sugar estates.

Ban Mai

Ban Mai is of a similar size to Ban Dong. It is located approximately 10 kilometres south-west, at the foot of Khao Manora Mountain, the beginning of the high mountain ranges (Figure 4.6). The prominent feature of Ban Mai's layout is the grid-pattern, nucleated settlement that forms the heart of the community and tells of the partially planned nature of settlement. However, scattered homesteads reveal the incompleteness of this attempt at directed resettlement.

Ban Mai lies at an altitude of approximately 200 metres above sea-level. The land is rolling, more level in the east but growing steeper toward the foot of the mountains and attaining steep gradients on the mountainsides. A small river, the Huai Nam Wing, runs past the village and drains the area into the Huai Khok Khwai. In 1986, the Huai Nam Wing was dammed, providing limited irrigation for vegetable plots. Soils are sandy, generally of low to moderate fertility, and without tree cover they have quickly lost their humic content.

Ban Mai is a more recently settled village than Ban Dong. The longest-standing resident in the area is an elderly Karen, who moved from the nearby Karen village of Ban I-Dang in 1960. Until 1978, most of the area was still under dense forest. Small clusters of houses, built by early

Figure 4.6
Ban Mai: Topography, Roads and Settlement

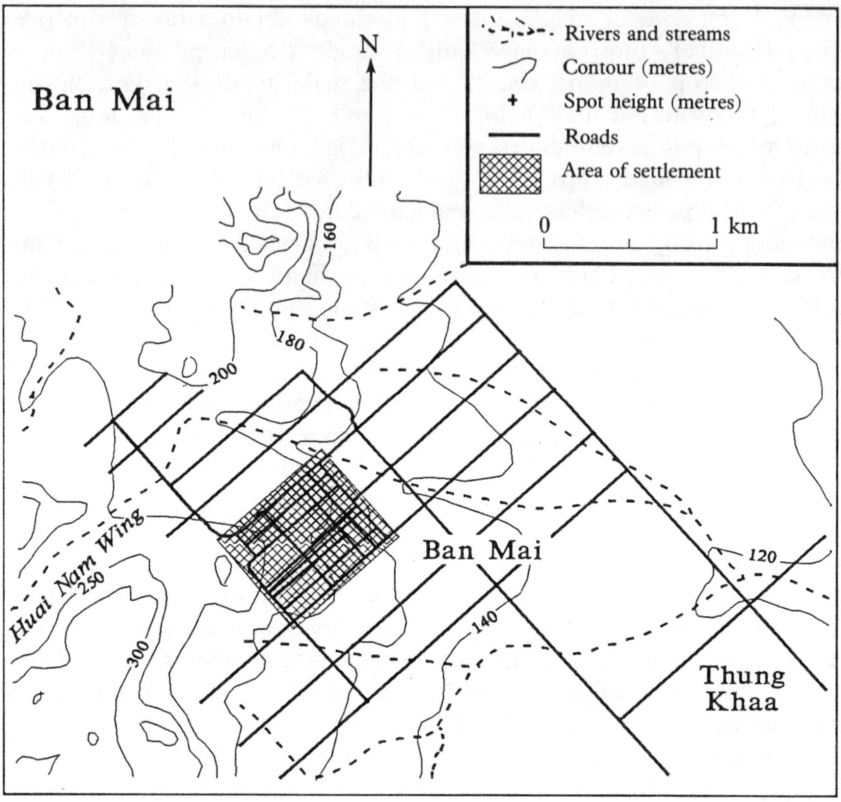

settlers who had moved out from Thung Khaa, of which Ban Mai was originally an extension, were scattered in small clearings in the forest. The economy was based on *yaang* resin tapping and subsistence agriculture. In 1978, the Agricultural Land Reform Office (ALRO) chose Ban Mai as the site for the first stage of the Tap Salao Land Reform Project, having failed to persuade villagers at the more established settlement of Thung Khaa to accede to land reform. This involved immediate clearance of the forest by TPC contractors, leaving the area within the land reform borders virtually treeless. Deforestation has since continued as land has been cleared well beyond the ALRO area.

Following land reform, migration into the newly cleared area was rapid. Initially, many settlers built their homesteads on or near their agricultural plots, despite provision of separate house plots by ALRO, in an area specially demarcated for this purpose and planned according to a grid-pattern of settlement. Later, ALRO stipulated that settlers had to reside in this area, but while some complied, others—up till today—have resisted doing so, many going to the lengths of building token shacks on their allocated house plots.

Until 1978, dry-season cart tracks were the only means of communication with the outside. With deforestation and land reform, the logging roads came first, followed by a network of all-weather gravel roads built by ALRO, which made Ban Mai physically one of the most accessible villages in the district despite its remoteness in terms of sheer distance. Flooding has sometimes disrupted communications, particularly in 1983, but ALRO maintains the roads at considerable cost. Under the ALRO programme, electricity came to the village in 1982, bypassing many others to make Ban Mai one of the first villages in Lan Sak to be electrified. Moreover, residents were exempted from the 30 per cent village connection charge, although individual houses have to pay for connection from the mains, so that it is mostly the houses of wealthier residents which have been connected.

Before 1978, the temple at Thung Khaa served as a focal point for the scattered community, and there was also a small temple in an outlying forest settlement. The temple at Thung Khaa and the school there had been built by villagers at the instigation of the *khon to* (the traditional leader), who was later to resist land reform. The school and temple in Ban Mai were established in 1978 after the forest was cleared, and in 1982 a large concrete primary school was built in the village. A health station and the ALRO office lie on the edge of the village.

A key feature of the ALRO project has been division of the area into rectangular plots of 24 *rai* each, with special title.[20] Prior to land reform, the forested area had been 'owned' mainly by Thung Khaa settlers who had staked a claim to the forest land and worked some of it for its *yaang* resin. By 1978, they had started to divide up some of these areas for sale. Upon the implementation of land reform, ALRO stipulated a single agricultural plot plus attached house per family, and set land prices at 210 baht per *rai*, irrespective of the location and quality of the land. ALRO loans were provided for land purchase and zinc roofing. Subsequently, certain settlers invited relatives and friends to sign their names to plots, without necessarily having to come and work them; these settlers are now the owners of large tracts of land. Other successful applicants sold their plots at a profit. ALRO's efforts had attracted a large number of settlers, so there was considerable demand for the plots which changed hands at prices well above the price stipulated by ALRO. As a result, poorer settlers went into debt or forwent the right to farm their plots until the covertly agreed price had been paid. Meanwhile, once the land in the ALRO area had been cleared, illegal logging and land clearance beyond the boundaries commenced, resulting in deforestation of many steep slopes on the mountains, Khao Manora and Khao Hin Lek Fai.

Except on low-lying land to the east of Ban Mai and in gullies where water can be retained, wet rice farming is not practicable. The field crops grown are maize, mung beans, soya beans, cassava, sorghum, cotton, and to a lesser extent groundnuts, castor beans, and sugar-cane. Despite the suitability of much of the area for tree crops, only a few scattered banana groves break the pattern of annual field-cropping. Fire is a major constraint to the establishment of orchards.

The nature of field-cropping changed drastically soon after deforestation. Planting in a forest or immediate post-forest environment requires few inputs. Ploughing is unnecessary since the soil is friable and a hoe suffices. Weeds and insects that affect monocropped annuals are generally not part of the forest habitat, nor of intercropped fields in forest clearings, and under forest cover the humic replenishment of the soil renders a natural fertility. The relative absence of weeds and the moistness of a forest environment, moreover, allows flexibility in the timing of planting, which means that family labour or reciprocal labour exchange predominates. However, once this environment changes, soil hardens under the impact of rain, pests find little competition in the absence of the forest, and soils quickly lose their fertility and dry out for lengthy periods. As a result, cropping requires increasing inputs, including hired labour, while yields decline significantly. In Ban Mai, this has affected poorer farmers the most, for they have to hire tractors for ploughing and obtain pesticides and sometimes fertilizers on high-interest credit. At the same time, they are the ones most likely to take up wage-labouring opportunities.

Most fields in Ban Mai are rain-fed. The exceptions are where rice is planted in stream gullies, and adjacent to a community fish pond built by ALRO, and latterly in the small area irrigable from the new dam. In addition, ALRO provides a land-levelling service and removes tree stumps from the fields to facilitate ploughing by tractor.

Tractors are now used for ploughing on every plot. A few owners hire out their tractors, often recouping their capital outlay in less than two years. Planting is done by hand, mostly using hired labour, although reciprocal labour arrangements are still in practice among poorer households. The same holds true for harvesting, while threshing and milling are now mostly by machine.

Full-time non-agricultural employment in Ban Mai is limited to a few retail traders, pick-up owners, and salaried officials. Occasional work with ALRO is available at minimum wage rates, which are nearly double the normal farm labour rate. Illegal forestry by influential local timber traders is another source of local employment. Petty trade provides a small income for many villagers: there are fifteen shops in the village, and home-made sweets and services such as hairdressing provide a small supplementary income. Non-local off-farm employment is much more common in Ban Mai than in Ban Dong. A large number of young people find work on construction sites and at factories in Bangkok, either during the dry season or year round. Increasingly, whole families are renting out their land to wealthier villagers and seeking urban employment, due to debt obligations and lack of capital to plant their own land. Several men from Ban Mai work in the Middle East on two-year contracts.

Change in Frontier Communities

Lan Sak as a whole and these two communities in particular have undergone recent and rapid change. On the surface, the most significant change in such frontier communities has been to the physical impact of human intervention. However, environmental change has in turn had important social implications, particularly concerning access to resources for production. This in turn is linked to changing structures of authority.

Environment

The most visible element of change in Lan Sak has been environmental change, in particular deforestation. This has affected not only the immediate vicinity of deforested areas. It has also had significant downstream effects in terms of factors related to water control.[21]

According to the reports of early settlers, rainfall in Lan Sak before deforestation was fairly consistent and extended over more months of the year than it does now. Maize planting in Ban Mai eight years ago took place in March, and in Ban Dong rice-fields were ready for transplanting by June or July each year. The alluvial soils of the eastern lowlands of Uthaithani have been worked as rain-fed rice-fields for many generations, suggesting that water was once sufficient for regular rice planting.

Deforestation has caused a radical change in the local hydrological cycle. Locally, rainfall is now inconsistent and, according to villagers, extends over a shorter period. Maize planting in Ban Mai now takes place in April and May, and rice in rain-fed fields in Ban Dong is often not planted until September. As a result, agriculture has become a marginal and risky activity where previously there was a great deal more certainty. Meanwhile, many fields in Nong Kha Yang District have lain idle for a number of years, due to a combination of drought and flooding.

Deforestation has also resulted in changed run-off patterns. Not only did trees increase the amount of water returned to the atmosphere, they also delayed the rate at which water ran off the soil and into streams and rivers. Water was thus held in the soil for a much longer period of time, and entered the streams mainly as ground water. This led to a relatively regular rate of stream-flow, with minor seasonal variation.

Deforestation has greatly increased the proportion of rainfall entering streams as surface run-off. Streams that used to flow year-round are now dry for several months of the year. Even the Tap Salao River is reduced to a trickle in the dry season. Flooding has become a major hazard, since trees and forest soils no longer inhibit immediate run-off by absorbing rainfall. In 1983, loss of life, crops, and livestock was widespread in Lan Sak and downstream. Even completion of the Tap Salao Dam in mid-1988 failed to prevent major flooding only a few months later. This is another factor leading to abandonment of rice-lands in Nong Kha Yang and Meuang Districts, which is in turn a cause of migration and further deforestation. A positive aspect of hydrological change associated with deforestation in both Ban Dong and Ban Mai is a rise in the water table for most of the year, resulting in more accessible well water.

Forest soils are productive as long as they are replenished with a humus input. Immediately following deforestation, soils appear fertile, and in some parts of Lan Sak they have maintained their fertility, in part by manure from draught animals (mainly buffalo), and in part due to a natural fertility and low gradients on lowlands immediately adjacent to the Tap Salao River, such as at Ban Dong. For the most part, however, soils are of low fertility and are fragile. In Ban Mai and some higher parts of Ban Dong, soil erosion is evident in gullying and washing away of topsoils, while reduced yields reveal the rapid loss of fertility resulting from monocropping on such soils. Meanwhile, flooding further east in Uthaithani has deposited infertile silt on the previously fertile alluvium, and soil erosion has also led to siltation of the Tap Salao weir, which is the distribution point for a 123,000-*rai* irrigation project in Nong Chang and Tab Tan Districts. Elderly residents of Ban Dong and Ban Mai attest to the siltation of local streams since deforestation.

Resource Situation

As abundance of local resources has declined, so access to these resources—particularly land and forests—has been governed by social relations. Land rights have changed from illegal but locally recognized control over indefinitely demarcated plots of mainly forested land to various forms of state-guaranteed control. In Ban Dong, NS3 and *chanood* certificates leave the individual owner with freedom to use and dispose of land as he or she wishes, while in Ban Mai ALRO retains a significant element of control over disposal of land. Outside the ALRO area, forest reserve land has now been claimed by influential individuals and is in the process of being parcelled out and sold off cheaply to small farmers, some of whom have also worked as illegal foresters for these landowners.

Ironically, the freedom to dispose of land in Ban Dong has led to only limited concentration of land holdings to date, whereas in Ban Mai the effective concentration of control over land (in as much as it was actually relinquished) has been much greater, albeit through indirect, covert, and therefore less visible means. This point is of interest in that it demonstrates the importance of power relationships based on other than state guarantees or free market exchange in determining control over resources, even in a community that has been affected to an unusually high degree by intrusions of State and capital. This will be discussed further in following chapters.

Before large-scale deforestation and extension of roads into the area, the utility of forests in Lan Sak was limited to their local use value. This included timber for local construction, charcoal, herbs that were used as medicines, the fish and wildlife that were part of the forest habitat, and an assured water supply. Certain items of exchange value were obtained, notably *yaang* resin and animal skins, but these left their exploiters with an incentive to maintain the forest for sustained natural production of what were virtually the only sources of cash income. In the words of one early settler, they refrained from clearing land for other than subsistence crops because they were 'concerned for the *yaang* trees' since clearing would expose the forest to fire and threaten their principal livelihood. Forest was an open resource, but its sheer abundance and lack of exchange value prevented competitive use. The only private control over this resource was the control over *yaang* trees established by prior claim.

Granting of concessions at once made the resource scarce and opened up the forest for a virtual free-for-all exploitation in a classic 'tragedy of the commons' situation (Hardin, 1968). Those who may previously have had a stake in maintaining forest, and in any case had little opportunity to exploit it other than for what it could produce on a replenishable basis, now had both the incentive (to make what they could before the TPC got to it) and the means (roads) to make quick profits from timber. The Forestry Department now maintains rights over both timber in forest reserve areas and that remaining on privately owned land. However, influential local people and even agents of the State (particularly the police) continue to make profits from illegal timber exploitation.

Other than for timber, forest is also exploited for charcoal. Previously, wood was abundant on individual plots in both villages. However, more complete clearing of fields for commercial cropping has removed this source of household fuel. Many households in Ban Dong now need to buy their charcoal, and most Ban Mai plots are virtually devoid of stumps. This leads to burning of the forest fringe, both for household use and as a source of cash income for those without alternative means of subsistence. Thus resource shortages in a lowland village such as Ban Dong intensifies the forest exploitation in more recently deforested areas such as Ban Mai.[22]

Before deforestation and commercialization of agriculture, inputs were minimal and yields were high. The land and associated forest resource itself provided all that was necessary for cultivation but the labour and seed—the former generally family or reciprocal labour, the latter kept over from the previous year's crop. With the radical change that has taken place in the agricultural regime, however, these resources are no longer available, nor are they sufficient. Most inputs must now be purchased, particularly in Ban Mai field-cropping, and to a lesser extent in Ban Dong rice farming. Most food protein must now be purchased, especially in Ban Mai, and comes mainly from pork raised by rice-mill owners and some farmers.

Another resource previously available and controlled locally was knowledge of a more or less stable environment, as evidenced by the detailed knowledge of the forest shown by longer-term residents. Such knowledge is less often recognized as a resource important for production, but like resources that can be applied or consumed more directly, it too has been exhausted (in terms of relevance) in Ban Dong and Ban Mai. This has given way to numerous uncertainties associated with the new inputs and technical knowledge that are a part of the environmental and agronomic change.

The common element in all these changes in the resource situation is the loss of local control in favour of dependence on non-local influences. In the case of land rights, forestry, agricultural inputs, knowledge, and other resources affecting production, the rapid environmental and agronomic change and the increased role of external forces in these two villages have placed the whole question of resource management beyond the capability of pre-existing local arrangements.

Production

A key element of peasant subsistence production such as that prevailing in the communities of Ban Dong and Ban Mai before deforestation is the non-class nature of the subsistence sector. Even in the exchange sector (in this case *yaang* oil and other forest products), production by individuals varied more in terms of quantity than in terms of the relation between labour and the means of production. Household labour was used in both the subsistence and exchange sectors, and reciprocal exchange labour in subsistence production, while trade was carried out by outsiders who brought their exchange goods by ox-cart to the villages. This did not mean an undifferentiated community: differential control over family labour and over *yaang* trees in the case of Ban Mai led to differences in economic status. However, these inequalities were based on differential access to certain resources, and not on unequal exchange, direct commoditization of labour (in the sense of labour becoming a freely exchanged good with a market price), nor on production relations within the community. Differences in status were associated with social power positions within the community, but only later were these to have a direct bearing on the production process.

A transitional period can be identified when agricultural production took on a secondary role to forestry and land sales as the dynamic of the local economy, although clearly this benefited different groups far from equally. During this period, those with the authority to lay claim to large areas of land enhanced their positions considerably through a combination of illegal forestry, subcontracting for the TPC, and selling off land to new settlers. These settlers, together with less influential members of the older communities, continued to make a subsistence living in a deteriorating environment and, in some cases, to take on wage-labouring jobs in forestry.

As has been described above, deforestation and access afforded by the new roads have transformed the agricultural regime. Particularly in Ban Mai, cash cropping is now predominant. Unlike the situation of the previous village economy, differentiation is rife under commercialized agriculture. In Ban Mai, tractor owners, shop owners, and creditors now control most sectors of the village economy, at the levels of provision of inputs and marketing of produce, in their strategic position as intermediaries between capital (in the form of suppliers and commodity markets) and peasant production. Increasingly, they are taking direct control over production by hiring labour to work land over which they have secured control. This is accomplished either by effective foreclosure of debtors' land or by renting land belonging to those without access to credit and equipment, and who therefore have no alternative but to rent out their land at a going rate of 100 baht per *rai*.

In Ban Dong, commoditization of labour has been less complete, due in part to the importance of rice as both a subsistence crop and a cash crop, and to the lower inputs necessary for production. Debt foreclosure is leading to a certain amount of land concentration, however, and rising land prices are inhibiting young farmers from buying land. In some cases, this is instead sold to outsiders who either rent out the land for cash or, in the case of rice-land, under sharecropping arrangements, or who plant sugar-cane on higher land.[23]

Leadership

Ban Dong has had formally appointed, and later elected, village heads for some time. In Ban Mai, the village head has only adopted his formal position since land reform. Before that, the *khon to* in Thung Khaa commanded authority and respect, as did lesser *khon to* in smaller outlying communities. Nevertheless, despite the more clear-cut break in Ban Mai from community-established leadership to formal, externally oriented leadership, the role of the village head or *kamnan* in Ban Dong has actually undergone some similar changes, notwithstanding an apparent continuity.

Ban Dong until the 1970s was remote from the Ban Rai district headquarters. As a result, the village head or *kamnan* rarely travelled to the district seat, and likewise district officials and police rarely had occasion to visit Ban Dong. This meant that the leader, despite being formally appointed, was answerable first and foremost to the community of which he[24] was a part, and would be seen as the community's spokesman in dealing with the administration. In one instance, Ban Dong villagers successfully petitioned for the removal from office of a *kamnan* who was embezzling registration fees. With state-led rural development in the form of increased accessibility due to road building, followed by designation of Lan Sak as a subdistrict and then as a National Economic and Social Development Board (NESDB) priority district under the Fifth Five-Year Plan, contact between the village and the administration has increased, and the *kamnan* has served as the principal intermediary. As rural development funds have been channelled into the area, opportunities for self-enrichment by village leaders have increased: they now have access to funds that have come from outside and that are thus also outside the sanction of the community. The point has been reached where the *kamnan* is seen principally as an agent of the district administration in the community, with substantial material interests in maintaining that position.[25] Meanwhile, his family economic interests extend far beyond Ban Dong, including ownership of an air-conditioned restaurant and a construction business in the provincial town 50 kilometres away.

Ban Mai, meanwhile, remained isolated for longer and more completely. The *khon to* referred to above resisted land reform and associated roads: in his words, 'You can have roads or you can eat rice', an allusion to the cultivable land that roads destroy. He was the undisputed authority in the area, and this he established by a combination of patronage (for example, by helping settlers to establish themselves as *yaang* tappers), fear (such as the sanction of violence in the case of infringement of strict rules against gambling and other unruly behaviour), and respect (for example, by organizing villagers to build the local school and temple in 1968 and 1972 respectively). Doubtless, one reason he and others resisted land reform was the loss of this leadership role that he was to suffer, since he was too old to be elected *kamnan*[26] and he disliked dealing with officialdom. On the other hand, he negotiated with officials to provide a teacher for the Thung Khaa school, whom he put up at his own house, thereby successfully resisting the authorities' desire to make the Thung Khaa school a branch of the Ban Dong school.

In the *khon to*'s words, problems came to the community 'with the election of a *kamnan* and village head'. The *kamnan* and village head who were to emerge in Thung Khaa and Ban Mai respectively (the latter was established as a separate village in 1978) were also influential villagers who were making large profits through the timber trade, the former as subcontractor for concessionaires besides being engaged in illegal timber operations. They differed significantly from the Thung Khaa *khon to*, however, in their outside connections, both in business and in contact with government officials. At the time of land reform, the present Ban Mai village head was a young and charismatic member of one of the outlying communities. He was well established in the area at a time when considerable upheaval and distrust was rife due to the influx of new settlers. He was chosen unopposed as head of the new village by a show of hands at a village meeting, and he will remain in that position until he is sixty in the year 2005. He now spends large amounts of time away from the village.[27] Many villagers are in debt to him, and he profits from the new roads with his daily pick-up service to Nong Chang, while retaining effective control over his lands by renting from debtors who cannot afford to plant their own land and now work for him and others as wage labourers.

The common element of change in leadership that can be observed in these two villages is thus an external orientation, and a reduced sanction over abuse of privilege. The point to note here is not just 'power corrupts', but rather that leadership changes in nature as a result of a change in its constituency. In making their increased connections with outsiders, villagers rely on the village head and, to a lesser extent, on the village committee as intermediaries. Members of the village committee obtain their positions by virtue of connections, patronage, or self-confidence arising from some other form of power base. At the same time, the district administration and interests of capital, in so far as they can be distinguished, rely on those same people, particularly the village head, as entry points into the village. With the resources at their disposal, they are making it both possible and more worthwhile for formal leaders to assume the position of representative of the State and of capital in the village, rather than representing the village in dealings with external interests. The greater a role external resources play in the village economy, the greater potential there is for economic gain by such intermediaries.

Development in Lan Sak

This, then, is the context in which rural development is taking place. Development is at once part of the change described and an attempt to direct that change. However, as is clear from the discussion in Chapter 2, development is not unidirectional change. An understanding of the parameters and contradictions of development in Lan Sak necessitates an examination of the local actors on this particular development stage.

The Local Developers

A number of activities termed 'rural development' are taking place in Ban Dong and Ban Mai, or are otherwise directly affecting them. A brief summary will help to set the scene for examining the actors themselves.

In both villages, the four principal ministries with statutory activities at the district level have a number of schemes. These include: housewives' groups and pre-school centres run by the Community Development Department (CDD); agricultural extension by the local agricultural extension officer of the Department of Agricultural Extension (DAE); activities associated with the village primary schools; health stations close to each village; frequent training programmes and intermittent 'advice' at village meetings; and administration of national programmes, such as the Rural Employment Generation Programme (REGP), and ideological training. The *tambon* council is instrumental in the administration of these programmes, but initiatives, final decisions, and budget allocations are made by district or provincial officials. Some other government agencies have occasional activities at the village level: the Land Development Department has carried out a soil survey of Ban Mai; the military hold occasional 'development' training programmes in both villages, the latest being the Army Reserve programme in Ban Dong and the National Defence Volunteers programme in Ban Mai; BAAC is the major institutional credit institution in both villages; and in Ban Mai, ALRO plays an important development role, both in land reform and in infrastructural development. Government is also active in road building and electrification, infrastructural development that affects both villages.

NGO activity in Ban Mai involves training of youths from poorer families in co-operative integrated farming methods and other skills at the youth training centre of the province-wide Nong Kha Yang Foundation for Rural Development (NKYFRD), with some follow-up work in the village, including activities of the associated Uthaithani Pig Raisers' Cooperative (UPRC). In Ban Dong, NGO activities are more community-based and involve a rice bank, a buffalo bank, and communal fish ponds.

Most of the state developers reside at the district headquarters or at the market of Paak Meuang. Senior officials are from various parts of the country, while many of the more junior officials, including those working at the *tambon* level, come from Uthaithani or surrounding provinces. With a few notable exceptions, these officials socialize among themselves, barring special occasions when a deliberate show of 'mixing' is made as a matter of policy, notably in the monthly 'mobile district', when officials spend an evening socializing and, the following day, providing various administrative services in one of the villages in the district.

Publicly, state developers present a show of unity, and in introducing programmes to villagers it is stressed that help is from the state bureaucracy rather than a particular department. There is a policy of focusing special attention on one village in each *tambon* as a show village for visiting provincial and other senior officials, and this brings various departments together. Training programmes involve officials from all four of the ministries with statutory duties at district level, and this often leads to a blurring of function as individual officials make semi-political speeches on subjects outside their own field of duty.

On the other hand, individual programmes are carried out independently of each other, and while not normally in open competition, departments tend to avoid treading on each others' toes. For example, the *tambon* DAE officer stated that she did not bother with Ban Mai since there are already ALRO officials working there, despite the fact that the latter have no training in, or activities concerning, agricultural extension. Meanwhile, duplication arises, for example in the provision of community rice barns by both DAE and CDD. The blurring of function is a product of the desire for each department to expand its range of activities. This brings the police, military, and other departments which would not normally be thought of as developers into the rural development field, and such activity also doubles as an image-building tool. On occasion, conflict between departments comes into the open, such as in 1986 when the Lan Sak police retaliated over confiscation of one of its illegal timber consignments by arresting a Forestry Department vehicle.

Developers' attitudes to development and the developed can be illustrated by reference to ALRO officials in Ban Mai and the CDD officer for Lan Sak. The official in charge of the ALRO Tap Salao Land Reform Scheme is based in Uthaithani but spends lengthy periods at the Ban Mai office. Unlike his predecessor, who was on close terms with many villagers and well liked, Pid[28] does not mix socially with Ban Mai villagers. Unlike most officials, however, he avoids official language and is direct and vernacular in his speech at village meetings, the main forum for communication between ALRO and villagers. He is said to be aggressive by villagers who have had to deal with him, but he is also seen as fair and uncorrupt. Pid privately considers Ban Mai villagers to have benefited unduly from ALRO's infrastructural provision and to be ungrateful in their lack of interest in ALRO projects. In particular, he sees failure by the villagers to repair roads following the 1983 floods as irresponsible, and he made a point of not repairing roads in the village, although ALRO undertook repair work on the agricultural roads outside the settlement.

The CDD officer for Lan Sak has little direct contact with villagers except as a speaker at training sessions and at village meetings; those with direct contact are the *tambon*-level officers. The present CDD officer has spent most of his career in politically sensitive areas in the North-east and sees his development role as part of the political side of counter-insurgency strategy. In practice, the CDD maintains a prominent position in state-led rural development as a co-ordinating agency between the *tambon* council and the district office, deciding which villages are most deserving of help. The CDD officer stresses the importance of finding appropriate local leaders. The first three things he says he looks for as a sign of quality are a clean and tidy house, a fence around the house, and a latrine in or near the house. He uses the standard examples of poverty, ignorance, and illness among villagers to illustrate the obstacles to development. Also prominent in his list of obstacles are Chinese merchants and 'influence' (as wielded by powerful persons). He suggests that one way to combat the latter is to co-opt *kamnan* and others with influence by sending them for training, such as for the *Phaen din tham, Phaen din tho'ng* scheme described in Chapter 2.

The Local 'Developed'

The increasingly ambiguous status of village élites has been noted. Since these key individuals within the village polity and economy are seen by fellow villagers at least partly as agents of the State, and since that status is enhanced by their role in various rural development programmes, they perhaps ought to be discussed along with other developers. However, due to their place of residence, inclusion as villagers, and continuity in social relations from a time when the distinction between State and village was more clear-cut, they are considered along with their fellow villagers as the 'developed', and their changing status is discussed more fully below.

As observed in Chapter 2, classification of Thai villagers along rigid class lines is not possible and is alien to indigenous categorization. Villagers in Ban Dong and Ban Mai do, however, have their own terms for distinguishing social status. A villager at a development meeting remarked in whispers that he would have liked to have talked to officials present, but was afraid to do so because of their status. The majority of poor villagers in the two communities refer to the wealthy élite as those with 'high status', 'people with money', or even 'the rich of the village'. In Ban Mai, they are often referred to by a more specific characteristic, such as their place in the local polity or economy, notably 'village heads' or 'tractor owners'. Such people are usually publicly keen to represent themselves as ordinary villagers or farmers, representing their own interests as those of the poor. The *kamnan* of Ban Dong, for example, frequently complains of the exploitation of 'us farmers' by BAAC and various government officials who join hands with the ethnic Chinese, despite the fact that he himself does not farm. In private discussion, however, many of the élite consciously or unconsciously distinguish themselves from poorer villagers by use of the term for villager in the third person, 'the majority', or more directly 'the poor'.

Differences in status can also be identified by certain social patterns. Although in village society there are few formally exclusive occasions,[29] socializing—in Ban Mai in particular—is to an increasing extent governed by economic status. However, such patterns are difficult to disentangle from other determinants, such as kinship, common place of origin, or present location of residence. Location of residence is important in the social cohesion of and identification of common interest within subcommunities of each of the administrative villages under study. In Ban Mai, these subcommunities are formed around small clusters of houses in outlying areas and around houses in the same lane in the grid settlement. In Ban Dong, common interest has been identified by larger communities such as Bung Khiew, where informal leadership in the person of Boi[30] is an important resource that has facilitated the establishment of rice and buffalo banks by villagers.

A clearer statement of status is that publicly pronounced by donations to the village temple in Ban Dong. Other distinguishing features are connections with outsiders, particularly local officials. The Ban Mai village head and Thung Khaa *kamnan* and his brother, the *tambon* doctor[31] (himself an influential Ban Mai resident), are frequently to be seen at the district offices. The DAE *tambon* worker in Ban Dong stays at the *kamnan*'s residence, making this the main point of contact for district officials. Another source of external contact and patronage comes from the local member of parliament, who owns, among his other interests, the largest pineapple estate and canning factory in Thailand, at Cha-am. In return for delivering votes at election time, several Ban Dong and Ban Mai villagers receive favours, and this may take them away from the village for periods of time. For example, the *tambon* doctor in Ban Dong, who also owns a small rice mill, arranges distribution of T-shirts for the member of parliament's Siam Democracy Party and organizes patronage of the local temple fair.

In terms of production relations, the major distinction recognized socially in Ban Mai is tractor ownership, while in Ban Dong it is position as a trader and money-lender. Materially, differentiation goes beyond this, and the following chapter illustrates the range of production constraints and opportunities faced by Ban Dong and Ban Mai villagers. The salient point is that the economic interests of the 'developed' are by no means convergent, and this has important implications for the direction of specific development projects.

Development, Change, and Participation on the Frontier

In Chapter 2, it was suggested that development is a generic cover for specific aspects of structural change, and that an ethos of development itself serves as an ideological instrument in bringing about certain forms of change. The present chapter has shown a context of rapid change in Lan Sak, change that has occurred by virtue of the location of the district at the frontier of agricultural land expansion, but which retrospectively has been termed 'development' and latterly has been shaped according to the interests of State and capital in securing control over the polity and economy of an area until recently on the periphery of such control. Control has been secured partly by means of an incorporative rural development strategy. Meanwhile, alternative attempts to direct change on the part of non-statist developers provide separate initiatives by and on behalf of villagers. Latterly, both sets of developers have emphasized villager participation as an essential aspect of rural development, and this raises the question of the role of villagers themselves in orienting change.

Early initiatives by Ban Dong and Ban Mai villagers were not considered at the time as 'participation' or even as 'development', but many of the activities (clearing tracks and roads, construction of schools, land improvement) are described retrospectively in developmental terms. These projects were undertaken by villagers themselves, using their own labour and latterly using pooled cash resources. Since most of such projects were on a small scale, they usually involved a common agreement among neighbours over fulfilling a mutual need or overcoming a mutual obstacle. Where direction was involved, for example in construction of the Thung Khaa school and temple, local forms of leadership in the person of the *khon to* were employed. This was at a time when production in the community was still relatively undifferentiated by function if not by scale. More recently, leadership in the context of development projects that orient change in Ban Dong and Ban Mai has come from the more powerful elements in increasingly differentiated communities. Alternative attempts to maintain control on the part of less powerful sections of the community in the context of change are less visible but will become apparent in the following chapters.

Thus change in the context of development involves an interplay between a variety of local and non-local actors. Initially posited as a dialectic between outside 'developers' and local 'developed,' this interplay in actuality involves a broad range of interest groups within which can be identified a number of subdialectics. The villager–outsider dichotomy becomes less relevant in the face of new divisions and new alliances. Participation in development by one or another of these groups means taking an active part in the direction of change or in controlling its effects. Since the emphasis is on development as incorporation, participatory development becomes a struggle over the terms of incorporation.

Conclusion

To recapitulate, change in Ban Dong and Ban Mai has resulted in a loss of control by a majority of villagers over resources and decisions affecting their use. Rural development appears to pull in a number of different directions with regard to maintaining, increasing, or decreasing such control. Hence, a key issue for participatory rural development is that of maintaining or increasing control. Broadly, initiatives along these lines involve one of two possible strategies. The first, which may be termed 'avoidance', is to re-emphasize local resources as the basis for the village economy in such a way as to give villagers sanction over resources for production. The problem is achieving this via a non-atavistic approach to development, which means accepting the need for new community-based institutions. Bung Khiew Rice Bank and Buffalo Bank may be seen as steps in such a direction. The second strategy is to accept, at least to some extent, the importance of external resources in rural development, particularly since there is already a net transfer of resources out of the community,[32] and to readjust the terms of control through 'engagement'. This means dealing with local power structures, which include not only the village élite but also state elements, although the former can increasingly be seen as coincident with the latter (Turton, 1989). Independent initiatives and representative leaders are of utmost importance in this respect, while obstacles include threat, long-standing patron–client relations, and the absolutism of state rural development strategy.

It is neither feasible nor, in the eyes of most of the developers and developed, desirable to pursue an atavistic course in search of a lost community that in all reality never existed, and in any case such an option is pre-empted in Lan Sak by permanent material transformations wrought by environmental change and infrastructural development. Having acknowledged change, the question for an analysis of the role of rural development *vis-à-vis* the position of villagers is, rather, how it relates to the power position of each of the developers and developed, and thus in what way the terms of participation are defined. This requires an analysis of the implications of various rural development initiatives as they affect participation by the villagers of Ban Dong and Ban Mai in controlling both local and supralocal resources and decisions affecting their use. The following chapter investigates the determinants of control over resources necessary for production in the two villages.

1. Western Uthaithani approximates roughly to what are now Ban Rai and Lan Sak districts (see Figure 4.2). Archaeological evidence shows that military campaigns of the Ayuthaya period probably used this area as a base of some sort during campaigns against the Burmese. Cave paintings provide evidence of prehistoric settlement.

2. 'Lao' is the ethnic name used by members of that group and by lowland Thais to refer to them. While this group did indeed originate in what is now Laos, 'Lao' is sometimes used more generally also to refer to people from the North-east of Thailand (*Isaan*).

3. *Yaang* resin is obtained by burning a hole near the base of the *mai yaang* tree (*Dipterocarpus alatus*). It is used in varnishes, and locally it is used in fire-lighters for charcoal stoves and for weather-proofing house stilts.

4. Land ownership, and therefore land transactions, had no legal basis. At this time the land area was classified as preparatory forest reserve.

5. Dry-foot annuals other than rice are hereafter referred to generically as 'field crops'.

6. Flooding in lowland Uthaithani has also become more severe due to the construction of the Chaophraya Dam at Chainat, 30 kilometres to the south. This has created a back-up, which raises the water level to several metres above the fields during September and October of some years (most recently, 1981, 1983, 1985, and 1988).

7. This somewhat paradoxical element of social cohesion conflicts with the popular and bureaucratic conceptions of frontier settlements as anarchic, free-for-all zones. In fact, the pattern is rather more akin to the traditional 'cellular' village structure described by Douglass (1984: 26) for pre-twentieth century Central Thailand.

8. In 1988, TPC made preparations for logging in the Huai Kha Khaeng sanctuary following a Judicial Council ruling allowing old concessions to be taken up. However, in January 1989, all such concessions were revoked by a Cabinet decision.

9. A revered monk, Phra Seemaa, proclaimed that ill-fortune would befall those who cut wood from this teak stand. True to his prediction, the few who failed to heed his word have, it is said, met premature and violent death.

10. Evidence for this comes mainly from accounts of longer-term residents of Lan Sak. Meteorological readings at the Lan Sak weather station date back only to 1981, hardly long enough to measure the effect of deforestation on rainfall. Records kept at Uthaithani weather station show a significant decline in annual rainfall over the period 1957–83.

11. Lan Sak DAE Office, 1985. DAE statistics are only rough estimates, based on assessments by *tambon*-level extension workers.

12. Irrigated rice-land sold in 1985 for 6,000–7,000 baht per *rai*. Rain-fed rice-land sold for about 2,000 baht, while upland crop-land sold from 100 to 2,000 baht, depending on land quality and title. Chayanov (1926) noted the over-capitalization of subsistence farmers due to their valuation of land suited to subsistence crops at above an economically rentable price.

13. Ninety per cent of Thai maize is exported, mostly to Japan and Taiwan for their livestock industries. The domestic market is growing, albeit slowly, with the involvement of agribusiness in intensive livestock rearing. Only small amounts of maize are used locally, for household pig-rearing and duck-raising.

14. At the time of the survey (1985), only a few farmers were growing cassava. However, by 1988, cassava had become a dominant field crop in Lan Sak.

15. The wealthiest landowner in Lan Sak has begun to acquire large amounts of land from indebted farmers. This he divides between a large sugar estate and buffalo-rearing on several thousand *rai* of land. Several traders and money-lenders in Paak Meuang market have bought or leased land from debtors for smaller-scale cattle raising.

16. The question of what constitutes a village or community is one that has been raised by Kemp (1987) and examined specifically in the Thai case by a number of authors (see Hirsch, 1990). Whatever the artificiality or otherwise of the administrative village as an imposed construct, it is used as a tool of rural development and thus serves as more than simply a convenient unit of study.

17. The most valuable timbers in this area were *yaang* (*Dipterocarpus alatus*), *makhaa* (*Ormosia*), *mai praduu* (*Pterocarpus macrocarpus*), *teng* (*Shorea obtusa*), *sadao* (*Margosa*), *takhien* (*Hopea* spp.), and *mai daeng* (*Xylia kerri*).

18. In 1988, after the main period of fieldwork for this study, Bung Khiew and other outlying settlements broke off to form a new administrative village.

19. In 1988, construction of the Tap Salao Dam was completed (see Hirsch, 1989). Following this, the Royal Irrigation Department plans to reconstruct and take over administration of Paak Meuang weir.

20. An ALRO land title can only be transferred by inheritance or with the approval of ALRO. This means that it cannot be used as collateral for commercial bank loans, nor can it be bought and sold freely on an open land market, although the deed can be used as collateral for loans from the Bank for Agriculture and Agricultural Co-operatives (BAAC).

21. It is also possible that there are down-wind effects resulting from altered patterns of rainfall (see Khan, 1986: 47). These are more speculative than are downstream effects, but measurements for Uthaithani show a significant decline in rainfall since the early 1970s, particularly for the month of March—early in the ploughing season. Oral evidence of farmers from many parts of Thailand supports the hypothesis that deforestation leads to reduced or altered rainfall in down-wind areas. The explanation for reduced rainfall lies in changed albedo and reduced evapotranspiration with loss of forest, together with reduced air turbulence resulting from a smoother land surface.

22. The effect of this is particularly localized due to the illegality of commercial charcoal production. This makes transport a risky business, which means that demand is usually satisfied by production nearby, or concomitantly that charcoal producers or traders prefer to sell locally despite the substantially higher price to be obtained in town. The risks involved in such trade are exemplified by a 20,000 baht 'fine' (bribe) paid to the police by one Ban Mai trader in 1984.

23. Because of its high investment requirement, the long wait necessary (two years) for economic returns, and the necessity of obtaining a quota from a refinery, sugar-cane tends to be a crop limited to large-scale farmers.

24. The masculine pronoun is used here because there are no women village heads or *kamnan* in Lan Sak. Indeed, it was only in 1981 that women were legally entitled to stand for such offices, since which time several have been elected in other parts of the country.

25. The *kamnan* in Ban Dong, for example, secures lucrative local contracts for his wife's construction business by virtue of his position. In 1984 he received a 100,000-baht contract for construction of a wooden bridge across the Tap Salao River to replace the one washed away in the 1983 floods. For this he used his position not only in securing the contract, but also in conscripting unpaid labour and using wood cut from forest reserve land in addition to that remaining from the previous bridge. In 1987 he was replaced.

26. Village heads and *kamnan* must retire at the age of sixty under Thai law.

27. So much so that the myna bird outside his house has learned to say '*Phuu yai mai yuu ro'k*' ('the headman's not in')! This has become something of a village joke.

28. All personal names used in this study are pseudonyms.

29. This appears to be changing with the recent issuing of invitation cards to ordination, wedding, and funeral ceremonies—all of which would normally have been open to all comers previously.

30. Following establishment of the new administrative village in 1988, Boi was elected formal village head.

31. The position of *tambon* doctor is statutory and not related to formal medical training. It gives an ex-officio position on the *tambon* council.

32. Scott (1976: 206) is critical of inward looking, self-help solutions for this reason. More concretely, it has been estimated that approximately half of pre-tax income of Thai villages was paid out via the rice premium, import duties, sales taxes, other taxes, and registration fees paid by villagers between 1965 and 1975. This exceeds the cost of education, public administration, irrigation, and other services received by villagers (Feeny, 1982: 116).

5

Production, Differentiation, Dearth

When the tractor owner comes to plough our land, we ask:
'How much?'
When the seed merchant sells us grain, we ask:
'How much?'
When the money lender sets the interest rate, we ask:
'How much?'
And when the middleman comes along to buy our crops, we ask:
'How much?'

Ban Mai villager

PRODUCTION of subsistence and commercial goods is central to development in two main respects. First, production relations provide the basis for social relations at a broader level. Thus they limit and to some extent determine the way in which society is organized,[1] particularly where the distribution of power at various levels is concerned. Second, production determines the material output of a society. As such, it is the basis for reproduction of material elements of the social order, and alternatively for extraction of surplus, for investment in new forms of production, or for redistribution of the social product. In as much as development is concerned with progressive change in social organization and with directing the social product, it is thereby intimately bound up with production.

Production is governed in the first place by resource availability, which in turn is limited on the one hand by social relations of production and on the other by natural availability and technology. Relations of production become relatively more important as a measure of control as natural resources become more scarce,[2] and social forms of control themselves change concurrently with, if not necessarily as a consequence of, increasing scarcities. Development therefore becomes more concerned with social change and less with opening up of untapped natural resources, while technological development plays an important part in integrating local and non-local resources for production.

There is thus a tension between development as increasing total production through intensification of resource use and development as a reorientation of production so as to effect more equitable social relations. As was shown in Chapter 2, rural development is concerned with equity in a spatial sense—that is, redressing imbalances between urban and rural areas. However, the involvement of State and capital in rural development raises serious distributional questions at a much more local level, since resources for production may be concentrated in the hands of a limited group. The processes lying behind this localized form of inequality fall under the rubric of rural differentiation.

Production and Rural Differentiation

Production in Lan Sak has undergone recent and rapid change. Individual producers have moved from reliance on an abundant natural environment to increased dependence on external inputs. Production has moved away from a subsistence orientation toward production for the market, partly as a result of change in ecological conditions and partly as a consequence of increased integration through communication links and marketing structures.

That this change has resulted in an increased total product, measured in cash-equivalent terms, is unquestionable. Less certain is whether this level of production can be sustained.[3] Yet what is clear from the examination of production in Lan Sak that follows is that this reorientation of production has been associated with changes in production relations which have affected access to resources. These changes have important implications for social differentiation among rural producers, a subject of long-standing and continuing debate.

Theoretical Aspects

The issue of differentiation of the peasantry as a result of agrarian change was brought into prominence by Lenin. Rejecting the Narodnik doctrine of the 'community' village, Lenin maintained first that the logic of capitalism as it spread to rural areas was to polarize the rural population into landowning and labouring classes, and second that this process had reached an advanced stage in early twentieth-century Russia. Describing differentiation as 'the sum total of all the economic contradictions among the peasantry', Lenin held that the process created new types of rural inhabitants and was referred to as 'depeasantizing' in peasant discourse. The new classes of agrarian bourgeoisie (comprising less than one-fifth of the rural population) and rural proletariat (more than half) were characterized above all by participation in the commoditized, monetized economy. This was in contrast to the middle peasants, who still worked their own land using family labour. However, agrarian conditions were such as to make the continued existence of this latter group precarious, since they could only make ends meet in good years and relied increasingly on the new 'masters of the contemporary countryside' for loans and labouring opportunities. Migration to the cities was highest among this group, who according to Lenin were rapidly being 'swept away' as a class (Lenin, 1899, in Harriss, 1982).

During this same period, an alternative interpretation of differentiation of the peasantry came from the populist Chayanov. Rather than seeing rising and falling fortunes of different members of the agrarian community as a unilinear polarization, Chayanov emphasized the cyclical nature of peasant livelihoods. He suggested that at different stages in the life cycle, peasant households are subject to varying labourer–dependent ratios and have access to different amounts of land within a basically homogeneous community. Rather than working within a capitalist, profit-oriented framework, the peasant maximizes utility by means of a trade-off between total factor income and leisure. Even though involved within a wider economy, the peasant family remains the basic unit of production, distribution, and exchange. The implication is that peasants continually adapt to changes in factors of production by reliance on domestic resources, sometimes in a 'self-exploitative' way, but in a way that preserves their existence against the apparent logic of capitalist relations of production (see Chayanov, 1926; Harrison, 1982).

More recent analysis of agrarian change in peasant societies has drawn widely on these early debates. The empirical problem facing a Leninist analysis is the apparent persistence in most agrarian societies (some argue even in western Europe) of smallholders who in certain aspects of production resemble Lenin's supposedly doomed middle peasantry. In suggesting ways out of empirical subjection to theory, White (1989) argues against rigid adherence to models developed in a specific historical and political context, as 'There is no universal or all-purpose "agrarian question" awaiting investigation, nor is there any universal form of "agrarian differentiation".'[4] This is not to reject entirely the relevance of classical analyses to current situations. Such relevance is, however, to be explored rather than assumed or imposed, for as White points out Lenin himself distinguished between underlying trends and specific situations, recognizing the incompleteness of 'proletarianization'. Even the Chayanovian and Leninist models are not entirely incompatible, and for White a key task is to disentangle cyclical and long-term trends. White (1989) goes on to say:

> Differentiation ... involves a cumulative and permanent (i.e. non-cyclical, which is not to say that it is never reversible) process of change in the ways in which different groups in rural society—and some outside it—gain access to the products of their own or others' labour, based on their differential control over the means of production and often, but not always, on increasing inequalities in access to land.

'Pumping out' of surplus labour is a key common denominator, but beyond this, concrete forms of differentiation are varied and complex. What is needed in place of the dichotomous focus either on polar extremes (such as landlord and labourer classes) or on small peasant households is explanation of the *coexistence* of the two forms.

Another recent departure in the analysis of differentiation has been to consider the political and ideological, as well as the economic. Hart (1989) considers the State's role in rural differentiation, in particular the creation of state-supported élites which fulfil a policing role for the State and in turn receive state patronage. However, the relationship between

States, rural élites, and poorer villagers varies according to specific aspects of the polity and social formation. Hart contrasts Thailand with Indonesia, for example. She shows that, in Indonesia, a highly centralized and exclusive state apparatus (Golkar) means that local élites invest in socializing with government officials in order to gain official standing themselves at a local level. In Thailand, however, a less powerful or centralized State results in 'local powers' having more independent authority and seeking constituencies not only among senior officials and representatives of capital, but also among village populations. Turton (1989) focuses on these local powers, emphasizing that they are to be found among village élites (typically 5 per cent of the village population) as well as among district-level officials and traders. Turton goes on to explain that the structural position of these élites is enhanced by their 'linkage' role, '. . . above all through relations which enable them to accumulate (or be the first stage in the accumulation of) village surplus through wages, commodity dealing, retail prices, rent, and interest'.

However, polarization in the ideological sphere is not as clear-cut, partly due to continuity in control over certain basic means of production. Thus despite being drawn increasingly into commodity currents in the sphere of exchange and being in a material sense 'wage labour equivalent', peasants *seem* to retain control over land and labour. The village community is maintained in part also by mitigation of contradictions by village élites, who use their new position in social and religious patronage to 'benefit from association with more traditional and village forms of relationship and legitimacy' (Turton, 1989).

Nevertheless, the new relationships entailed in this specific variant of rural differentiation give rise to transformations, not only in structural or material position but also in the ideological sphere. Turton has demonstrated elsewhere (1984b) how peasant discourse reveals emergent forms of consciousness. Anan (1984; 1989) shows how rapid differentiation in a northern Thai village leads to new alliances and cleavages despite the only partially developed nature of markets in land, labour, inputs, and products, and he highlights constraints on capitalist development such as efforts by poorer villagers to hold on to small plots for subsistence production. If we are to follow Hart (1989) in seeing change as a dialectical rather than a linear process, it is essential to focus on these specific contexts and draw patterns from reality rather than vice versa. The reality here is studied in terms of control over resources for production.

Control over Resources for Production[5]

Compared with Ban Ping farmers in Chiang Rai Province in 1960, whose basic option was between plough and tractor agriculture (Moerman, 1968), Lan Sak farmers a quarter of a century later would at first sight appear to be veritably spoilt for choice (Table 5.1). Not only are there several crops to choose between, but each crop can be cultivated at each stage by one of a number of methods. Moreover, options concerning

Production Possibilities for Rice and Maize in Lan Sak

	Rice		*Maize*	
	Method	*Input/Output*	*Method*	*Input/Output*
Seed	**Keep over**/ exchange/buy	**Foregone Consumption**/ cash	**Buy**/ keep over	**Cash**/ foregone sale
Preparation	**Burn**/ plough	**Household Labour**	**Cut and Burn**/ burn/plough	**Labour**/ tractor
Ploughing	**Buffalo**/power tiller/tractor	**Own**/rice/cash	**Tractor**/ power tiller	**Cash**/own
Planting	**Transplant**/ broadcast	**Household Labour**/ reciprocal labour/ hired labour	**Sow**	**Hired Labour**/ reciprocal labour/ household labour
Pest control	**None**	**None**	**Herbicide**/ weeding	**Cash, Household Labour**/ hired labour/ reciprocal labour
Fertilizer	**Buffalo Manure**/ none/chemical	**Own**/rice/ none/cash	**None**/chemical compost	**None**/cash
Harvest	**By Hand**	**Reciprocal Labour**/ household labour/ hired labour	**By Hand**	**Hired Labour**/household labour/reciprocal labour
Threshing/ husking	**Buffalo**/power tiller/machine/ by hand/tractor	**Household Labour**/ reciprocal labour/ cash	**Machine**/ by hand	**Cash**/reciprocal labour/ household labour
Use	**Consumption**/ sale/keep over	**Food**/ cash/seed	**Sale**/ keep over	**Cash**/seed

Source: Field survey, 1985.
Note: The existing predominant form under each category is indicated in bold.

labour and capital input are numerous. However, this choice is largely illusory, since choices of crop, cultivation method, and inputs are dictated by factors largely and increasingly beyond the small farmer's control. In particular, Uhlig (1984: 166) points out:

> The choice of crops [in newly cleared upland cropping areas] . . . is a result of the dependence of the farmer on the trader. As a result of the pressure of paying back his debts and his resulting obligation to deliver all yields after the harvest, the farmer has practically no other choice than to cultivate on his land only those crops which are of interest to the trader.

Even more significant is the fact that the very choices that small farmers are forced to make move them toward a system of agriculture in which they no longer control key factors of production.

Control over production means securing access to resources or to means of production. Such access is determined by production relations through arrangements determining *de jure* ownership, via state-guaranteed property rights, and *de facto* control that may not be legally guaranteed. Ultimately, control may depend more or less on either of these: there is no guarantee that *de jure* rights will be associated with enhanced control over production if other influences undermine the significance of those rights (see Witayakorn, 1983: 102–3). This is particularly relevant where agents of the State are unable or unwilling to enforce, or are collusive in infringing, such rights. This aspect is crucial in that it underlies one of the principal contradictions of change that are the focus of this study—that is, the less than total switch to a market economy controlled by 'rational', capitalist relations of production, under which access to land, labour, and capital are the product of monetized relations. The persistence of other means of access to resources for production reflects power relations that are not simply anachronistic remnants of pre-capitalist production, but are an integral part of the change that has been taking place.

Land

Control over land in Ban Dong and Ban Mai varies both in terms of *de jure* ownership and *de facto* control. In Ban Dong, land ownership is certified by the State with NS3 exploitation testimonials, which serve to all intents and purposes as land title deeds, giving the holder control over the use and transfer of the land. Some Ban Dong residents own land overlapping the boundary into neighbouring villages which have not yet been granted land titles. Here, tax certificates are treated by landholders as title deeds for purposes of purchase, inheritance, and even informal collateral, but they have no legal basis. Unlike NS3 certificates, therefore, they cannot be used as collateral for bank loans.

In Ban Mai, land within the ALRO area is held under the special ALRO land title. This guarantees rights of the holder for use, but it restricts transfer except through inheritance. As a result, this land title cannot be used as collateral except with BAAC under an agreement with ALRO. Other restrictions include a ban on rental of ALRO land. Land outside the ALRO area is forest reserve and holders have no documentary proof of ownership. Ownership of such land is established by verbal agreement.

Control over land is achieved in any one of a number of ways. Purchase of NS3 land is a free and straightforward transaction, despite nominal approval that is required from the district land office. Purchase of land without title is also relatively unrestricted, although in the case of land without tax certificates conflicts can arise. In 1984, a Bung Khiew villager found that his land in a nearby forest reserve area had been sold by someone else to a third party: only a direct and potentially dangerous intervention redeemed him his land.

Purchase of land with NS3 title is increasingly difficult for young families. This is due to the steeply rising price of land. Land that sold for 200 baht per *rai* in 1975 sold for 2,000 baht ten years later, and the best partially irrigated land in Ban Dong commanded 7,000 baht per *rai*. Ban Mai land has always been sold covertly for more than the ALRO-stipulated price. Cheap land is still available in hilly forest reserve areas at 100 baht per *rai*, but this is land of poor quality and carries with it the risk of arrest for illegal settlement. Thus there exists a steep land price gradient, prices rising with both quality of land and security of title. As a result, the best land is falling into the hands of those with ready capital—increasingly, in the case of Ban Dong, to wealthy outsiders.

Land can be acquired through inheritance, but the traditional division of land among offspring is inhibited by a number of factors.[6] In Ban Dong, debt has forced a number of elderly farmers to sell rather than to pass on their land. In Bung Khiew, in 1984–5, for example, two of the longer-term residents divided up their land. One sold a large portion to an outsider from Nong Chang to pay off 50,000 baht in debts to BAAC, to a commercial bank, and to neighbours. The other sold his land to his children at half the going price of 2,000 baht per *rai* in order to meet family debts. Some of these children themselves had to borrow to buy the land. While this is not a direct form of debt foreclosure, it represents a long-term trend toward loss of control over land and an inability to reproduce the family production unit; even in the second case just described, young families are starting off with the burden of a land debt. Loss of inheritable assets is an important part of the process of differentiation.

In Ban Mai, inheritance of the family plot is only possible for one of the family, since subdivision of holdings is prohibited. It is too early to assess the long-term effect of this or to determine how it will affect inheritance patterns: but, already, the solution for some has been to move on to clear or purchase forest reserve land, and for others to take on wage labour in Ban Mai or elsewhere.

In some cases, state-guaranteed rights to land are not sufficient. An example in the case of Ban Mai is that of Dam, a migrant from Ban Dong who helped Pot, a friend, clear land in 1975. In exchange, he was given 25 *rai* of this land at a time when its cash value was minimal. This land was duly allocated to Dam with land reform in 1978. In 1984, Pot turned up to demand 15,000 baht for 'his' land. Unable to pay and feeling the demand unjustified, Dam refused. Pot reacted by renting the land to another villager. Frightened of Pot (two people were killed in a nearby village the previous year in similar circumstances), Dam went into the forest at Thong Lang to rent *yaang* trees for tapping in the hope of raising the cash. However, he only just broke even, the whole family having caught malaria, and in early 1985 was unable to pay Pot when he again demanded money for the land. By April 1985, Pot had raised the demand to 20,000 baht, with threats to Dam's life if he could not raise the money within a week. Dam spoke informally with the village head, who suggested he tell ALRO, but the village head declined to intervene on Dam's behalf. Dam felt that going to ALRO would only make Pot more violent, and ALRO is seen not to intervene in such cases. Dam fled with his family back to relatives in Ban Dong, and Pot continues to rent out the land. Dam summarizes his rationale quite clearly: 'Having no land is better than my children having no father and my wife no husband.'

Less extreme cases result from the ability of influential villagers to rent debtors' land at token rates and, in some cases, in lieu of interest. ALRO rules prohibit rental of land, since the land reform ideal is to encourage equal family-sized plots. However, the people involved in illegal renting include the village head, *tambon* doctor, and other influential moneylenders within the village. ALRO has neither the will nor the means to enforce its rules against such people, some of whom are by virtue of their position minor state functionaries. The same held true of sales of land by influential local people to newcomers entitled to land under the land reform programme, at rates in excess of the ALRO price, which in many cases meant that the ALRO loan to these newcomers was insufficient for full purchase. In some cases, this has meant that Ban Mai families are unable to work the land that is legally theirs, and fear of the owner prevents them from bringing the matter into the open. While ALRO is aware of the problem, it admits helplessness in enforcing its own rules.

Foreclosure is still uncommon but nevertheless an increasingly important means of land acquisition in Ban Dong. In Bung Khiew, for example, one farmer had to sell all his rice-land in 1984 to pay off a debt to a Ban Dong villager. His intention was to move on to newly cleared forest land in Bung Waeng along with another landless Bung Khiew villager. More common, but less overt, is the rental of Ban Mai land by wealthy farmers, as described above, which often amounts to foreclosure in all but name. The owners of rented land express uncertainty as to the period of rental. In some cases, such land has been put over to sugar-cane, which is at least a three-year and sometimes a four-year investment.

Whereas rental is a strategy of the better-off for control over land in Ban Mai, in Ban Dong it tends to be the landless or near-landless who rent land (Table 5.2). Usually, the land rented is sufficient for subsistence requirements only. Three broad types of rental contracts exist: cash, *ka*, and *baeng suan*. The first involves a fixed payment in cash, the second in rice. The last is a share-cropping agreement, with one-third to two-fifths of the rice crop the normal payment; a second crop of mung beans may

TABLE 5.2
Tenant Characteristics in Ban Dong and Ban Mai

	Percentage of Villagers Who Rent Land	*Average Land Owned (rai)*	*Income as Percentage of Village Average*
Ban Dong	29	13	44
Ban Mai	21	33	150

Source: Field survey, 1985.

be cultivated without charge. The operator is responsible for all inputs. In the case of *baeng suan*, the rent may be reduced at the discretion of the owner in a bad year. Fixed payments are increasingly preferred by landlords as giving a predictable income.[7] Even tenants with assured income sometimes prefer the *ka* system. They see it as giving more incentive to increase yields, and also prefer being able to sell rice immediately after it is harvested and threshed.

The original means of securing control over land—staking claim to it—is more or less precluded now that even the steepest land behind Ban Mai has been claimed. Much of this land has been claimed by influential people in Ban Mai, Thung Khaa, and surrounding villages. Some of these influential villagers staked out or bought this land as a result of having had to sell land within the ALRO area to beneficiaries of the land reform programme. Hill land is sold off to landless families as far afield as Ban Dong for the same price as they would pay to rent land for a single year in their own villages.

Despite the complexity of control over land in Ban Dong and Ban Mai, certain significant points can be drawn from the above patterns. Legal ownership and actual control over land do not necessarily move in the same direction. Aspects of power, inability of household production units to reproduce themselves in an increasingly commercialized village economy, and discrepancies between state guarantees and their praxis all work against control over land by the poorer, less powerful sections, both inside and outside the two villages. In Ban Dong, where state control over land is restricted to guarantees over property rights, such processes are above board and to some extent visible, but usually take the form of undramatic intergenerational trends rather than blatant dispossession. In Ban Mai, where state controls are greater and nominally more equitable, most of the processes are covert and thus largely invisible to outsiders, but more sharply felt by those affected.[8]

Water

For most Ban Dong and Ban Mai villagers, water is controlled by *thewadaa* (the gods). Although the ritual of parading a cat in a cage (*hae maew*) is still practised occasionally if the first rains are late, for most it is a matter of chance and, where possible, risk minimization strategies are taken accordingly. In Ban Dong, water storage in rice paddies is maximized by the usual practice of diking. In some cases, paddies have been created by levelling. The availability of commercial machinery on hire has led some farmers with sufficient capital to undertake such levelling, and many even in Ban Mai express a desire to use any capital that should come their way for levelling, to enable them to store water and plant rice.

In Ban Dong, water is controlled communally through an elected irrigation committee. This committee looks after the bamboo and log weir at Paak Meuang and the channels that divert water from the Tap Salao River to the lower-lying rice-fields of Ban Dong. Although this is an indigenous group, district authorities have recently attempted to formalize control and now attend group meetings. Several attempts have been made by Bung Khiew villagers to divert water to their fields, but so far without success. One such attempt is documented in detail in the next chapter.

Both in Ban Dong and in Ban Mai, natural streams provide an intermittent source of water for rice cultivation. Water can be diverted by the owners of land adjoining these streams. In a few cases, it may be possible to practise fish farming where enough water can be held back. Since there is no community or legal sanction governing the use of this resource, upstream farmers have the advantage of prior access.

On a larger scale, two projects that affect Ban Dong and Ban Mai have been provided by the State. One is the large 565-million-baht Tap Salao Dam at Rabam, which stores water in an 18-square kilometre reservoir as part of the larger Tap Salao irrigation project. Because this was first planned in the early 1970s when little of Lan Sak was under cultivation, no provision has been made for diversion of irrigation water to Lan Sak fields except for a resettlement site at Phet Nam Pheung, 10 kilometres downstream from the dam (Hirsch, 1989). This project provides water for 123,000 *rai* of land in Nong Chang. It involves no local planning or management of irrigation. The project is supposed to benefit Ban Dong by reducing flood risk, but during the rains following completion of the dam in 1988, the bridge linking Ban Dong with the main road was again washed away. The other project is a smaller dam that cost about 3 million baht (excluding distribution channels), built above Ban Mai in 1986. Irrigation potential is limited to vegetable plots near the Nam Wing stream. Ban Mai villagers had no part in the planning of this dam.

In so far as trends in control over water are discernible, one tendency is worthy of mention. This is a deteriorating natural situation, which farmers at least had the means of adapting to if not controlling absolutely, matched by a compensatory programme of large-scale works. However, where control by adaptation in the past was in the hands of individual farmers and water-user groups, the large-scale programmes are run by the bureaucracy. In one important respect, there is thus declining control over this resource for production.

Capital

The agricultural economy of Lan Sak villages is becoming more and more externally oriented. This, together with the deteriorating natural resource situation means that local resources are insufficient for sustained or increased production. As a result, control over non-local inputs to agriculture assumes importance. This is determined by access to both short-term capital for seasonal production inputs and long-term capital for control over non-local factors of production.

Except for those whose income is surplus to consumption and minimum production requirements, access to credit is the means of securing control over capital. Credit is usually divided into institutional (formal) credit and non-institutional (informal) credit. The former is at fixed and relatively low interest rates, but limited to those who fulfil set conditions regarding collateral or other forms of guarantee. The latter is at variable and relatively high interest rates, but is accessible to those who would otherwise not qualify for an equivalent loan from institutional sources. This is often because the guarantees covering the latter type of loan are not based on legally foreclosable assets, but rather on unofficial tenure of land, even less tangible ties of patron–client relations, or exertion of authority. Table 5.3 shows the proportion of credit received from each source in the two villages.

Ban Dong and Ban Mai farmers have four potential sources of institutional credit. These are briefly outlined below, as are parameters affecting their importance to various groups.

1. *Commercial Bank Loans*. These are limited to wealthier villagers. The normal collateral is land with NS3 or full (*chanood*) title. However, machinery or other readily saleable assets can also be used. The advantage of such credit is that a loan can normally be obtained of up to half the value of proffered collateral. Moreover, the loan is arranged on an individual basis. Only 4 per cent of Ban Dong households and no Ban Mai households report having such loans. In 1984–5, the interest rate for short- and medium-term loans was 18.5 per cent per annum.

2. *Bank for Agriculture and Agricultural Co-operatives (BAAC)*. This is the most important source of institutional agricultural credit. Hypothetically, any farmer is entitled to a BAAC loan. The need for individual collateral as guarantee is replaced by the joint liability system, whereby any number of farmers from six upward guarantee each other's repayment. It is possible, therefore, that even landless farmers can qualify for loans. In practice, however, there are considerable obstacles to poorer farmers obtaining loans. Local BAAC loan officers are reluctant to accept landless or otherwise-assetless new members. Likewise, local groups are reluctant to guarantee members who may be unable to repay their loans. The bias of BAAC loans in favour of larger farmers has been adequately documented (see, for example, Lightfoot and Fox, 1983: 43). In fact, BAAC figures show that in Uthaithani as a whole, this bias is considerably less severe than elsewhere: 40 per cent of BAAC clients in the province have farms below median size, compared with 19 per cent nationally (Lightfoot, 1985: Table 1). In 1984, one-third of Ban Dong farmers and one-quarter of Ban Mai farmers took out BAAC loans. In 1984–5, the BAAC annual rate of interest was 14 per cent, rising to 17 per cent on default of the one-year loan contract.

In addition to one-year (short-term) loans, medium- and long-term

TABLE 5.3
Access to Credit in Ban Dong and Ban Mai

Cumulative Number of Debts	*Ban Dong*			*Ban Mai*		
	Percentage of Households			*Percentage of Households*		
1 debts		66			81	
2 debts		23			43	
3 debts		4			8	
Creditors	*Percentage of Villagers Receiving Credit*	*Credit Given (baht)*	*Percentage of Total Credit*	*Percentage of Villagers Receiving Credit*	*Credit Given (baht)*	*Percentage of Total Credit*
Commercial banks	4	172,000	6.1	0	0	0.0
BAAC	33	844,000	29.8	25	792,000	18.2
Co-operatives	11	132,000	4.7	15	332,000	7.6
Agricultural middlemen	7	478,000	16.9	67	2,290,000	52.6
Village traders	26	562,000	19.8	20	756,400	17.4
Relatives	11	644,000*	22.7	5	184,000	4.2
Total	93	2,832,000	100.0	132	4,354,400	100 0

Source: Field survey, 1985.
Notes: Total amounts of credit are estimated by multiplying the 25 per cent sample total by 4. Numbers of debts and creditors may not tally due to rounding.

*More than 90 per cent of this is accounted for by two debts, those incurred by a school teacher and a village trader.

finance is offered by BAAC at slightly higher interest rates. This is secured almost exclusively by better-off farmers and used for purchase of agricultural machinery. In 1985, a wealthy Ban Dong resident built a rice mill in Bung Khiew, using a 250,000 baht five-year BAAC loan. The formation and operation of BAAC groups is described further in Chapter 6.

3. *Government Co-operatives and Farmers' Associations*. These organizations exist mainly as sources of agricultural credit. They obtain finance from BAAC at an interest rate 3 per cent below their lending rate, which is in line with that of BAAC. Repayment records of these organizations are very poor when compared with direct lending. This is largely due to their lack of personnel or sanction when compared with other creditors. As a result, BAAC now allocates little credit via these organizations. In 1984, 11 per cent of Ban Dong farmers took co-operative credit from Lan Sak Agricultural Co-operative (LSAC) and Ban Dong Farmers' Association (BDFA). This amounted to less than 5 per cent of total and only 11 per cent of institutional credit in Ban Dong. BDFA now gets no support from BAAC, so its credit operation is relatively insignificant, relying on members' subscriptions as a pool of revolving credit. Its other function of selling rice via the Farmers' Marketing Organization (FMO), for which many farmers originally joined, lapsed after a year as FMO did not continue its preferential marketing service. In Ban Mai, ALRO set up a co-operative, membership of which is compulsory for all non-BAAC members. It has no function other than supplying agricultural credit, and it has a poor repayment record: in 1984, 139 out of 145 borrowers defaulted. Fifteen per cent of Ban Mai farmers took out co-operative credit in 1984, accounting for 30 per cent of institutional credit.

4. *Hire-purchase*. In Ban Mai, this is used mainly for financing purchase of consumer goods such as refrigerators and televisions. However, vehicles, power tillers, and other items of agricultural machinery are also commonly sold under such schemes, and most Ban Dong hire-purchase loans are for the multi-purpose power tillers and trailer attachments. Effective interest rates are usually in excess of 20 per cent per annum. The hire-purchase item itself serves as collateral. This necessitates a steady income, since several consecutive missed payments enable the hire-purchase company to repossess without compensation, as frequently happens in Ban Dong and Ban Mai when aggressive sales tactics result in villagers' making purchases beyond their means.

Non-institutional credit is of three main types. Although the discussion here is limited to cash borrowing, loans in kind are also common, particularly for rice. Whether or not this is considered as borrowing for production depends on our conceptions and functional differentiation of the peasant household economy. This type of borrowing is discussed further in the next chapter.

1. *Agricultural Middlemen*. This is the main form of non-institutional credit in Ban Mai. Agricultural middlemen have as their principal security the crop itself, since debtors are obliged to sell their produce to

them. They thereby establish a monopoly position. Interest is usually paid in cash, at 5 per cent per month for an ordinary loan. In Ban Dong, only 7 per cent of villagers borrow from agricultural middlemen, whereas in Ban Mai 67 per cent of all villagers borrow from this source. Most Ban Dong villagers borrow from middlemen in nearby Paak Meuang, while Ban Mai villagers go further afield: many borrow from middlemen in Nong Chang or Uthaithani, and some go as far as Lopburi and Takhli in neighbouring provinces. In one respect, this demonstrates the patron–client nature of the creditor–debtor relationship, since most of the more distant links are remnants of past ties in areas from which the debtor has migrated.

2. *Village Traders*. For those unable to secure an outside loan due to insufficient connections or lack of tangible collateral, wealthy villagers provide an increasingly important source of credit. Most of these are village traders, and in Ban Mai they are known as 'agents' of middlemen, since they obtain credit from middlemen typically at 2–3 per cent per month. They lend in cash; the principal is repaid in cash, but the interest is often repaid in kind, typically 20–30 *tang* of rice or maize per thousand baht borrowed. With a maximum five-month period between borrowing and repayment, this works out to the equivalent of at least 12 per cent and as much as 24 per cent per month interest. Sometimes, the entire crop goes towards paying off interest, and an even larger amount needs to be borrowed to get through the following year. Debtors are obliged to buy their inputs, sell their produce, and often to plough their land using the services of this same creditor. In Ban Dong, village traders serve as a source of security in that they can be called on for cash loans at any time, but in Ban Mai poorer villagers complain that the shopowners now have to see the crop in the fields before they will advance any cash credit. In Ban Dong, 26 per cent of villagers borrow from village traders, while in Ban Mai 20 per cent borrow from this source. In Ban Mai, certain creditors lend to poor families who would otherwise have no source of capital. They are able to do this due to their reputation of being able to exert authority. It is alleged, for example, that Saeng, a wealthy trader and tractor owner, killed a man in his youth, and this is linked to his ability to extract payment without the need for collateral ('He doesn't have to raise his voice: no one would dare cross him . . .').

3. *Family and Close Relatives*. If loans from relatives are of short duration, no interest is charged. In any case, such loans are generally of small amounts. In some cases, they are a matter of reciprocity, whereby two distantly related households, who might otherwise expect interest, tacitly agree to help each other over periods of shortage.

Many households depend on more than one source of credit. This strategy is necessary for a number of reasons. BAAC credit is popular for its low interest, but other factors drive small farmers back toward dependence on the same informal lenders that institutional credit is supposed to replace. One is that BAAC credit is insufficient in both quantity and flexibility to cover both production and consumption requirements. BAAC adopts the conventional capitalist separation of production from consumption. It therefore sees its concern with the limited role of the peasant household as a production unit and lends accordingly, failing to take into account even imputed family labour costs in agricultural production. As a result, most households do not have enough cash to see themselves through the year. This is particularly true in Ban Mai, where virtually everything necessary for subsistence must be bought, including rice. In addition, timing of BAAC loans is inflexible. Borrowing is once a year, to be repaid within twelve months for short-term loans. As a result, many are forced to resort to interim loans from middlemen or wealthy villagers, and to a lesser extent relatives, in order to make ends meet throughout the year. A further problem with BAAC credit is the stipulation that seed and fertilizer must be taken in kind as part of the loan, otherwise no entitlement to credit is given.[9] This is despite the fact that many farmers have reservations about the suitability of the seed given out by BAAC as compared with local varieties in this marginal environment; there is, for example, particular concern over the ability of this strain to withstand drought during middle growth. Fertilizer is of even more uncertain suitability, and it is clear that most farmers do not want it. This is evidenced by the fact that, in 1985, Ban Mai clients of BAAC sold their fertilizer to Paak Meuang traders at less than the BAAC price at which they were forced to buy it.

Middlemen and wealthy villagers maintain a hold on their debtors in a number of ways. One is the increasingly insatiable demand for credit with commercialization of agriculture and the corresponding increase in inputs. Another is the debt cycle, whereby outstanding debts are carrieed over (with interest accruing) on the understanding that the debtor will continue to use the trading and mechanical services of the same merchant and tractor owner the following year. This is a remnant tie of patron–clientage, although its multiplexity has diminished. However, the attitude of creditor as provider remains strong. Moreover, there is usually a greater urgency to repay a non-institutional loan before an institutional loan, due to the pressure—social, moral, and sometimes physical—brought to bear on the borrower, as well as the higher interest rate accruing.[10]

The difference between formal and informal debtor–creditor relations is reflected in the actual priority for repayment. Altogether, 24 of 148 Ban Dong and Ban Mai villagers interviewed defaulted on one or more debts while paying back the other. Table 5.4 shows in which cases debts were repaid first and in which they were outstanding. It is interesting to note that, overall, debt is repaid more promptly to informal than formal lenders. Latterly, many BAAC members have in fact made desperate attempts to pay back their loans so as not to 'spoil' their records and disqualify themselves from further credit. This was evident in Ban Mai in 1985, when groups of BAAC clients arranged to borrow from village traders at an interest rate of 10 per cent for a single month in order to repay their BAAC loans and obtain the following year's loan, which was immediately used to repay the trader. This is one of the clearest examples of the downward slide into permanent multiple debt faced by many Ban Mai villagers.

Among informal lenders, middlemen are repaid most promptly, village

TABLE 5.4

Priority in Debt Repayment in Ban Dong and Ban Mai as Ranked by Twenty-four Debtors

Priority Ranking	*Number of Debtors Ranking Priority in Debt Repayment by Creditor Category*						
by Debtors	*Relative*	*Village Trader*	*Middleman*	*BAAC*	*Co-operative*	*Commercial Bank*	*Total Debts*
High	1	7	15	3	1	1	28
Low	4	3	1	6	14	0	28

Source: Field survey, 1985.
Note: The total number of debts is 28 in each case because 4 of the 24 debtors defaulted on two debts, and are thus counted twice.

traders next, and relatives last, since greater flexibility is possible in a more intimate debtor–creditor relationship. It is also possible for kin or fellow villagers to repay partially in kind, for example in labour services.[11]

In summary, the expansion of institutional credit has increased the overall level of debt rather than replaced exploitative non-institutional debt. In Ban Dong the average outstanding farmer debt is 6,400 baht, in Ban Mai 9,400 baht. Less than half of this is left over from the previous year's current debt, the remainder representing debt from previous years. This long-term debt is increasing rapidly in both communities, particularly in the commercialized economy of Ban Mai.

The demand for credit and resulting debt arises from the need for ever greater inputs in commercial agriculture. Use of seed distributed by BAAC is a pre-condition for credit for other purposes. Given freedom of action, most farmers would utilize a single stock of seed for about three years before purchasing new stock even if they were to use the high yielding varieties (HYVs), Suwan 1 or Suwan 2. An aggressive policy of marketing by the Charoen Pokaphan (CP) Company, which uses BAAC meetings as a forum, also plays a part. Impressive charts show the yield to be expected with CP seed compared with local varieties, backed up by evidence from demonstration plots which have been intensively cared for, watered, and fertilized on top-grade soils in Lopburi Province. This is recognized by local farmers who comment, 'They [CP] have time to mollycoddle [the plots] twenty-four hours a day.' Seed accounts for 15 per cent of cash inputs in first-crop maize planting, but only 1.5 per cent for the second crop since seed is kept over from the first harvest. For rice, seed accounts for only 5 per cent of cash inputs (Table 5.5a), although Ban Mai rice farmers spend 22 per cent on seed (Table 5.5c) while Ban Dong farmers, who plant rice every year, have no cash outlays for seed (Table 5.5b).

Herbicides are necessary for maize cultivation in particular. Since the forest environment has been altered, weeds have become a major problem. Particularly rampant are *Pennisetum polystachyon*, *Imperata cylindrica*, and *Thysanolaena maxima Ktze*. The first of these has little use, except potentially for compost. *Imperata* is used for thatching and *Thysanolaena* for making brooms, but they are otherwise seen as pests. Two types of herbicide are used: weed control and weed-killer toxins. The first of these has detrimental effects on the soil, felt in particular by those who plant mung beans as a second crop. Herbicides account for 10 per cent of cash outlays for the first crop of maize, 5 per cent for the second crop.

Potentially more hazardous both directly to human health and indirectly in their effects on wildlife are insecticides. Every year, farmers spraying insecticides suffer serious reactions.[12] These chemicals have become necessary, in particular for mung beans and cotton, both affected by caterpillars. However, the various pests quickly acquire a resistance to the pesticides. Moreover, those using little or no pesticide protection come off worse if their neighbours use it than if none is used at all, since the damage is then concentrated in their fields. As a result, farmers are forced into an ever less effective cycle of insecticide use. The precise

TABLE 5.5a
Proportion of Cash Expenses Incurred at Each Stage of Cultivation for Various Crops: Ban Dong and Ban Mai

	Cash Expenditure at Each Stage of Cultivation as Percentage of Total Cash Expenditure for Cultivation													
Crop	*Tillage*	*Seed*	*Planting*	*Herbicide*	*Insecticide*	*Fertilizer*	*Spraying*	*Weeding*	*Harvest*	*Milling*	*Transport*	*Outlay per Rai (baht)*	*Income per Rai (baht)*	*Average Area Planted (Rai)*
Rice 1	49.3	5.1	9.3	0.3	0.0	0.2	0.2	0.2	13.4	19.0	3.1	105	866	16.1
Rice 2	0.0	0.0	35.2	0.0	0.0	3.1	0.0	0.0	58.8	2.9	0.0	269	1,088	5.0
Rice 3	0.0	0.0	0.0	0.0	0.0	0.0	0.0	0.0	0.0	0.0	0.0	0	n.a.	1.0
Maize 1	40.7	15.0	3.7	10.0	0.2	0.1	1.2	3.3	12.3	7.5	6.0	295	646	23.4
Maize 2	69.4	1.5	3.1	5.1	0.2	0.3	0.2	0.6	9.9	6.9	2.6	118	219	21.4
Maize 3	0.0	0.0	0.0	0.0	12.5	87.5	0.0	0.0	0.0	0.0	0.0	160	900	1.0
Mung 1	35.5	12.1	0.0	0.0	16.1	0.2	2.0	0.0	28.1	4.7	1.4	267	405	16.6
Mung 2	26.8	9.8	0.0	0.0	26.0	0.0	3.9	0.0	32.6	0.7	0.1	215	496	11.2
Cassava	54.3	2.5	3.3	0.0	0.0	0.0	0.0	0.0	36.6	0.0	3.3	406	699	17.7
Soya	30.8	12.1	0.0	0.0	6.4	0.0	0.0	0.0	25.7	16.6	8.4	389	1,575	20.0
Cotton	10.2	8.1	0.0	0.4	68.8	0.0	0.0	4.5	6.1	0.0	1.9	966	2,740	4.2
Sorghum	57.3	10.3	1.4	0.0	1.4	0.0	0.5	0.0	14.5	10.6	4.0	144	246	16.1
Cow-pea	14.0	46.4	0.1	0.0	17.1	0.0	5.9	0.0	11.1	0.0	5.4	153	146	10.5
Castor	0.0	0.0	0.0	0.0	0.0	0.0	0.0	0.0	0.0	0.0	0.0	0	1,500	2.0
Total	38.1	9.6	4.2	6.0	6.0	0.2	1.5	1.7	22.3	6.1	4.2			

Source: Field survey, 1985.

Notes: 1. Rice 1 is the principal rice crop; Rice 2 is the secondary, irrigated rice crop; Rice 3 is glutinous rice; Maize 1 is the principal maize crop; Maize 2 is the secondary maize crop; Maize 3 is sweetcorn; Mung 1 is the upland mung bean crop following maize 1; Mung 2 is the rice-land mung bean crop following Rice 1.

2. The income from unsold rice is calculated at 29 baht per *tang*.

3. Totals may not add up to 100 due to rounding.

TABLE 5.5b

Proportion of Cash Expenses Incurred at Each Stage of Cultivation for Various Crops: Ban Dong

Crop	*Cash Expenditure at Each Stage of Cultivation as Percentage of Total Cash Expenditure for Cultivation*													
	Tillage	*Seed*	*Planting*	*Herbicide*	*Insecticide*	*Fertilizer*	*Spraying*	*Weeding*	*Harvest*	*Milling*	*Transport*	*Outlay per Rai (baht)*	*Income per Rai (baht)*	*Average Area Planted (Rai)*
Rice 1	46.3	0.0	10.6	0.4	0.0	0.1	0.2	0.2	16.0	23.0	3.2	100	938	18.5
Rice 2	0.0	0.0	35.2	0.0	0.0	3.1	0.0	0.0	58.8	2.9	0.0	269	1,088	5.0
Rice 3	0.0	0.0	0.0	0.0	0.0	0.0	0.0	0.0	0.0	0.0	0.0	0	n.a	1.0
Maize 1	37.7	22.5	3.3	7.1	0.0	0.0	1.0	5.6	8.4	8.1	6.2	214	n.a.	14.2
Maize 2	85.8	0.0	0.0	0.0	0.0	0.0	0.0	0.0	8.0	5.1	1.1	83	120	12.5
Maize 3	0.0	0.0	0.0	0.0	12.5	87.5	0.0	0.0	0.0	0.0	0.0	160	900	1.0
Mung 1	37.2	6.1	0.0	0.0	19.2	0.0	2.0	0.0	29.5	4.9	1.0	235	463	8.4
Mung 2	27.4	10.3	0.0	0.0	25.9	0.0	3.5	0.0	32.3	0.6	0.1	204	473	11.2
Cassava	–	–	–	–	–	–	–	–	–	–	–	–	–	
Soya	–	–	–	–	–	–	–	–	–	–	–	–	–	
Cotton	9.2	17.2	0.0	0.0	73.6	0.0	0.0	0.0	0.0	0.0	0.0	820	2,700	4.5
Sorghum	44.8	11.3	2.0	0.0	3.7	0.0	1.2	0.0	18.0	17.2	1.9	144	413	14.0
Cow-pea	16.9	50.0	0.0	0.0	8.1	0.0	4.8	0.0	20.2	0.0	0.0	112	156	6.5
Castor	0.0	0.0	0.0	0.0	0.0	0.0	0.0	0.0	0.0	0.0	0.0	0	1,500	2.0
Total	35.1	7.6	7.8	3.4	7.5	0.3	1.7	2.3	24.9	7.1	2.2			

Source: Field survey, 1985.

Notes: As for Table 5.5a.

Dash indicates crop not grown in this village.

TABLE 5.5c
Proportion of Cash Expenses Incurred at Each Stage of Cultivation for Various Crops: Ban Mai

Crop	*Cash Expenditure at Each Stage of Cultivation as Percentage of Total Cash Expenditure for Cultivation*													
	Tillage	*Seed*	*Planting*	*Herbicide*	*Insecticide*	*Fertilizer*	*Spraying*	*Weeding*	*Harvest*	*Milling*	*Transport*	*Outlay per Rai (baht)*	*Income per Rai (baht)*	*Average Area Planted (Rai)*
Rice 1	59.3	21.9	5.1	0.1	0.0	0.3	0.0	0.0	4.9	5.8	2.7	119	660	9.1
Rice 2	–	–	–	–	–	–	–	–	–	–	–	–	–	
Rice 3	–	–	–	–	–	–	–	–	–	–	–	–	–	
Maize 1	42.2	11.2	3.9	11.6	0.3	0.2	1.3	2.1	14.3	7.1	5.9	337	768	28.1
Maize 2	62.8	2.2	4.4	7.1	0.3	0.4	0.3	0.5	10.7	7.6	3.3	131	259	25.0
Maize 3	–	–	–	–	–	–	–	–	–	–	–	–	–	
Mung 1	34.9	14.2	0.0	0.0	15.1	0.2	1.9	0.0	27.6	4.6	1.5	278	384	19.5
Mung 2	14.4	0.0	0.0	0.0	28.8	0.0	12.3	0.0	41.2	3.3	0.0	486	1,035	5.1
Cassava	54.3	2.5	3.3	0.0	0.0	0.0	0.0	0.0	36.6	0.0	3.3	406	699	17.7
Soya	30.8	12.1	0.0	0.0	6.4	0.0	0.0	0.0	25.7	16.6	8.4	389	1,575	20.0
Cotton	10.9	1.9	0.0	0.6	65.6	0.0	0.0	7.5	10.2	0.0	3.1	1,063	2,767	4.0
Sorghum	65.2	9.7	1.0	0.0	0.0	0.0	0.0	0.0	12.4	6.4	5.3	144	142	17.4
Cow-pea	11.1	42.8	2.3	0.0	26.1	0.0	7.0	0.0	2.1	0.0	10.7	193	136	14.5
Castor	–	–	–	–	–	–	–	–	–	–	–	–	–	
Total	39.0	10.2	3.1	6.8	5.5	0.2	1.5	1.5	21.4	5.8	4.9			

Source: Field survey, 1985.
Notes: As for Table 5.5a.
Dash indicates crop not grown in this village.

nature of the pollutant effect on water sources is unknown, but fish disease is evident.[13] Insecticides account for 16 and 26 per cent respectively of investment for upland and rice-land mung bean cultivation, and fully 69 per cent for cotton.

Until 1985, fertilizer use in Ban Dong and Ban Mai was minimal. In rice agriculture it was limited to the small areas of dry-season irrigated crops, while it was only used in a few cases and in small quantities for other crops. The reasons for such low usage are manifold. The principal reason is the uncertainty of rainfall and lack of confidence that the expense is warranted. Many fear the dependence on fertilizer that the soil acquires once fertilizer is used, and the hardening of the soil that results from protracted use. Many of the negative ideas that Lan Sak farmers have about fertilizer come from first- or second-hand experience in other areas, since many retain links with the district or province from which they moved to Lan Sak. Another reason is that the soil is still productive, characterized as 'new' or 'unspoilt', since it has only been used for a short time. The district DAE office has a policy of achieving a standard fertilizer usage of 25 kilos per *rai* and does not differentiate between soils. This crude approach does little to raise farmers' confidence in chemical fertilizer use. It is not surprising, therefore, that when BAAC stipulated in 1985 that its clients take fertilizer as part of their loan, the reaction was one of feeling 'forced', and evidence of the aversion to fertilizer use is its resale as described above. On the other side, DAE and BAAC regard the low use of fertilizer as symptomatic of the ignorance (euphemistically phrased as 'lack of knowledge') of farmers, although individual field officers understand and sometimes accept as valid the farmers' case, but are powerless to contravene official policy.

The other major use of capital in seasonal production is in the hire or purchase of machinery. The most important item here is outlay for ploughing.

In Ban Dong rice agriculture, ploughing by buffalo is still prominent, but power tillers are increasingly popular. This involves a capital outlay of 30,000–40,000 baht, depending on terms of purchase and what accessories (such as trailer or pump) are acquired. If they are not bought outright, BAAC medium- or long-term credit is available for some, but most depend on hire-purchase. In the two communities, 18 per cent of farmers have power tillers, and of these two-thirds use them only for their own fields.

Four-wheel tractor owners, on the other hand, use their machines principally for hiring out to other villagers. Not even the largest farms warrant full-time use of a tractor. Nevertheless, ploughing for upland cropping is now almost exclusively by means of tractor. Rates vary from 70–120 baht per *rai* for a single tillage, although more is charged if the land is newly cleared or heavily overgrown with weeds. To purchase a second-hand Ford 5000 tractor requires at least 200,000 baht and is thus limited to those with substantial capital.[14] In Ban Dong and Ban Mai, such capital has been acquired through land sales, illegal forestry, or trade. On the other hand, the cost can be recouped in less than two years if the tractor is put to full use. This means being able to hire it out elsewhere during the local slack seasons. One Ban Mai tractor goes as far afield as Paak Chong in the north-eastern province of Korat after the second ploughing. Personal connections external to the village are important in this case. For the majority of upland farmers, particularly in Ban Mai, hire of a tractor is the single most costly cash input. It accounts for 38.1 per cent as a whole (looking at both Ban Dong and Ban Mai), 35.1 per cent in Ban Dong, and 39.0 per cent in Ban Mai. For maize cultivation, it accounts for 40.7 per cent of inputs. For cassava and sorghum respectively, 54.3 and 57.3 per cent of costs go on tractor ploughing. Even for rice, tractor ploughing now accounts for nearly half of all cash inputs, but this is half of a smaller outlay (Tables 5.5a, b, and c).

Labour

Labour for production is secured in three main ways. First, household labour provides the basis for peasant production.[15] Second, reciprocal labour provides the means for social mobilization of labour for tasks beyond the capacity of household labour. Third, waged employment commoditizes labour within the monetized economy. Two additional forms of labour are free labour given to relatives and neighbours, and community labour secured by dictate or agreement.

Household labour is the form of labour over which the household production unit has most direct control. Control over household labour depends first and foremost on reproduction of the family unit. This in turn requires adequate levels of food consumption and health, both traditionally secured largely from the family's own production and locally available resources. However, recent changes have altered this situation greatly, and cash is now important for both forms of bodily sustenance. Most families in Ban Mai purchase the bulk of their food requirements, including rice. In Ban Dong, subsistence production still commonly provides basic food needs, although most families supplement this with cash purchases. However, in the case of medicine, cash has become necessary with the decline in traditional herbal practices, reliance on modern drugs and hospitals, and the need for cash payment to local doctors who in the past would have taken payment in kind (for example, rice, chickens, labour services). The slide into debt is commonly precipitated by medical expenses, and these often arise from illness related to production.

Traditionally, control over household labour would have been a vital asset in a situation of relative land abundance and low capital inputs. In particular, clearing of forest land in Lan Sak and maintaining a claim to land depended on 'having a following, or "mates"', in one farmer's words, at the heart of which would have been a close and preferably large family (see also Ananya, 1985: 83–4). Several of the most influential villagers in Ban Mai, for example, the village head and the *tambon* doctor, come from large Thung Khaa families. With increasing land scarcity,

1 Huai Kha Khaeng Sanctuary: Lan Sak's last remaining forest.

2 *Yaang* oil tapping.

3 Ban Dong Bridge destroyed by floods on the Tap Salao River.

4 Continued clearing in the hills behind Ban Mai.

5 Dry season fields near Ban Mai, cleared after 1978.

Ban Mai agriculture depends heavily on purchased inputs.

7 Farmers at Bank for Agriculture and Agricultural Co-operatives (BAAC).

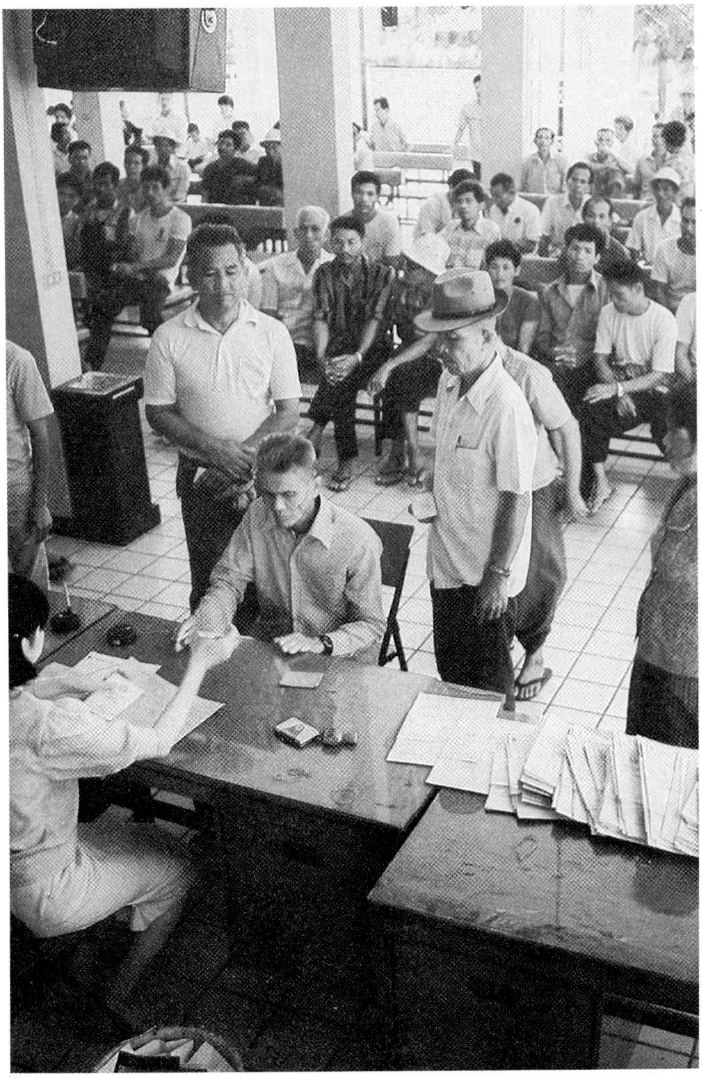

8 Harvesting after drought in Bung Khiew.

9 *Ao raeng* (reciprocal) labour in Bung Khiew for rice harvest.

10 Measuring rice for milling.

11 Wealthier villager's house in Ban Mai.

12 Poorer villager's house in Ban Mai.

13 Isolated homestead in Bung Khiew.

14 Official symbolism of development in Ban Dong.

15 Ban Dong *kamnan* at village meeting.

16 Co-operation in Bung Khiew: Strengthening the bridge into the village.

changing means of securing control over land, and the growing importance of capital inputs in the production process, the advantages of control over household labour diminish in relative significance. Indeed, an excess of household members can be a liability in terms of increased consumption demands.[16] Furthermore, in the relatively closed village economy, household labour was fully under the control of the household production unit. Declining opportunities for employment of such labour and increasing off-farm employment, on the other hand, cause young people to leave their families at an age where they are most productive.[17] Many of the young people who leave Ban Mai lose contact with their parents, and large remittances from children working in Bangkok or elsewhere are the exception rather than the rule. Forty per cent in Ban Mai and 26 per cent in Ban Dong who live away from home send no remittance at all. Despite these changes, a certain amount of household labour is still important for most stages in the agricultural production process, as is evident from Table 5.1.

The major exceptions are in non-rice agriculture, where ploughing is done mostly by tractor because of two main environmental constraints. One is the hardening of the soil that has taken place following deforestation, which makes the use of draught animals difficult. This is compounded by the effect of tractor ploughing itself, which further compresses the soil and leads to the formation of a hardpan, while not providing nutrients and the healthy structural effect that animal manure has on the soil. The other constraint is the shortened planting season, which means that the period for ploughing is short. Delays are therefore risky, and ploughing early is not practicable because of weeds. The need to get produce sold quickly means that milling, husking, and threshing is mainly by machine, which usually belongs to the buyer.

Household labour is not sufficient for many of the stages of the cropping process, since there is only a window of a few days due to weather-related factors or to the need for even planting and harvesting. This has always been true in rice cultivation. Reciprocal arrangements have been a traditional method of securing control over village labour within the community but beyond the individual household. These arrangements are discussed in more detail in the next chapter; for the time being, discussion is limited to the trends in the use of this form of labour.

Reciprocal labour has diminished in importance rapidly throughout the Central Plains (Ananya, 1985: 92; Girling, 1981: 45). In Lan Sak, it is still common in rice harvesting and in maize planting, but otherwise it is used decreasingly (Table 5.6a). Previously, reciprocal labour would be used for rice transplanting and other parts of the agricultural production cycle. Control over such labour depends not on access to capital or other external resources, but on two intrinsically domestic resources—namely, household labour and social relations within the community.[18] Meanwhile, Table 5.7 shows that ability to depend solely on household and reciprocal labour varies both between crops and between communities for the same crop. In general, subsistence rather than cash crops can be produced using these domestic labour resources only, and the less commercialized economy of Ban Dong shows a greater reliance on household and reciprocal labour than does that of Ban Mai, even for cash crops.

While the importance of household labour and reciprocal labour has been diminishing, hiring of labour has been on the increase. In Ban Dong 62 per cent and in Ban Mai 68 per cent of households are engaged in paid agricultural employment. Although the wealthier farmers are the larger employers, even small, capital-deficient households employ labour at some stages of the agricultural production process. As a result, 40 per cent of Ban Dong and 57 per cent of Ban Mai households are simultaneously agricultural labourers and employers of labour. Tables 5.6b and 5.6c show the extent hired labour is used relative to reciprocal labour in each stage of cultivation of various crops in the two villages.

It should be noted that securing even wage labour is not entirely independent of social relations. Use of the term *khaek* (guest) as opposed to *luuk jaang* (employee) is a continuity of discourse that underlies a certain continuity of functional status in the producer–labourer relationship. Evidence of this lies in the treatment of wage labourers working alongside reciprocal labourers as ordinary *khaek*, whereas quite different expectations are held of teams of wholly hired labour. Wealthier farmers

TABLE 5.6a

Proportion of Non-household Labour which is Hired or Reciprocal at Different Stages of Cultivation for Various Crops: Ban Dong and Ban Mai

	Percentage of Non-household Labour which is Hired (H) or Reciprocal (R) at Different Stages of Cultivation			
Crop	*Planting*	*Spraying*	*Weeding*	*Harvesting*
Rice 1	65 R	87 H	100 H	70 R
Rice 2	82 H	–	–	100 H
Rice 3	–	–	–	–
Maize 1	54 H	97 H	63 H	85 H
Maize 2	92 H	100 H	100 H	80 H
Maize 3	–	–	–	–
Mung 1	90 R	95 H	–	97 H
Mung 2	–	100 H	–	94 H
Cassava	88 R	–	–	81 H
Soya	–	–	–	100 H
Cotton	100 R	–	100 H	65 H
Sorghum	100 H	100 H	–	76 H
Cow-pea	79 R	100 H	–	100 H
Castor	–	–	–	–

Source: Field survey, 1985.
Notes: As for Table 5.5a.
H = Hired labour.
R = Reciprocal labour.
Dash indicates non-household labour is not used for these tasks/crops.

TABLE 5.6b

Proportion of Non-household Labour which is Hired or Reciprocal at Different Stages of Cultivation for Various Crops: Ban Dong

Crop	*Percentage of Non-household Labour which is Hired (H) or Reciprocal (R) at Different Stages of Cultivation*			
	Planting	*Spraying*	*Weeding*	*Harvesting*
Rice 1	67 R	100 H	100 H	69 R
Rice 2	82 H	–	–	100 H
Rice 3	–	–	–	–
Maize 1	53 R	100 H	62 H	60 H
Maize 2	–	–	–	100 H
Maize 3	–	–	–	–
Mung 1	–	100 H	–	91 H
Mung 2	–	100 H	–	94 H
Cassava	–	–	–	–
Soya	–	–	–	–
Cotton	–	–	–	–
Sorghum	100 H	100 H	–	82 H
Cow-pea	100 R	100 H	–	100 H
Castor	–	–	–	–

Source: Field survey, 1985.
Notes: As for Tables 5.5a and 5.6a.

TABLE 5.6c

Proportion of Non-household Labour which is Hired or Reciprocal at Different Stages of Cultivation for Various Crops: Ban Mai

Crop	*Percentage of Non-household Labour which is Hired (H) or Reciprocal (R) at Different Stages of Cultivation*			
	Planting	*Spraying*	*Weeding*	*Harvesting*
Rice 1	55 H	100 R	–	79 R
Rice 2	–	–	–	–
Rice 3	–	–	–	–
Maize 1	56 H	97 H	63 H	89 H
Maize 2	92 H	100 H	100 H	79 H
Maize 3	–	–	–	–
Mung 1	90 R	94 H	–	98 H
Mung 2	–	100 H	–	100 H
Cassava	88 R	–	–	81 H
Soya	–	–	–	100 H
Cotton	100 R	–	100 H	65 H
Sorghum	100 H	–	–	70 H
Cow-pea	100 H	100 H	–	100 H
Castor	–	–	–	–

Source: Field survey, 1985.
Notes: As for Tables 5.5a and 5.6a.

who employ solely or mainly wage labour recruit from large pools all round the village, although practicality often involves having to recruit workers who live close to each other in order to save time in summoning labour. Smaller farmers recruit from within a limited circle, often employing families who later employ them. Teams of reciprocating families during the planting season will hire labour first and foremost within the circle when it comes to harvesting.

Nevertheless, even though wage labour does not entirely undermine the importance of social relations, control over agricultural labour depends to a decreasing extent on intrinsic household resources and to a greater extent on the ability to hire labour. This in turn requires access to capital. As a result, poorer households suffer a loss of control over labour for production, since they are at once unable to summon reciprocal labour, as in the past, and at the same time are constrained in their ability to hire wage labour. Such households thus become net suppliers of wage labour, while wealthier households manage to secure labour beyond what could be achieved using only household resources.

Management of labour shows a qualitative change in the move from household and reciprocal labour to hired labour. No supervision is required for household labour, since those involved are all part of the same production and consumption unit. Villagers often express a preference for working on their own land, since rewards are commensurate

TABLE 5.7

Percentage of Households Using Only Own and Reciprocal Labour in Labour-intensive Stages of Production* for Various Crops

	Ban Dong		*Ban Mai*	
Crop	*Percentage of Households Using Only Own and Reciprocal Labour*	*Percentage of Households Planting that Crop*	*Percentage of Households Using Only Own and Reciprocal Labour*	*Percentage of Households Planting that Crop*
Rice 1	62.7	69.8	83.3	24.0
Rice 2	33.3	4.1	–	0
Rice 3	100.0	1.4	–	0
Maize 1	38.2	46.6	12.3	86.7
Maize 2	50.0	2.7	40.0	6.7
Maize 3	100.0	1.4	–	0
Mung 1	31.6	26.0	14.8	72.0
Mung 2	12.5	32.9	0	1.3
Cassava	–	0	33.3	4.0
Soya	–	0	0	1.3
Cotton	100.0	2.7	33.3	4.0
Sorghum	40.0	6.8	12.5	10.7
Cow-pea	50.0	2.7	50.0	2.7
Castor	100.0	1.4	–	0

Source: Field survey, 1985.

Notes: As for Table 5.5a.

*Planting, spraying, weeding, harvesting.

with effort. In the case of reciprocal labour, supervision is limited to pointing out which fields are to be planted when. Any member of the 'host' household in the fields will work alongside the 'guests', while rests are taken by common agreement. The knowledge that the task is to be reciprocated prevents shirking, but the work is more relaxed and timing more flexible than in the case of hired labour. If a field is finished early, 'guests' may go home early; if a small amount remains to be done at going-home time, they often stay to finish the job as they would on their own fields. For hired labour, on the other hand, supervision is much stricter. An adult member of the hiring household supervises the work, calls the breaks, and occasionally admonishes slackers. Timing is strictly by the clock.

Agricultural wage labour rates are well below the legal minimum wage in Uthaithani province of 54 baht per day. In Ban Dong and Ban Mai in 1985, the standard rate was 30 baht. Occasionally this rises to 35 baht at times of peak demand, such as the height of the planting season in Ban Mai. Larger employers of labour even bring in teams from lowland villages during such periods. An increasing incidence of reliance on cash income from wage labour means that the availability of such labour has increased, especially in Ban Mai. This has been accompanied by stagnant or falling wage rates. Despite inflation, the normal rate did not rise in the seven years prior to 1988. Even more telling is the rice wage as alternative to cash payment in Ban Dong. The eldest residents report that this once-standard form of payment has stood at one *tang* of paddy for as long as they can remember. This same *tang* payment is for the employer equivalent to slightly less than the 30-baht cash wage, and for the employee it amounts to slightly more than the rice that could be obtained for the cash wage.[19] Meanwhile, the price of rice has fallen steadily relative to the overall price index. The downward pressure on wages is felt acutely by those most affected. It is explained by one Ban Mai landless labourer thus: 'This year there are many labourers who've gone under, so they have no capital to plant their own field crops.' Harvesting wages for field crops are usually at piece rate, by the sack for maize and by the basket for mung beans. Piece-work harvest rates in Ban Mai have fallen recently with declining crop prices and reduced yields.

In summary, traditional forms of labour were controlled within the household and the community. Commoditization of labour removes these limitations. It gives those with capital potential control over a much wider pool of labour than they could secure by traditional means. At the same time, it means that those without capital become themselves the commodity, subject to control by monetized relations.

Fuel

Until recently, fuel for cooking was plentiful in Lan Sak in the form of charcoal. Even after deforestation, tree stumps burnt in the fields provided a source of wood. In Ban Dong, many families (41 per cent) now need to buy all or some of their requirements. In Ban Mai, wood is also becoming increasingly scarce, as a result of which forest reserve land close by is encroached upon with severe environmental consequences.

Eighty per cent of households still manage without having to purchase charcoal, but this number can be expected to decrease rapidly. Charcoal in Ban Dong is purchased mainly from villages to the north, which were settled more recently and still have a supply of wood and stumps. Charcoal is sold in these villages for 30–35 baht per sack. In Ban Dong the price can reach as much as 50–60 baht. The reason for this differential is not just the cost of transport *per se*: more important is the risk involved, since transporting charcoal is in contravention of forest protection laws and heavy fines can be imposed. In Ban Mai, such a differential is absent, since charcoal is available on the fringes of the village. However, some traders (Ban Mai pick-up owners) buy charcoal for 30–40 baht per sack in Ban Mai, mostly from landless or near-landless families, and sell it at Nong Chang market for double the price. This is risky for those not on good terms with the police. In Ban Dong, a few wealthy households have begun to follow the trend elsewhere in the Central Plains of switching to cooking on gas stoves.

Motive power for ploughing and transport is increasingly dependent on petrol or diesel engines, as indicated above. Draught animals are still used widely for ploughing rice-fields, but relatively rarely are they now used for drawing carts, as in the past. The exceptions are in carting home the rice harvest from distant fields and in (illegal) transport of logs, usually at night, from villages near Ban Dong into the village.

Whereas fuel was until recently an abundant resource over which control was universal, it is now in short supply and increasingly secured within the monetized economy. One side of this monetized fuel economy is covert, since the law proscribes manufacture of charcoal for any purpose other than one's own consumption.

Knowledge

> I am master of [this] college;
> . . . what I don't know isn't knowledge!
> Epigram on Benjamin Jowett

> I am native of this village;
> how can what *I* know be knowledge?
> Author

Long-term residents of Ban Dong and Ban Mai have an intimate knowledge of the forest environment. Early settlers in both communities quickly adapted to the exigencies of subsistence production and *yaang* resin tapping by acquiring an extensive knowledge of flora and fauna, soils and water resources. Settlement was governed by the use of natural resources, particularly water courses. Traditional land preparation, ploughing, selection of seed, harvesting, and threshing techniques were adapted to the constraints of the environment and locally available resources. Knowledge was acquired through direct experience, learning from neighbours—by observation and communication—and by passing on from one generation to the next. Of course, such knowledge (*khwaamruu*) was not perceived of as such, for *khwaamruu* is something that one gets at school or from official training. Rather, such knowledge was part of a 'practical consciousness' (see Giddens, 1984: xxiii, xxx, 41–5).

As long as the production regime remained the same within a not greatly altered environment, possession of such knowledge gave Ban Dong and Ban Mai settlers an advantage over outsiders in terms of control over production. However, several changes have taken place to undermine this control. Loss of the forest environment has meant a rapid disappearance of many elements fundamental to the subsistence production regime. Large and small wildlife, assured rainfall and fluvial water sources, forest shrubs and herbs, *yaang* trees, and a replenished soil were all part of the disappearing system. The result has been uncertainty, where traditional knowledge is insufficient to cope with the pace of environmental change. Change to market-oriented production has meant introduction of new crops, new methods, and new inputs which require a new stock of knowledge for successful production.

Despite rapid adaptation and adoption of new methods, Ban Dong and Ban Mai farmers do not maintain the same advantage as they did with indigenous production in a less altered system. From the official's point of view, the basic obstacle to villagers' improving their situation in the given circumstances is that they 'lack knowledge'. Villagers themselves jest to an outsider in this way: 'We're stupid; we don't possess knowledge.' The old *khon to* in Thung Khaa says of outside events that are known to affect farmers, such as the 1984 devaluation of the baht, that it is not worth trying to explain them over the radio: 'It's like playing the violin to a buffalo.'

What has been lost is not the essence of the knowledge itself. Rather, it is first the relevance of that knowledge in a changed situation, and second, even where indigenous knowledge maintains its relevance or has been adapted or supplemented so as to suit the new situation, the status of indigenous knowledge has diminished. As mentioned above, *khwaamruu* is used to apply only to formally recognized information, skills, or techniques that have been passed on in a situation of DAE official, schoolteacher, or other outsider conveying 'knowledge' to an ignorant peasantry. It is thus by definition that 'villagers are without knowledge', for what they know is not knowledge as defined by the dominant discourse.

Production and Differentiation in Lan Sak

The preceding discussion examined the means by which individual households gain control over production via resources and social relations governing access to them. The emphasis has been on change and the ways in which it has affected control. These points are now illustrated by reference to production in the villages of Ban Dong and Ban Mai. For each village, there is a description of the agricultural production cycle and an analysis of individual livelihoods, and this is followed by a comparison.

Production and Differentiation in Ban Dong

Ban Dong is primarily a rice-growing village, but most farmers also grow field crops. Ban Dong farmers consider and refer to themselves as *chaonaa*, or rice cultivators. This is despite the fact that non-rice production may be a larger portion of some farmers' agricultural activities, measured in time spent, area planted, or income derived. Overall, rice accounted for 80 per cent of crop production by value and 66 per cent of total area planted in the 1984 main crop season, while secondary crops grown on rice-land made up 57 per cent of production and 51 per cent of area. Considered alternatively, 60 per cent of Ban Dong villagers who cultivated crops in 1984 produced mainly rice (measured in cash value of yield), and 69 per cent planted mainly rice-land (measured in area planted). Table 5.8 shows the relative importance of the various crops planted in Ban Dong.

Control over land, water, and household labour are clearly the key factors in rice production. Average land ownership in Ban Dong is 24 *rai*, or 33 *rai* if land owned outside the village is included, and ranges from none to 139 *rai*, or 180 *rai* including land owned elsewhere. Most of the non-local land is forest reserve or preparatory forest reserve land owned elsewhere in the district, and much of it has yet to be cleared and put under permanent cultivation. Twenty per cent of villagers are landless, while another 17 per cent own less than 5 *rai* in the village. Of those farming, less than 25 per cent have mainly irrigated or semi-irrigated fields, but 37 per cent gain at least some benefit of irrigation water.

TABLE 5.8
Ban Dong Cropping

Crop	*Percentage of Households Planting that Crop*	*Percentage of Area Planted with that Crop*	*Yield Per Rai*
Rice 1	70	47.3	32.4 *tang*
Rice 2	4	0.8	37.5 *tang*
Rice 3	1	0.1	25.0 *tang*
Maize 1	47	24.3	13.0 *tang*
Maize 2	3	1.3	3.8 *tang*
Maize 3	1	0.1	1500 cobs
Mung 1	26	8.0	4.3 *tang*
Mung 2	33	13.5	4.6 *tang*
Cassava	0	0	–
Soya	0	0	–
Cotton	3	0.5	208.3 kg
Sorghum	7	3.5	12.3 *tang*
Cow-pea	3	0.7	1.7 *tang*
Castor	1	0.1	10.0 *tang*

Source: Field survey, 1985.
Notes: As for Table 5.5a.

Technically, most of the rice-land in Ban Dong is at least semi-irrigable, but various factors to be discussed in the next chapter leave large areas, including almost the whole of Bung Khiew, to rely on rainfall. Household labour is still mostly locally employed, although nearly one in three households had at least one member absent for part of 1984. Of these, many were only away for the dry season.

Rice is planted from June onward. Timing of planting depends both on the rains in any one year and on the situation of particular fields with regard to water. Fields are ploughed once the soil has been softened by the first rains. If possible, rice is sown in nursery beds and transplanted. This is more labour intensive than broadcasting, but it gives higher yields and facilitates harvesting.[20] In nearly two-thirds of cases, only family labour is used. Of the non-household labour used for transplanting, one-third is hired labour and two-thirds reciprocal labour. In 1984, the drought was such that Ban Dong farmers could not inundate rain-fed fields, so they had to resort to broadcasting using family labour.

Between planting and harvesting, there is little to attend to in Ban Dong rice farming. Those with upland (51 per cent) manage to intersperse maize and secondary crops.[21] Approximately ten days before harvesting, the tall traditional varieties of rice are deliberately toppled so as to fall neatly in one direction and ease harvesting. A few days before the day of the harvest, labour is summoned for that particular day. Most of these labourers come under reciprocal labour agreements, but some are hired. The harvest is usually completed within one or two days, those with larger fields inviting more 'guests'.

Threshing and winnowing of rice is done in any one of a number of ways. Those with buffalo often maintain the traditional practice of stamping, with the grain laid out on an earth threshing floor and buffalo driven around a stake planted in the middle. Winnowing is then done using trays. This process may be mechanized partially by driving a small tractor or power tiller over the grain in place of a buffalo. Full mechanization in the form of threshing machines is becoming more popular, however, at a charge of 1 baht per *tang*. These machines are owned by wealthy villagers.

Three out of five Ban Dong villagers have small granaries, but surplus rice is nevertheless usually sold within a short time after threshing and winnowing are completed. This is due to the immediate need for cash, both for consumption and for paying off debt. Rice is either sold directly to Uthaithani or Nong Chang middlemen who come with a lorry to the farmstead, or to the Lan Sak rice mill, or to village brokers—of whom two get most of the trade. Many have to sell through the latter due to debt obligation. Middlemen are seen as exploitative not so much in the low price they offer as in the discounts they claim for broken rice and the cheating they practise with the scales. Paddy is sold unmilled, but rice for home consumption is milled mechanically. Until 1985, rice in Ban Dong was milled at the small mills of one of the two village millers or at the larger Lan Sak rice mill. In 1985, a small mill was constructed at Bung Khiew by a wealthy Ban Dong family.

The dry-season mung bean crop is planted immediately following the rice harvest. Planting is broadcast and cultivation is not as intensive as it is in the north of Thailand. Lack of water control is a major uncertainty. Intensive spraying of pesticides is necessary to protect against caterpillars. Harvesting normally takes place during March or April, using hired labour for those with larger areas under cultivation. Husking can be carried out using traditional rice-threshing methods or by machine.

To describe agricultural production as such is to risk presenting an over-simplified picture of the agricultural community as an undifferentiated production system with minor variations due to varying preferences or micro-environmental constraints. To do so would be misleading, for the possibilities and actualities facing individual households (the basic production unit) are varied, dependent to a large degree on control over resources for production and the relations governing such control. As we saw in the preceding section, such control is changing as access to resources for production is increasingly monetized, concentrated, and subject to external influences.

Production based on a subsistence crop with an as yet low level of capitalization does in fact lead to a more homogeneous community than where commercialization is more advanced. But this homogeneity is only relative. Key factors of production are unequally distributed within the community. To illustrate the effect this has on household production, the cases of six Ban Dong households are presented below. Each household is referred to by a pseudonym for the reported household head, and this is used also to refer to the entire household. Although it usually refers to a male, this is not to imply that the male head of household is the dominant individual regarding household production, for example in land ownership or labour input.

1. ***Nid, Landless Labourer***. Nid has never owned land. Before coming to Ban Dong, Nid's family rented land in Nong Chang, but the land was poor and the family moved to Lad Yao in Nakorn Sawan in the hope of being able to buy cheap land. They were unsuccessful and moved to Ban Dong in 1974, where they reside on a sister's land. Some years, they rent 23 *rai* of rain-fed rice-land, but in 1984 they did not plant because of drought. Since they are sharecroppers, the landowner agreed not to take any rent.

There are five people in Nid's household. Two of the daughters, aged seventeen and twelve, have finished school, and the youngest is about to start. Their mother complains about the cost of sending children to school. In particular, she resents the cost of sweets at the village shop. In the past, children would ask for a baht once a week or once a fortnight for home-made sweets wrapped in banana leaves. Now it is two or three baht per child per day for plastic-wrapped sweets with no nutritional value. If the children cannot buy the same sweets as their schoolmates, they complain that they are ashamed.

Although two children have now finished school and can contribute to the family's labour, Nid himself is unable to work in most jobs following a pillion motor cycle accident which left him permanently crippled. In

1984, the entire family income of about 9,000 baht came from local agricultural wage labouring. Half of this was required just for the purchase of rice and charcoal. They are also in debt to a neighbour for 3,000 baht, on which they pay 1,800 baht per year in interest.

Only a small proportion of Nid's family consumption needs can be satisfied by use of local resources. Without land, access to rice and other necessities requires cash. They grow some vegetables on their home plot and manage to make some of their own charcoal on wasteland, but neither is enough to last all year round. A few chickens provide an occasional source of food. Their only major possession other than their small thatched bamboo and timber shack is a bicycle.

2. *Nai, Tenant Farmer*. Nai has also never had land of his own. He lives in Bung Khiew on his brother's land and rents poor quality land from one of Ban Dong's larger landowners who is a member of the village committee. Nai moved to Ban Dong with his parents in 1974. They had been affected by drought on their rain-fed rice-land in Lad Yao, and consequently moved to Lan Sak. Nai's parents and sisters work a small plot of land on the edge of the village. Since Nai now has a family of his own, he and Lad, his wife, have built their own tiny house. They have a seven-year-old son.

In 1984, Nai rented 30 *rai*, but because of drought only planted 13 *rai* on a sharecropping basis. In 1983, he had lost part of the crop because of flooding. Apart from cultivating 5 *rai* of the traditional *luang prathaan* variety of rice, Nai also planted 8 *rai* of maize, followed by a second crop of sorghum. Nai uses household labour or reciprocal labour wherever possible. However, for harvesting the field crops in 1984, it was necessary to hire labour. Significantly, for the rice crop, no hired labour was used at all, whereas for cash crops it accounted for approximately three-quarters of non-household labour.

Nai had to rent two buffalo for 50 *tang* of rice each. In this way, he could use his own labour for ploughing, threshing, and winnowing the rice crop. For the cash crops, however, he relied on hiring a tractor to plough the fields and a machine for husking the maize and sorghum. He also had to use chemical pesticides for the maize and millet and hire a sprayer. For all these cash inputs, Nai relied on family wage labour and a small loan from a village trader, to whom he was obliged to sell his crop.

In a good year, Nai could expect to harvest up to 6 *kwien* (600 *tang*) of paddy. However, in 1984 he only managed 2 *kwien*. Half of this went on buffalo rent, and another quarter on land rent. The land rent was reduced by the landlord because of the poor crop, as is common in sharecropping arrangements, making them less risky for the tenant than fixed rice or cash payment. The remaining 50 *tang* was not enough to see two adults and a child through the year. The previous year, Nai had purchased three sacks of rice at 600 baht each because of crop loss from flooding. Cash for purchase of rice is obtained in part from profit from field-cropping, which in 1984 yielded just under 5,000 baht net. This would have been reduced by half had Nai had to pay interest on debt incurred by borrowing for inputs.

Nai raises a few chickens and plants vegetables for home consumption. He hopes to make some supplementary income by raising buffalo for a wealthy villager. However, Nai does not see a long-term future in Ban Dong. Even off-season work or activity such as sawing wood and house construction is now scarce. Nai spends periods during the dry season hunting with his father in the mountains beyond Ban Mai. One such trip has taken him to Thong Laang, where he has met Karens on an ALRO–military scheme to settle hill people in permanent agriculture. However, since this conflicts with traditional Karen shifting cultivation (in Nai's words, 'Karens don't like cleared land'), the Karen are secretly selling off the forest reserve land allocated to them by ALRO to lowland Thais at 300 baht per *rai*, and Nai expects to move there soon. Nai believes that education beyond the compulsory six years is out of the question for children of someone of his means, and he expects them to be farmers, which is one reason why he would like to obtain his own land.

3. ***Norm, Part Tenant***. Norm moved to Ban Dong as a child from Wat Singh in Chainat Province in 1966. His parents were among the first settlers in Bung Khiew. They used the proceeds from selling the little land they had in Wat Singh to buy a larger area of uncleared forest from earlier Lao settlers. However, Norm's father has been unable to give his land to his married children, as would be customary, because of debt. Instead, he has sold them each a plot of 10 *rai* for half the going price. Norm now farms this land but also rents 15 *rai* from a wealthier neighbour, Thiip, for whom Norm used to work as a mahout until Thiip's work-elephant died in 1983. Norm and his wife Sao live with their two young children in a small hut next to their fields.

In 1984, Norm planted 15 *rai* of the hardy local *khaao leuang* rice, a drought- and disease-resistant strain that nevertheless commands a poor price. He also planted small areas of maize and mung beans, with two crops of the latter. Like Nai, Norm rented two buffalo and used mostly household or reciprocal labour for the rice crop, whereas the field crops required cash inputs. However, Norm started working in late 1984 as a Provincial Volunteer, under a military programme recruiting villagers to help in the 'psychological warfare' village development scheme in Ban Rai.[22] This takes Norm away from Ban Dong for fifteen to twenty days per month, but it also provides a steady income of 1,500 baht per month. As a result, labour was hired for the rice harvest and the paddy was machine-threshed. On the other hand, the small yields of mung beans were husked using household labour, since this could be done by Sao at home. Sao is now left to cope with most of the domestic and agricultural work.

In 1984, Norm's fields yielded 450 *tang* of paddy. Of this, 250 *tang* had to be sold immediately in order to raise cash to pay his parents for land. The remainder was not enough even to cover land and buffalo rent and interest on a cash loan paid in rice, which meant that he had to buy rice until the following harvest. The maize and second mung bean crops were severely affected by drought, and Norm made a loss on both, not even taking into account labour expended. Again not taking into account labour, these losses were barely made up by a small profit on the first mung bean crop. If the interest in grain on the loan required for inputs for the field crops is also taken into account, it transpires that Norm's rice crop in effect subsidized losses on his cash crops.

Despite the seeming irrationality of such a move, Norm is rapidly changing to cash-oriented production. However, the security of a salary ('monthly money') is an attractive alternative to living 'by the stars'—this is a comparison often made by villagers to contrast their livelihoods with those of officials. Norm's salaried work makes it both possible and necessary to hire labour. Whereas previously he would have expressly avoided debt to outsiders, even BAAC, he is now paying off a 600-baht per month hire-purchase loan for a television set run by a car battery. The incongruous sight of a television aerial rising out of Norm's small hut in the middle of rice paddies testifies to the consumerist influences brought to bear by increased involvement with the outside world.

4. *Sud, Self-sufficient*. Sud lives with his wife and two children in Nong Sung, where he himself was born. Nong Sung is another small outlying community of Ban Dong. Sud's father moved there from Ban Dong when it was still dense forest. Still a relatively isolated community, Nong Sung is connected to Ban Dong only by a footpath. However, it has been cleared of forest for some time: according to Sud, the main influx of settlers occurred when 'people came from "down below" [that is, to the East] when the price of maize rose [in the early 1970s]'.

Sud owns 28 *rai* of land in Nong Sung, of which 15 *rai* are semi-irrigated rice-land and 11 *rai* upland. The remaining 2 *rai* make up the house plot. He bought this land in 1978 for an average of 2,500 baht per *rai* from a villager who had staked it out. In early 1984, Sud spent 11,000 baht on levelling his rice-land, part of which he irrigates by means of a pump powered by the engine of his power tiller, for which he also has a trailer attachment. Sud uses his tiller on his own and his mother's land, but he does not hire it out.

In 1984, Sud planted 15 *rai* of rice-land using the new variety RD7, and 8 *rai* of maize. Secondary crops of mung beans were planted on 14 *rai* following the maize and rice harvests. Sud used his power tiller to do all his own ploughing, threshing and husking of mung beans and rice, and transporting produce from the fields. The only machinery he needed to hire was for husking maize. Planting was done using family labour, reciprocal labour in the case of rice transplanting. Family labour was used for weeding in the case of maize and for spraying insecticide to protect mung beans. The rice harvest used household and reciprocal labour, the maize harvest only household labour. The only labour hired was for harvesting mung beans. Cash inputs were limited to petrol, maize and mung bean seed, and insecticide. These were obtained on a 2,000-baht BAAC loan, using Sud's father's membership.

The rice harvest yielded 6 *kwien*, of which 5 *kwien* were sold. Seventy *tang* each of maize and mung beans were obtained; overall, Sud's crops yielded a net cash income of just over 20,000 baht, after deducting inputs and interest on Sud's loan, and enough rice for annual consumption needs.

Other than cropping, Sud engages in occasional labouring for neighbours. Fruit trees also yield a minor income, and duck eggs provide small but steady cash earnings. Chickens are raised for home consumption. To date, Sud has never had to purchase charcoal, but the supply of wood is nearly exhausted.

Sud is an example of a more or less self-sufficient farmer. He has control over most of the basic means of production, sufficient for but not surplus to his own household needs. Capital is used mainly for improving on-farm production, such as by levelling land and pumping irrigation water. Involvement in the wage labour economy is minimal, despite the fact that most of Sud's crops are produced for the market. Sud would like his children to study if they are up to it ('if they have good minds'); otherwise, he expects them to be rice farmers. In the latter case, Sud would seek to purchase additional rice-land.

5. *Thii, Extensive Farmer*. Thii was born in Ban Rai and moved to Ban Dong in 1953 when he married Jai, the then *kamnan*'s daughter. Both Thii and Jai are Lao, Jai from one of the old Ban Dong families. They still farm with three of their children and son-in-law (temporarily away on military conscription), and also have living at home with them one child studying at secondary school and one infant grandchild.

Thii is a large landowner, with 139 *rai* of land in Ban Dong. Of this, 80 *rai* is rice-land and 55 *rai* upland; the remainder is a large house plot. Nearly half of Thii's land was staked out by his father-in-law during the 1930s, while the remainder was bought cheaply by Thii in 1964. Thii has a small tractor, which he uses exclusively on his own and his children's land.

In 1984, Thii let his children work 40 *rai* of his land. An additional 25 *rai* were let to a relative for 180 *tang* on a fixed rice-payment contract. Of the remainder, 50 *rai* were planted with *luang prathaan* rice, 20 *rai* each with maize, sorghum, and mung beans, the latter two intercropped. Those of Thii's children who still live at home planted mung beans on rice-land after the harvest, but separately from the main household in which they are otherwise included.

Thii relies heavily on cash inputs. In 1984, his tractor developed mechanical trouble, and he had to hire a large tractor for ploughing. No reciprocal labour is used, even in rice cultivation. Rice is broadcast, as are millet and mung beans. Other than household labour, hired labour is used for maize planting, weeding, spraying herbicide, and harvesting for all crops. Herbicides and insecticides are purchased, and rice and maize are threshed and husked by machine. These are financed in part by a 10,000-baht BAAC loan. Thii also borrowed 1,500 baht from Maen, a village trader, with no interest but an obligation to sell his maize crop to him. The small tractor is used to thresh the sorghum and mung bean crops.

Drought affected the rice and maize crops; birds and caterpillars the sorghum and mung beans. Of the 5 *kwien* of rice harvested, 2 *kwien* were to be kept for home consumption. Overall, each of the cash crops made Thii a small profit, with a net income of just under 10,000 baht, allowing for interest on the BAAC loan. In addition, the rice harvest yielded a 2,000-baht profit and enough rice for annual home consumption. Other than their own crop cultivation, Thii's children work as occasional wage labourers. Otherwise, Thii raises chickens and ducks for home consumption. Charcoal is produced for home use.

Thus Thii, despite being one of the largest landowners in the village and having relatively easy access to capital, chooses to farm extensively. He is a large net employer of labour.

6. *Maen, Village Trader*. Maen moved to Ban Dong from Sawang Arom district in 1970. The family had been farmers, but drought was such that they decided to sell up and follow relatives to Ban Dong. They opened a small shop, and this has become one of Ban Dong's three main general goods suppliers. Their two children study at secondary school, one in Lan Sak and the other in Uthaithani. Maen is a member of the Village Committee, and Aa, his wife, is vice-president of the government-initiated Housewives' Group.

Maen owns 8 *rai* of land which he bought from a relative in 1974. Part of his land has a strategic road frontage location. In 1984, Maen planted 5 *rai* of maize, using hired labour for planting, weeding, and harvesting. A tractor and husking machine were hired for ploughing and husking, and seed was purchased from BAAC. Maen made a small profit on this crop, despite drought.

Maen's principal activity is trade. Apart from running a general goods store, which Aa looks after most of the time, Maen is one of the two main village traders in rice and field crops. He lends cash, usually charging interest in rice and maize, but sometimes in cash at 5 per cent per month. He obtained 12,000 baht credit himself from BAAC in 1984, but most of the cash he lends out is either his own or is obtained from urban wholesalers. Maen owns a pick-up and also makes about 6,000 baht per year driving a lorry. Apart from a few chickens, Maen produces little directly for subsistence. Rice and charcoal are bought.

Maen faces two main problems with his trade. The first is that retail trade has gone down with improvement of roads, since mobile traders now come into the village and it is easier for villagers to shop at Paak Meuang or even Nong Chang and Uthaithani. The improved communications do, however, benefit Maen in encouraging cash crop production and thereby increasing the volume of agricultural trade. The second problem is theft: Maen suffered a loss of 5,000 baht in 1984. Maen would like his children to study and become government officials. One difficulty is having to buy expensive clothes for their son who studies in Uthaithani, who would otherwise (like Nid's children: Case 1) be 'ashamed'. Even Maen, whose current income derives mainly from trade rather than direct agricultural production and who does not expect his children to farm, feels a desire to acquire rice-land as a nest-egg.

These six cases demonstrate the very different measures of control over production achieved by various Ban Dong families, and the implications this has for reproduction of the household production unit. Unequal control over land as the key factor of subsistence production is compounded by different capacities to secure labour, water, and motive power. The result is greatly differing surpluses. Accumulation is mainly through rent, trade, and interest, rather than in direct control over factors of production.

Of particular note is the propensity to hire labour with increasing scale of operation. Whereas Nid (Case 1) is solely a labourer and Thii (Case 5) almost solely an employer of labour, Nai (Case 2) and Norm (Case 3) are net suppliers of labour (in the case of Norm an external wage income may make him a net employer at the local level), and Sud (Case 4) is marginally a net employer, albeit at a very low level. This is paralleled by a tendency for those at either extreme of wealth to engage relatively more in wage labour arrangements compared with those in between, who maintain reciprocal arrangements where possible and have control over the necessary factors of production to utilize their own labour more fully.

Finally, it must be stressed that production in Ban Dong continues to change, and trends in relations determining control over factors of production can be summarized as follows. Ploughing and threshing are slowly becoming mechanized even though those with buffalo retain the means for their reproduction. This is due to three main pressures: decapitalization, since debt is forcing some farmers to sell buffalo; limited natural resources in the form of space for grazing and watering; and social factors, notably the rise in buffalo theft. A minority of families are able to afford power tillers. In 1984, 44 per cent of Ban Dong farmers had no implements for ploughing or threshing and husking.

Land shortage and consequent landlessness is increasing for several reasons. Most families have more than two children, which means that subdivision or unequal inheritance of holdings is inevitable. Land prices are rising, and outsiders are buying up land. Debt is forcing sale of land. Slowly declining soil fertility and uncertain rainfall take small farmers below subsistence level.

Labour is still mostly employed locally. Use of reciprocal labour is on the decline. While this is replaced by hired labour in most cases, the opportunities for off-season employment are declining as traditional non-agricultural subsistence occupations such as house construction, sawing wood, and charcoal burning are limited by the resource situation. Meanwhile, mechanization decreases total labour requirements in seasonal cropping.

Production and Differentiation in Ban Mai

In contrast to Ban Dong, Ban Mai is primarily an upland or field-cropping village. Ban Mai farmers speak of themselves as *chaorai*, or non-rice cultivators. Wherever possible according to the micro-environment, Ban Mai farmers will grow rice, but opportunities are so limited that, on local land, field-cropping is the overwhelmingly predominant activity. Only 7 per cent of land owned by Ban Mai villagers is suited to rice farming, and much of this is non-local land (that is, land located elsewhere). Rice accounts for only 8 per cent of the area cultivated and 7 per cent of the cash-equivalent value of Ban Mai crops during the main planting season.

Ban Mai is heavily commercialized. Aside from that which is kept over for seed or for animal feed, all produce is sold. Inputs of purchased seed, herbicides, insecticides, and latterly of fertilizer, require capital, as does hire of machinery for ploughing and husking and hire of labour for planting, weeding, and harvesting. Moreover, to treat the household in cash calculations merely as a production unit does not conform with the material realities of the situation faced by most Ban Mai families. Cash is needed also to purchase most food for sustenance and, by extension, for continued use of household labour for production. Moreover, commercialization and electrification of the village increase the need for cash still further.

The standard double-cropping regime followed by 72 per cent of farmers is of maize followed by mung beans, yet the range of field crops grown in Ban Mai is considerable. Up to five crops are planted by individual farmers, but most grow two or three. A second crop of maize, millet, and black cow-pea are alternative second-cropping field crops. Cassava is an extensive alternative to double cropping, while cotton is an intensive alternative on small plots (Table 5.9).

Land preparation for all forms of field-cropping begins in March or April with the clearing and burning of weeds. This is usually done using household labour. During this period, fire is a serious hazard to houses roofed with *Imperata* grass. In the winds of the hot season, fire can cross

TABLE 5.9
Ban Mai Cropping

Crop	*Percentage of Households Planting that Crop*	*Percentage of Area Planted with that Crop*	*Yield Per Rai*
Rice 1	24	4.8	22.7 *tang*
Rice 2	0	0	–
Rice 3	0	0	–
Maize 1	87	53.3	24.6 *tang*
Maize 2	7	3.6	7.3 *tang*
Maize 3	0	0	–
Mung 1	72	30.7	3.4 *tang*
Mung 2	1	0.1	9.0 *tang*
Cassava	4	1.5	8.4 tonne
Soya	1	0.6	15.8 *tang*
Cotton	4	0.4	208.3 kg
Sorghum	11	4.1	4.1 *tang*
Cow-pea	1	0.8	1.6 *tang*
Castor	0	0	–

Source: Field survey, 1985.
Notes: As for Table 5.5a.

roadways, and in 1985 it spread to the main village settlement. Not only houses are at risk. Of the few attempts at tree-cropping (mainly bananas and mangoes), most have been destroyed by fire. This danger is a major obstacle to the establishment of perennials, particularly since most farmers live at some distance from their fields.

Ploughing commences in April. There are eight tractors in Ban Mai, and these plough most of the area. Each plot needs to be ploughed twice. Some farmers use power tillers, and those with newly cleared hill land use just a hoe, but otherwise dependence on tractors is the norm. Timing of planting is important for two main reasons. For the first crop, it is important to take advantage of the early part of the monsoon, since there is often a tapering off in July and August, and late ploughing can mean drought at a critical stage of growth. Double-cropping also means that if the first crop is harvested late, the second is susceptible to drought if the monsoon finishes early. At the same time, premature planting of the first crop can lead to its failure in the event of a false start to the monsoon. In 1984, the early planters did well, whereas the reverse was true in 1985. Because of this uncertainty, the ploughing and planting period is a tense time of year. This tension can turn to exasperation or anger at the tractor owners on whom villagers are dependent if they do not plough at the time promised. Few have sanction over the tractor owners, however, since many are also creditors and the ploughing operation is an expensive part of field-cropping (Table 5.5c).

Planting of maize usually takes place in May. Those with sufficient capital hire labour. Large farmers sometimes bring in labour from nearby rice-farming villages. Those without capital make use of reciprocal labour in teams of fifteen to twenty, sufficient to plant a 24 *rai* plot in one or two days. Rodenticide is mixed in with the seed. While the maize is still short, herbicide is usually sprayed. Alternatively or additionally, manual weeding is carried out once or twice. Spraying usually uses household labour, although a machine sprayer may need to be hired, and weeding involves reciprocal, hired, and household labour (Tables 5.6c and 5.7).

Harvesting of maize is by hand. Mostly this requires hiring of labour, but some use reciprocal arrangements. Either way, labour is rewarded by piecework: 10 baht per sack or one sack's labour debt. Husking is mostly by machine, at a standard rate of 7 baht per sack of husked maize. Transport of maize from field to homestead is an extra expense for many because of the distance they have to live from their fields.

Immediately following the maize harvest in August, tractors are in action again for the second crop, having been employed in neighbouring villages and districts in the intervening period. A single ploughing suffices. Mung beans and sorghum are broadcast almost exclusively with household labour, usually taking no more than one day. Insecticide to protect against caterpillars is the major input for mung beans. Spraying machines sometimes have to be hired, but most use manual sprayers. Harvesting mung beans involves labour hired on a piecework basis, paid by the basket.

Cassava differs from maize and mung beans in that it takes almost a full year to mature and can be left in the ground without ill-effect. Planting, harvesting, and slicing require hired labour, but for the rest of the year little attention is required. It is thus favoured by two main groups: large-scale farmers who wish to minimize supervision find cassava attractive, and debt-ridden farmers with off-farm employment combine cassava with urban wage labouring. This is despite an awareness of cassava's destructive impact on the soil: in the case of large-scale farmers, it usually involves rented land with little concern for long-term fertility, while in the latter pressures of debt do not allow long-term considerations to carry much weight.

An interesting feature of production in Ban Mai that is a distinctive characteristic of a recently settled community is the importance of kinship ties in maintaining diversified production. Several Ban Mai families spend part of the year working on relatives' land at some distance from the village. This is reciprocated either in labour, during periods of peak activity in Ban Mai's upland cropping, or in rice, but since the exchange is usually between close relatives, it is normally not on a calculated basis. The family of Tu, for example, lives for part of the year at Thung Naa where they rent rice-land, and labour is shared between the two sites. Another family, that of Pik, helps out on their parents' rice-land at Pradahak in exchange for rice, and they work some of a relative's irrigated rice-land during the dry season in exchange for letting the same relative work some upland in Ban Mai. Khao works land in Ban Mai with the help of relatives from Nam Phu and Nong Chang, and in turn Khao helps out in their rice-fields in an uncalculated labour exchange; machinery is also shared between the families.

As in the case of Ban Dong, Ban Mai is a heterogeneous community. However, the basis for Ban Mai's heterogeneity is more stark than in Ban Dong. This is largely to do with the influence of capital in mediating social relations of production. This influence might be expected to cause Ban Mai to conform more neatly with the classic differentiation model. However, a number of factors complicate the picture. One is land reform, which gives a nominally egalitarian and fixed pattern of land ownership. This means that control over production is secured in ways other than straightforward land alienation through foreclosure on land title. Aspects of power beyond the rational-legal framework are important determinants of control over production. This leads to a situation of starker differentiation than found in Ban Dong. The variety of situations faced by and strategies open to Ban Mai villagers can be illustrated by the cases of six households.

7. *Phad, Landless Labourer*. Phad moved to Ban Mai with his wife Nuai and three children from Nong Kha Yang in 1980. Phad had never owned any land and had worked in Bangkok and elsewhere as an itinerant labourer. Land reform attracted Phad as it presented him with his first opportunity to acquire land, since ALRO provided loans and was supposed to facilitate purchase of land at a low stipulated price of 210 baht per *rai*. The 24 *rai* of land Phad was supposed to get comprised a hilly plot on the edge of the land reform area, and it was adjacent to

land owned by three earlier settlers. Phad obtained an ALRO loan sufficient to buy the plot at the price stipulated, but the owners would not sell at this price. Phad used the loan to place a down payment on a 9-*rai* section of the land belonging to Raeng, who wanted nearly four times the ALRO price. Phad hoped to raise the remaining cash by labouring, but to date has been unable to do so. Raeng has been renting out the land in contravention of the ALRO rules, but Phad is afraid of him and does not dare to bring the matter into the open. Raeng let Phad work the land for a single crop of mung beans in 1982, but the crop failed because of drought, and all Phad has to show for his efforts is an 8,000-baht BAAC debt with accumulated interest. He has also been unable to repay the ALRO loan and has accumulated small debts elsewhere.

In effect, Phad is still landless apart from a 1-*rai* house plot in the village. Until 1984, the family had been relying on local wage employment, mostly agricultural labouring at the standard 30 baht per day. During the dry season, Phad occasionally works as a labourer for his carpenter neighbour Wan (Case 11), mainly planing wood for house construction. In May 1984, Phad and his two teenage children went to Bangkok for construction and welding work with a Chinese firm subcontracting to a Japanese company in Rangsit. After receiving two weeks' pay, Phad and his son worked for a further three months without getting paid, and in August the subcontractor went bankrupt without paying outstanding wage bills. Meanwhile Mii, Phad's daughter, went to work in a small textile factory. Her wages supported her brother and father for the period. They came back to Ban Mai empty-handed, and the family is again labouring locally except for Mii, who is working at a shop in Thung Naa for 400 baht per month. Their existence once again conforms closely to the local idiom of '*haa chao kin kham*' (look for [food] in the morning, eat in the evening'). During the 1986 planting season, Phad was hospitalized after suffering a reaction to the rodenticide mixed in with the hand-planted maize seed, thereby threatening the family with further debt.

Khiang, Phad's son, has received periods of training at the NGO youth training centres run by the Nong Kha Yang Foundation for Rural Development (NKYFRD) near Uthaithani. These centres emphasize integrated farming, particularly based around pig rearing. Latterly, co-operative training has been emphasized. As yet, Khiang has not been able to put the training into effect to help the family situation, but the course is seen as a source of employment and the Foundation and associated pig raisers' co-operative as a patron. Phad and Khiang talk of raising chickens in the future, but lack of capital is a major obstacle.

8. ***Porn, Dispossessed Farmer***. Porn moved to Ban Mai in 1977 from Kamphaengphet, where he had been renting upland. Upon land reform, he bought 25 *rai* from a Thung Khaa landowner at slightly higher than the ALRO-stipulated price, and he is still in debt to ALRO. For the first few years, Porn managed to farm his plot, but faced deterioration ('hardening') of the soil and uncertain rainfall: 'You used to be able to plant maize in the fourth month [March]; now you have to wait for the

sixth month [May]. . . .' Porn could continue cultivating only by getting into debt to the village head, who charges 5 per cent per month interest, and to BAAC. The debt was compounded by hospital bills for treatment of malaria, and by bills for amenities that are part and parcel of the 'model village'—namely, electricity connection and purchase of a television set. Porn and Mai, his wife, have two teenage children, two children still at school, and one infant son.

By 1984, debt had accumulated to the extent that Porn was unable to raise the capital necessary for cultivation, and the land was rented out to their village creditor—namely, the village head. The rent they received (100 baht per *rai*) was about half the amount they pay in interest alone on the village head's loan. Porn and his two teenage children went to Bangkok to seek employment in construction work, while Mai stayed to look after the children. Nine months in Bangkok provided Porn with a much higher gross income than could be expected in Ban Mai, but costs of living in Bangkok are so high that they barely managed to save enough for subsistence needs. Porn is vague about being able to plant his land again.

Porn has not been dispossessed in a legal sense, but *de facto* control of the land has gone to the village head. Meanwhile, Porn expects to go on working as a labourer for the time being. In the longer run, he is considering moving on to clear more land if things do not improve, since he expects his children to be farmers.

9. *Som, Subsistence Farmer*. Som moved to Lan Sak from Nong Chang in 1976, where she and her husband had been labourers. Initially, they moved to a mainly rice-growing village beyond Thung Khaa, but upon land reform, Ad (Case 12), a Ban Mai landowner afraid of being dispossessed, asked Som if Som would come and take over her land in name, while selling only 8 *rai* to Som for nearly four times the ALRO price. Ad maintains control over another 9 *rai* of the 24-*rai* plot, while a third owner Tuk still owns the rest.

In 1983, Som's husband left her but has been back since and beaten her severely. Som and her common-law husband now live with her teenage daughter, two school-age children, and one infant daughter in a tiny shack on her land. Som also maintains a token residence in the village in compliance with ALRO regulations. ALRO stipulated that all village residences were to have zinc roofs, and Som's only financial debt is an outstanding ALRO loan for purchase of roofing. In 1984, she also incurred a rice debt, on which 10 *tang* interest was paid on a loan of 25 *tang*. Som had to purchase four sacks of rice in 1984, but managed to produce all her own charcoal. She raised chickens and ducks for home consumption, but in 1984 they were all killed by a neighbour's dog.

Som would desperately like to purchase the remainder of the plot and to this end is sending her teenage daughter to work as a housemaid in Nong Chang: this will enable her to borrow 6,000 baht from her daughter's employer as a down payment on Tuk's 6 *rai* of rice-land. This rice-land is rain-fed, but co-operation between neighbours in digging an irrigation channel from a nearby stream could partially irrigate the fields.

Som cannot obtain credit from BAAC, since she would require her husband's signature as joint owner of the land; moreover, he refuses to divorce her.

Som farms her 2 *rai* of rice-land and 6 *rai* of upland intensively, using household labour for the most part. In 1984, she planted rice, maize, and mung beans, and the only non-household labour she used was reciprocal labour for the rice harvest and weeding the maize crop. A buffalo was rented and used for ploughing the rice-land and for the mung bean crop, and it was also used to thresh the rice by trampling. The only mechanical inputs were a tractor for maize cultivation and husking machines for the maize and mung beans. Herbicide was used for the maize crop, but household labour was also used for weeding. Mung bean seed and insecticide had to be purchased for the mung bean crop. Thus with low cash inputs, Som managed to maximize on use of household resources and obtained a rice yield of over 1 *kwien*, while making a profit of about 1,350 baht on the field crops. Of the rice, just over half went in rent for the buffalo and repayment of the rice loan, which meant having to take out another small rice loan to survive the year.

Som's common-law husband now supplements the family income by doing a bicycle ice-cream round. He cycles over a rough track from the homestead 4 kilometres into Paak Meuang each day to pick up the ice-cream, and cycles the 6 kilometres back to Ban Mai to sell to villagers. Som occasionally supplements her income by selling home-grown bananas and wild vegetables in Paak Meuang. The three working members of the family also derive a small cash income from occasional wage labouring. Ultimately Som sees her future in acquiring and working the remainder of her plot of land and having her children provide for her in her old age. Her husband had wanted her to accept an offer of 17,000 baht for their land, arguing that the children would go their own way and having cash in hand now was the safest course of action: this was one of the main points of contention that led to their separation.

10. ***Lak, Debt-ridden Small Farmer***. Lak moved to Ban Mai with his wife Rat and four children from Chainat in 1978. They had previously been landless, but when they arrived in the year of land reform, they bought 30 *rai* of land on the edge of the village from a local landowner. Of this, 6 *rai* are outside the ALRO area. They live in the village. Since 1978, they have been cultivating maize and mung beans, but Rat complains that the soil has been hardening steadily.

Other than their land, house plot, and zinc-roofed house, Lak's family owns nothing of significant value. They are dependent on a Paak Meuang tractor owner, working through a village agent of a middleman, as creditor, tiller of their land, and as purchaser of their produce. In 1984, Lak was promised that their land would be ploughed by late April, in time for optimum planting, but the tractor owner kept putting off the ploughing since the tractor was busy on other fields and Lak had no option but to fret and wait for the land to be tilled. It was June by the time the land was finally ready for cultivation, and by this time the prospects for maize were too risky to rely on this crop alone, and in any case it was going to be too late to plant a second crop. Therefore Lak planted only 20 *rai* of maize and put the remaining 10 *rai* to cassava, using left-over stems given by a neighbour.

In the event, the maize crop failed because of the late ploughing. Although Lak maximized use of household and reciprocal labour, the need for cash inputs of seed, hiring the tractor, herbicide, transport, and husking meant that the entire yield of 100 *tang* only offset the interest on the 5,000-baht loan required for investment in cultivation. For planting, weeding, and slicing the cassava, household and reciprocal labour sufficed, but labour was hired for the harvest. Additional cash inputs were required for ploughing and transport from the fields. Proximity to the edge of the forest led to the crop being ravaged by wild boar, but 3 tonnes were nevertheless salvaged. In 1984, the 850 baht per tonne price of cassava was well below the price of the previous year, and Lak only broke even on the crop, not even taking into account household labour input.

Not surprisingly, therefore, Lak is heavily debt ridden. He owes 18,000 baht to the Paak Meuang middleman and another 14,000 baht to a village trader who charges interest in maize. The whole family engages in occasional wage labour, but this is only sufficient for subsistence, since rice and other commodities have to be purchased and only charcoal can be home-produced. The prospect for clearing debts is thus remote, and the village creditor is threatening to sue. Lak is considering selling and moving back to Chainat, where at least they have relatives. There is an obstacle to this in that, if they went, they would want to dismantle and move their house with them,[23] and to do this they would have to obtain permission from the provincial authorities via the village head. He will not help without a 3,000-baht bribe, in which case he would agree to turn a blind eye and avoid the need for official permission altogether.

11. ***Wan, Farmer–Artisan.*** Wan moved to Ban Mai in 1976 from Ban Rai, where he had owned only a small plot of land. He purchased 25 *rai* of land cheaply from the *kamnan*, who was at that time starting to sell off his large holdings in anticipation of land reform. Wan lives in the village with his wife, two teenage daughters, and a school-age son, although during the cultivation season he spends long periods in the shelter on his land, which is about 2 kilometres from the village.

Wan is a self-taught carpenter and latterly has made a modest income from house construction. The dry season is the busiest time, but work is available throughout the year in 'even' [lunar] months, which are the auspicious months for house building. He owns an electric plane and in this way has benefited economically from electrification of the village, although even in surrounding villages which have not been electrified, a generator is often set up. Wan sometimes employs Phad (Case 7) and another villager on the same *soi* (lane, often now used to specify where in the village one lives).

Far from carpentry's reducing farming as part of Wan's enterprise, an income of approximately 30,000 baht actually enables him to extend cultivation. In 1984, Wan rented 19 *rai* of upland from a poorer villager, and these he planted in addition to his own 22 *rai* of upland and 2 *rai* of rice-land. On the 41 *rai* of upland, Wan planted maize and followed this with mung beans and sorghum. His cash inputs were high, including purchase of seed for all the field crops, hiring a tractor for the ploughing, hiring labour for maize planting and harvesting and for sorghum harvesting, purchase of pesticides for maize and mung beans, hiring a machine for husking the field crops, and transporting maize, sorghum and rice from the fields to his house plot in the village. Otherwise, mainly household labour was used, although reciprocal labour was used for maize planting and weeding. In addition to obtaining 50 *tang* of rice to cover part of subsistence needs, Wan made a large profit on the maize crop, so that despite a small loss on the sorghum and a minor profit on the mung beans, he still cleared nearly 20,000 baht net after rent on land and interest on loans had been paid.

Wan borrowed 6,000 baht at 5 per cent per month from village creditor Ad (see below), to whom he had to sell his crop, and 8,000 baht from BAAC. He is head of a BAAC group and also works for the BAAC 'welfare fund' at Paak Meuang, for which he receives a *per diem*. His wife and daughters take on occasional agricultural wage labour, and in 1985 his eldest daughter went to work in a textile factory in Bangkok. Wan's main expenses are purchase of rice and other necessities, and between 1984 and 1985 he extended his own house. Wan still manages to produce charcoal sufficient for home use.

12. ***Ad, Tractor Owner and Trader***. Ad moved to Ban Mai in 1972 from Nong Chang. Before that, her husband Jon had been a monk in Pitsanulok Province for ten years. Ad bought land from a previous resident, at a time when it was still largely forested. Upon land reform, Ad sold all but a single plot, though as the case of Som (Case 9) shows, she actually retained control over a larger area than the stipulated 24 *rai* plus house plot.

Latterly, direct agricultural production has become less important to Ad than other activities. She runs one of the larger general stores in Ban Mai and is a major agricultural supplier, and like Maen (Case 6) in Ban Dong, she uses this as the basis for trade in grain and associated money-lending. Ad has become wealthy as a consequence and, in 1985, bought a Ford 5000 tractor, which will be the basis for even larger accumulation.

Nevertheless, Ad and Jon continue to farm their land and, in 1985, expanded production by renting another plot. They rely mostly on hired labour, although household labour and even reciprocal labour is also used. In 1984, the 19 *rai* of upland were planted with two crops of maize, and the 5 *rai* of rice-land were planted with *luang prathaan* rice. Overall, they made a profit of nearly 14,000 baht on the maize, despite having to invest cash in every stage of the production process. Labour was hired for most of the rice cultivation, and the harvest of just over 1 *kwien* is plenty to see the family of three through the year.

Ad is a member of the village committee. She is seen as one of the 'village bosses' who run affairs in the village. She is reticent about her own economic situation. Neighbours, debtors, and others talk of her and other shopowners in indirect but often bitter tones.

These cases illustrate the parameters affecting control over production in Ban Mai. The most immediate and salient points, which are interrelated, can be summed up as follows. First, legal control over land does not in itself assure or limit control over production. In the cases of Porn (Case 8) and Lak (Case 10), for example, control is almost entirely in the hands of money-lenders and tractor owners. In the case of Lak, crucial control over timing of ploughing and planting is lost, and this in turn means loss of control even over crop choice. In the former case, control over land for agricultural production has been lost indefinitely. The second point is the degree to which control over labour has moved away from the household. This has allowed those with capital to expand agricultural production by means of securing control over land and labour through both monetary and other means, as the examples of both Wan (Case 11) and Ad (Case 12) demonstrate. The third point is the increasingly dominant role of capital in determining production relations in this commercialized village economy, where key means of production are beyond the control of all but a few individuals. The fourth point, significant for the political economy of the village, is the way in which aspects of power other than legal guarantee and 'rational' economic relations determine control over production. This means, on the one hand, that Phad (Case 7), Porn (Case 8), and Som (Case 9) lose control over land that is legally theirs. On the other hand, the alternative of withdrawal and maximal use of household resources for subsistence production, as evidenced by Som's case, involves Chayanovian self-exploitation in the form of labour inputs and valuation of land that bear no relation to opportunity costs of these two domestic factors of production.[24]

The mechanisms that determine trends in control over production in Ban Mai can be summarized in terms of three interrelated processes. First is the increasing indebtedness of the less well-off farmers. Second is capital accumulation by a few traders-cum-tractor owners. Third is the declining fertility of the soil and other environmental change. The first and third factors make it increasingly difficult for farmers to work their own land, since they suffer declining access to capital at a time when required inputs are ever greater. Fully 81 per cent of Ban Mai farmers lack control over ploughing implements. Wealthy farmers take advantage of this, renting (as tenants) land at low cost, often securing control for three years. This they can manage due to the enlarged pool of wage labour, their access to capital, and their control over a key factor of production—namely, tractors. They can also pay little regard to soil conservation by planting cassava, for example, and neglecting contour ploughing, since they have little long-term interest in land quality on rented land and even less in land on which their tractors are hired for ploughing.

Comparison

Comparison of two communities is usually an outsider's indulgence. However, in the case of Ban Dong and Ban Mai, certain interactions enable us at least to start off with a villager's perspective. Many upland farmers of Ban Mai have been rice farmers in the past. For many of them, field-cropping seems in retrospect a hazardous and strenuous occupation. For one Ban Mai farmer, 'At least you have rice to eat' if you are a rice farmer. 'If I had rice [no matter how much my debt], no creditor would dare take sacks of rice from my house.' With cash or other assets it is a different matter. The hardiness required of upland farmers is expressed in the common comparison, 'Rice farmers have to work in the rain, but [we] upland farmers have to work under the blazing sun.'

Several families have direct experience of both communities. Two Ban Dong families, both Lao kin of one of Ban Dong's oldest families, have returned to Ban Dong after a period in Ban Mai. One is the family of Dam forced out by threat, described in the above section on land. The other could not stand the pressures of Ban Mai life and speaks with bitterness of the village leaders, the factionalism, and the 'oppressive feeling', complaining that in Ban Mai 'there is no freedom at all'—for example, in having to pay a bribe of 5,000 baht to the village committee just to sell your land. Things are summed up as, 'This kind of wealth I can live without.' The family has left land in Ban Mai and the husband has gone to Malaysia as a construction worker for two years. On the other hand, some Ban Dong villagers who have visited Ban Mai on hunting trips, or to see relatives, speak of *Baan Tua Yaang* (Model Village) as it is known locally as 'prosperous' and 'civilized' due to its being provided with roads, electricity, large concrete school, and other material evidence of government attention.

Table 5.10 shows the distribution of local and non-local land in Ban Dong and Ban Mai. Average land ownership is the same, but Ban Dong land is much less evenly distributed. More than one in three Ban Dong villagers have little or no local land, compared with less than one in twelve for

TABLE 5.10

Land Distribution in Ban Dong and Ban Mai

	Percentage of Households Owning Land by Size of Land Holding							
Location	*No Land*	*1–5 Rai*	*6–15 Rai*	*16–30 Rai*	*31–50 Rai*	*51+ Rai*	*Mean*	*Standard Deviation*
Ban Dong	20.5	16.5	8.2	26.0	20.6	8.2	24.1	26.3
	(15.1)	(10.9)	(8.2)	(28.8)	(19.2)	(17.8)	(33.5)	(35.8)
Ban Mai	2.7	5.3	2.7	81.3	8.0	0	24.1	9.4
	(0)	(2.7)	(2.6)	(70.7)	(14.7)	(9.3)	(33.1)	(23.5)

Source: Field survey, 1985.

Notes: Figures in brackets indicate percentage of non-local land owned with that category of land holding.

Ban Mai. In the latter village, more than four-fifths are within the medium range of land ownership, with three-quarters owning the standard ALRO 25 *rai*. If land owned outside the village is taken into account, the average land ownership for the two villages remains similar, but the distribution of land among Ban Mai residents becomes markedly less evenly distributed.

The low variation in local land ownership in Ban Mai is due to its status as a land reform village. The 37 per cent of households who do *not* conform to ALRO rules on tenure grounds and the many more who infringe on grounds of tenancy are significant in demonstrating the persistence of alternative sources of control over land. In Ban Dong, differential access to land is a product both of historical processes and of dynamics of current production relations. Historically, access to land depended upon ability to lay claim to a tract, which in turn required authority. Latterly, capital or trust has been more important for the acquisition of land. Trust was important in the case of landless settlers who would buy on credit from earlier settlers. Loss of land by those who once held it is usually due to debt, which arises either by unsuccessful involvement in the commercial economy or through other expenses, often unavoidable, such as in the case of illness. This is often an intergenerational process, and as such it is less immediate and hence less salient than stark foreclosure.

Capital in the form of implements necessary for production is heavily concentrated in Ban Mai, less so in Ban Dong (Table 5.11). Overall, 56 per cent and 19 per cent of farmers in Ban Dong and Ban Mai, respectively, own some form of ploughing implement. Only about 5 per cent of Ban Mai villagers own a tractor. These implements account for roughly half of all cash investments in field-cropping (Table 5.5c). Although ploughing also accounts for half the cash investment cost of rice planting, this is half of a much smaller amount, and non-cash inputs (household and reciprocal labour, household resources) are considerably more important. Overall, inputs as measured in cash equivalent are lower for rice in proportion to the value of output.

The main contrast between rice farming and field-cropping, therefore, is the relative significance of land and capital. This is reflected in Ban Dong and Ban Mai, where the significant variables in control over production are respectively land ownership and access to short- and long-term capital. Average cash inputs in Ban Mai are three times those in

TABLE 5.11
Control over Tillage in Ban Dong and Ban Mai

	Percentage of Households Owning		
Location	*Tractors*	*Power Tillers*	*Buffalo*
Ban Dong	5.5	24.7	24.7
Ban Mai	5.3	12.0	0

Source: Field survey, 1985.

Ban Dong. Although in Ban Dong capital is becoming more important, mainly as a means of gaining access to hired labour with the decline of reciprocal labour, subsistence farming is still practicable with little capital input and opportunity costs incurred by domestic production. With sufficient rice-land, it is within the means of most households to secure additional resources for subsistence production. The most important of these are water, buffalo, and household labour. In Ban Mai, on the other hand, land ownership is supposedly equal. Even were the ideal conformed to, formal land holding is itself no guarantee of control over production. Without capital for annual production, field-cropping is not feasible. Control over production is concentrated in the hands of those with such capital, particularly those with the machinery for ploughing, husking, and transport. This control is noted even by villagers who farm their own plots but depend on other villagers for ploughing of their fields, husking and sale of their produce, and capital inputs: 'We are like their employees'; or even, 'We just become their low-down slaves'. A discussion of this subjective alienation is presented in Chapter 7. In many cases, Ban Mai villagers do in fact become wage labourers, having rented out their land to those with sufficient capital to work it. The point is that the subjective experience of proletarianization as an alienation from control over the means of production commences before this point is reached, if in fact it is reached at all.

Accumulation through surplus appropriation is generated in three main ways in Ban Dong and Ban Mai: money-lending, trading, and renting out of factors of production. Money-lending is an important means of surplus accumulation in both communities. It is also an effective means of alienating control over means of production from debtors. This is particularly so in the case of conditional credit—for example, the stipulation to use a creditor's tractor and sell produce to a village merchant or to buy inputs from BAAC.[25]

The second principal means of surplus appropriation that leads to lifferentiation within the village is trade. In the past, trade was mainly carried out by non-local middlemen. Now 52 per cent of rice is sold to village traders, 14 per cent of maize, and 13 per cent of mung beans. This is particularly important in Ban Dong, where the corresponding figures are 55, 51, and 70 per cent respectively. In Ban Mai, no rice and only 9 per cent of maize and 2 per cent of mung beans are sold to village traders. Dominance by village traders does not necessarily reflect an absence of opportunities for villagers. What they lose in lower prices given by village traders is made up in part by lower transport costs and flexibility in timing of sales. It does, however, enhance intra-village differentiation and dependency relationships that result. In turn, this has profound implications for the village as a community of interest, in as much as this ever existed, and it bolsters the position of those who are increasingly identified with State and outside commercial interests. This is in part due also to their role as village-level mediators of state-led rural development, as for example in the cases of village committee members Maen and Ad (Cases 6 and 12 respectively; see also Ananya, 1985: 169, 205).

Surplus appropriation by the renting out of factors of production varies between Ban Dong and Ban Mai. Renting out of land is most important in Ban Dong, where 29 per cent of farmers are tenants, accounting for 17 per cent of cultivable land. As we observed in Table 5.2, these are mostly land-short farmers. In Ban Mai, on the other hand, renting land as a tenant helps generate surplus for wealthier farmers since they employ wage labour (often including the nominal owner of the land rented). Renting out of tractors is the principal form of *rentier* surplus in Ban Mai, and as we have seen from Table 5.5c, this accounts for an important part of the Ban Mai economy. Money-lenders, traders, and tractor owners are the same few people in Ban Mai. In Ban Dong, money-lending is combined with trading, but this is not coincident with large-scale land ownership. Less conventional means of surplus appropriation include running or serving as agent to illegal lotteries as in the case of the *kamnan*'s wife in Ban Dong and the village head in Ban Mai. Use of political office for personal gain, such as by charging a 'fee' for registration of births and deaths and pocketing portions of development project allocations, is common practice in both communities.

Response to Resource Shortage

The problems of the rural poor are a product both of factors concerning resource endowment and of social relations of production. As agriculture moves away from production based on use of local resources toward linkage with the wider economy, so access to resources is less bound or guaranteed by the local resource situation. Therefore, resource shortage cannot be calculated merely in terms of such indices as person to land ratios. It also involves social aspects of differential control over resources.

Chapter 4 revealed rapid changes in the natural resource situation in Lan Sak over the past ten years. These have resulted in restricted opportunities for subsistence production. At the same time, cash cropping has become more marginal. The need for cash is greater now both for consumption and production, in as much as these can be delimited in peasant agriculture. Response to resource shortage thus consists of attempts to secure control both over traditional subsistence resources and over the exchange economy via cash. This dual strategy is a product of the dual character of resource shortage described above—namely, natural resource shortage and shortage resulting from relations of production. It can be characterized as attempts to deal with the larger system by avoidance and by engagement. Although the strategy is presented in dichotomous terms, the two types of option are by no means mutually exclusive to individual households, and each is contained within the four types of response to resource shortage presented below.

Local Resources

A number of traditional responses to resource shortage are available to Ban Dong and Ban Mai villagers, albeit in an altered form. Shortage of land and shortage of draught animals can both be overcome by renting, a strategy followed by both Nai (Case 2) and Norm (Case 3). Rice-land is rented by one of three types of contract. Upland is rented only for cash. However, renting in Ban Mai does not represent a response to resource shortage so much as a way of taking advantage by wealthier farmers and money-lenders, such as Ad (Case 12), of others' shortage of capital. Buffalo are still rented mainly for rice. In 1984, 22 per cent of Ban Dong villagers rented buffalo, most of them renting a pair in order to be able to harrow. Rent is paid in rice, 40 or 50 *tang* per animal being standard rents.

In the event of a shortfall in rice in Ban Dong, rice can be borrowed from relatives who have a surplus. Otherwise, as in the case of Som in Ban Mai (Case 9), rice must be borrowed from wealthier villagers at high interest rates, usually 40–50 per cent, payable the following rice harvest. The practice of selling 'green rice', which involves selling part of the future harvest at well below the expected price, is not as common in Ban Dong as it is elsewhere in Thailand, particularly in the north (see Moerman, 1968: 74).

Until recently in Ban Dong, and still in Ban Mai, a strategy for the landless has been to make use of the local forest resources. One way is to burn charcoal for sale. As seen in the case of Lak (Case 10), it is not only the landless who are responsible for encroachment on the forest for charcoal, but it is only they who make a significant proportion of their cash income from it. A second way is to farm steep forest land. Even some Ban Dong villagers now farm land on the mountain behind Ban Mai, having lost their rental contracts in Ban Dong. The forest resource is also a supplementary source of protein (skink, wild boar, monkeys, bear, monitor lizard, and other wild animals are hunted), of fruit (wild bananas, *mafai* [*Baccaurea ramiflora*]), of bamboo and more permanent building materials, and of herbs used in traditional medicines. Nai of Ban Dong (Case 2) and Phad of Ban Mai (Case 7) both spend time hunting during the dry season, and in Ban Mai, forest products provide a potential source of cash income if sold to wealthy villagers or government officials at Paak Meuang.

There are many other means of survival based on use of local resources. One is to sell assets that are or would once have been redeemable from the local environment. A common strategy is to sell a house, since this is a means of selling timber quite openly; wood can then be cut to build a new house. The father of Norm (Case 3) has done this twice, but with the near-complete clearance of the forest in Ban Dong and increasing surveillance by the Forestry Department in Ban Mai, this option is now severely limited. Buffalo can also be sold, as can land, but these latter are harder to redeem, particularly as prices rise faster than cash income from selling agricultural produce.

With closure of traditional outlets, some resort to more desperate means. Buffalo theft has always existed, but it has increased greatly over the past few years. Long-term Ban Dong residents speak of the time they used to leave buffalo to graze unattended for several days. Now, few farmers let buffalo out of their sight even during the daytime, and at night they are shut in pens adjoining the owners' houses. The switch to power tillers is partly due to the ease of locking up a machine, compared with keeping an eye on buffalo. In Ban Mai, petty theft is rampant. Villagers complain that they cannot leave tools unlocked, and they cannot raise chickens or grow vegetables in the village unless there is someone at home all day, which is difficult to guarantee as wage labouring becomes necessary for survival. Violent incidents occur regularly in Ban Mai due to actual or suspected theft. Villagers report that local theft is particularly common in bad agricultural years—in other words, it is directly associated with shortage.[26]

A final way of responding to resource shortage—that of reverting to the use of locally available resources—is one that is atavistic by most 'rational' economic considerations, but characterized by its own peasant logic. This way is to respond to shortage of capital in a capital-oriented agricultural regime, such as that of Ban Mai, by withdrawal from the monetized system and by pursuit of a labour-intensive, subsistence-first strategy. This may be termed the 'self-exploitative' option, after Chayanov (1926), as it involves highly labour-intensive cultivation in place of modern inputs. Such an option is taken in different forms and to varying degrees, from those who reluctantly use reciprocal labour in place of a now more standard wage labour, to Som (Case 9) and a few others like her (usually women coping on their own) who work towards an ideal of this kind of self-sufficiency.

Local Cash Economy

The need for capital for production and cash for consumption rises due to changes in the agricultural regime and the absence of opportunities for subsistence production, particularly in Ban Mai. Consumerism as part of development also increases the desire for cash, which is now most readily fulfilled by local wage labour. In Ban Mai agriculture, wage labour predominates, and it is becoming more prevalent in Ban Dong. However, the low wage (30 baht per day) and the seasonal nature of production limits this option as a survival strategy. Households, such as that of Phad in Ban Mai (Case 7), which rely entirely on local wage labour, are among the poorest in both villages.

On the other hand, differentiation increases potential for cash income through specialization. The example of Wan in Ban Mai (Case 11) shows that an artisan skill can be a vital supplementary source of income. The local cash economy is put to use by fifteen Ban Mai villagers who now engage in petty trade, mostly in combination with agricultural production. Other forms of cash earnings are on the decline or becoming more risky, notably logging.

Cash Borrowing

Although borrowing is by no means a novel response to shortage, the scale and form it has taken in both Ban Dong and Ban Mai differ from traditional borrowing. The change from borrowing in kind to borrowing in cash, and from borrowing for urgent consumption needs to borrowing for production inputs has altered the nature of borrower–lender relationships. Interest is calculated on all but short-term loans to immediate kin. Since a cash debt is universal, precise, and can be allowed to accumulate indefinitely, it tends to undermine forms of reciprocable assistance and redistribution within the community. New dependency relationships are established by this form of debt, whereby debtors surrender partial control over production to the creditor who determines when and by whom land should be ploughed, crops processed and transported from the farmstead, and what price should be given for them. For most, debt is an inescapable response to seasonal or longer-term resource shortage, but it is not surprising that many try to avoid it. When in debt, 'You can't sleep, you can't eat properly'. On the other hand, debt can become habitual. One medium-scale farmer reports being so used to borrowing that he borrows even in years when it is not absolutely necessary. It is commonly seen as and expressed as being a failure of self-discipline or resolution to fall into debt, and as such it is a demoralizing response to shortage.

Migration

Migration has long been a common response to resource shortage in South-East Asia and elsewhere. In Lan Sak, most of the present inhabitants have quite recently taken this option: if they had not, Lan Sak would still be sparsely populated. Of these migrants, many have moved more than once. While it would be wrong to overstate the itinerant nature of the population, the recent establishment of the communities nevertheless reduces cultural barriers to migration that exist elsewhere.

Ban Dong and Ban Mai villagers possess two types of migration option. The first is the traditional option of seeking out new land in forest areas. This opportunity is restricted by the virtually complete occupation of land well-suited to agriculture, but pockets of unoccupied land still exist. Nevertheless, farmers making such a move are usually on the limits of subsistence, and long-term potential of the land is secondary to subsistence needs. This renders large areas of steep forest land susceptible to encroachment, often facilitated by influential timber traders who offer land in exchange for help in logging. A Ban Mai informant estimates that at least twenty families moved on to settle new forest land in the two years prior to 1985. Permanent movement from Ban Dong is less rapid, but a number of families have moved to newly cleared areas to the north. In 1984–5, many families in both communities were considering moving to new forest areas, mostly as a way out of debt or landlessness, others as a form of insurance for their children. Two areas are particularly popular: Thong Lang in Ban Rai (see the case of Nai of Bung Khiew (Case 2) above) and the area past the end of the uncompleted Nong Chang–Umphang road in Nakorn Sawan. More distant destinations include Kamphaengphet, Tak, and Petchaboon Provinces.

A decision to move to a frontier area is not taken lightly. The hardships of frontier life have been described in Chapter 4. Insecurity is increased by the Forestry Department policy of occasionally clearing settlers off forest reserve land.[27] Thus permanent migration of this type may be seen as a strategy of last resort for gaining control over the basic means of subsistence production, namely land.

The alternative means of securing a livelihood by migration from the village is urban employment. Opportunities for waged employment are made more accessible by roads and daily transport between Lan Sak and Bangkok via Uthaithani. Several Ban Mai families have moved to Bangkok, either through having lost their land entirely or having mortgaged it to local money-lenders.

Nevertheless, permanent migration is a last-resort response, and temporary migration is more common both in use of the forest resource and in urban migration (raiding the natural economy or 'raiding the cash economy' (Scott, 1976: 212ff.)). Moreover, temporary migration almost always precedes a permanent move. Urban-bound migrants from Ban Mai, who rent out their land by the year due to lack of capital but who maintain a house in the village while they move to the city as construction workers (such as Porn (Case 8)), pursue an alternative form of temporary migration as a survival strategy.

Not only is migration often not permanent; it is also not necessarily a unitary strategy. Some members of the household may remain to make use of local opportunities while others supplement the household income by temporary wage employment elsewhere. In Ban Mai, this is common and oriented mainly to other Central Plains towns and Bangkok—for example, Phạd (Case 7), but the Middle East is also a sought-after destination.[28] In Ban Dong, such migration is less prevalent but is still common and ranges from driving a tractor on newly cleared land in Tak Province to construction work in Malaysia.

Conclusion

To recapitulate, control over resources for production is unevenly distributed within the two communities under study. Control is determined both by the natural resource situation and by social structures influencing production relations. Land is of primary importance in Ban Dong, in its own right and in as much as it is the key to control over the secondary factor of production—capital. In Ban Mai, capital is the key variable, and it is this that is the key to *de facto* control over land. Ownership is distinct from control. In one Ban Mai farmer's words, land 'is in the name of the poor but in the hands of the rich'.

In order to determine control over a particular factor of production, its place in the entire production process must be established. In Ban Dong, variation in ownership of land is considerable, but ownership of a large amount of land does not in itself establish control over production of those with less. With a subsistence crop, it is feasible for a household to be involved in producing it more or less independently of the wider system. In Ban Mai, no such option exists for the majority of farmers. For a commercial crop, capital secures control not only over one's own production, but also over the production of one's capital-short neighbour, irrespective of the relative size of land plots.

The implications of these changes in control over production for the development of the community are many. We are most concerned here with the dual relationship between production and development with which we started this chapter—that is, the way in which production affects social relations in the community and its place in the mobilization of resources. The chapter has examined these issues in two main ways, both with important developmental implications. First, it has been concerned with differentiation of the community and the resulting heterogeneity of interest. Social equity is clearly not enhanced by the divergence of economic fortunes entailed in differentiation. A community of interest becomes more difficult to establish for future joint development initiatives as exploitative relations become internal to the community. Second, this chapter has examined the range of existing responses by those who lose out in their attempt to retain control over production. Differentiation encourages short-term uses of local resources that lead to medium- or long-term deterioration. On the part of wealthier farmers in Ban Mai, this includes 'mining' of soils on land rented from debtors. On the part of the poorer, marginal farmers, it includes a range of short-term responses for survival and debt clearance, including a similar mining of soils on their own land, exploitation of forestry resources for wood-fuel and cash income, depletion of fish and wildlife, and underutilization of farmland due to lack of capital inputs.

The joint consequences of these processes include local social tension and resource depletion, and on a wider scale the costs of urban squalor and environmental deterioration. In both these ways, the priorities for a development strategy oriented towards less powerful sections of the community become clearer. Movement along a more equitable and sustainable path can only be achieved by a reorientation towards the rural poor in a way that addresses the question of control over resources for production. Local initiatives need to be directed by and on behalf of the rural poor. Under existing power structures, the rural poor are individually at a social and political disadvantage to the better off members of the community. This leads to a need for consideration of the place of joint initiatives for control over production on behalf of the poor. The next chapter addresses this important development issue.

1. The extent to which social organization is or is not determined by relations of production—that is, the economic 'base'—is a subject of controversy in the Marxist debate on economism. Lenin attacked the deterministic concept as stunting of political action through its 'worship of spontaneity' (Lenin, 1902: 93) and its 'downgrading of the conscious element in social life' (Bottomore, 1983: 143). For present purposes, production relations are seen as limiting rather than determining in any absolute manner, but wherever possible the way in which changing production relations affect social relations (or are affected by them) is pointed out.

2. This may also be seen as the process of progressive incorporation in the destruction

of the 'natural economy' by capitalism, as postulated by Rosa Luxembourg (1913). However, seventy years on, this process is far from complete.

3. A number of indicators demonstrate the instability of the present regime. These include the near universal reports of drops in yields, increase in frequency of symptoms normally associated with soil exhaustion, increased inputs that are necessary, and expressed uncertainty by farmers themselves as to the sustainability of the regime. In addition, a Land Development Department (LDD) study of Ban Mai soils shows that large parts of the area presently under field-cropping are only suited to tree crops or extensive cattle rearing in the long run (LDD, 1984). Moreover, even those areas suited in principle to field crops are only sustainable with inputs of fertilizer and land improvements that are uneconomic given conditions of production and current crop prices.

4. White (1989) reminds us that the Lenin–Chayanov debate was not a purely academic confrontation, but rather one between the Bolshevik (socialist) and Narodnik (populist) points of view in a concrete situation.

5. Unless otherwise indicated, figures in this and following sections are derived from a survey carried out by the author among 148 Ban Dong and Ban Mai households in 1985.

6. The customary practice of inheritance in most of Thailand is equal division among all the children. An exception to this is when a son moves to clear new land, in which case land is divided up among those remaining at home. The homestead and house usually go to the youngest daughter. Moerman (1968) suggests that this is not so much a case of formal ultimogeniture as a matter of circumstance, since the youngest usually stays at home to take care of the parents until they die, by which time other siblings will have married and established separate households. This is borne out by inheritance patterns in Lan Sak, among both Lao and Thai villagers.

7. Scott (1976: Ch. 1) gives a detailed analysis of the effect of a change from share-cropping to fixed payments on distribution of risks between tenant and landlord. Share-cropping minimizes risks for the tenant, whereas fixed payments assure the landlord a predictable income. There is some evidence in Ban Dong that this is taken into account in the relative terms of rental—that is, that over the long run, sharecroppers would pay a higher rental in exchange for increased security. This would in turn help explain why farmers not on the borderline of subsistence prefer fixed payments, although there is no evidence that this plays a conscious part in their preference.

8. This leads to an interesting divergence in subjective assessment of these two types of process by 'developers' and 'developed', for what is comprehensible from the perspective of the outsider and thus visible may be different from the stark experience of villagers affected by covert processes. Chambers' (1983) concept of 'visibility' as applied to rural development shows that there is a dynamic in rural processes and the way in which rural development administrators view them that leads to bias through oversight, as is the situation in Ban Mai's hidden transactions. On the other hand, piecemeal change that fits more readily into conventional analyses of land alienation impinge less forcefully on the consciousness of those affected (see Scott, 1986: 13), as is the case in Ban Dong.

9. This is actually in breach of BAAC policy. When the issue was raised at BAAC headquarters in Bangkok in 1985, it was suggested that this was a case of local officers getting carried away with the idea of delegated responsibility. However, as of 1988, members were still being penalized for not buying BAAC fertilizer.

10. In Ban Mai, 95 per cent of BAAC debtors take additional loans from other sources; in Ban Dong, the corresponding figure is 42 per cent. The implication of dual loans is serious for BAAC objectives. Since BAAC loan amounts are fixed while informal loans are flexible, the marginal rate of interest on capital is more likely to be calculated by the debtor as that which the middleman or village trader charges, rather than the BAAC rate. As the BAAC objective in lending to small farmers is to allow them to intensify agriculture through capitalization on the basis of cheap loans, this objective is largely nullified by the irrelevance of the BAAC rate in the farmer's calculation of the marginal cost of capital.

11. In Ban Mai, for example, there is *Khruu* Cherd, a local schoolteacher, who farms and raises pigs and whose wife is a machinery contractor. Theirs is one of the wealthiest families in the village. They get paid in kind by poorer neighbours. The son of a local debtor helps out in *Khruu* Cherd's pig-raising activities by collecting rice-water from nearby houses of those 'who sometimes receive favours from *Khruu* Cherd'. The daughter of another debtor

is a live-in help. Sometimes, someone will bring a monitor lizard or other delicacy back from a hunting trip for *Khruu* Cherd's consumption.

12. The author witnessed several cases of unconsciousness as a delayed reaction after a day's spraying. Many regularly complain of stomach-ache and 'heart flutters' soon after spraying or maize planting when rodenticide is used. Eckholm (1977), in a chapter entitled 'Who Pays for Production?', suggests that the health cost borne by producers is greater than normally accounted for, and he specifically mentions pesticide use in developing countries (Eckholm, 1977: 154–5). According to a World Health Organization (WHO) survey in several countries, 40 per cent of sprayers show symptoms of poisoning (Eckholm, 1977: 165). A report based on detailed surveys in each of Thailand's regions reveals widespread health problems related to pesticide use (Supot, 1982).

13. Fish disease has been occurring on a national scale since the 1982 outbreak in twenty-one provinces. Despite a great deal of scientific research into the causes of this, no firm conclusions have been reached. However, a report published by the Department of Fisheries suggests that pesticides have a role in lowering the resistance of fish to disease (see also Wattana *et al.*, 1985).

14. This amount, 200,000 baht (about US$8,000), is the equivalent of ten times a good annual agricultural income in Lan Sak.

15. Household labour as the basis for production is often cited as one of the primary criteria in the definition of 'peasant' as distinct from 'farmer' (for example, Johnston, 1981: 250). Wolf (1966: 2) points out that the peasant runs a household rather than a business concern. He quotes Chayanov to show that the peasant will utilize labour differently from a capitalistic enterprise: if land is locally abundant, it will be farmed less intensively than under capitalist enterprise, while land scarcity will lead to more intensive use, a low imputed wage, and high valuation of rented or purchased land in order to make use of surplus (household) labour (Wolf, 1966: 14–15). Meanwhile, Foster (1967) stresses the structural and relational aspects of peasant livelihood as being of more definitive significance than the occupational, and primary among these former aspects are the peasant's use of labour and relations of exchange deriving therefrom.

16. Part of Chayanov's analysis was to show how peasant households tend to work with decreasing returns to labour as land scarcity increases, in order to maintain a subsistence livelihood. An important factor affecting the welfare of the peasant household at any one time is the ratio of productive to non-productive workers in the household (see Harrison, 1982; Scarborough, 1985: 30–3).

17. Even Moerman (1968) in Ban Ping noted this process of individualization of production at the expense of the household as a unitary production unit. In the case of Ban Ping farmers, it was commercial rice production at Thunglor using tractors that offered young people the possibility of a cash income partly independent of the larger household; in Lan Sak, it tended to be the non-farm economy that presented such opportunities. Uhlig (1984: 164) notes the breakup of the extended family unit in spontaneous land clearance, as a result of which families have less access to household labour and depend on hired labour, thereby increasing the cost of dry-land cropping.

18. Moerman (1968: 129) suggests that social relations are as important a resource for production as are material goods, particularly in the case of mobilizing labour.

19. A *tang* of paddy could be sold for 28 or 29 baht in 1984. One hundred kilograms of milled rice cost at least 500 baht. At 15 kilograms per *tang*, this amounts to 75 baht per *tang* of milled rice. At the usual volume conversion rate of 42 per cent, the milled equivalent of one *tang* of paddy yields rice worth at least 31.5 baht. Since the standard daily harvesting wage is 30 baht, both employer and rice-deficient employee thus benefit by payment in paddy.

20. See Johnston (1975: 200–2) and Hanks (1972: 23–68) for comparison of broadcasting and transplanting. Ananya (1985: 238–9) documents a switch from transplanting to broadcasting by larger farmers as a means of reducing labour costs, assisted by new pre-germination techniques made possible by improved water control.

21. Field-cropping will be described in detail in the section on Ban Mai. Certain specifications differ, but the production process is basically the same for the same crops in the two villages.

22. This is one of a number of paramilitary schemes established following the 1980

policy of using political as well as military tactics for 'pacifying' the countryside (see Suchit, 1987; and Hirsch, 1987).

23. A normal village house is quite mobile. Consisting basically of posts, planks, and roofing panels (zinc or thatch), dismantling and transport is not only easy but also common. Thus farmers will often literally 'move house' when they change their location of residence. It is also common practice to sell all or part of a house for cash in case of emergency and build a new one or re-extend the old one little by little with hand-sawn planks.

24. Scott (1976: 14–15) shows that Chayanovian self-exploitation can be explained in terms of neoclassical micro-economic theory as a rational use of factors of production in the absence of opportunity costs. In one sense, these opportunity costs do exist in Ban Mai (local and non-local wage labouring, rental price of land) and prevent many people from taking a course of action such as that of Som. A neoclassical economist would thus take issue with the rationality of Som's decisions, and Chayanov would cite her as an example of the divergence of peasant mentality from neoclassic rationality. However, understood subjectively from the point of view of the farmer involved, the uncertainty and loss of control over production associated with these new 'opportunities' must be included in the equation, in which case opportunity costs of the 'safety first' course are correspondingly diminished and the micro-economic rationality of the peasant remains intact. A less theoretical objection to economists' consideration of household labour in terms of 'imputed wages' is put forward elsewhere (Moerman, 1968: 159):

'Since family members have not made an economic decision when they work for their household, there is little theoretical justification for imputing a 'wage' to them. Assigning cash value to all the factors in rice farming would be misleading socially and offensive morally to the villagers who do not live in a world where everything and everyone has a price.'

25. See Bharadwaj (1985) on interlinked markets in land, labour, and credit. Bharadwaj (1985: 12) maintains that the resource position of a small farmer determines not only the *scale*, but also the *type* of exchange relations entered into, so that 'it is the production relations which socially interrelate both the parties to the transaction that influence the form of the exchange relation'.

26. Johnston (1975: 152) notes the inverse relationship between rural crime and village welfare early in the century—for example, relating outbreaks of crime to crop failures.

27. For 'security reasons' there is a reluctance to antagonize illegal squatters on forest land by evicting them. This reluctance has declined since about 1981 with diminished concerns about the possibility of villagers going over to 'the other side' (that is, to the CPT), and the Forestry Department has become more aggressive in its evictions. According to the long-time manager of the TPC in Uthaithani, influential illegal timber traders would encourage landless farmers to settle on forest reserve land in exchange for help in logging operations, assuring them that the Government would not dare alienate them by driving them off the land for fear they would join the Communists.

28. Employment in the Middle East is highly prized, but a large amount of capital is necessary to pay the agent's fees and other associated fees necessary for going there. It is also a notoriously risky investment, as stories abound of people getting cheated out of large sums by agents. At least 30,000 baht is required, and relatives are often called upon to provide their NS3 land title deeds as security in order to raise the loan from a commercial bank. Many Middle East workers spend a year or more of their two-year contract just paying off the debt incurred in getting there.

6

Co-operation and Development

Reality had taught them the value of joint action during peaceful times, such as during *long khaek* (reciprocal labour sharing) for transplanting and harvesting. Large jobs got done with the strength of the many who joined as one. These lessons enabled them to join together to get at the roots of the injustices that oppressed them.

Seni Saowapong, in the novel *Pisat*, p. 253 (Author's translation)

In the past we used to help each other; now we step on one another to get ahead. It's everyone for himself.

Ban Dong villager returned from Ban Mai

Just imagine if next year farmers agreed not to sell any rice. If only we [*sic*] *chaonaa* could stick together.

Ban Dong *kamnan* ruminating

Working on your own you're like single fingers on a hand; work as a group and you're like a fist.

NGO worker talking to villagers

The trouble with us Thais is that we don't work together. Groups are what is needed for village development.

District official at a public meeting

THE ethos of development in Thailand is imbued with the need for co-operation. Concern over lack of farmer bargaining power, fragmentation of village communities, decline of traditional co-operation, and the administrative difficulties associated with an individualistic attitude all contribute to a discourse, ideology, and new structures that stress co-operative endeavour. At the same time, processes are at work that place the emphasis on the individual. Individualization of production, differentiation of the village community, and increased importance of monetized relations within communities all work against co-operation as an ideal or a practicality. This fundamental contradiction is the subject of the present chapter.

Neither traditionally nor formally established co-operation are new concepts on the Thai scene. Traditional village structures contain many co-operative elements, despite certain prevailing official myths to the contrary. Formal co-operatives were established as long ago as 1916, although they have rarely moved beyond a credit function—and a notoriously unsuccessful one at that.[1] What is more recent is the association of co-operative activity at all levels with rural development, and the associated proliferation of groups (*klum*).

In this chapter, the contradiction inherent in pursuing co-operative forms within an individualistic ethos is first examined in terms of theories and local realities of peasant economy. This is followed by a consideration of the rationale of co-operation, particularly as it applies to production in Ban Dong and Ban Mai. Development is reconsidered with respect to the co-operative–individualism dichotomy, and consideration is given to the concept of *klum* as it applies to the ideology of State, NGO, and villagers. Specific instances of co-operative development are described, with particular emphasis on one project that spans indigenous initiative, NGO, and state rural development structures and with which the writer was directly involved. Finally, potential areas for co-operation are examined with reference to Ban Dong and Ban Mai production, and obstacles to their achievement are identified.

Collectivism and Individualism in Peasant Economy

The collectivist versus individualist debate has historically taken on many forms. It is linked to the basic communal and 'rational' self-maximizing principles underlying socialist and capitalist social and economic systems respectively. In terms of peasant systems, the main debate has in recent years revolved around the moral versus political economy arguments of James Scott and Samuel Popkin. Underpinning these arguments are conflicting accounts of village structure from different parts of the world in different periods, but much of the recent debate has drawn on evidence from South-East Asia in the context of colonial and capitalist change. The debate can be extended beyond academic theorizing into popular notions of traditional village structure as reflected in various discourses. An analysis of indigenous production arrangements as described in the previous chapter shows that neither corporate nor individualist notions explain in isolation what arrangements are arrived at, particularly in the context of rapid change in production relations occurring in Lan Sak. The following discussion suggests that a major omission in the moral versus political economy debate is that of the reflexivity of change on peasant social structure, where the latter is all too often taken as a given, and where response or reaction to change is used to prove the nature of this given.

Theories of Peasant Economy and Village Structure

The principal opposing theories of village structure as interpreted through peasant economy are James Scott's (1976) moral economy approach and Samuel Popkin's (1979) political economy approach. Scott uses evidence from Burma and Vietnam to suggest a morally-based world-view of peasants, founded on the principles of reciprocity and assured subsistence. Popkin counters with evidence from Vietnam to suggest that Scott's ascription of atavism to peasants is unjustified, and that peasants are in fact forward-looking, self-maximizing individuals with a universalistic investment logic.

Scott develops his argument by first considering the basis for the 'subsistence ethic' as he terms it. The peasant household enterprise as consumption as well as production unit places assured subsistence before long-term income maximization. This leads to norms of reciprocity and exchange relationships that may appear exploitative but form the moral basis for peasant society. What peasants sacrifice to their village betters in status and long-term income, they gain by way of insurance against starvation. This is mediated by collective village institutions, patron-clientage, expectations by peasants of better-off members of the community, and reciprocity, all of which serve to keep peasants in moral debt for most of the time but enable them to call on a wealthy fellow villager or on community resources in times of need. These norms were infringed by the claims of the colonial economy and State, which shifted risk onto the peasantry so that in times of shortage they paid proportionately more rather than less in order to stabilize colonial revenues. It was this infringement that led to peasant rebellions even against enormous odds. Rebellions are, however, rare, and Scott shows that the moral economy more often leads to redistributive and self-help solutions that are concerned above all with assuring subsistence of the household. A number of alternatives to outright rebellion are suggested as indicators of whether the moral economy has been infringed in concrete situations.

Popkin rejects the moral economy analysis on four main grounds. First, while acknowledging that peasants are concerned with short-term survival, he suggests that the 'safety first' emphasis takes insufficient account of investments and even gambles made by peasants when opportunities present themselves. Second, he questions the efficiency of village institutions in guaranteeing subsistence through redistribution, maintaining that needs are normative and norms are flexible and therefore subject to uncertainty. Third, the potential of villagers to act collectively is thrown into question by the problem of free-riders. Finally, patron-clientage is seen by Popkin as continually open to change depending on the relative bargaining power of the sides involved, and such relations are governed by endogenous circumstances rather than by a culturally determined, fixed ethic of reciprocity. Popkin supports his argument by showing that traditional villages were far from harmonious, that individual maximization preceded village-level strategies, and that élites appropriated community resources for themselves. Rebellion is shown to be a response to opportunities in the specific context of strong leadership rather than a retreatist attempt at regaining a lost harmony.

The two theories thus differ fundamentally on the issue of what causes peasants to act, specifically in response to changes affecting the village influenced by outside events. Scott's peasants react to change in a negative way when the moral premises of subsistence guarantees are threatened or actually infringed. Popkin's peasants are astute respondents to opportunities presented by change. At one level, Scott's cutters of losses and Popkin's maximizers of gains are the same peasants cast on swings and roundabouts. More fundamentally, however, implicit and explicit assumptions about village structures underly the two principal arguments.

Whereas Scott uses as his starting point the collectively organized and harmonious village, Popkin questions the validity of both of these characterizations of traditional village structure. On the one hand, he questions village communality by showing that collective institutions are difficult to establish and that peasants are motivated primarily by an individualistic investment logic. On the other, he raises numerous examples of exclusion of segments of the village population from involvement in village affairs and infringement of community institutions by village élites. The implications of these disagreements over peasant motivations and village structures range from response of peasants to market opportunities through constraints on community development to potential for revolutionary action.

On the Thai scene, popular, populist, and other non-academic versions of history contain their own discourses on the nature of the traditional Thai village and its inhabitants. The urbanite conception is of the village as containing the source of the true Thai character. Villages are places where the *chaobaan*[2] are poor but content, where people help each other, where poverty is shared, where honesty and simplicity border on stupidity—hence the dual connotation of the word *seu*, meaning both 'honest' and 'naïve to the point of ignorance'. Among those with a more intimate acquaintance with the realities of village life, there is a range of theorizing about the true nature of the village, and this is complicated by the realities of change and substantial variation between regions. Among NGOs, for example, there is a tendency in the North and North-east to work according to an undifferentiated model of village structure, a rejection of concepts of class, and a consensus approach to decision making. Those working in the more 'developed' Central Region, and this includes Uthaithani, work to a model of differentiated villages in which identification of 'target groups' (despite much consternation over this term) is necessary. Among officials, in as much as they can be seen as distinct from the general urbanite population, the village is differentiated not so much in economic terms as in the quality of its inhabitants in the way they respond, acquiesce, or react in other ways to official contact. Meanwhile, there is an official exasperation at the perceived inability of villagers to work together on official projects. The principal oppositionist element in Thai society until the 1980s, the CPT, split seriously over its own conceptualization of the Thai social formation, including village structures, as either semi-feudal and semi-colonial, or semi-colonial and semi-capitalist.

Academic analyses of the structure of traditional Thai village society are manifold, and there is only room to provide a brief guide to them here. Scholarship was for long distracted by the debate on the supposed 'loose structure' of Thai society, based on Embree's (1950) observations (see Evers, 1969, for aspects of this debate). Potter's (1976) study attempted to refute the loose-structure paradigm. Meanwhile, Thai political economists take a more dynamic approach, focusing on the impact of State and capital in specific historic contexts rather than trying to identify the nature of a primeval village society (see, for example, Chatthip and Suthy, 1981; and Chatthip *et al.*, 1981). Specifically in the frontier village context, Johnston (1975: 152ff.) makes the interesting observation that redistributive mechanisms existed within a village society whose inhabitants perceived a 'limited good' (see Foster, 1967) and thus saw loss and gain in terms of the community rather than specific individuals.[3]

Peasant Economy and Village Structure in Lan Sak

Just as no amount of theorizing, academic or otherwise, will arrive at a definitive formulation of the nature of village structure or peasant economy, so no isolated case-study can provide proof or vindication for a particular theory. However, theories that have been built upon general experience can help in the interpretation of specific structures, processes, and contradictions, while concrete and empirical studies shed light on the appropriateness or otherwise of assumptions underlying more abstract theorizing.

The practical and ideological discourse of Lan Sak peasants is to be found in village-level arrangements. Since Lan Sak villages are relatively young, these are a combination of traditional arrangements that were carried over from settlers' home villages, together with adaptations that were made to suit the demands of a new type of environment, novel production constraints and opportunities, the peculiarities of frontier life, and rapid changes in all of these.

What is the evidence concerning collectivism versus individualism during early Lan Sak settlement? Evidence from Ban Dong and Ban Mai (and the latter's parent settlement at Thung Khaa) shows that elements of both are strong, and that the predominance of one or the other in peasant actions and evolution of village structure is governed by local and historical circumstances—not by given 'peasant' characteristics. This fluidity subsequently helps explain the rapid shifts that are apparent with changes resulting from external events.

Co-operation in early Lan Sak settlements was essential for survival. Construction of the settlement involved co-operative effort in many tasks. House-building, cutting of paths and later of tracks, construction of temples and in the case of Thung Khaa also of the village school, were all indigenously organized co-operative activities. Labour could be summoned from each house in the community during the agricultural off-season: people lent 'a piece of wood each, a hand each'. Natural and human hazards encouraged an attitude as well as settlement patterns that diverged from those associated with the settlers' previous experiences. In the case of Bung Khiew, for example, early settlers from different locations, even from different provinces, established a concentrated settlement in order to guard against natural and supernatural dangers of the forest. Communities relied on mutual protection, and outsiders were distrusted. Yet trust within the community was strong. In Ban Dong, long-term Lao settlers speak of having been able to leave buffalo out to graze for days on end. In Ban Mai, early forest settlers talk of the time when a house would remain unguarded; if neighbours arrived and nobody was at home, the neighbours could help themselves to 'enough rice for a meal and charcoal to cook it'. All of this produced a cohesion that is rarely associated with frontier life in the minds of outsiders.

Meanwhile, activities more directly concerned with production involved several important elements of co-operation. The most ubiquitous and the one least specific to the locality is that of reciprocal labour (*ao raeng*). In the past, many tasks had involved mutual help on an uncalculated basis, and among these some survive—such as moving house (literally) and preparing food for a household feast. However, most *ao raeng* is on a strictly calculated basis, whereby one day's labour is returned in kind, almost always for the same task. As is evident from the previous chapter, *ao raeng* is more prevalent in some agricultural tasks than in others. In Ban Dong, it is most commonly used in rice harvesting, while in Ban Mai it is used mainly for maize planting. In the past, Ban Dong farmers would use this arrangement for other agricultural tasks that involved a large number of people—notably, transplanting.

Ao raeng labour is summoned a few days in advance by the 'host' household. On the day, most 'guests' (labourers) are in the fields by about 8.00 a.m., but some may arrive a little late. Several members of the host household remain at home to prepare the midday meal for as many as fifty or more people, but at least one member will work in the fields and supervise the work. Shortly before noon, the guests stop work and, in the case of Ban Dong, go to the host's house where lunch is waiting. It is a matter of pride that a meal above the usual standard should be provided, with several dishes and plenty of meat. Guests are exhorted to eat their fill, and the bowls of curry that are set in the middle of each circle of rice bowls are constantly refilled from large tureens. In the case of Ban Mai, this important social aspect of *ao raeng* is lost, since fields are usually too far from the host's house to go back for lunch, and the meal provided at the field shelter is more modest. Work resumes at 2.00 p.m., although some may arrive slightly late if they have been home after lunch to attend to household tasks. Half-way through the afternoon, there is a short break at which a home-made rice brew is usually served; this is one of the few occasions when home-made liquor is consumed openly and liberally, by women as well as men. In the case of the rice harvest, the remainder of the afternoon's work is often boisterous, with much singing and joking.

Despite the social importance of *ao raeng* to the co-operative spirit of the community and the enjoyable aspect it brings to what is otherwise hard toil, its operability depends on a number of key conditions. Since *ao raeng* depends above all on reciprocation, it is important that a sufficient number of members of the community continue to use it. Although co-operating households do not have to have identical labour requirements, it would clearly be impossible for a family with a large number of fields to fulfil its reciprocal obligations were it to utilize *ao raeng* labour. By the same token, it would be pointless for a family with few fields to engage more *ao raeng* workers than it could employ, and it is entirely irrelevant to the landless. Thus *ao raeng* requires a moderately egalitarian scale of production between participating households. It is also important that the tasks for which *ao raeng* is used are flexible in their timing, otherwise all will attend to their own fields or employ hired labour at the optimum times. A third condition for successful *ao raeng* arrangements is the relative social cohesion of the community or section of the community participating, since the social element is still a strong one and there is at least some degree of trust involved in expecting obligations to be fulfilled in an only partly mensurable way.

Other than co-operative arrangements in early establishment of the community and in agricultural tasks, indigenous co-operation is also evident in the mobilization of an important factor of production in Ban Dong—namely, water. From the 1960s when farmers first practised settled rice farming on any scale in Lan Sak, they have dug irrigation channels and constructed weirs on the Tap Salao River. Ban Dong fields are partially irrigated by water diverted at Paak Meuang (whose name means 'head [mouth] of the irrigation channel') via a channel that also makes use of natural streams and another small weir at Khong Chai (see Figure 4.5). This channel was dug by hand under the co-operative effort of Ban Dong residents when much of its course was still forest or scrub. Since its inception, this mini-irrigation system has been administered by an indigenous irrigation committee akin to the type of arrangement more commonly found in the north of Thailand (Vanpen, 1986). This committee is elected annually, with individuals putting out tenders to the members (that is, beneficiaries of the system) and mustering their own team if elected head. In exchange for constant control of the water level by adjustments to the bamboo and log weir and distribution of water fairly among the hundred or so members in Ban Dong and further downstream, the committee receives an agreed rice payment of 2 *tang* of rice for every 3 *rai* of land harvested. The committee members generally have little land of their own, since most of their time is taken up by administering the system. During the agricultural off-season, the committee summons labour from the member households, which each has to provide an agreed amount of materials in the form of bamboo and timber.

Finally, the household as a co-operative unit should be mentioned, since it is so often taken for granted as being such without consideration of its potential divisibility. Traditionally the household functions as a co-operative unit, with little or no differentiation of rewards accruing to its constituent members according to the amount of labour they perform in its name. Ideological differentiation of tasks there is: in traditional rice agriculture, men are responsible for the 'heavy' tasks—notably, ploughing, while women perform most of the 'fiddly' tasks—notably, transplanting. Both men and women take part in the harvest. In fact, this division of labour is more ideal than real, and it is common to see women ploughing and men transplanting if there is a shortage of male or female labour in a particular household. The household itself is often defined by 'those who eat from the same pot', and the word for family is *khro'bkhrua* (a common hearth); in the village, it is more often referred to as a *langkhaa baan*, or 'those living under the same roof', or simply as *baan* (house). However, this sharing is limited to production activities utilizing indigenous factors of production—notably, local land. If children or other members of the household work for a wage elsewhere, they may or may not pool their earnings in the family kitty. Men from Ban Mai working in the Middle East often remit only a small part of their savings, preferring to carry the bulk back with them. Thus change towards an externally oriented economy has significant implications for the co-operative nature of the household, particularly in the area of gender and generational relations.

These are the main indigenous aspects of co-operation in the field of production to be found in Lan Sak villages. In counterbalance, it is necessary also to mention some individualistic aspects of traditional life. To begin with, the decision to migrate is itself an individual one, and despite the fact that many choose to settle near friends or relatives who have made the move before them, the uprooting of whole villages or large parts of them is the exception rather than the rule. Thus Ban Dong and even more so Ban Mai are inhabited by settlers from a diverse range of locations, and village cohesion that has developed over generations in established villages has only had a short period to develop in Lan Sak villages. The common perception of frontier life as individualistic and thus ruled by the law of the gun is distorted, but there is an element of truth in as much as boundaries are as yet poorly defined, leadership is up for grabs, and social and legal controls are weakly established.

Another aspect of individualism is the preferred residence pattern of Thai settlers. Living close to one's land is partly a matter of convenience, since many economic activities are only possible in proximity to the homestead, and farmers prefer not to have to walk long distances to their fields each day. However, such a preference is also ideologically expressed, and lowland Thais see themselves as different from Lao in this respect, since the latter prefer to settle in a clustered community. When forced to settle in such a community, as in the case of Ban Mai, many villagers complain not only of the material inconvenience of having to spend up to two hours travelling to and from their land and of not being able to raise ducks and chickens or plant fruit trees, but also of discomfort, unease, and feeling constantly pestered or annoyed.

The seemingly contradictory notions of self-perceived individualism as a Thai trait and the normative ideal of co-operation are expressed ideologically in a number of ways. The most powerful element in the discourse of villagers on individualism in everyday life is the phrasal pattern ____ *khrai* ____ *man*. Thus *thii khrai thii man* (each to his or her own), *baan khrai baan man* (each house(hold) for itself), *reuang khrai reuang man* (each person's affair is their own concern), and so on. The Buddhist concept of *kama* (karma) holds that each individual is responsible for his or her own fate. On the other hand, joint support for monks and the temple is an important ideological co-operative arrangement. One often hears the need to 'join hands' (co-operate), and *ao raeng* is seen as much as a way of helping neighbours as a matter of self-interest. The distinction between self-perception and the ideal is apparent in the frequent admiring comments made by Thais about other ethnic groups. On the Lao (Isaan) in a neighbouring village, for example, is often heard the comment that they 'co-operate well together'. Despite resentment of the Chinese traders in Paak Meuang and elsewhere, their success is admired and ascribed not only to hard work but also to the fact that 'the Chinese help and support each other, they don't exploit each other like [us] Thais'.

Co-operation and Change

At no point in time can villages or villagers be characterized as exclusively collective or individualist, but rather elements of each are manifested according to the pertaining material and ideological situation—both of which are subject to change. Changes are accompanied both by disruptions in the rationale for traditional co-operation and by emergence of new forms in response to change. Since co-operative practices require rules, mutual expectations, and even moral codes, they take time to get established. At the same time, infringement of these rules, expectations, and codes can quickly undermine established forms, and it is therefore unsurprising that co-operative endeavour suffers in the context of rapid change.

In Lan Sak, a number of changes have resulted in a decline in traditional co-operation. One is the dispersal of communities away from village clusters with more complete deforestation and decline in the dangers that produced co-operation through safety in numbers. Another is the large size of most villages, making co-operation based on kinship or affinity difficult to establish on a village-wide basis. However, more fundamental changes have been due to external influences, in particular the State and the market economy.

As was noted above, an important form of co-operation in early Lan Sak settlements was the joint construction of infrastructural projects such as roads, irrigation canals, and even schools. Since the State has started to provide resources for such projects, the need for community co-operation has declined and only the temple is still entirely a joint village responsibility. The State also impinges on the irrigation administration, village leadership in general, and other spheres of village life.

Monetization, debt, and differentiation produce a change in production relations that makes traditional co-operation difficult to sustain. In particular, the decline of *ao raeng* can be attributed to these factors. *Ao raeng* depends on the more or less equal valuation of a day's labour by participating households, otherwise households with more ready cash will be more likely to hire labour so as to avoid having to fulfil what are seen as tedious reciprocal obligations. Differentiation in control over land makes it unlikely that those at either end of the spectrum will engage in *ao raeng*, and after a point the pool of participants is too small for continued viability of the system (see Anan, 1984: 461; Ananya, 1985: 92, 164). Intensification of cultivation by double-cropping makes for more critical peaks of labour demand, which in turn makes it more difficult for *ao raeng* for a particular task to be spread over two or more weeks, and labour is hired in preference. These periods have become known as times of 'fighting over [hired] labour', and the wage rate rises temporarily to 35 baht at such a time.

Ao raeng persists in part due to its adaptability to changed circumstances. In Ban Dong and Ban Mai, it is not uncommon to find reciprocal and hired labourers working alongside each other. In this case, the hired labourers have to provide their own lunch or have a small amount (usually 5 baht) deducted from their day's wage. Monetary relations also help introduce an element of flexibility into the reciprocal relationship by allowing a household unable to fulfil its obligations of *ao raeng* to a second household to hire labour from a third household to work on the day in question. Alternatively, outstanding obligations are cleared in cash if not reciprocated by the end of the season.

A combination of differentiation, monetization, and natural resource scarcity also effects changes in village arrangements. A case in point is the irrigation administration in Ban Dong. Until 1984, the committee was paid in rice and members contributed labour and materials for the upkeep of the weir and channels. In 1985, for the first time, it was decided at the annual meeting to contract out the administration to the lowest bidder, dispensing with the need for labour and material inputs from the members. Such contributions are increasingly difficult to organize as wealthier farmers place a higher valuation on their time, and bamboo and timber are difficult to find. As a result, these inputs are now to be replaced by equal cash contributions from the members, which is of course regressive in its effect on those landholders with smaller holdings. Rice is still paid to the irrigation committee for administration, but this could eventually also be replaced by a cash payment.

In Ban Mai, the individualization of production has affected the household. Young people who seek employment in Bangkok and elsewhere, and even some who work locally, keep most or all of their wages for themselves. This is influenced in large part by the consumerist culture that has developed in the competitive environment of the village, which means that young people value the independent income that wage labour gives them for purchase of material goods such as clothes, radios and cassette players, and motor cycles.

The response of villagers to the changed production relations brought about by these trends can be summarized by a brief comparison of *ao raeng* as seen by Ban Dong and Ban Mai villagers. *Ao raeng* still fulfils an important co-operative social function in Ban Dong, whereas in Ban Mai some of the traditional and enjoyable aspects that distinguish reciprocal from hired labour in a qualitative way have been lost. The following two paraphrased statements of Ban Dong and Ban Mai villagers respectively, comparing *ao raeng* with hiring, speak for themselves. In the words of one Ban Dong villager, 'Given the choice, I'd rather work under *ao raeng* any day. If you're a bit late it doesn't matter. You don't feel you have to be at it every minute of the day, and you can talk and joke as you work. There's the fun of the midday meal and the afternoon break; generally it's more fun, and you don't have to have cash.' In contrast, a Ban Mai villager complains, 'I wish I had the cash like some to hire labour. Reciprocal labourers ['guests'] turn up late and horse around instead of putting in a proper day's work like hired labourers. *Ao raeng* is only for us poor lot who haven't the cash to hire.'

In response to changed conditions and outside influences, new forms of co-operation are emerging. Most of these are discussed below under the heading of development initiatives since they are specifically associated as such, but three new forms of co-operative endeavour are spontaneous enough to be considered primarily as indigenous responses. The first is the pooling of cash for joint infrastructural projects that are urgently desired, but for which the district authorities have not budgeted. Examples are road improvement and an attempt at irrigation channel construction by Bung Khiew villagers, both of which were carried out using machinery belonging to private contractors and hired using funds collected specifically for the purpose. In the past, joint labour would have been used in the agricultural off-season to perform the same tasks. The second is the spontaneous mobilization of villagers for an appeal to government authorities when an issue too urgent to be left to formal village leadership arises. In September 1984, one such issue arose in Ban Mai, when ALRO brought in machinery to remove tree stumps from fields that had already been planted with mung beans. About fifty Ban Mai villagers, whose crops were threatened, went to the ALRO office 60 kilometres away in Uthaithani to petition the provincial authorities, and they were successful in having the work put off until after the harvest. In May 1985, Bung Khiew villagers, angered by substandard work on a community granary constructed by a contractor commissioned by the provincial DAE office, appealed through a local leader over the heads of local officials to have the work inspected. Eventually, they not only got a new granary but also persuaded the provincial DAE officer to award the reconstruction contract to a team of five Bung Khiew villagers. A third example of indigenous co-operation in response to change also comes from Bung Khiew, in the donation of land by several villagers for community projects.

Development and the Concept of *Klum*

The tension between individual and co-operative modes is clearly dynamic, and as such it is closely tied to processes subsumed under the term 'development'. In so far as arrangements for the mobilization, distribution, and exchange of resources can be individually or co-operatively organized, the alternatives for development can also be categorized as such. This conceptualization is not out of line with village categories. In local discourse, one can either do things 'each to himself or herself' or one can do them 'jointly'. With regard to development, however, we find a blatant contradiction between an ethos that places increasing emphasis on the individual as the primary agent for development and specific programmes that involve co-operative effort. The ethos is inherent in the background ideology, discourse, and structures involved in promoting capitalist development of the countryside. Specific programmes are those initiated by state and NGO developers.

Individualistic Ethos

The ideology of capitalist development places stress on individual advancement. Capitalist monetized relations of production free individual producers from the social constraints imposed by existing relationships for mobilization of labour and other factors of production. Commoditization of labour turns individuals into marketable factors of production, control over which (whom) is potentially unlimited, with cash as the sole constraint. Thus the underlying national strategy of capitalist development of the countryside itself is a powerful ideological instrument toward individualization. It is evidenced in Lan Sak above all in the decline of reciprocal labour in favour of hiring arrangements as the means for securing control over labour, and by the concentration of control over a key factor of production, namely tractors in the case of Ban Mai.

In addition to the individualistic logic of capitalist relations of production, a number of other effects of the national development strategy favour individual advancement. Most powerful of all is the consumerist culture that is produced by availability of goods, conspicuous consumption by village élites, association of material goods with social status, and the embarrassment of those unable to keep up with the consumption standards of their neighbours. Introduction of electricity into the village, such as in Ban Mai, is a major stimulus to promulgation of such a culture. On the heels of electrification follow vans of travelling salesmen from Singer and other companies, and many of these have commissioned agents within the village. This is the most sharply felt aspect of the ideology of competition, whereby individuals are not only released from social constraints over getting ahead independent of their neighbours, but actually see getting ahead in material terms as their goal. In Ban Mai, only half have been able to afford electricity connection costs (despite not having to pay anything toward village connection costs and only paying for individual household connection of electricity), yet many even of these have incurred debt by spending beyond their means.

The competitive approach is promoted by state rural developers as a key incentive for village development. Village competitions are held at the district, provincial, regional, and national levels. Within the village, competitions are held for best-kept households. The emphasis is on outdoing others and feeling ashamed at being outdone. Another aspect of such competitions, and their use by officials to impose their own standards on village life and village development and to co-opt local leaders, is discussed in the following chapter.

Officials often have a differentiated view of the village based on the moral character of its citizens. This is imparted in district development training programmes. An example is a nation-wide programme that places emphasis on the moral fibre of villagers, while the vices condemned in Buddhist discourse, notably gambling and drinking, are held up as the greatest obstacles to development. By implication, development is above all an individual path. A sign placed at the Ban Dong temple in 1985 reads: 'Obstacles to development: selfishness, bickering, laziness, stupidity and bragging, and vice.' The concept of spiritual development as originally coined by NGO workers in opposition to the exploitative, self-oriented mores associated with capitalist development, has been taken by state developers to mean an individual path of development through abstention. The dominant discourse ties national salvation to personal salvation through individual discipline. Meanwhile, the individualistic emphasis on moral character overlaps into state discourse on co-operation. The Uthaithani ALRO head attributes problems in Ban Mai to the fact that villagers 'don't give co-operation' (to ALRO), and there is thus a need to 'develop the [co-operative] spirit' of villagers.

An elaboration on this general emphasis was made during a training programme for village heads in Lan Sak in April 1985. There are, it was explained by the district DAE officer, six types of people. The first is 'quick witted and resilient', always looking for new ideas. The second is 'wait and see'; these are willing to listen but are not active seekers. Third are those who 'look on hesitantly'; they sit on the sidelines and are slow to get involved in new ideas. Type four is 'stubborn': it is difficult for anything to get through to them. Fifth are those who 'sit hugging their knees': they are almost beyond help. The last group is 'good for nothing'. The first three groups are classified as 'lotuses above water', which in popular Buddhist terms means 'enlightened'. The lower three types, on the other hand, are 'lotuses under water', or those with the potential for enlightenment but not yet ready. This is a modification of popular Buddhist terminology,[4] used to differentiate people in their willingness to accept new ideas, where most of these are concerned with 'modernity'; coming from the district agricultural officer, this implies fertilizer, pesticides, and other aspects of capital-intensive farming. The implication is that the lotuses above water are those deserving of help, whereas those below the surface are not worth bothering with.

The individualistic, competitive ethos is evident in several aspects of village discourse. Ban Dong returnees from Ban Mai complain that they dislike the competitive spirit and the currying of favour in order to get ahead in the latter village. Shame is commonly expressed at inability to keep up in consumption standards. Differentiation is accompanied by mutual resentment between different social strata in the village. In Ban Mai, one of the village traders who is also a tractor owner and influential village committee member is said to 'exploit the poor' (of the village)—for example, by the low wages he pays for menial work like humping sacks of grain onto his lorry. He in turn says of the majority of villagers that they 'are not serious' about farming; his wife ascribes the problems of the village to the fact that 'people are not willing to listen to (*cheua fang*) the [village] leaders'.[5] Mutual interdependence between the better-off and poorer villagers has lost its reciprocative social content, yielding to individualistic priorities and opportunities for gain.

Co-operative Programmes

Despite the emphasis on the individual and the divergence of individual fortunes that is inherent in capitalist development and evident in associated discourse, the actual programmes that come under the aegis of rural development are co-operative in orientation. The emphasis on farmer co-operation in small groups originated in Thailand with the NGO movement in the 1970s. The problems of farmers were interpreted as being due to lack of bargaining power *vis-à-vis* money-lenders, traders, and the State. Collective action by formation of groups was seen as the basis for increasing the power of small farmers to act within a political economy that stacked the odds against them. Such groups were a sensitive political issue at the local level, and NGO workers who tried to set up co-operative schemes at the village level were often accused of trying to 'mobilize', or stir up trouble.

However, with the Government's rural development programme and poverty alleviation scheme starting under the 1982–6 Five-Year Plan, the idea of setting up groups at the village level has been taken up. 'Development' is now associated closely with *klum* (groups), to the extent that for a village to be entered for a competition, it is mandatory that groups are set up as evidence of the developed state of the village. These include housewives' groups, young farmers' groups, youth groups, village scouts, and others set up by various branches of the district administration. In addition, other state agencies utilize groups in their programme strategies at the village level—for example, the BAAC joint-liability groups and military reserves. NGOs still place emphasis on co-operative action, and rice bank and buffalo bank projects are examples of NGO-initiated groups in Ban Dong. The only indigenous group of any permanence to be found in either of the two villages is the Ban Dong water users' group described above. Before going on to examine specific projects in Ban Dong and Ban Mai, it is useful to consider the principle of co-operation as seen by the various actors on the development stage. To this end, the concept of *klum* (group) is considered from the viewpoint of state developers, NGO workers, and villagers affected by *klum*.[6]

State Concepts of Klum

State developers attach importance to the formal establishment of development groups at the village level. The stated objective of such groups is to encourage self-help, using the group as a forum. Varying degrees of pressure are put on villagers at monthly village meetings to join the group. For the official involved, the establishment of groups is an objective in itself, since merit points are gained within each department at the district level by setting up formal groups. Each department in turn vies for influence at the village level in order to secure increased budget allocations. Each group has a name that delimits its membership and its function to some extent, but there is overlap of both. Thus it is possible to be a member of several groups and, at the same time, activities may be similar in each of these.

In fact, activities of most of these groups are limited to training sessions, often lasting several days, at which instructors from different government departments, from the Buddhist clergy, from the military, and sometimes from NGOs are invited to speak. Most of the time is spent teaching civic virtues, explaining government policy on various issues, speaking on the need for security, the need for vigilance, and on the threat posed by Vietnam.[7] Training on some programmes includes humiliation, using psychological methods to incur a sense of unity and loyalty to the group in a way similar to that used in the Village Scout movement (see Muecke, 1980).

The function of these development groups, then, is first and foremost to give district officials a forum for access to the village population. By electing villagers as president and committee members, groups have a semblance of independence. In fact, both group officials and government officials claim that the primary use of groups is 'to ease administration'. Communicating with villagers via groups means having only to contact the head of the group. In an important sense, therefore, *klum* in the State's terms is a means of extending the pyramidal hierarchy down to the village level, bringing with it the features of duplication, top-downward orientation, lack of co-ordination, and stress on formal rules.

NGO Concepts of Klum

As already noted, collective action by farmers is the basic philosophy of non-governmental organizations in increasing bargaining power *vis-à-vis* exploitative outside forces. Like state-initiated schemes, NGO groups are characterized as self-help organizations. Unlike state-initiated groups, NGOs are concerned that group members themselves initiate these new institutions from the design stage, and membership is voluntary or by peer pressure rather than by pressure from an external authority. The problems faced by NGOs in establishing groups at the village level are precisely those concerned with giving villagers a sense of proprietorship over the groups.

Until approximately 1981, NGOs working at the village level had to proceed extremely cautiously with the setting up of farmers' groups. At the local level, genuine bargaining power in the hands of farmers threatened local monopoly interests. On a wider scale, the Government regarded many such groups as Communist front organizations. As a result, groups were open to accusation and, where they did operate, it was within a politically sensitive context. Consequently, farmers' groups were not directly confrontational, they relied mainly on indigenous resources, and their discourse was as politically neutral as was possible given their function.[8]

Following state interest in setting up groups, the concept of *klum* has acquired a new legitimacy, and the scope for NGO action has to this extent been enhanced. Indeed, much of the statist rhetoric on development and *klum* is borrowed from NGO discourse. However, the NGO concept of *klum* as a power instrument in the hands of villagers differs fundamentally from that of state developers' notion of *klum* as an instrument of administration and dissemination of official policy.

Indigenous Concepts of Klum

The concept of *klum* is not entirely alien to the indigenous community. The Ban Dong irrigation group described above is an indigenous community institution. The group head and his team are not very different from the group presidents and committees of externally initiated groups. Thus when collective effort is required to secure control over a basic factor of production, in this case water, co-operative practice is the norm. It is recognized that an authority is required both to summon the resources (labour and materials, latterly cash) to maintain the system and to adjudicate in allocation of resources, in this case the protection of those whose fields are downstream from those upstream with prior access. This authority is legitimated by annual selection from within the ranks of the group.

Also not entirely alien to indigenous experience are collective involvement in ideological activities and instances of collective bargaining with outside authorities. In the first case, the village temple is administered by a temple committee, traditionally selected from among elders of the village, for administration of what is the villagers' principal ideological institution. In the second case, petitioning of state authorities is not unknown. An example in Ban Dong is the successful unseating in the 1960s of a *kamnan* who had been appropriating registration fees instead of sending them on to the district authorities at Ban Rai.

Klum that exist as channels for dissemination of statist ideology are, however, alien. So are multi-purpose or vague groups based on membership rather than function, such as housewives' or youth groups. In bargaining with outside interests, local leadership is called on to deal with specific issues as they arise, and permanent functional groups to this purpose are superfluous in the traditional close-knit community. The alienation of most villagers in Ban Dong and Ban Mai is evidenced in a number of aspects of their discourse, most simply by use of the third person pronoun in referring to the groups. Alienation is also shown in the confusion over the proliferation of *klum* and their associated acronyms.[9]

Co-operative Development in Lan Sak

Discussion so far has dealt with concepts and ideology. What of the actual structures and initiatives behind co-operative development? The present section provides an empirical examination of specific projects in Ban Dong and Ban Mai. State, NGO, and indigenous co-operative schemes are described in turn, and the section is concluded by an extended account of one project that incorporates all three sectors, illustrating the potentials and pitfalls of co-operation between as well as within sectors.

State Schemes

The proliferation of state schemes at the village level is detailed in Table 6.1, which lists the various groups that have been established in the two study villages. Two of these are examined here in order to illustrate the way in which groups are set up, run, and led.

Housewives' Groups. Housewives' groups were set up in Ban Dong and Ban Mai by the Community Development Department (CDD). This department was established in the 1960s, and for much of its existence it has been concerned with rural pacification through social programmes. Housewives' groups were conceived of ostensibly to give women a role in community development. They provide a forum for training programmes in domestic skills and hygiene and in handicrafts such as crochet.

The housewives' groups are started in the following manner. The (male) district CDD officer speaks at a monthly village meeting, announcing that a group is to be set up and a training programme is to be held at the village temple on a certain date. A member of every household is supposed to attend, and it is said by the officer to be a matter of shame for the village if attendance is less than that avowedly achieved in surrounding villages. This is an extra incentive for the village head to exhort villagers to attend the training, and response varies from those who see such occasions as fun to those who feel pressured into attending despite urgent tasks at home. At the training session, instructors speak on various matters of government policy and on the importance of unity and loyalty to the group. Group officials are elected by a vote, candidates often having been suggested by the officials present or by the village head; rarely is there more than one candidate for a post.

In Ban Dong, the president of the Housewives' Group is the wife of one of the village traders who is also the *kamnan*'s assistant. The vice-president is the wife of Maen, the village trader and village committee member mentioned (Case 6) in the previous chapter. In Ban Mai, the president of the Housewives' Group is wife of the village head, the vice-president is wife of a village trader and member of the village committee, and the treasurer is wife of the *tambon* doctor—the *tambon* doctor is also a village committee member and an ex-officio *tambon* council member, wealthy trader, and lorry and tractor owner.

In the case of the Ban Dong group, activities since initial training in 1982 have mostly consisted of providing support for official training programmes at the village and district levels. Housewives' groups are expected to provide the food and clean up afterwards at such events. In April 1985, housewives' groups from the four *tambon* of Lan Sak had to provide food at a five-day training session of village heads. This labour had to be provided free of charge, and in the case of the Ban Dong group there was exasperation at the fact that they had to contribute out of their own pockets since the money (200 baht) allocated to feed fifty people for

TABLE 6.1
Permanent Groups in Ban Dong and Ban Mai

State-initiated	*NGO-initiated*	*Indigenous*
Housewives' group	Rice Bank	Water users' group
BAAC group	Buffalo Bank	Temple committee
Farmers' association		
Young farmers' group		
Co-operative branch		
Funeral association		
Village scouts		
National defence volunteers		
Reserve volunteers		
Development groups		

Source: Fieldwork, 1984–5.

three meals was not enough, and pride meant that a decent meal had to be provided. The Ban Mai group was set up in 1983, and since the initial training the only activities have involved members of the group committee, who have been sent on training courses at which they are provided with a *per diem* that exceeds the normal daily wage.

Another function of the housewives' groups is to establish savings groups, whereby members save 10–20 baht each per month. This money is paid into a common fund to be used for a communal purpose at a later date. The Ban Dong fund is inactive, while in Ban Mai small interest-free loans are made. The treasurer is adamant that such loans go only to those who in her judgement will be able to repay, and this effectively restricts membership of the savings group. The amounts of money involved are insignificant: from the point of view of the CDD, the purpose is more to get people into the habit of saving rather than to accumulate any large fund of major utility to the community.

Housewives' groups are thus used as instruments of the State in three main ways. First, they give access to a section of the community who tend otherwise to have less contact with officials than do their male counterparts. Second, they serve (literally) as useful resources for the State in organizing events at the village level. Third, they provide a forum for dissemination of official ideology in the form of encouraging espousal of civic virtues. Some of these are conservative urbanite conceptions concerning the role of women as providers of domestic service, occupationally most proficient in light cottage industry rather than agricultural or other heavy work, and supportive of men in the 'real' work of administration or agricultural production (see Rogers, 1980). Others are more general aspects of capitalist production ideology, particularly the need for cash savings in place of (the common official notion of) profligate spending.

BAAC Groups. BAAC groups have mushroomed throughout Lan Sak in recent years. This is a result both of the increased demand for credit with the move into commercialized agricultural production and of the increased amount of credit provided by the Bank.[10] BAAC operates quite separately from the district administration. It maintains an office at Paak Meuang, at some distance from the district offices. It arranges its own meetings with villagers, separate from the monthly village meetings. BAAC field officers operate independently from district officials, such as DAE extension officers. Nevertheless, BAAC is a state institution and is perceived as such by villagers: this is evident, for example, in their unfulfilled expectations of BAAC in activity areas such as marketing (hence comments such as this: 'If the Government guarantees the rice price at 3,300 baht per *kwien*, why doesn't BAAC set up a scheme to buy it at that price?').

BAAC groups are set up at the initiative of individual villagers. BAAC credit is well enough known in its availability and low cost so that it does not have to be very actively promoted. A group of neighbours usually appoints one among its number to obtain application forms from the office at Paak Meuang. Once at least six separate applications have been made to set up a group, a BAAC field officer will come around to interview each of the applicants. These officers are informal in their manner when compared with district officials, and they have a strict code of conduct in dealing with villagers. For example, they are not supposed to accept food or drink or any other form of deferential hospitality, and although this goes against traditional interaction between villagers and outsiders, villagers frequently mention it in a positive light and attest to its veracity. This is in stark contrast to senior district officials, for whom considerable preparations have to be made.

In principle, any group of six or more honest, able-bodied farmers over the age of twenty are eligible for BAAC credit through a joint-liability group. In fact, several factors tend to prevent the poorest farmers from joining such a group. One is the reluctance or refusal of local BAAC officers to accept applications from those without individual collateral in the form of land or a house. This suggests that the joint-liability principle fails in local officials' eyes to provide an effective mutual guarantee, and this is borne out by the rarity of groups being called on to pay up for a defaulting fellow member; the exception seems to be when such a defaulter actually disappears and cannot be accounted for. This brings in another factor, which is that the joint liability is real enough to make farmers reluctant to accept as a fellow member someone with insufficient personal collateral, who would thereby make it more likely that fellow group members would have to pay up in the event of default. A final factor is the reluctance of many of the poorest villagers to entertain the idea of institutional debt, preferring either to avoid borrowing altogether or to maintain the flexibility afforded by village creditors.

Credit given via the group rather than individually makes sense to BAAC and the members involved in a number of ways. In addition to the potentially reduced need for individual collateral that joint liability affords, a group with a responsible leader provides the peer pressure on the one hand, and a convenient point of contact on the other, for eased administration by BAAC officers. At the same time, small-group action gives members a certain solidarity, and this is not utilized only in deference to BAAC rules. Quite the contrary was the case, for example, in Ban Mai where a BAAC group was used to acquire credit from a village trader in order to pay off BAAC, and where the BAAC group was a forum for comparing notes on the best way to get rid of unwanted BAAC fertilizer!

The irony of BAAC groups is that they represent the most enthusiastic co-operative action by farmers under the aegis of state-led rural development, while at the same time playing a key role in the processes leading to the individualization of production. Farmers join BAAC groups to obtain credit for themselves or their household production unit, not in an effort to raise the productivity of the group as a whole. Group solidarity is limited strictly to the functions directly served by BAAC operations; production, marketing, and non-BAAC inputs are still arranged individually.

NGO Schemes

The principal local NGO operating in Lan Sak is the Uthaithani-based Nong Kha Yang Foundation for Rural Development (NKYFRD). Two village-based schemes are described below. Both are based in Bung Khiew, the Ban Dong subcommunity of approximately forty-five households described in Chapter 4.

In late 1983, workers of the NKYFRD spent several days in Bung Khiew speaking with farmers about their debt and production problems. Bung Khiew was chosen as a village of interest for two main reasons. One was the precariousness of production and consequent poverty in this rain-fed area. The other was the role of Boi, a Bung Khiew villager who is also a volunteer who helps co-ordinate the activities of NKYFRD in Lan Sak and further afield. Three principal and immediate problems emerged from talking with villagers: the uncertainty of rice production that leads to villagers having to borrow rice, or cash to buy rice, at high interest rates; lack of means of tillage, which means that farmers must rent buffalo and surrender a significant portion of their rice crop in return; and lack of an assured water supply for rice cultivation.

Rice Bank. The first of these problems has two deleterious effects, one at the level of the household and the other at the level of the community. At the household level, having to borrow rice and pay interest in kind of 50 per cent over the space of an agricultural season means a loss of surplus and the continual cycle of debt and dependence on the creditor that results. Since most of the creditors are from outside Bung Khiew, mainly from Ban Dong, this loss of surplus also represents a loss of resources to the community, even though the community as a whole may not face a rice deficit. In response to this problem, it was suggested to Boi and other villagers that a meeting be called to propose the setting up of a rice bank.

The purpose of a rice bank is to establish a community store of paddy from which members can borrow in times of shortage. The advantage to individual members is that the interest paid is low, at a rate agreed on by the members themselves. At the community level, the advantage is that this surplus remains within the community, and the community is thus able to use it to increase the stock available for lending, to pay out as dividends to members, or to use for some other community purpose. The functioning of a rice bank relies on an initial stock of paddy, and this can be secured by voluntary donations, purchase of shares in paddy, or institutional support.

Bung Khiew Rice Bank was started after a meeting in March 1984 at Boi's homestead, a common meeting place for Bung Khiew villagers. A worker from NKYFRD came to talk about the principles of co-operation and, in particular, the way in which a rice bank might work. Details were discussed by villagers themselves, and representatives of most households were present. This discussion covered topics such as whether contributions should be equal and calculated or dependent on each household's capacity to contribute, what interest rate should be charged, and what provision for payment of dividends should be made. A group president and committee were elected. Boi declined being elected since he was keen to get other villagers involved in responsibility for community affairs. It was decided to make provision both for donations and shareholding, the latter limited to group members. The interest rate was set at 20 per cent, higher than what the NGO workers had in mind. Two weeks later, rice was deposited in shares of 5 *tang* each.

Lending is decided by the Rice Bank committee, which it was decided should be put up for election every two years. Some even suggested annual elections, and this element of leadership accountability is seen as important. This is also evidenced in the annual elections held for the Ban Dong irrigation committee (which does not involve any Bung Khiew villagers).

In 1984, the stock of paddy was still small, with an initial deposit of 5 *tang* each from 29 households. As a result, only the poorest could borrow, and these borrowed a maximum of 25 *tang* per household. Because the 1984–5 harvest was so severely affected by drought, some of these were unable to repay in rice the following year, and those who planted mung beans were allowed to repay in this crop to a sale value equivalent to the amount of rice owed. Others had to carry their debts over to 1986, but even with interest accruing this still amounted to less than they would have had to pay in interest for a single year to a private creditor. The 1985–6 harvest was a good one, and by mid-1986, with all debts being cleared and new deposits made, villagers had accumulated a total of 14 *kwien*, half held in individual shares, the rest consisting of donations and institutional support. In January 1986, visiting NGO workers from neighbouring Nakorn Sawan Province were impressed to see Rice Bank members depositing their shares on a trust basis, and both NKYFRD and villagers themselves hold it as a matter of pride that the Rice Bank should be based on mutual trust. In 1987, the Rice Bank had sufficient grain to help several villagers affected by severe drought. After a good harvest in 1988, the accumulated stock in 1989 had reached 60 *kwien*.

Initially, the Rice Bank relied on support from NKYFRD since there was no community granary. The paddy was transported to, stored, and milled at the integrated agricultural training centre at Nong Kha Yang, 50 kilometres away. In 1985, Boi requested that the DAE in Lan Sak provide funds and the standard 5-*kwien* paddy grant for a community granary, which was to be built on land donated by three villagers. DAE agreed, and a commercial tender was put out for construction. Villagers suggested that they carry out the construction themselves, but DAE maintained that only licensed contractors could put in a bid. Furthermore, the granary had to be built according to official specifications, which conflicted with the requirements of the villagers in size (the 10-*kwien* capacity allowed for is too small for the Rice Bank store), shape, and alignment of the roof. In the event, the contract went to an influential provincial assembly member, said to have (corrupt) connections with certain senior provincial officials. The amount of the bid (40,000 baht) was at least four times as high as the villagers would have charged. A team of labourers from neighbouring Chainat Province was sent in by the contractor, having been hired on a contract basis for 5,000 baht. They had to wait three days before the materials (wood, zinc, and concrete piles) arrived. By this time, Boi had left for a two-day training course in Pitsanulok, but other villagers noticed that the wood was inferior quality softwood that would not last more than a year; the materials were estimated to have cost the contractor a maximum of 5,000 baht. The workmen were asked to wait until the specifications could be checked, but by this time they were impatient to get started, so the concrete piles were set in and construction of the granary was well under way when Boi returned. On seeing the wood, some of which was termite-infested, he used his position as village committee member to radio the provincial office from the local DAE office, and the workmen agreed to stop work until an inspection could be made. The following day, the deputy provincial DAE officer, who had approved the contract in the first place, arrived while Boi was away on his rounds as family planning volunteer,[11] and told the workmen 'not to listen to any daft old villager who pokes his nose in'. The granary was thus completed using the substandard materials and with the roof in alignment contrary to village practice (east–west instead of north–south). Within two weeks the roof had blown off, since the workmen had had to supply nails out of their own pockets and had therefore used nails that were too short; fortunately, this occurred before any rice had been deposited. Boi and Bung Khiew villagers had an unexpected success, however, since the widely respected and down-to-earth provincial DAE officer made a visit after a chance meeting with Boi, and on inspecting the granary immediately ordered that it should be dismantled and reconstructed by contracted Bung Khiew villagers using new materials.

The Rice Bank is thus an externally initiated project based on locally expressed needs and relying in the first instance on endogenous resources.

Of key importance in its functioning are broad participation of the community from the start, not in joining an exogenous project but in setting the rules and establishing a strong but accountable leadership. This depends in turn on the structure of the community itself and the nature of the leadership, issues that are discussed below and in the next chapter.

Buffalo Bank. The second production problem faced by Bung Khiew villagers is tillage. Many have to rent buffalo at 50 *tang* of paddy per season. Since all of these are rented from outsiders, this also represents a loss to the community. In late 1983, during negotiations with a small international aid agency for a larger project, NKYFRD also successfully requested assistance in setting up a buffalo bank at Bung Khiew. Ten animals were purchased, and a committee consisting of sixteen group members was elected to allocate the animals based on need.

The Buffalo Bank works on the following principles. The buffalo remain the common property of the Bank, which is a community institution. All the initial buffalo purchased were cows in calf. After weaning, the first calf is returned to the Bank for reallocation, although it cannot be used for work until it is three years old. Male calves are sold in exchange for females, prices being roughly equal. The second calf becomes the property of the member renting the cow, the third goes back to the Bank, and the fourth calf goes to the member, the cow at this stage being returned to the Bank. In this way, each member ideally ends up with a team of two buffalo, and the stock of buffalo in the Bank is built up.

Initially, Bung Khiew Buffalo Bank members elected to charge a rental of 10 *tang* of paddy per year. However, it was then felt that this would antagonize those who normally rented out buffalo to Bung Khiew villagers, going by experience elsewhere recounted by NKYFRD workers of buffalo that had been poisoned by those who stood to lose. It was decided instead to take 40 *tang*, only 10 *tang* less than the private rate. However, 30 of the 40 *tang* are deposited in the Rice Bank (to which all Buffalo Bank members belong), and this can be reclaimed after three years. This also helps to build up the stocks of the Rice Bank.

Bung Khiew Buffalo Bank has been faced with a number of problems. One is the long time it takes for such a project to become a full community institution, since the gestation period of buffalo is long (fourteen months) and animals are not fertile or ready for work until their fourth year. This was compounded in Bung Khiew early on by the death of several of the Bank buffalo, so that by 1986, after two years of operation, there were still only 20 cows and calves from the original 10 pregnant cows. This led to a certain amount of gossip that 'people don't look after a "project" (lit. royal (*luang*), based on the royally donated buffalo) like they'd look after their own'. There was no evidence to suggest that the buffalo died due to any form of neglect, but this shows the jealousies that can be generated by such a scheme.

The Buffalo Bank, like the Rice Bank, is a group initiated externally but based on local participation and responsibility. It differs in the key respects that it was founded with external resources and in that it takes many years before the whole community can become involved in its benefits. By 1989, it had accumulated about 40 animals.

Indigenous Schemes

In discussing indigenous co-operation for development, a problem arises as to what is to be discussed as development and what is to be treated as indigenous work practices. The state and NGO schemes described above come under 'development' in the discourses of villagers and outsiders alike. Since this is a category exogenous to the community, but since certain aspects of indigenous co-operation are now often spoken of as development, we can for present purposes follow the local discourse as a guide to what is and what is not development.

High on the list of concrete examples of development—as locally defined—come roads. Although these are commonly a state responsibility and state emphasis, road building is also undertaken in some circumstances by villagers without any direct involvement of the Government. It may be recalled that the original communications into Lan Sak were constructed entirely by villagers, although some recently established communities had more assistance than earlier ones in road construction.

A comparison of road construction into Bung Khiew with that into Ban Mai reveals some interesting features of indigenous co-operation for development. Bung Khiew villagers were connected to the outside world only by footpath via Ban Dong until 1978. In this year, villagers co-operated by giving land and labour for the construction of a dry-season cart track into Bung Khiew, and this track was later extended to villages to the north. During the dry season the track was rough, but during the rains it was impassable. Moreover, it entered Bung Khiew via a precarious log bridge over the irrigation channel, which under no circumstances was passable by anything larger than a pick-up. In early 1984, Bung Khiew villagers got together to improve the road by levelling, with the promise that laterite would be laid at the district authorities' expense. This time, a bulldozer was hired in place of manual labour, with each household contributing an hour's vehicle time (600 baht) in cash, although those who could not afford the cost were exempted and some households paid more. It was also agreed that a proper bridge, passable by vehicles of up to 6 tonnes, be constructed. This involved three days' labour from each household in Bung Khiew. Materials were obtained in the form of planks from the bridge over the Tap Salao River into Ban Dong that had been washed away in the previous year's floods. This wood had originally been donated by villagers from the village adjoining Bung Khiew to the north, since the road also provided their only access, and it had been transported using the free services of a Bung Khiew villager's work elephant.

Once the levelling and bridge building were complete in April 1984, villagers were anxious to have the laterite laid before the onset of the rains. They had to wait a further month for the *tambon* council to arrange the laying, using a Nong Chang contractor. In the event, the material laid was too soft, and villagers intimated that half of the money made available had gone into the pockets of the *kamnan* and other council members. After much complaint, the road was relaid with firm laterite.

This local initiative contrasts sharply with the situation in Ban Mai. The original tracks into this area had been cleared by *yaang* oil tappers, but the first roads passable by motorized vehicles were the logging roads constructed by TPC contractors. The major road construction was carried out by ALRO, which provided a dense grid of roads inside the village, linking the agricultural plots and linking the village to the outside.

The effect of this state provision has been to make roads for Ban Mai villagers state property and hence state responsibility. In 1983, floods destroyed or cut off many of the roads and bridges, both inside and outside the village, including the bridge across the Tap Salao River linking Ban Mai with Paak Meuang. The officer in charge of the ALRO Tap Salao project, whose headquarters is half a kilometre outside Ban Mai, complains that villagers are not interested in maintaining the roads, even those directly in front of their own houses. He made a point of only repairing the 'agricultural roads' so that the roads within the village remained unrepaired two years after the floods. Villagers, on the other hand, complain that ALRO does not maintain its roads, and the *khon to* who was opposed to their construction in the first place cites this as an example of official irresponsibility. The bridge across the Tap Salao River was repaired partly using villagers' contributions, but only on the initiative of a neighbouring village, and this bridge is outside the ALRO area. Indigenous co-operative initiative, responsibility, and commitment to particular projects clearly depends on the degree to which communal ownership is established.

Bung Khiew Irrigation Channel

State, NGO, and indigenous schemes are not mutually exclusive. Each relies to some extent on the other, and in an alternative sense the very term 'co-operative development' has been taken to mean co-operation between these various sectors rather than within them. The saga of Bung Khiew Irrigation Channel is an example of the problems encountered in intersector and intrasector co-operation for development.

Meuang Bung Khiew, as the project came to be known, has a history going back to the late 1970s. All Bung Khiew rice-fields are rain-fed, as are those in villages upstream and downstream at a similar distance from the Tap Salao River. Unreliable rainfall is a recurrent problem and, in 1976, money from the *tambon* revolving fund scheme[12] was used to dig a channel leading from the channel serving Ban Dong just below Paak Meuang, through Bung Khiew, and on to villages lower down, using both hired labour and digging equipment. However, the course had not been surveyed, and when a section across a granite rise at Khao Din was traversed, the depth required of the channel was greater than the depth of laterite covering bedrock. The blasting required would have cost far more than the funds available for the project, and the project was abandoned despite the fact that a 7-kilometre-long channel had been dug over a period of two years and the obstruction was less than 200 metres long.

In 1981, Bung Khiew villagers decided to make another attempt at securing irrigation water. In order to avoid the obstacle of Khao Din, it was decided to divert water lower down the Ban Dong channel, and to dig a short 500-metre link to the lower end of the channel that had been dug in 1976. This would serve most of Bung Khiew and villages below it, but several villagers would not be able to get water via this channel. The thirty households who expected to get water agreed to contribute 1,700 baht per household, a considerable sum in local terms, to hire a mechanical digger for the job. Again there was no means of surveying, and the project failed due to unstable soil over part of the section to be dug and unexpectedly hard rock over a short portion. Since the digger was paid by the hour, all the risk was placed on the shoulders of the villagers, who say that they were quite aware of the gamble involved.

By 1984, Bung Khiew villagers were once again talking of reviving the *meuang* project. At the same time, NKYFRD had become involved in the village through the Rice and Buffalo Banks and was aware of the uncertainties of rain-fed cultivation. In May 1984, discussions between NKYFRD, Boi, and other villagers established that irrigation water was still the most pressing need in the community, and NKYFRD suggested that if villagers were prepared to put in resources of their own, external help might be available. The villagers hastily called a meeting to discuss what could be proposed and how much each household could be called on to contribute. A contribution of 1,000 baht per household was agreed on, and initially it was decided to opt for the link channel, since it was not thought that sufficient resources would be available for the larger project, despite the fact that the latter was favoured in terms of the reliability of water and number of beneficiaries. From the information and suggestions put forward, a short proposal was written in Thai and English (the latter for application to foreign aid agencies) by Boi and the author. This was discussed with the NKYFRD in the chance presence of a representative of NKYFRD's overseas sponsor, who took an immediate interest and provisionally agreed to fund the project, provided a technical survey was carried out in advance.

Two weeks later, NKYFRD workers visited Bung Khiew to inspect the options. The nature of the soil, the lack of gradient over the link, and the fact that more resources appeared to be available than was first thought led to examination of the Khao Din option as well. Villagers were enthusiastic at the possibilities of either using explosives to deepen the existing channel or of circumventing Khao Din by digging a new section, approximately 2 kilometres long, to the north. It was decided that the feasibility of the various options would be left to surveyors from the Royal Irrigation Department (RID) to establish and make recommendations upon.

The Khao Din options posed a number of potential problems over and above the technicalities mentioned above. Since the channel had originally been dug, a fisheries project had been established at Bung Lom, and it would be necessary to cross this. It was not known whether the *kamnan* of *tambon* Lan Sak, in whose area Bung Lom lies, would agree, or whether permission would be required from the Fisheries Department, since a fish grate would have to be installed and there was a risk of siltation. If Khao Din was to be circumvented, the owners of the land would have to give their permission, although this was not thought to be a major obstacle since they would benefit from the irrigation water and money could be made available for compensation if necessary. It was decided to leave this until other problems had been cleared. Another task was to obtain permission from the RID for extension of the agricultural area irrigable from Paak Meuang weir, since in the original Tap Salao project, an area of only 3,000 *rai* was allocated and this was already taken up in Ban Dong. The amount of money available was also still uncertain. The project now involved villagers, and NGO, state, and international aid staff.

Despite the uncertainties and complexity of the project, villagers were keen to go ahead. The first step was for the director of NKYFRD to use his influence and connections, as president of the Uthaithani branch of the Kasetsart University Alumni Association, to arrange for the chief engineer of the Tap Salao project to make a preliminary assessment of the project, and then to approach the chief of the regional Small Projects Division at Chainat. The Small Projects Division chief rejected the possibility of blasting as too expensive, but suggested that RID surveyors from the Tap Salao project could be made available to establish the feasibility of the circumventing route and measure the amount of earth to be moved. Following this, a meeting was held at the Small Projects Division, and the regional manager was enthusiastic at the combination of villager initiative and NGO and foreign interest. It was agreed to waive the 3,000 *rai* limit, provided no formal request was made, and surveyors were put at the disposal of the project. It was then confirmed with the Lan Sak *kamnan* and the Fisheries Department that no objection would be raised, since silt content was not in fact great and the fisheries project had not materialized. The funder confirmed that at least 90,000 baht and up to 120,000 baht would be made available. Several delays in surveying and estimating the amount of earth to be moved ensued due to the surveyors' not turning up as appointed; this disappointed the Bung Khiew villagers, who had prepared food. They had also provided manual help and advice based on local knowledge for the outsiders involved at each stage. Conversation in Bung Khiew for several months centred on the progress of the *meuang*. Another initiative was to approach villagers upstream and downstream to secure a commitment to help top up the funds, and enthusiasm was extended to neighbouring communities.

It was not until February 1985 that the technical feasibility of the project was confirmed by the surveyors and the scale of the job calculated. At commercial rates, it would have been beyond the combined resources available. The *tambon* council was in the process of deciding on how the Rural Employment Generation Programme funds were to be spent that year, and the *kamnan*, in whose area the benefit from the channel was to be obtained, pressed for part of the money to be spent on the channel. However, the technical advisers from the district office had another project in mind and used various means to get this through.[13] The apparent shortage of funds was overcome when a committee member of NKYFRD, an equipment contractor, offered to dig the channel on a non-profit basis as a contribution to the NKYFRD, quoting a figure of 80,000 baht, well within the resources available.

Owners of the land to be crossed by the channel had been consulted informally by Boi and other villagers at an early stage, but until the route, feasibility, and resources available were known, no definite arrangement could be established. Altogether, land belonging to six farmers was to be crossed. Four of these farmers lived permanently near their land, while two were large landowning brothers in Ban Dong. (One of these is Thii—Case 5 in Chapter 5). All six had expressed a willingness to make land available for the channel, and those living locally were enthusiastic at the prospect of obtaining irrigation water themselves.

A meeting was called in March 1985. This was attended also by the owner of the digger that was to carry out the work: he came for a final inspection before the work was to begin two days later. Quite unexpectedly, Thii's wife Jai and their nephew raised an objection to the channel crossing their land where it had been surveyed, asking that it follow the land boundaries on either side. Technically, this is impossible, since the northern boundary is too low-lying for a diverted channel to rejoin the old one, while the southern boundary is so high as to mean that any new digging would have to go almost as deep as that which caused the original channel to be abandoned. Thii and his brother Lek were concerned that the channel would divide their land.

There followed a long period of escalating negotiation and conflict, backed by an urgency due to the limited time for which the digger could be made available at cost and the impending rains that would make work impossible. A delegation of Thii and Lek's closest associates in Bung Khiew went to see each of them in turn, negotiating and offering compensation for any land lost to the channel. After several visits, positions only seemed to be further entrenched, and Nii, a Bung Khiew villager and long-time friend of Lek, decided on an alternative, confrontational course of action. Until then, Lek had only been able to get his tractor to his land by means of crossing Nii's land. Now Nii blocked the track with posts and organized the other two Bung Khiew villagers with access tracks to Lek's land to do the same, receiving help in this from other Bung Khiew villagers. The only alternative access involved a diversion of several kilometres. They let it be known that the posts would only be removed when Lek and Thii agreed to let the channel cross their land: 'If he crosses our land, why shouldn't we be able to cross his?' was the reasoning. This only hardened Lek's resolve and reduced the possibilities for compromise. The next step was for villagers to urge Boi and the author to talk with the brothers, and a meeting was arranged at Thii's house. The temple abbot, *kamnan*, Boi, Nii, and the author attended this meeting which took up an evening, the abbot and *kamnan* doing most of the talking. Thii said little except that his wife and children were the ones who objected more than he did, and they were not present. Lek refused to speak even to the *kamnan* or abbot about it, and a village committee meeting was called to which Lek's wife was summoned. Four of the nine committee members are from Bung Khiew, so there was considerable interest, but the *kamnan* did not turn up, and this reduced the authority present. It was threatened that the matter would be taken to the district authorities, but no progress was made.

By this stage, many of the villagers were suggesting that the channel be dug to either side of the approximately 300-metre stretch crossing Thii and Lek's land, in order to pressure them into giving in. NKYFRD and Boi were reluctant to raise the level of conflict further, and their fears were justified by the words of some villagers who, when asked what might happen if Thii and Lek still refused access once the channel was dug, replied, 'Someone might get killed.'

The last resort was to take the matter to the district office. Boi served as intermediary, and after several trips the deputy district officer agreed to speak to Lek and Thii. On his next trip, Boi was told that they had agreed to let the channel cross their land provided compensation was provided. Believing that all was set, Boi and several villagers arranged with Lek and Thii to point out the definite route and discuss terms of compensation; by now it was the last opportunity to start work before the rains. On the appointed day, Lek and Thii were at their land and said that they had decided once again only to allow the channel to follow the boundaries.

The project was abandoned.

A compensation for Bung Khiew villagers was that the funding agency agreed to allow the money allocated for the irrigation channel to be spent on another community project. At a village meeting, it was decided that two large village fish-ponds be constructed on land donated by seven villagers. The water in these ponds is insufficient for full irrigation, but some supplementary irrigation can be provided to nearby fields using a pump. Fish fry was supplied by the Fisheries Department. In fact, villagers would have preferred to have dug individual fish-ponds, but the funders and NKYFRD were insistent that this must be a joint project.

The lessons to be learned from this failed initiative are many, involving aspects of villager co-operation, co-operation and co-ordination between villagers, NGOs, state authorities, and international aid agencies, various means of conflict resolution, and participation of villagers in concrete development projects for communal mobilization of production resources.

Potential for and Obstacles to Co-operation

Neither co-operation nor conflict are new to Ban Dong or Ban Mai. The parameters affecting co-operation change as new opportunities present themselves and as new obstacles are placed in the way. Lack of co-operation does not in itself imply conflict, just as projects involving co-operation themselves can heighten the potential for conflict. Peasants in Ban Dong and Ban Mai avidly seek out new opportunities in both individual and collective ways; yet peasants in both communities place a high priority on securing control over the resources necessary to assure subsistence production, be they collectively or individually mobilized. Moral norms do not entirely overcome the problem of free-riders, but at the same time non-contributors are accommodated where their incapacity to contribute is appreciated by the remainder of the community.[14] Moral and rational, collectivist and individualist attributes are determined by locally and historically specific circumstances.

If it is accepted that these circumstances provide the key parameters, it should be possible to make certain statements about the basis for co-operation or otherwise from the concrete situations described above. Changes in production relations have diminished the extent to which individual producers are constrained by reciprocal arrangements with the advent of monetization and differentiation of the respective communities. On the other hand, differentiation as expressed in the alienation of individual producers from the means of production and concentration of these means in the hands of others can provide new scope for co-operation. This is particularly true in the case of 'lumpy' items of technology. In Ban Mai and Ban Dong, farmers have discussed and rejected the possibility of joint ownership of power tillers and tractors, revealing some illuminating factors concerning co-operation in production. Both of these items of machinery are beyond the means of most individual farmers, particularly tractors, and both if put to full use would be superfluous to the needs of most individual farms, particularly so in the case of tractors. Why then has there not been a single case of co-operative purchase?

Power tillers are in fact often used on more than one farm, not so often on a rental arrangement as in helping out close kin, often an elderly parent. However, this is quite different from joint ownership. In the case of power tillers, two factors are raised as obstacles to co-operation. The first is the problem of maintenance and repairs. If the machine were to break down, it is considered inevitable that quarrelling would arise over responsibility for fixing it. The second obstacle is the issue of allocating usage, since ploughing even with a power tiller can take several days and, as described above, intensification of production limits flexibility in timing. The maintenance problem arises also in the case of tractor sharing, and with such an expensive item of machinery the stakes are much higher. Timing is not so great a problem, since a single day is sufficient in most cases for ploughing land owned by a single farmer, provided a large tractor is used. A much more considerable problem is raised by the schedule of tractor usage. In order to be used to the full, a tractor must be able to plough fields in neighbouring districts and provinces or even further afield outside the periods of local peak demand. This is accomplished by wealthy tractor owners with outside connections, means of collecting payment, and time to expend on the considerable managerial task involved. Such a task is beyond the individual and co-operative capabilities of small farmers in Ban Dong and Ban Mai.[15]

Other than the rationale for co-operation as delimited by material aspects of production relations, a number of ideological factors present potentials and obstacles. Interaction with outsiders, specifically with 'developers' is one such factor. As is apparent from the ideology of NGOs and the experience, for example, of Bung Khiew Rice Bank, the stimulus of ideas and institutional support provided from the outside can enhance co-operative development. On the other hand, other aspects of exogenous ideology and structures can work against co-operative effort. Some of the determinants of the effect of external involvement are set out below.

In terms of interaction, the type of approach made by external agents affects the degree to which co-operation is promoted or otherwise. Three principal approaches can be identified from the examples raised above. The first is what can be termed the 'cadre' approach, whereby outsiders spend time among the villagers and differences in status are minimized. This has the benefits of enhancing communication, increasing the outsiders' understanding of the problems of the community, and minimizing the power difference between the actors involved. The second approach can be termed the 'friendly technocrat' approach, whereby an externally determined policy that requires set patterns of villager co-operation is put into effect by fieldworkers who try to reduce the gap between themselves and villagers. BAAC approximates this type of approach. It is successful in ensuring co-operation within the limits of its objectives but, as was suggested earlier, it involves a contradiction in a wider sense in that it is part of the promotion of change in production relations that is actually individualizing production. The third approach suggested here is the 'hegemonic technocrat' approach, which is used to implement state policy at the village level in the name of co-operation and benefit to the community that is to arise therefrom, but with little or no diminution of the power or status gap between 'developer' and 'developed'. This issue of power is dwelt on at greater length in the following chapter.

A second issue of outsider influence is the extent to which over-involvement of outsiders and consequent demands made on villagers' time and other resources can sap latent co-operative potential. State schemes are often overlapping and mutually competitive, with villagers being pressed into joining many different groups each. There is often a minimal understanding of the purpose of these groups, apart from vague ideas that they are to promote 'unity'.[16] Moreover, use of NGO discourse as part of the state rhetoric leads to confusion over what are often already terms alien to village discourse. It thus ironically becomes more difficult for NGOs or others to involve the community despite the apparently liberalized political environment, as connotations shift and confusion reigns. For villagers, it takes time for the cadre approach of NGO workers to distinguish them from state officials, given the traditional dualistic class distinction described in Chapter 2. Official schemes may thus insert an intended or unintended 'static' that inhibits the emergence of indigenously organized groups, either out of sheer overwhelming by the proliferation of *klum*, or by usurping potentially useful discourses necessary in the establishment of independent forms.[17]

A third aspect of relations with outside 'developers' and the implications for co-operation concerns the direction of communication. If co-operation is to make use of external resources in a way that gives participants a sense of responsibility through common 'ownership', the initiative must come from below as in the case of Bung Khiew Irrigation Channel. In this case, a literate villager with outside connections was able to make the necessary link such that villagers were able co-operatively to call on external resources. An advance in enhancing this potential more widely was made with the foundation of the Local Development Assistance Programme (LDAP) by the Canadian International Development Agency (CIDA), the main Canadian government development agency working in Thailand, which seeks short proposals in Thai from villagers themselves, although the NGO network is used for most applications.[18] The government has followed this idea by establishing a Village Development Fund under the Sixth National Economic and Social Development Plan, but the fact that proposals will have to be channelled through village committees and *tambon* councils poses potential problems to be discussed in the following chapter.

A final pair of factors influencing co-operation is related to the community itself. First, the size of the community can have a key influence on the practicability of co-operative arrangements. In the case of Bung Khiew Rice Bank, trust plays an important part in the success of such a scheme. Bung Khiew's cohesion, partly based on kinship ties, was discussed in Chapter 4. It is unlikely that any such scheme could be established on the same basis in a village as large as the Ban Dong or Ban Mai administrative villages.[19] Bung Khiew's achievement of separate administrative status, encompassing two other small clusters (Nong Sung and Khao Din), under the leadership of Boi in 1988 enhances the potential for co-operation within official structures. While no set figure can be placed on size, larger communities are clearly more easily fractionalized than are small ones, which are bound to a considerable degree by kinship. Here, NGOs show a flexibility that is difficult to achieve within the rigid structures of the State, where administrative boundaries precede natural communities for most considerations. One attempt was made by the Ban Dong *kamnan* to overcome the size problem when he ordered that 'development groups' be set up to ease administration, in particular for the compulsory fence-building programme.

The other factor concerning the community is the extent to which it is actually a community of interest. Differentiation of the community clearly reduces the commonality of interest as economic fortunes diverge, systems of production vary from one household to another, and conflicts of interest arise. Thus it is unlikely that a village trader who is also a money-lender and buffalo *rentier* or tractor owner is going to support co-operative marketing, indigenous co-operative credit, or buffalo banks. The fact that no Bung Khiew villagers are major rice lenders or buffalo *rentier* meant that there was not the conflict of interest that would have arisen in a Ban Dong-wide scheme. Increasing the power of villagers through co-operative action is bound to involve conflicts of interest, but the key aspect of this is whether or not this conflict is internal or external to the co-operative endeavour. A common external adversary can enhance as much as threaten group solidarity.[20]

Conclusion

The parameters affecting co-operation for development are complex and contextually bound. The NGO analysis expressed succinctly in the quote at the head of this chapter still pertains. However, without a recognition of the limits to, constraints on, and lack of inherent sanctity of co-operative in preference to individual action, neither state nor NGO development efforts at encouraging co-operation can succeed. Ultimately 'the answers lie in the village', but this still covers a lot of ground figuratively as well as physiographically in the scattered, differentiated villages of Lan Sak. It can be held that for small, powerless farmers, co-operation is necessary if participation in factors controlling one's life is to be achieved, but this cannot be drawn independently of wider issues of power associated with the various co-operative forms that come under the aegis of development. It is to these issues that the next chapter is addressed.

1. Even earlier institutional means for co-operation had been suggested by the Assistant Minister for Agriculture, Chaophraya Wongsanupraphat, in 1905. He suggested the formation of farming associations as vehicles for government promotion of technical improvements, such as use of fertilizers and improved seed (Johnston, 1975: 356). However, no action was taken on this, and action following the establishment of formal co-operatives was similarly sluggish: by 1926, there were only 1,414 co-operative members in the country (Johnston, 1975: 399).

2. '*Chaobaan*' used by an urbanite is a distinctive category that refers to a different, lesser educated sort of people. It can be used to mean 'the common people' even if they live in town. Used (less frequently) by a villager, *chaobaan* refers to people of the speaker's village or a village specifically mentioned.

3. Chayan (1990) identifies five traditions of village study, each of which contains explicit and implicit assumptions of village structure.

4. The popular Buddhist classification of people is actually as follows. Lotuses above the water have reached enlightenment, although not of course in the strict Buddhist sense. Lotuses on the surface are prime for enlightenment and just need some help in getting there. Lotuses under water are not yet ready, but they have the potential for enlightenment. Lotuses stuck in the mud at the bottom have no hope of attaining enlightenment.

5. The word *fang*, literally 'listen', contains a connotation of obeisance (see Turton, 1984b: 46).

6. The conceptualizations presented here are culled from observation of specific programmes at the village level and discussions with the people involved, rather than from formal interviewing or abstract questioning along the lines of 'what do you understand by "*klum*"?'.

7. Irvine (1982) discusses at length the way in which Communism is posed as a threat to the developing, modernizing Thai nation. Since Irvine did his fieldwork, the situation has changed somewhat, in that the 'internal' (that is, CPT) threat has declined, and in

compensation the 'external' (that is, Vietnamese) threat increased in government rhetoric with the occupation of Cambodia in the 1980s and Vietnam's presence in Laos. Even in a province as far from these borders as Uthaithani, the Vietnamese are continually posed as a threat, and official myths such as the poisoning of coffee that supposedly led to the 'shrinking penis syndrome' (see Irvine, 1982: Ch. 8) are still purveyed.

8. This situation refers to the period subsequent to the 1976 coup. Prior to this, farmers' organizations were more open and political, notably in the case of the Farmers' Federation of Thailand (see Kanoksak and Kanchana, 1985; Turton, 1984b: 58). The example of this organization, thirty of whose leaders were assassinated by right-wing elements in 1975, shows the dangers for farmers of overt political organization even during a nationally liberal period.

9. At one Lan Sak development training meeting, for example, the DAE officer opened the meeting by instructing that 'the most important thing to learn for development is the meaning of acronyms'. Use of acronyms rather than more direct description of project activities has a number of interesting implications. It gives programmes an official ring to them, implying a status distinction from independent initiatives. It serves to take the emphasis off the name of the programme which contains the original intention, so that for example the Rural Employment Generation Programme (REGP) has become associated with infrastructural projects rather than employment generation. It adds to the specialized vocabulary of development discourse that is used at meetings, and it serves to limit participation of those not adept at use of official language.

10. BAAC credit increased at more than 6 per cent per year in real terms between 1976 and 1980 (Lightfoot and Fox, 1983: 11).

11. Boi's role as volunteer co-ordinator for the Meechai organization in Lan Sak takes him to every village in the district once a month. This has allowed him to make external connections and to make frequent stops at the district offices, which have in turn proved important in making the connections necessary for co-ordination of projects in Bung Khiew that rely on external resources.

12. The Rural Employment Generation Programme (REGP) is a continuation of the revolving fund programme initiated by Prime Minister Kukrit Pramote in 1975. This programme divided 2,500 million baht equally among *tambon* for local infrastructural programmes that were in principle designed to create local employment during the agricultural off-season. Although numerous local roads have been constructed under these programmes, employment effects have been limited in part by the use of heavy machinery in place of labour, and this has gone hand-in-hand with a high level of corruption in connection with these funds, since the allocation of funds is decided on by *kamnan* who may have direct or indirect interests in heavy machinery contracting.

13. In 1985, the Ban Dong *tambon* council was presented with two major projects on which to spend its annual allocation under REGP. The *kamnan* and several other village headmen were in favour of supporting the Bung Khiew Irrigation Channel, while the 'technical advisers' from the district office had decided to press for a water jar construction project. The *kamnan* and others claimed that the irrigation channel would give by far the greater benefit. However, health officials, despite not being allowed in principle to speak other than to give technical advice, made an impassioned case for the water jar project, stressing that all villages would be able to share in the benefits. Since only five of the *tambon*'s fourteen villages stood to benefit from the irrigation channel, most headmen were in favour of the water jars. In the event, the council voted two-thirds of the funds to the water jars and one-third to the channel; however, the district office subsequently disqualified the allocation to the channel project, since it was claimed that only one project was to be allowed (despite precedents for multiple projects elsewhere). In the event, no local employment was created since contractors were brought in from another province to construct the jars. This illustrates the considerable bureaucratic control over supposedly participatory bodies such as the *tambon* council.

14. Bung Khiew is an example of where the 'free-rider' problem posed by Popkin is overcome by village solidarity in a community bound by strong social ties, partly based on kinship and partly based on relative lack of differentiation when compared with the larger community. In such a situation, norms of mutual assistance are operable for four main reasons:

—The community is tightly knit enough so that those receiving assistance at the expense of others are identifiable, as is their material situation, making it difficult for anyone to become an anonymous free-rider;
—Affectual relations within the community are strong, based on kinship and neighbourliness;
—New institutions of mutual assistance overlap with traditional forms;
—It is clear to the majority that if they do not include some element of subsidy to the less well-off, the project will not come off at all, and when the scale is limited it is relatively easy to achieve consensus over who is to contribute what.

A case from the same community shows an awareness of potential free-rider problems. In helping surveyors on the Bung Khiew Irrigation Channel, villagers insisted on sending a member from every household, so as to avoid 'bias', even though fewer helpers would have sufficed.

15. See Moerman (1968: 69–70) on why Ban Ping villagers did not buy a tractor co-operatively. 'The natural environment of Thunglor requires the tractor; the social environment of Ban Ping prevents villagers from owning one.' This is because no individual is wealthy enough to purchase a tractor, while no social institution exists for joint ownership. It was envisaged, just as in Ban Dong and Ban Mai, that joint ownership would lead to bickering over maintenance and ploughing schedules. Where the situation of Lan Sak in 1985 differs significantly from Ban Ping a quarter of a century earlier is in the ability of *individuals within the village* to purchase such a large item of machinery.

16. The word for 'unity' (*saamakhii*) is used ambiguously in the sense of implying unity alternatively as solidarity and as prohibiting dissenting voices. This is another example of the importance of context in interpreting the discourse of development.

17. Maurice Bloch discusses 'exercise of power through formalization' (1975: 10) in Merina society in Madagascar, as a result of restrictive formal discourses effectively pre-empting alternative or countervailing speech. The restriction of choice as to what can be said, a restriction entailed in formalization (p. 17), extends into what can be done, and in this way formalization of *klum* can be seen as a pre-emptive exercise of power. On the other hand, Bloch notes certain limitations to the power of formalization, namely that it must be restricted through skills necessary for formal articulation or by a restrictive political situation. The implication is that given a more liberal political environment, it is possible for individuals such as Boi to acquire the formalistic skills necessary for exercise of countervailing power.

18. In 1987, Boi secured LDAP funding for a buffalo-rearing project specifically aimed at alleviating debt. It has been particularly successful, partly as a result of its combination of group responsibility with attention to individual problems.

19. Similar problems have been described in achieving villager co-operation in large, recently settled villages in Sri Lanka (Harriss, 1982b: 328).

20. An interesting political use of the 'common adversary' is detectable in the Ban Dong *kamnan*'s frequent outbursts against Chinese traders, officials (especially schoolteachers), BAAC and other banks, and politicians. Despite not having been directly involved in agricultural production for some time, he frequently speaks of 'us farmers' (see the quotation at the beginning of this chapter).

7
Participation and Power in Development

> We poor have no right to speak, no right to voice opinions.
>
> Ban Mai villager

> Now it is the people who are the regulators.
>
> Lan Sak District Officer

THE recent emphasis on participation in development is based on the premise that 'taking part' is something new for villagers. In the past, it is reasoned, villagers were excluded (from what, for the moment, being a moot point). Development programmes that came from the outside were initiated and run by, and often for, outsiders. The principal issue for development thus became how to involve local people in these schemes.

This emphasis has gone hand in hand with the linking of the village to wider political and economic systems. As the village polity has become integrated into the nation-state and as the village economy has become linked increasingly to the national and international capitalist systems, so influences of these wider systems have affected villagers to an increasing extent. At one level, therefore participation in the wider system has already been established by means of the general incorporative rural development strategy. However, the passive and dependent nature of this incorporation places most villagers at a disadvantage in terms of political and economic bargaining power.

The initial premise stated above needs to be examined more closely. In the past, it is true, villagers did not take part in the wider system to any significant extent, but at the same time decisions taken at a supravillage level had only a limited effect on village life and production. Meanwhile, villagers did have an active part in the decisions affecting community affairs and household production—that is, the affairs that most directly affected them. These latter were based not on formal committee decisions but rather on local cultural norms and informal relationships in which kinship and social obligation played an important part. Local leadership was established by acceptance and respect rather than by formal election. The main function of the local leader was to manage or arbitrate affairs within the community, while contact with external authorities played only a secondary role. It is only latterly, particularly in the case of recently settled forest communities, that dealings with the wider system have raised the issue of participation. These very linkages now pose questions concerning participation internal to the village community.

Participation and Development

The difficulty of discussing a concept such as participation stems from the very looseness with which the term is used and the resulting ambiguity it takes on. Indeed, it is this ambiguity that underlies the contradictions to be expanded on presently. Like democracy and motherhood, everyone must be for participation: precisely because of this vagueness, there is everything to play for.[1] The value of examining the concept thus lies not in achieving any universal measure of participation that can be used to determine the relative participatory merits of specific rural development schemes, but rather in a contextual identification of the term within various discourses. It is therefore insufficient to list a variety of definitions and then select the one we deem best suited to our own purposes without having first outlined discursive evolution of the term.

The literature on participation is vast, and the present discussion simply summarizes interpretations that have been used both implicitly and explicitly.[2] Any meaningful use of the terms under consideration is highly context-bound (ideologically, historically, and spatially), so the contextual approach of the United Nations Research Institute for Social Development (UNRISD) and the specific manipulations of 'participatory development' in the Thai context are given particular attention. Four main sources are used for the latter case, representing the principal strands of discourse on participation influencing current debates. These are, respectively: World Bank conceptualizations; the Thai section of the UNRISD project on popular participation; a conference of prominent Thai academics, civil servants, and development workers; and local-level discourse as witnessed in Lan Sak during 1984–5.

General Conceptualizations of Participation

Early post-war discourse on development contained little that dealt specifically with issues of participation. The participatory role of the masses in development was seen as one of taking part in economic development as producers by provision of cheap labour and, in the longer run through 'trickle down' effects, as consumers of the enlarged national products that development would bring about (Stiefel and Wolfe, 1984). Decisions on the direction of development were to be left to the technocrats: such deliberations were seen as basically management decisions to be made by experts concerning the best way to move along the unitary path of growth, industrialization, and increased productivity. In the Thai context, this was epitomized by Sarit's doctrine of concentrating on economic development while stifling all forms of popular political participation in the early 1960s (Morell and Chai-anan, 1981: 5–6; Chai-anan, 1984: 34–5).

However, it soon became apparent that two sets of factors were inhibiting development of the kind the technocrats had envisaged. The first had to do with the unequal distribution of the benefits of growth, with élites adopting Western lifestyles at the expense of the impoverished masses, leading to 'apathy' and 'unresponsiveness'. The latter term itself indicates the way in which participation of the rural population was seen as the following of directions set by policy makers at a higher level. The second inhibiting element was what is sometimes summed up as 'cultural inertia', which may be translated as a failure to recognize the benefits of accumulation via participation in the capitalist economy. The answer to this was 'modernization', requiring new attitudes, institutions, and a culture of consumerism and efficiency, such that, as explained by Stiefel and Wolfe (1984: 10): 'Popular participation was a form of therapy, the purpose of which was to transform "backward", "traditional", "unresponsive" populations into "modern, responsive" citizens ready to assume their duties and obligations in a predetermined development process.' This led to the establishment of channels and superficial mechanisms for participation based on Western models, but it left unchanged existing structures of exploitation and inequality.

Conceptualizations of participation have changed along with other strands of thought in the wider development debate. The rejection of modernization theory and the emergence of models of dependency and modes of production, and the consequent political and economic emphasis that was thrust into the debate led to political formulations that approached participation from the point of view of the poor, the powerless, and above all the excluded. Exclusion of the rural poor from the fruits of capitalist development led to a set of analyses concerning the failure of trickle-down mechanisms. These ranged from urban bias (Lipton, 1977), imperfect factor markets (Griffin, 1979), superficiality of understanding by national planners (Chambers, 1983), to world system models of dependency (Frank, 1967), modes of production (Hindess and Hirst, 1975), and unequal exchange (Amin, 1976).

As to how these mechanisms actually affected the rural poor, these biases, imperfections, and injustices were articulated initially in terms of problems of 'access' (Buijs, 1982). Yet, irrespective of whether access is defined generally as 'including the excluded' (Palmer, 1975: 1), or more specifically as 'the relation between the administrative allocation of goods and services and the people who need them, and for whom they are intended' (Shaffer, 1975: 3), it clearly places people as passive objects rather than active subjects.

The search for a more active way of involving the rural poor in development led to increasing reference to the need for participation, not only as passive recipients but as formulators, planners, doers, and beneficiaries of various programmes. Nevertheless, despite the fact that the debate had stepped back from the *how* of participation in a mechanical sense to consider the *why*, many still saw participation primarily as a means to achieve predefined objectives and only secondarily as an end in itself. Kent (1981) sees the advantages of participation in three main dimensions: contextually, local people know their own social and physical environment and can be expected to use this knowledge to increase the effectiveness of decision making; practically, participation in planning and decision making enhances the probability of participation in implementation, where imposed programmes may be ignored or avoided; morally, people have a right to take part in making decisions that affect their own lives.

A common aspect of the writing on participation has been a programme orientation, a focus on what makes specifically identified development programmes more or less effective. While this is of interest to development workers involved in such programmes, participation seen from the perspective of the rural poor involves a range of social, political, and economic processes that are included in many structural analyses of development, but ignored or taken as givens by those concerned with specific development programmes. It is the recognition of the importance of these processes as fundamental to the issue of participation that makes the UNRISD popular participation programme a novel departure.

The UNRISD programme stressed from the start the irrelevance of selecting specific 'experimental' participatory programmes in isolation as objects of study, since these are marginal to the experience of most Third World rural producers. Likewise, it stressed that the objective was not to utilize or devise any body of 'participation theory'. Rather, such areas as social change, class, power, hierarchy, ideology would provide the theoretical background to an analysis of the constraints and openings for participation in a variety of social situations. Moreover, participation was seen not as a way of altering backward societies so as to emulate more participatory systems that had developed in the West or, alternatively, the socialist bloc. It was specified from the start that the battle against domination and stifling of creative powers is a universal one, albeit fought in many ways. Thus in the West, democracy and trade union rights have been won, yet industrial society still faces growing alienation from responsibility and creativity. In revolutionary societies where formal class structures have been abolished, bureaucracies and political power monopolies have taken choice away from the mass of individuals.[3] And in the Third World, new forms of oppression are continually taking shape (Pearse and Stiefel, 1979). As such, forms, emphases, and even definitions of participation are necessarily highly context-bound, hence the commitment to avoiding universalistic prescriptions (Stiefel and Wolfe, 1984).

A tenet of the UNRISD approach is that participation is a basic element in reversing the trend toward dependence and marginalization of the masses, and so 'the central issue of popular participation has to do with power' (Pearse and Stiefel, 1979: 5). Early on, as stated by UNRISD (1978: 2), participation was seen as: '(A)ctive and meaningful involvement of the masses of people at different levels: (a) in the decision making process for the determination of societal goals and the allocation of resources to achieve them and (b) in the execution of resulting programmes and projects.' A distinction was thus made between active and passive participation, the latter being the provision of cheap or free labour to community development programmes, and therefore being rejected in the terms defined by UNRISD, above.

In its effort to establish 'outer obstacles' (structures inimical to participation) and 'inner limits' (contradictions between central and local authority), UNRISD was committing itself to a political-economic approach. More specifically, as Pearse and Stiefel (1979: 5) stress:

> The study of poverty and the political economy of the production of wealth during the last few decades has shown convincingly that the generation of poverty is a function of the concentration of power and the monopolization of resources, which puts the cheap and obedient labour of the poor at the disposal of the monopolizers, thereby increasing their power. It must be accepted, therefore, that the struggle for people's participation implies an attempted redistribution of both control of resources and power in favour of those who live by their own productive labour.

This commitment to get to grips with issues of control and ultimately of power represents a departure from previous work in two main respects. First, it links what is commonly regarded as a programme-related issue, namely participation, with underlying structural phenomena, enhancing the understanding of issues within mainstream development debates. Second, it tackles head-on the association of participation with issues of existing or potential conflict. The realization that such issues must not be side-stepped led to a revised working definition of participation as 'the organized efforts to increase control over resources and regulative institutions in given social situations on the part of groups and movements of those hitherto excluded from such control' (Pearse and Stiefel, 1979: 8). Participation thus defined represents an unambiguous identification with disadvantaged social groups.

Participation is seen in a number of different dimensions.[4] Primary for UNRISD are analyses of the anti-participatory structures and ideologies, as outlined above, and encounters between the excluded and those that maintain exclusion. Such encounter may take on many forms, from bargaining to armed struggle, between groups, classes, or organizations. An encounter model is devised, whereby participation is seen as being concerned with 'struggle over terms of incorporation' (Pearse, 1980: 2) in the context of change and loss of effectiveness and relevance of traditional institutions. Moreover, as explained by Pearse (1980: 6), the struggle is not seen as a simple encounter of village with State or any other defined rural social unit with the larger system, for:

> the fact of participation by the village in regional and national affairs (i.e. as political force, source of commodities, recipient of services, as supplier of labour, etc.) is no guarantee that it acts as an agent of popular participation, though indeed it may *if national class divisions do not penetrate and divide it too deeply*. (Emphasis added.)

The importance of this proviso will become apparent in discussion of the terms of participation in Lan Sak below.

The discussion has dwelt at some length on the UNRISD formulation of participation for two main reasons. First, the importance attached to underlying structural aspects of the political economy corresponds with the production approach used in this study, and the resulting emphasis on control is of value for the following analysis of participation in the context of changing production relations in Lan Sak. Second, the rigorous avoidance by the UNRISD studies of universalist applications and consequent focus on regional, national, and local contexts is of value in a locally bound study such as this one.

Indeed, UNRISD as part of its continuing programme has revised its approach for different world regions. The initial regional distinction is between the Asian and Latin American contexts, due to the different constraints faced by alternative movements in the two sets of studies. Whereas in Latin America popular autonomous action has a long tradition, in the Asian case the more pervasive power of the State allows less space for such movements. Thus where the working definition of participation stated above is still applied in the Latin American studies, it has been amended in light of experience in the Asian context to include 'reference to policies of particular states and governments whose purported aim is to devolve such control to the people' (Pearse and Stiefel, 1979). The approach is modified yet further within individual national contexts.

Thai Conceptualizations of Participation

The World Bank has long held influence in orientation of the Thai national development strategy. Since the early 1960s, with the start of national economic planning, the Bank has promoted a growth-oriented strategy in which traditional economic indicators have been used to reflect a buoyant economy and remarkable success in the Bank's own terms (IBRD, 1959). Yet towards the end of the 1970s, as the negative side of this strategy became ever more apparent in steadily increasing inequalities between town and countryside, between regions, and between social groups within each of these, the Bank turned itself towards issues of redistribution. In part, this represented a shift in thinking among conventional development economists towards the 'redistribution with growth' orthodoxy that had emerged in the 1970s.[5] In the Thai case, it led to a report entitled 'Thailand: Toward a Strategy of Full Participation' (IBRD, 1980).

The Bank's interpretation of participation is clear from this report, even though it is not explicit. The problems of past development strategy, according to the Bank's analysis, stem not from the capitalist penetration of the Thai economy; rather, they stem from the fact that it has not gone far enough, that it has not involved all in its benefits. Those who have participated most fully to date are those on the edges of the Central Plains who have managed to diversify by movement into non-rice agriculture in response to market signals. In the local terms of the present study, this makes Lan Sak farmers exemplary participants, more so in Ban Mai than in Ban Dong. Wider participation is to be achieved by ensuring more complete involvement of the mass of the population in the capitalist economy. Non-capitalist elements are to be ironed out by road construction, extension of credit, improved marketing, and other measures designed to increase the cash income of the rural poor.

Although this analysis clearly represents exogenous influence, it cannot be represented in isolation from Thai discourse on development. The approach is essentially that adopted by the mainstream macro-economic planners of the NESDB. Indeed, this strand of discourse has been prominent ever since the early 1960s, with the popular slogan of then Prime Minister Field Marshall Sarit, 'Work is money, money is work, happiness abounds'.

A contrasting Thai discourse on participation is contained in the UNRISD project on Thailand (see Turton, 1989). This involved a group of Thai academics, development workers, and the rural poor themselves in an attempt 'to document and contribute to a popular history of organized and everyday efforts made in the past few years by (and on behalf of) the rural poor to enhance their livelihood and social power [and to] assess the potentialities, obstacles, and limitations of such efforts' (Turton, 1984a: 2).

Not only was the analysis broadened beyond simple participation in the market, but the market itself—or rather lack of control over it—emerged as a ubiquitous problem.

The UNRISD studies identify power as a key element in participatory struggles of the rural poor. In line with the focus on the power of the State in the Asian context, Turton (1984a: 4) concludes:

> While the public statements of governments may give some currency to values of democracy, pluralism, self-reliance, and popular initiative, in practice government policies and agencies have largely had the effect of fragmenting, demobilizing, and preventing autonomous forms of solidarity among and between various strata and sectors of the people.

This is not to say that individual government officials, groups, or programmes are not supportive of participation. Indeed, this study found that no particular form of organization was itself enabling or limiting in any absolute sense. However, it was found that, for the most part, official groups stifle initiative, work to rigid bureaucratic standards, and provide unrepresentative leadership. In order to meet with success in terms of participation as set out in the UNRISD definition, groups have to overcome these drawbacks.

More important than the nature of specific groups, however, are underlying cultural and political-economic aspects that explain the anti-participatory organization of Thai society. A 'culture of subordination' is identified, and Turton speaks of the fragmenting effect of the increasing variety of labour processes and the intensification of labour. At the local level, socio-economic differentiation of the village and the links between village élites and the State are identified as the first stage in surplus accumulation. Because conflicts of interest are already so firmly established, conflict and participation are seen to be inseparable. Participation at present is suppressed not so much by an absence of a sense of injustice as a lack of 'space' (in the legal, institutional, and linguistic sense) for criticism of the social order, given the close association of government, state, nation, religion, and monarchy.

A third set of discourses on participation on the Thai development scene emerged from a conference held in February 1984 involving Thai civil servants, academics, and non-governmental development workers. The resulting publication (Thawithong, 1984) reflects the variety of interpretations of participatory development held among different sections of the intelligentsia, but at the same time it points to an apparent consensus on the need for broader involvement in the development process than has taken place hitherto. The principal differences concern the terms of participation involved.

The contributions fall roughly into three categories, in line with the three groups of participants in this dialogue. First, there are civil servants expounding the official version and policies of popular participation, with heavy emphasis on officially designated institutions. Most of these are senior officials whose statements reflect accurately the rhetoric but not necessarily the local practice of the State in promoting its particular form of participation. Participation is defined by the Director of the Community Development Department (see Phairat, 1984: 6; author's translation) as:

> the process by which the government promotes, persuades, supports, and provides the opportunities for people in the community, whether they be individuals, groups, clubs, associations, foundations, or voluntary organizations, to take part in carrying out any piece(s) of work . . . in order to fulfil stipulated development objectives and policy.

Participation is something sponsored by outsiders, and its aim is to encourage local involvement in achieving objectives that are stipulated elsewhere. Vehicles for participation other than formal government institutions (for example, co-operatives, farmers' groups, *tambon* councils) are permissible, but the examples of 'non-formal' organizations given—Village Scouts, National Defence Volunteers, Rotary Clubs, Lions Clubs[6]—are hardly independent or representative initiatives. The emphasis in these contributions is on improving the efficiency of specific mechanisms such as the administrative framework of the *tambon* council (Chit, 1984). The starting point is that of encouraging a hitherto apathetic or ignorant village population to take an interest in official projects.

The academic contributions are critical of this project orientation and the emphasis on official channels as media for participation. Thawithong criticizes the ambiguity of the Fifth Plan regarding the place of popular participation in development policy, especially in the political-economic sphere. In particular, he regards official conceptions of participation as misguided, since they are concerned primarily with expanding activities of each department (or 'empire' in political scientist Chai-anan's words), and with increasing the number of villages rather than the quality of work in any one project. As Thawithong (1984: 2–3; author's translation) puts it: 'The (official) meaning of participation tends to be used as a means to get people to co-operate in activities or projects that the State or its officials have stipulated. . . . Most state officials think that participation is a new instrument or technique for getting villagers to accept the activities already laid out by those officials.' This leads to the forcing of villagers into numerous activities that increase not only their burden but also their dependence on outsiders. Saneh Jamrik (1984) in his critique of Phairat's approach (see Thawithong, 1984: 24; author's translation) criticizes the idea that initiatives and forms must be external to the community, ignoring the potential of what is already there. He is particularly worried about the use of participatory development as a tool for imposition of alien structures: 'We overlook the resources that already exist. What is already there is like a local plant whose growth ought to be supported. Instead, what is being done now is equivalent to uprooting and discarding this plant and replacing it with one unsuited to local conditions. In the end, the plant dies.' Saneh defines participation as developing and using local people's full potential, starting with what is already there.

A prominent Thai political scientist deals more directly with participation as involving issues of power and broader structural aspects of the social formation. Since participation is concerned primarily with the devolution of power from those who have it to those who do not, it cannot be divorced from the political process. In the Thai context, monopolization of legitimacy by the civil service system means that it is above all the role and internal functioning of this system that needs to be addressed. In achieving participatory aims, there are essentially two alternatives: voluntary evolution of power on the part of those with, versus use of pressure tactics by those without (Chai-anan, 1984).

Those closest to the practical concerns of participatory development are the non-governmental development workers. One such prominent worker of many years' experience questions the premise that villagers have not participated in the past. On the contrary, enthusiasm was at first great, with villagers expending large amounts of time and other resources on projects, meetings, and new forms of production brought in from the outside by developers. Many local village leaders were used by outsiders to the extent that these leaders' own families suffered hardship, and the fruits of this development went to a minority of better-off villagers. Meanwhile, the result for most was increasing indebtedness, loss of land, and destruction of traditional ways of life. More fundamentally, and going even further back, villagers were not without their own ways of making decisions, working in groups, and changing things for the better. Outside interference in the name of development has, over the past thirty years or so, tended to undermine such indigenous organization. Recent concern to enable villagers to participate is often illusory, since participation is within a predetermined framework established by non-villagers, and participation is considered simply as a technique; meanwhile, it is a convenient way of blaming failures on local-level deficiencies, neglecting to take account of how nationally set priorities limit and determine local action. True participation (though not explicitly defined as such) must involve villagers as the main actors, outsiders being relegated to a support role. This involves a re-evaluation of past development by villagers and a reassessment of their own attitudes by outside development workers, who must seek to build on the existing community rather than try to replace it with alien forms. Finally, there is a need for reconsideration of the relationship between community and national objectives: to date, the community's task has always been to accommodate nationally set priorities and interpret them into local action; there is a need to reverse this in order that national direction is set at the local level (see Bamrung, 1984).

Structures of and Discourse on Participation in Lan Sak

Participation has become a catchword attached to, if not quite as pervasive as, development. It has worked its way through all levels, from the conventional and more radical international organizations concerned with development, such as the World Bank and UNRISD, through mainstream and alternative national development organizations, to local-level structures. At one level, this merely reflects the desire of each of the developers to involve people in a particular form of development. More fundamentally, however, it relates to the terms of involvement. This can be illustrated by reference to structures of and discourse on participation in Lan Sak, particularly as observed in Ban Dong and Ban Mai.

The two key official structures for participation are the *tambon* council (TC) and the village committee (VC). Although the TC has been in existence since 1956, it has gone through several modifications, and only since the Fifth Plan has it been stressed as the principal vehicle for popular participation in development. As in every other *tambon* in Thailand, the councils in Ban Dong and Thung Khaa are presided over by their respective *kamnan*. In addition, all village headmen and elected elders sit on the council, as do a local headmaster as secretary and the *tambon* doctor. All these must be approved by the district officer. Local health and community development officials attend the council in an advisory capacity. Meanwhile, the VC is presided over by the village head and is made up of several other elected members.

Through such bodies, according to the Lan Sak district officer, 'villagers are now the regulators'. However, a closer examination of these structures in the two study villages reveals two substantial weaknesses *vis-à-vis* participation in any other than the formal senses outlined in the previous section. The first weakness has to do with official conceptualizations of the role of TC and VC. The second is the extent to which these bodies represent the interests of all sections of the community.

The synaptic role of officially sanctioned village institutions and leaders[7] places them in an ambivalent situation with respect to relations between villagers and the wider polity. At a development training programme for village heads in Lan Sak in 1985, the senior deputy district officer summed up the function of the VC in the following words, 'The VC gives approval to government units within the bounds of the village.' This legitimization role as expressed in local official development discourse is a reiteration of wider official conceptualizations such as the following statement concerning the TC: 'It is not an organization for local administration. Nor does it have independent legal status. Rather, it is the basic unit of government administration' (Chit, 1984: 54–5; author's translation).

These expressions conflict sharply with participatory notions conceived by academics and non-governmental development workers. Many high-level bureaucrats have taken progressive ideas concerning participation on board, recommending for example that participation of villagers must involve decision making, planning, carrying out work, benefits, and evaluation, and that officials should take a back-seat role as 'advisers' rather than 'doers' (Chit, 1984). However, the reality of the functioning of the VC and TC as observed in Lan Sak shows them to be more relevant as tools of state power at the village and subdistrict level than as vehicles for articulation of community interests in dealings with the state authorities.

If the VC and TC serve primarily as vehicles for official entry to local communities, what of their role in serving the communities by representative leadership? In both Ban Dong and Ban Mai, VCs are dominated by the village head and one or two cronies, in all cases men of exceptional economic status in the village context. The TC in Ban Dong and Thung Khaa are both heavily dominated by their respective *kamnan*. In both these cases, the head of the VC or TC is an ex-officio member who remains in office up to the age of sixty, and who has an exceptional status by virtue of his position in the village or *tambon*. As a result, VC and TC meetings are dominated by these persons who, because of their economic status, are not seen as representative by the majority of villagers. This pattern, although not universal, is typical of VCs and TCs all over Thailand (Pathaan, 1984; Turton, 1984b).

The main official forum for participation in village activities is the monthly village meeting. In Ban Mai, attendance is compulsory on penalty of a 50-baht fine. The meeting is dominated by the VC, in particular by its president, the village head. The meeting takes place at the temple hall or at the village school. A microphone is used to address the 400 or so villagers present in Ban Mai (fewer in Ban Dong), and the VC sits at the front. Up to two hours may be spent reading official announcements from the district office. Occasional proposals are presented by district officials or the village head, who require a yes or no vote rather than a choice between alternatives. Government personnel, including police and army officers, to whom a show of deference is made by the village head, regularly use the meeting as a forum for dissemination of official policy; indeed, the meeting is timed to occur a few days after the meeting of village heads at the district office at the beginning of each month.[8] Any other business is then called for, this in the knowledge that there is up to an hour and a half's roll call before anyone can leave for lunch and what is left of the day's work, and rarely does any other business arise. There is occasional contribution from the floor, but too much spontaneous interjection evokes a reprimand from the village head, who insists that anyone who wants to speak must first raise a hand and wait to be called upon before being given the floor, unaided by microphone.

Another official forum for participation is the array of training programmes provided by various government departments at the village level. These take place mainly during the agricultural off-season (February to April). Attendance is often compulsory. A common method is for district officials to state publicly at a village meeting that it would reflect badly on the village if any household failed to send a representative, placing the onus on the village head to ensure that all households participate.

Villagers themselves frequently express the feeling of being forced into attending numerous meetings and training sessions. The content of the training is largely ideological, with emphasis on loyalty to the nation, religion, and monarchy, as well as on duties as a citizen, unity, and anti-Vietnamese rhetoric. Another aspect of coercion is mandatory participation in 'development days' proclaimed by the district office, when the VC is responsible for organizing activities such as roadside grass cutting. In 1984, village heads were chided by officials for not being zealous enough in securing participation.

Non-governmental structures of participation in Ban Dong and Ban Mai are few, and participation has yet to enter into non-official discourse. Even the Bung Khiew Rice Bank and Buffalo Bank, perhaps the most genuinely participatory structures in either of the two communities, are not spoken of by members in terms of participation as such, but rather in terms of mutual help and co-operation. Discourse and structures are thus independent and not always coincident articulations of participation in any situation, and in the case of structures, participation must be interpreted according to criteria implicit in the various conceptualizations set out above.

The more radical of these include non-institutional action and expression of power by the powerless as important elements of participation, which might be taken to include resistance to official or hegemonic programmes.[9] The reluctance of villagers to attend meetings is a form of resistance in Ban Dong; the fact that they have to be forced under penalty of fine in Ban Mai also indicates a resistance of consciousness, if not of action. Scott (1976: 230) suggests that an increase in repressive powers is itself evidence that compliance is achieved through means other than passive acceptance of authority. In this sense, resistance to resettlement by Ban Mai villagers is a move to retain control over livelihood and is thus participatory in the terms outlined above. Many other examples of passive resistance (Scott's 'foot-dragging') are evident in the two communities.

Revised Concepts of Participation

Discussion so far has avoided a definitive or universalist approach to participatory development. It has also revealed that any notion as widely applicable—and applied—is capable of considerable ideological manipulation, and moreover that its application and interpretation are highly context-bound. A revised approach is now expounded that utilizes strands from the various interpretations outlined above and that is of relevance in examining issues of participatory development in the context of changing production relations in areas such as Lan Sak.

Two emergent themes in the foregoing discussion of participation have been the determination by various actors of the course of their own lives and the involvement of those hitherto excluded. More generally expressed, these are the basic themes of control and power. These themes relate directly to issues of production and co-operation discussed in the two preceding chapters, necessitating a reconsideration of participation as it applies to the political economy of Lan Sak agriculture.

Participation and Production

A striking feature of the programmes involving the discourse of participation in Lan Sak described above is that they are only marginally concerned with production *per se*. Some of the training programmes include agricultural advice and some of the TC projects involve construction of infrastructure with a direct or indirect bearing on production—such as irrigation facilities or roads, but most activities under this heading are concerned with administrative or ideological aspects of development. None enter into the area of production relations. This tendency follows experience elsewhere in Asia, as evidenced by a set of ten participatory studies in seven countries, which show that the majority of participatory projects are peripheral to the economic mainstream and therefore have little effect on productivity of the poor. The reason for this is that most projects bypass the issue of the share of the poor in the main production process (for example, wages, tenants' shares, access to inputs) and try to work outside the main economy, where the resource base is correspondingly small (Mehta, 1981). In Lan Sak, most of the project-oriented participation is likewise peripheral to the main economy.

A starting point is the role of participation in increasing (or maintaining) control over factors influencing one's own life as well as over power *vis-à-vis* the wider system, but it is considered vital to address these primary issues to areas of villagers' lives that affect their circumstances most directly. For this reason, the emphasis is on production, based on the premise that production is of importance both in itself and as a determinant of wider social relations. Since production is the basis for livelihood, the link between control over influences affecting one's life and control over factors of production is inextricable. Moreover, power within the communities under study and in relations between the communities and outside influences (notably State and capital) are closely related to production.

Movement from subsistence-oriented production towards capitalist relations of production involves steady erosion of decision-making power in a number of respects. Most basic in the political economic analysis is the alienation of labour by capital—that is, the treatment of labour as a commodity, which ultimately leads to its subsumption by capital. The process by which this occurs is complex and extremely varied, and in peasant agriculture it often occurs in disguise, in the sense that it may not involve clear-cut or immediate alienation of land or other means of production as in the classic Leninist model. Moreover, superficially capitalist specialization often provides an appearance of diversified production choices. However, from the point of view of the rural producer, these choices are increasingly illusory as parameters affecting the ultimate choice recede ever further beyond the producer's control.

It is useful to divide these parameters affecting production into two categories. The first has to do with the fact of producing for the market rather than for one's own use. This involves such areas as prices, marketing structures, transport of goods to market. In such a case, loss of control is over the value of the product, while its production may remain unchanged from subsistence methods. In an ideal case with no other influences, a producer faces a straight trade-off between personal consumption of the product and sale, retaining control over everything but the terms of sale. The second set of parameters has to do with restructuring of the production process itself, whereby control is lost over factors of production. These include land, labour, tillage, and material inputs. The first case is one of commoditization of produce, the second of commoditization of factors of production. The first is typical of peasant agriculture,[10] while the second is a common feature of Green Revolution technologies and associated changes in production relations. In the context of the present study, the first is an idealized representation of Ban Dong rice agriculture, whereby traditional production methods are utilized and only rice surplus to subsistence requirements is sold. The second case, however, is representative of Ban Mai, where production is not only almost entirely market-oriented, but also itself heavily commoditized.

Alternatively, the subjective experience of rural producers can be considered. This reveals a progressive loss of control over work processes in the move from use of family labour and reciprocal labour exchange to day labouring and contracted extended employment. In addition, subsumption leads to subjective experience of loss of control over what is normally classed as family labour. This phenomenology of class process is an important reminder of the non-materialist aspect of polarization. Together with the changes described in Chapter 5, such an analysis suggests that, hitherto, development has been notably anti-participatory in effect. Given that commoditization, first of agricultural produce and then of the production process itself, involves progressive loss of control, participation as a regaining, maintaining, or increasing of control cannot side-step the issue of production relations.

While official participatory development schemes fail to attack this problem, NGOs concern themselves both in their analyses and in some cases in practical action with production. Broadly, there are two schools of thought among NGO developers. The first, which may be termed 'avoidance', is to aim for self-sufficiency, concentrating first and foremost on subsistence production.[11] Many regard this approach as trying to 'swim against the current', for many determinants of production (for example, debt, consumer ideology) pre-empt any such return. Atavism is criticized by Scott (1976: 206), who regards the self-help approach as retreatist, for

> it involves 'making do' with the resources at hand rather than recapturing the surplus taken in taxes and rents by the state and landowners. A large share of the community's land and its product, after all, is now controlled by outsiders. Most of the opportunities for employment, education, and assistance are no longer in the hands of villagers and even the effort to minimize external demands for taxes and rents requires connections, directly or indirectly [*sic*], with the external world.

The alternative strategy, which can be termed 'engagement', involves altering the power balance within the system in order to increase control over production. Because of the limited power of the individual rural producer, this usually involves co-operative efforts.

Participation and Co-operation

The main NGO rationale for co-operation is to allow individuals greater bargaining power and potential for mobilization of resources as a group than any of them would have on their own. In seeking greater control over production, therefore, co-operative endeavour is often a necessary aspect of participation. Co-operative marketing is the main way of increasing bargaining power so as to establish control over the value of produce. In the case of controlling the production process itself, co-operation extends to credit arrangements, labour organization, tillage, and in exceptional cases communal production.

The problem for co-operation is determining who co-operates with whom, for what, and for whose benefit. The difficulty of establishing norms and preventing free-riders in any co-operative enterprise has been noted. In the struggle for participation through increased control, the problem can only start to be resolved by consideration of where or to whom control has gone. For example, has control over surplus gone to persons or mechanisms external to the community? Is production controlled by key individuals within the community? Only when such questions are answered can forms of co-operation be established.

This raises a common dilemma faced by co-operative initiatives in the context of village society: should co-operative action involve a relatively homogeneous socio-economic group, or should a heterogeneous group be involved? The advantages of the former rest with the commonality of interest that lies within a more uniform group and the correspondingly reduced potential for internal conflict. The advantages of the latter include the increased material resources and social influence that can be brought to bear on behalf of the group by inclusion of more powerful elements within the community. The generally non-exclusive nature of Thai village society, in which there are no traditional caste boundaries, does not lend itself to exclusive organization of the poor. Latterly, exclusion has occurred at the other end of the spectrum where a village '(high) society' has emerged (Turton, 1984b: 30–1). This clearly poses a problem for co-operative attempts to establish control that has been usurped within the community.

Participation and Lan Sak Agriculture

Broadly formulated, participation is concerned with establishing control over factors determining production decisions, and in redressing power imbalances that result from iniquitous production relations. A general desire for participation in this wider sense explains many courses of action taken by rural producers in the two communities under study, and subjective experiences reveal the importance of control and power in determining strategies of livelihood.

In Chapter 5, we saw evidence of loss of control over factors of production as a result of the change from subsistence-oriented production in the relatively isolated forest community to commercialization in the context of rural development. Family and reciprocal labour, determined by social relations internal to the community and established by the participants themselves, have given way to wage labour controlled by cash arrangements, placing control in the hands of those with cash resources—that is, the more powerful within and even outside the community. Control over land has in many cases passed out of the hands of poorer villagers as a result of debt obligation, either through outright sale or through effective mortgaging to debtors. Rising land prices are another way of concentrating land ownership in the hands of a few villagers or outsiders. Control over production has been further undermined by changes in the production process itself. Control over tillage is often in the hands of a few tractor owners, while control over inputs rests with village traders. Access to these increasingly essential factors of agricultural production requires cash, control over which is concentrated in the hands of village traders, agricultural middlemen, and state credit institutions, who use this as leverage for control over agricultural production decisions. One stage removed, production decisions are affected by price changes that are determined in Bangkok and Chicago, over which producers have no control.

The subjective experience of this loss of control is expressed in a number of ways. One such expression is found in the categorization of forms of labour control, from own-account production, through reciprocal labourer to hired day labourer, extended contract labourer, and (figuratively) 'low-down slave'. The implication is that own-account production involves greatest control over one's own labour and, by extension, over production. This is evidenced by the fact that family labour is almost exclusively used before any other type of labour, except by the few households with sufficient means to be able to limit family-labour use to a supervisory role. Particularly indicative of the premium placed on control afforded by use of family labour is its use in tasks where the implicit return is substantially below the going wage rate. The maintenance of reciprocal exchange arrangements where possible demonstrates a preference for relying on resources over which family and community maintain intrinsic control. The uncertainty of relying on hired labour arrangements is twofold. In periods of peak activity, competition with better-off members of the community means having to pay higher wage rates to secure labour. Meanwhile, an existence as permanent labourer is precarious, involving day-to-day uncertainty over livelihood. The contrast between being a labourer and working for oneself is expressed in the feeling that as a debtor of middlemen, village traders, or even BAAC, one becomes a labourer on one's own land, since production decisions and even choice of crop may be determined by the creditor. The low status of having to depend on day-to-day employment for livelihood is expressed by one landless labourer in the expectation that his teenage children, currently working in Bangkok, 'probably won't *escape* [in the sense of rise above] labouring'. Many debt-ridden farmers see full-time labouring as a last resort in case of destitution through bankruptcy. In extreme cases, where the creditor's choice of crop, timing of production, or other decisions conflict most sharply with preferences of the producer, it is not uncommon to hear the expressed feeling of being 'their low-down slave'. Where the control is lost to less readily identifiable or more anonymous factors, expressions such as 'being squeezed by the economy' are common.

Loss of control by one group is complemented by its assumption by another. Control over labour is enhanced by those with access to cash. Control over land by creditors and control over specific aspects of production by tractor owners and village traders gives them control over production in a wider sense. Control over production by capital, including international capital, is mediated by local credit and marketing structures. Whereas loss of control over the value of produce in the relatively isolated and undifferentiated community was to outside traders, the loss of control over production suffered in the differentiated community is in the first instance to fellow villagers. The implications for co-operative attempts to increase participation through re-establishment of such control are clear, and they signal the repeated failure of community development efforts that take an undifferentiated approach.

If Ban Dong actually matched the ideal case postulated above, loss of control would be primarily to external traders who would have little control over production within the community. In fact, debt, diversification into market-oriented cash cropping, and village-level differentiation have led to increased control over production by key village traders. Nevertheless, the dominance of rice in the village economy and the maintenance of traditional methods of tillage and labour sharing have made it possible for many to retain control over most aspects of production. This is particularly true in subcommunities such as Bung Khiew, where differentiation is relatively minor and is based on ownership of different amounts of land rather than on exploitative relations between villagers. However, consumerism and crop failures as a result of inability to secure control over water have exacerbated debt, giving outsiders increased control over production within the community.

In Ban Mai, this process is much further advanced, both because of the ecology of the area which restricts subsistence-based production, and because of the accessibility afforded by the ALRO road network that enables specialization in production for the market. In Ban Mai, loss of control has been to three main groups: tractor owners, village traders and suppliers, and creditors. However, as we saw in Chapter 5, these are largely the same few influential villagers who invest surplus capital in all three of these lucrative enterprises, securing increasing control over village production.

So far, the role of the State in this loss of control by the majority of rural producers has not been discussed. At a basic level, it can be seen that the emphasis on roads, electricity and associated consumer culture, together with an ideology of bringing prosperity or civilization as described in Chapter 2, plus BAAC credit and associated high-input agriculture are all part of the ethos of individualistic capitalist development. Specifically in the case of Ban Mai, state control is heavily felt in the stipulated settlement pattern, which places important constraints on production. Resistance to residence in the nucleated settlement can be seen as an expression of a desire for control in the area of production. Invariably, ability to keep a close eye on one's land, raise chickens, plant fruit trees, get in some work before breakfast, and other aspects of the convenience of production on the isolated homestead were advantages most keenly extolled by those who had held out against resettlement in 1984–5.

More fundamental is the role of rural development in providing the State with access to village structures. The principal official structures for villager participation are now the TC and VC. Yet if we examine the membership of these bodies, we find that they are in the hands of the same people who are assuming control of the village economy, particularly in Ban Mai. At the same time, they are taking on the role of minor state functionaries by virtue of their new rural development role.

In the context of Lan Sak agriculture, what participatory strategies exist to regain control over production? Certain individual strategies were discussed in Chapter 5, and these included moving from the area altogether. Forest encroachment is a means of regaining control over the basic factor of production—land—and escaping from the constraints of capital in a subsistence-oriented existence. Urban migration represents an adaptation to the market economy, in which cash is the means of securing control over key factors of production. This latter move is more often a desperate attempt to avoid further loss of control, rather than a means of enhancing long-term control over agricultural production.

Within the community, constraints imposed by local conditions impair participatory co-operation. The intensification of work in Ban Mai leaves the majority with little free time for socializing, not to mention involvement in meetings; such are the luxuries of village élites. This is not such a problem in Ban Dong where the agricultural off-season is a period of socializing and co-operative activity, and when there is still considerable time available for organizing co-operative activity. However, in

Ban Dong as in Ban Mai, the very size of the administrative community until the 1988 subdivision represented an obstacle to co-operative development, since the increasing role of the State meant that organization was more along lines of administrative convenience than of natural communities. The success of Bung Khiew initiatives can be traced partly to the involvement of a cohesive natural community rather than an artificial and cumbersome administrative unit.

Issues of Control

We now turn to specific issues of control faced by villagers in Ban Dong and Ban Mai in the context of change. Control is a two-way process in that individuals can control and can be controlled. The tension that this creates underlies the following discussion of social and administrative structures, leadership, and uncertainty and threat in the two communities under study.

Social and Administrative Structures

Traditional structures in Lan Sak such as kinship, patron-clientage, land rights, and water users' groups have emerged as a set of implicit agreements legitimized in local cultural norms and expectations. Control over labour is achieved by means of family bonds and neighbourly reciprocation. Control over land is secured by recognition of rights by others in the community, despite the fact that no legal title deeds have been issued. Control over water is attained by establishment of a co-operative group within the community. The means by which such structures are established are indigenous to the community, affording an inherent legitimacy.

New forms, on the other hand, are exogenous. Rural development provides an aegis under which standardized structures can be imposed on village society. Most of these are implemented in the name of enhancing control by villagers over wider societal resources as part of the incorporative process. However, the terms under which such control is exercised are themselves controlled by the designers of the new development structures, and in as much as they replace indigenous forms, they may thus represent a loss of control within the community. This contradiction can be illustrated by reference to specific programmes in state-led rural development strategy, under which apparently co-operative structures may serve to accelerate processes of individualization and lead to a loss of control by poorer rural producers.

As was illustrated by the account in Chapter 5, a major problem faced by producers, especially in Ban Mai, is the rising investment cost of commercial agriculture, due both to inflated costs of inputs and to changing ecological conditions. Demand for credit and associated usury have been eased by the expansion of institutional co-operative credit, particularly that of BAAC. Such a trend may be seen to represent a step towards rational, equitable, and co-operative participation in the market economy by small farmers. Certainly such credits represent one of the government's major financial commitments in its rural development programme and are presented as welfare measures to ease the burden of usury from the small farmer's back.

Yet any programme that increases the involvement of rural producers in commercial agriculture also serves to remove them from decisions affecting production. Associated with BAAC credit, moreover, are stipulations as to the type and quantity of inputs to be used, and credit is given partly in kind. The only credit normally given in cash is expressly for payment of wages or hire of machinery. BAAC credit is thus heavily biased against peasant agriculture and is designed to hasten adoption of capitalist production relations. It is also biased against any major change in the agricultural regime, particularly relevant in Ban Mai where present agricultural practices are causing rapid environmental deterioration. While this is not to suggest that BAAC itself is responsible for adoption of such practices, these biases do mean a loss of control over production, and they represent a contradiction in terms of survival of the small independent producer. Meanwhile, the co-operative element is for the convenience and security of BAAC rather than a means of enhancing the bargaining position of group members, and the credit provided is part of the individualization of production that was described in the previous chapter.

Another form of co-operation that is supposed to increase community control over resources is the range of projects initiated by the Community Development Department (CDD). CDD discourse emphasizes its own mode of community participation, expressed as 'coming in to take part' (*kaankhaomaa mii suanruam*). CDD provides no budget, and villagers provide unpaid labour and donate materials for schemes such as a day-care centre. The housewives' and associated savings groups are run by villagers through committees. In principle, therefore, these group projects of *klum* offer villagers increased opportunities for improving control over their own welfare.

In fact, these *klum* have been used as a means of enforcing participation on the terms of outsiders and key individuals within the village, as in the case of housewives' groups described in the previous chapter. Control of the terms of participation is in the hands of state functionaries, who determine the standardized forms of such groups. Day-to-day running of and benefit from the groups is controlled by a small minority of village 'society', while the only association related to production, the savings group, is limited to better-off members of the community, since the treasurer refuses loans to anyone of insufficient status so as to ensure prompt repayment.

Bureaucratization of procedure is another aspect of innovation on outsiders' terms. Supposedly participatory structures become channels of access from State into village. Proliferation of committees and rules is a component of *klum* in general, but most prominent in the current rural development strategy is the *tambon* council as the corner-stone of the popular participation programme. Through a combination of bureaucratic and nominally democratic procedures, villagers now have, in principle, a say in requesting certain projects and thereby gaining access to state development resources. Yet the TC is merely consultative *vis-à-vis* the state bureaucracy. Actual decisions over the use of resources are made by the latter, and the TC has no independent source of revenue or independent legal status. The five-year plan presented by the TC was described to the author by one NESDB official as being a kind of 'menu' from which government departments could order at their own whim (or, incidentally, have dishes made to order). The drawing up of projects is done by the village elders, village heads, and *kamnan* who make up the TC, with advice from technical personnel provided by the district office and local headmaster, who acts as secretary. The status and education of the latter give them a disproportionate say that easily goes beyond their advisory role. Village representatives are free to consult villagers—or not to consult them—in their proposal of projects, and the nature of village meetings is such as to minimize participation in project formulation or other TC responsibilities.

Leadership

Control through social and administrative structures is not established by an automatic process of mutual assent, even in the relatively cohesive indigenous community. As we saw in Chapter 2, early leadership in the person of the *khon to* was an important element in the making and enforcing of rules in Ban Dong and Thung Khaa. Likewise, development initiatives rely on new forms or adaptation of older forms of leadership. However, control through leaders first implies control over leaders by their constituency, so that leaders are representative of their communities. The corollary is that non-representative leaders reduce control exercised by the community as a whole and may increase outside control over it.

The concept of leader (*phuu nam*) is indigenous to the community. Several categories embrace this position. Other than *khon to*, another category is the *phuu yai*, used for someone of exceptional status. Thai social hierarchy is often defined in terms of *phuu yai* and *phuu noi* (literally, large and small people respectively; see Girling, 1981: 38–9). *Hua naa* means 'head', or someone with some authority. *Naai*, or 'boss' is a remnant of the quasi-feudal (*sakdina*) division of Thai society into *naai* and *phrai* (serfs). The formal leadership posts are *kamnan*, the top leadership position in Ban Dong for some fifty years, and *phuu yai baan* (village head). A recent category is that of *phuu mii ithiphon*, or simply *ithiphon*, meaning 'those with influence', referring to persons with unofficial and often illegally wielded authority.

The extent to which leadership and feared authority are coincident in the indigenous community is illustrated by the terms given to the two wild animals most feared in the early Ban Dong and Ban Mai communities. Tigers were known as *kamnan*, while elephants were referred to as *phuu yai baan*. The *khon to* attained and maintained his position by a combination of patronage, respect, and fear. Yet, ultimately, a leader depended on resources that could be mustered from within the community. Local resources were the basis of the village economy and the polity was such that support came from within rather than without the community. In the limited dealings with state authorities, the leader served as representative of the community, and in the case of Thung Khaa this for long involved a resistance to state intervention through land reform, deforestation, and construction of roads. Negotiations for supplying a village teacher were carried out by the *khon to*, whom both villagers and government officials saw as representative of the community in dealings with the outside as well as in organization and adjudication of village affairs.

It is a misconception to view the isolated forest village as a homogeneous and democratic community. Differences in economic status predate changes in production relations, and leadership was exercised according to 'the law of the forest' (*kodmaai paa*).[12] However, differences in economic status were limited and based on varying scales of production in an undifferentiated production regime, so that exploitative relations were external to the community. While the law of the forest appears undemocratic in form, it is based on normative concepts of justice established by the villagers themselves. The ultimate sanction over village leaders rests with villagers, and the outcome of struggles depends on the resources that the leader is able to muster within the community. The *khon to*'s resistance to changes associated with land reform was in part due to a sense of responsibility to the community if, as he expected, things were to go wrong.

Opening up of the community involves a number of changes with regard to control over, and control through, leadership. On the one hand, incorporation into the national polity and rural development programmes means adherence to apparently democratic norms. The village heads and *kamnan* must now be elected, committees are set up in the name of community participation, and apparently arbitrary systems of justice and enforcement are replaced by defined legal statutes. However, the role of the new leaders can only be properly understood in terms of changing production relations alongside the changing polity. Opening up of the village and associated differentiation results not only in increasingly divergent economic fortunes of individual members of the community, but also in internalization of exploitative relationships within the community. Meanwhile, as the village economy and polity becomes ever more dependent on external forces, the position of village leaders as representatives of the community is diminished as they come to depend on external resources and hence are seen as representatives of State and capital within the village. This is best exemplified by the position of the *kamnan*, village heads, and village committees in Ban Dong and Ban Mai.

The Ban Dong *kamnan* have always come from among the Lao section of the community. In the past there was little to distinguish the *kamnan* from others in economic status. Contact with officials was rare. In the one instance of abuse of position, the *kamnan* was replaced by the community. In contrast, the present *kamnan* (also village head) is exceptionally wealthy. Following forest clearance by TPC, he sold off large areas of land in Bung Khiew and elsewhere at many times the price he had paid for them. Although he still rents out land, he does not farm, and his main business interests lie outside the community. Until 1984, he owned the only air-conditioned restaurant in the provincial town 50 kilometres away. More importantly, his wife, who is a Provincial Assembly member, runs a construction business, and this wins contracts for most local development schemes, in particular road construction. In 1984, she won a 100,000-baht tender for reconstruction of the bridge that had been washed away in the previous year's floods. The *kamnan* used his position to summon labour from within the village, and wood was cut from nearby forest reserve land. Villagers received little or no payment and estimate that a profit of at least 50,000 baht was made. A similar case of corrupt practice was recounted in the case of the previous year's road construction into Bung Khiew. Meanwhile, the position of the *kamnan* as village head provides opportunities for self-enrichment and patronage. Registration of births and deaths requires a small 'service charge'. At election time, the local member of parliament (MP) disburses large sums via the *kamnan*. State welfare is at the discretion of the *kamnan*, involving hand-outs of blankets, relief in case of flooding or fire, and free health treatment cards for the poor. Awareness of corruption and favouritism is evident in local discourse, particularly that of the poor. There is talk of 'leaky money' in the context of development funds, together with complaints that the only ones to benefit from the *kamnan*'s use of funds are his relatives and underlings.

The Thung Khaa *kamnan*'s wealth is based more on local resources. Following land reform and deforestation, he made large sums in land sales to new settlers in Ban Mai and through forestry subcontracting and illegal forest poaching. He gained favour with the district office by supporting land reform and road construction, and he enjoys the same benefits by virtue of his position as does the Ban Dong *kamnan*. The Ban Mai village head is also from one of the older Thung Khaa families. He was elected unopposed for his youthfulness and energy, but there is now general disillusionment with his favouritism, inefficiency, and corrupt practices. In one incident witnessed by the author, his position as minor state functionary enhanced his ability to summon labour from a household that had its own urgent tasks to attend to, but which dared not refuse for fear of being unable to call on his help in dealing with the authorities in the future. He runs one of the two local bus services to Uthaithani, acts as a money-lender, and rents land belonging to debtors; he is a large employer of labour for his cassava planting and processing. Both he and the *kamnan* have received sums of money from the local MP at election time and in exchange for recruiting labour for the MP's pineapple plantation in Cha-am.

The VCs in the two villages are somewhat more heterogeneous in composition, although the poorest sections are not represented in either community. However, the VC is dominated by the village head and one or two other influential people. In Ban Mai, the *kamnan*'s eldest brother, who is also *tambon* doctor and one of the wealthiest traders and tractor owners in Ban Mai, is also an influential member of the VC. The same is true of Maen (Case 6, in Chapter 5) in Ban Dong. In Ban Mai, as of 1986, the VC members are allowed to carry shotguns as part of the self-defence development village scheme, adding a potentially repressive aspect to their role. They are identified closely with the tractor owners and traders and referred to collectively as the 'heads of the village'. Their position is clearest at village meetings and on community work days. In 1984, the King's birthday was set aside by the district office as such a work day, and the village head decreed that grass along the road edges should be cut. The VC took up a supervisory role, not actually taking part in the manual work, provoking comments that 'the VC ride on [our] backs [literally, necks]', a traditional expression of exploitation.

The connection between economic status and official leadership position is not coincidental. To begin with, the amount of time that a village head has to spend at meetings and other official engagements would make it difficult for most villagers to take on the position. In the local cultural context, 'to be of consequence' (literally, 'to have face and eyes') is increasingly linked to economic status, and this is a prerequisite to election. More directly, large sums are now spent by contenders for such positions since the potential rewards are large, though not so if measured only in terms of official salary (400 baht per month for a village head in 1984–5). The village head is expected to be able to entertain officials or other outsiders, and this is financially impossible for most villagers.

This is not to suggest that all leaders are concerned purely with personal benefit or that those so motivated are entirely devoid of respect from within the community. The culmination of the *Songkran* new year water festival, bathing of the Buddha image, is preceded in Ban Dong by bathing of the *kamnan* as a sign of respect and ritual washing away of antagonisms. Until recently, the *kamnan* was popular for his informality and, significantly, in that he 'left (you) alone' (from official matters). However, the trend is for leaders to depend less and less on the indigenous economic and social resources of the community for their position and more and more on external resources of State and capital. Many of these resources enter the village via such leaders in the name of rural development programmes or as indirect results of changes in production relations that are themselves part of the underlying rural development strategy.

A final point to note is that so called 'natural leaders' do emerge, such as in the case of Boi in Bung Khiew. A key role played by such leaders is as a link with the outside, as spokesperson who can represent villagers' interests. Boi's role in the rice barn controversy and the Bung Khiew irrigation channel, both described in the previous chapter, demonstrates this clearly. Such a leader requires a number of qualities, including willingness to represent community before personal interests, ability to communicate in official language, a non-confrontational approach which often means involvement in many official programmes (see Turton,

1984a: 104), and the trust of the local community.

In summary, the opening up of the village is not the beginning of the process of differentiation. Rather, it marks a change in the control exercised through village leadership as a result of the changed structural position of such leaders. The leadership function is increasingly oriented to that of intermediary between village and bureaucracy and between petty producer and external capital, giving external resources a more important place in maintaining the leader's standing as they play an increasingly important role in the political economy of the village. At the same time, differentiation is a consequence of increasing internal commoditization of labour, which means that those in positions of power are now in direct exploitative relationships with other villagers. Lost is the sanction that dependence on local or internal resources afforded. Meanwhile, control over village institutions and economy by State and external capital is facilitated by the minor functionary status that formal leaders now take on. In this context, leadership of participatory initiatives usually requires the emergence of alternative leaders who may or may not pose a challenge to existing formal leaders.

Uncertainty and Threat

A third dimension of control relates to the certainty or otherwise that decisions or courses of action are going to lead to the intended results. Peasant livelihood is normally considered to be one fraught with uncertainty, and many of the measures associated with rural development are at least nominally concerned with reducing this uncertainty. In particular, the vagaries of the weather and other natural elements are to be overcome by technological innovations that are commonly associated with 'green revolution' measures. However, the alternative face of such change is a different sort of uncertainty that results from changes in production relations as a part of the incorporative rural development strategy: 'The consequence [of change] is a substantial loss of autonomy and the exchange of one type of uncertainty for another involving greater dependency on others, on remote economic developments, and on shifting priorities in government policy' (Hainsworth, 1982: 16). This new uncertainty serves as an obstacle to increasing popular participation through control over production.

A recently deforested area such as Lan Sak differs from other contexts of rural development in that natural uncertainties actually increase over time. The degradation of soils, variability of rainfall, and increase in pests was documented in Chapter 4, and these have led to decreased control over the environment by agricultural producers. It is thus easy to understand why Lan Sak farmers see many of the modern inputs of fertilizer, irrigation, and pesticides as compensatory rather than as positive measures of improvement in line with the extension worker's perspective. This is particularly the case in a situation of declining yields.

A second set of uncertainties results from the commercial orientation of agriculture. Whereas in the subsistence-oriented community, local resources could be used for production, control over which was achieved by community-based arrangements, credit is now needed for the increasingly capital-intensive production. Uncertainty over credit stems from the dependence on middlemen or BAAC, both outside community control. Equally important, creditors gain control over debtors' production, leading for example to uncertainties in ploughing schedules as in the case of Lak (Case 10 in Chapter 5). Increased dependence on the market leads to uncertainties over prices, and Table 7.1 shows the basis for this uncertainty in terms of fluctuation of crop prices observed in Ban Dong and Ban Mai. Marketing is one of the main uncertainties for producers in Ban Dong and Ban Mai. Most depend on the middleman coming to the homestead, and prices can vary from week to week. A common tactic in Ban Dong is to agree provisionally on a price; a fortnight later, when the lorry arrives and the sale is made, the price has fallen. Middlemen use their access to marketing information, control over the scales, and determination of quality to their own advantage, at least in the eyes of the farmer. Indeed, so low are the margins that it would be difficult for the local middleman to make any substantial profit without some cheating.

Another uncertainty arises from the increasing dependence on labouring income for subsistence. Whereas a certain amount of planning is possible in one's own production, day-to-day wage labouring depends on the demands of the labour market, which in agriculture vary from season to season and from year to year. In Ban Mai, there are many occasions when an employer requests labour for the following day at distant fields and then fails to turn up to collect the day labourers, by which time it is too late to arrange an alternative daily income. In the longer run, families planning on a more steady income can be similarly misled. Two examples occurred during 1984–5. The first was a proposal by the local MP to employ labour from Ban Mai and surrounding villages on his pineapple plantation in Cha-am. The *kamnan* and village head were to arrange transport, charging each labourer 300 baht (the return fare by public transport would have cost less than 200 baht). Originally, the leaving date was to be the end of March. This was repeatedly delayed, until finally at the end of the dry season the scheme was called off, and those waiting to go had little or no chance of local employment in the meantime. In the event, several ended up seeking work in Bangkok

TABLE 7.1
Crop Prices Received by Farmers in Lan Sak, 1984–1986

	Crop Prices in Baht per Kwien	
Year	*Rice*	*Maize*
1984	2,700–2,900	4,000–4,200
1985	2,900–3,100	3,200–3,800
1986	1,700–2,400	2,300–2,600

Source: Fieldwork, 1984–5; follow-up visit.

instead, including Phad (Case 7, Chapter 5). A second prospect of sustained employment that fell through was the reservoir built by ALRO above Ban Mai. The planning of this was done without consulting villagers, but it was rumoured that it would employ many labourers for several months at ALRO minimum-wage rates, nearly double the agricultural wage. In the event, ALRO brought in its own contractors, and much of the construction was carried out using heavy machinery.[13]

An important aspect of uncertainty in connection with changes in agricultural production pertains to knowledge systems. Local knowledge has been downgraded, not only in terms of its status but also in terms of its relevance to the new production regime. Whereas subsistence production in the isolated community utilized a body of locally acquired and adapted knowledge, use of new inputs and production techniques requires a body of knowledge that cannot as readily be assimilated by local producers. As a result, crop failures may be wrongly interpreted, effects of applications of new inputs may lead to unexpected side-effects on both plants and users, and long-term effects of new inputs may not appear until it is too late to rectify. This uncertainty is reinforced by a lack of knowledge of local conditions by extension workers, making it difficult for farmers to turn to them in adapting new inputs.

On the project side of rural development, uncertainty takes on many forms. A basic element of uncertainty concerns responsibility for infrastructural work. In the isolated community, all community schemes were the joint responsibility of villagers, usually at the behest of a community leader. In Bung Khiew, for example, roads were constructed by the villagers, while in Thung Khaa villagers constructed their own school. At present, the uncertainty over whether Government or villagers are responsible for such projects often leaves work undone, as in the case of road repair after the 1983 floods. The result is described by the old *khon to* in Thung Khaa as follows: 'now you can't go anywhere [literally, walk], nor can you plant rice [in reference to the land the roads have "eaten"]'. The piecemeal and haphazard way in which the REGP scheme is carried out also leads to uncertainty and work left undone. One reason is the uncertainty both by villagers and local government officials over whether the principal aim of work is to create employment or to build up rural infrastructure. In 1984, work on a dike around Ban Dong school to prevent flooding was stopped halfway through construction since the piecework rates, measured in cubic metres of earth, became less and less attractive as earth needed to be brought from further and further afield. Eventually machinery had to be brought in to finish the job. In 1985 and 1986, no local labour was used at all in the water jar construction for which REGP money was used, since skilled artisans were required for the standardized model of jar stipulated by the district office. Instead, a contractor was brought in with his own team, making a profit of over 100,000 baht after labour and materials.

Such uncertainty about government programmes among villagers, resulting from deviation from principles or lack of clarity about such principles in the first place, is paralleled by uncertainty within the local administration over responsibility for particular programmes. The duplication and lack of co-ordination among departments at every level was noted in Chapter 2. This impinges most strongly on villagers' experience at village meetings or training programmes, where it is not uncommon to hear the district agricultural officer talking about the benefits of giving up drink, the police chief about raising chickens, the community development officer on the dangers of communism, the health officer about loyalty to the King, the local headmaster about the need for vigilance and national security in the face of imminent invasion by the Vietnamese, and the abbot about the need to follow the Government's advice on rural development.

Associated with the contradictions inherent in State-led rural development is uncertainty produced by an ambiguous development discourse. The very word 'development' is at once associated with general improvement in livelihood and with programmes that impinge on one's time and freedom of action. The term for civilization or prosperity, which is often equated with development, is also associated with debt and other consequences of commercialization. In the words of one long-standing Ban Dong resident, buffalo theft commenced 'when civilization started to arrive [from lower down—that is, on the plains]'. Convenience that is often associated with roads and electricity benefits those who can afford transport and connection costs. Yet longer-standing Ban Mai residents associate the coming of money-lenders with the coming of the roads. The term 'to watch over' as a paternalistic aim of development is used ambiguously in the need for those in positions of authority to 'watch over everyone', translatable alternately as 'take care of' in the welfare sense and 'keep an eye on' in the sense of surveillance. Similarly, 'security' implies safety against external threat while giving powers that increase repressive potential within the village. The ambiguity of the idea of unity has been referred to in Chapter 6, footnote 16. Last, participation itself is used to mean semi-compulsory joining of official schemes in the name of giving villagers a say in their own lives.

A final aspect of uncertainty concerns the issue of legitimacy. In the face of rapid expansion of state involvement in village affairs through its rural development strategy, the legitimacy of initiatives that do not conform with the recognized structures is called into question. An example of this uncertainty came early on in the setting up of Bung Khiew Rice Bank, whose status *vis-à-vis* the district office was a subject of some doubt and concern. A month after the first rice deposits had been made, a group of NGO workers from Chiengmai came to visit and exchange experiences with Bung Khiew villagers. The thrust of the exchange was to compare similarities and differences. This, combined with the manner of one of the visiting development workers, caused several of the villagers to suspect that they were government officials sent to spy on the group. The reasons for concern were the apparent nonconformity between the Bung Khiew group and that of the visitors, and the assumption that any visitors who were not farmers must be officials (some villagers commented, 'You only have to look at their feet to see that they have never planted rice!').

Uncertainty and control impinge most forcefully in the form of threat. This can initially be divided into two areas, threat by the State and threat by non-state influences, but it will become apparent that the two are ultimately inseparable. Fear of state reprisal for illegal initiatives, as evidenced by the above account, are not unjustified. Until approximately the start of the Fifth Plan (1982), the climate of suspicion in rural Thailand was extreme. Use of particular words by villagers, association with visiting students or NGO workers, voluntary spirit, and a number of other traits were enough to place someone under suspicion (see Turton, 1984b: 51). Although this climate has relaxed considerably, there are still many ways in which the watchful eye of the administration is kept on any potential dissidence. Every village has 'volunteers' who 'listen out'. The CDD's *tambon*-level workers are responsible for keeping an ear to the ground and reporting any suspicious activity.[14] The danger of 'communist menace' is still frequently invoked, and it can be used as a generic form of accusation against non-conformists. In one Lan Sak *kamnan*'s words, you can always pick out a communist from among villagers, for 'whoever does not rely on a [money-lender] patron must have a [subversive] patron behind [him or her]'. Such insinuation is not mere rhetoric in terms of state threat, for the history of violence against leaders of movements of the rural poor is well known.[15] The policy of selective killing off of undesirables—criminals and political dissidents alike—is applied widely, particularly in northern Thailand, but also in frontier areas such as Lan Sak. At a less overtly political level, the local police are generally feared and detested in Lan Sak, commonly being referred to as 'thieves in uniform'.

However, the climate of rural violence is not generally perceived as being perpetrated directly by state authorities. More commonly feared are certain influential people, and these are increasingly those in official leadership positions. When asked in private conversation why no voice of protest is raised at the sometimes blatant abuses of position by the Ban Dong *kamnan*, villagers who complain of such abuse commonly reply that they are 'afraid of being shot in the head'. The general level of violence in Lan Sak over relatively minor conflicts of interest provides a constant reminder of the basis for such fears. The case of Dam in Chapter 5 illustrates the extent to which blatant injustices will be borne as a result of threat. Although the level of violence has declined greatly since the late 1970s (the peak period of settlement), the murder rate in 1984 was still four times the (already high) national average of 25 murders per 100,000 population. A surprisingly uniform figure of 70,000–80,000 baht was quoted on a number of occasions as the amount needed to get away with murder (literally) by bribing the local authorities.

Returning to the theme of control, we find that the uncertainty imparted by the atmosphere of threat is a means of maintaining control over action and discourse on the one hand, and preventing the assumption of control by independent bargaining power on the other, through what Turton (1984b: 59ff.) terms 'the ideological mediation of fear'. This is the combination of hegemonic rule by establishment of legitimacy and forceful suppression by creation of a climate of fear of dissidence. In Lan Sak in 1984–5, rural development programmes loomed large in the legitimization of the State at the village level, giving state functionaries control over village affairs through key intermediaries, whose position relied increasingly on power divested legitimately via external links, and semi-legally or illegally as part of the collusion of what Turton (1989) refers to as 'local powers'.

Issues of Power

A political-economic interpretation of participation concerns basic issues of power. In the UNRISD analysis, the aim of participation is to empower the powerless. Accordingly, participation involves the recognition and resolution of certain contradictions. This inevitably addresses conflicts of interest. In most community development analyses, such conflicts are seen, if at all, as existing between the community and the outside—for example, between village and external State. However, differentiation associated with incorporation of village by State and capital alters the axes of power struggle, and many contradictions are internalized within the community. The emergence of these contradictions internal to village polity and economy can be traced to local transformations of state power and production relations.

State Power and Participation

Stephen Young (1968) characterized the Thai village of the 1960s as a 'non-participatory democracy'. It is a democracy because of the sanction held by villagers over their leaders. It is non-participatory because of four axiomatic principles guiding action in the political sphere: limited government; minimal public involvement with government; government legitimization through concern with the public interest; and obedience to authority. These guides to political behaviour reflect the traditional separation between State and village affairs, whereby state authorities have responsibility for defined functions, mostly connected with the provision of public infrastructure. The separation of functions or duties is such that villagers play no part in state affairs, which are thus left to those who wish to get involved in politics. Young (1968) was cautious about the likely participation of villagers to be expected in the Developing Democracies Programme (part of the Thai–US development–containment programme in the 1960s) with which he was concerned; he placed greater faith in establishing the presence of state power or authority at the village level, in line with his fourth axiom, so as to maintain its role as the 'significant other' (Young, 1968: 873–86). The rural development strategy pursued since that time has involved a combination of this presence with a more visible incorporation.

The normal rationalization of the incorporative rural development strategy is that villagers have hitherto been excluded from the management and fruits of extra-village resources, so that the village has not played its due role in state affairs. Democratization means providing the structures that give villagers some hold over supravillage resources, in principle making state authorities accountable to villagers rather than vice versa. As we have seen, however, the reality of incorporation is that state authorities gain an increasing influence in village affairs, and this is done partly by means of a co-optive strategy involving certain powerful individuals within the village. Thus profusion of committees, *klum*, and individual 'volunteer' positions represents an entry of the State into village affairs, in the name of villager participation in affairs of the wider polity. The potentially repressive element of such an entry is expressed clearly by one such volunteer, the deputy village head of Ban Mai, who sees in his intelligence role a duty to collect information on anyone who tries to form an independent group or stir up trouble.

The hold that this entry gives state developers over village affairs can be illustrated by reference to a key aspect of the state rural development strategy, that of holding village competitions. This epitomizes the shift in the state–village power balance in a number of ways. First, it is part of the standardization that is basic to state-led rural development. Second, it involves co-optation of village leaders. Third, it enhances the competitive element in the ethos of rural development. Fourth, it places state officials as instigators, arbiters, and beneficiaries in programmes that are, at best, of marginal relevance to the needs of the majority of villagers. Fifth, it favours short-term reward-oriented projects at the expense of long-term structural change.

A typical village competition is that held in Ban Dong in 1985. At the instigation of the district office, the Ban Dong *kamnan* entered the village for the provincial competition. The normal practice is for each district to concentrate its resources on a single village that it can show to visiting senior officials as an example of development. In this case, village development involved a number of steps. The first and most visible effort was to build bamboo fences around each house plot, in line with the current policy of having every village fenced. The purpose of this is twofold from the point of view of the administration. First, it gives the village an appearance of 'civilization' compared with the 'messy' appearance of an unfenced village. Second, it enhances control by district and village officials over villagers, expressed as 'ease of administration', since it allows for easy identification of house plots and residents. This is further enhanced by the construction of awnings and name signs at the front of each house. The fence building was effected by the constant exhortation of the *kamnan*, who threatened to withdraw all co-operation (that is, statutory services, such as issuing identity cards) from anyone who refused to comply. Villagers had to provide materials themselves, involving wood for posts, bamboo, and nails: this involved some expense, due to the shortage of naturally available materials. Despite some grumbling, most of the Ban Dong road frontage was fenced. The backs of houses were not fenced, and in Bung Khiew it was decided to take a common stand against fence building unless the *kamnan* could provide the materials, since it was felt that the fences provided no tangible benefit and that, in any case, they would soon fall into disrepair. This united stand at the regular meeting of Bung Khiew villagers to discuss the Rice Bank and other community matters raised the confidence of individuals to resist the scheme.

The non-material side of preparation for the competition was to set up eight development groups. This was done at a Ban Dong village meeting by the *kamnan*, who divided up the village and appointed group heads to be responsible for each group. Some of these were absent at the time of the meeting—for example, Yot, a Bung Khiew resident who normally has little to do with the rest of the community, now found himself head of the Bung Khiew group. The *kamnan* has since used these groups for relaying orders via the group heads, placing them in often uncomfortable positions since they are not natural leaders and the orders they carry are perceived to be the whim of the *kamnan*. The first duty was for each group to provide several 'volunteers' to go on a trip to visit a village in a neighbouring province that had won the previous year's regional competition. Those who went had to provide the 70-baht bus fare themselves, and on the day only about half the bus load turned up; after some discussion the *kamnan* agreed to pay the remainder of the charter fee. Before entering the village, the district officer gave a welcoming talk to the visiting Ban Dong villagers, in which he gave advice on how to win a competition. Most of this consisted of how to take good care of the judging committee and how to catch their eye—for example, by selecting a pretty girl to welcome the judges and to know what they were looking for. This was followed by a visit to the village, at which the villagers provided a hospitable welcome and showed the group around the model houses that had been selected for their cleanliness and conformity to set criteria.

At the meeting following the Ban Dong fence building, the district DAE officer spoke of his admiration at how the village had developed almost overnight. The material effect was less enthusiastically appreciated by some villagers, who in the past would have been able to cut across each other's land but now had to go the long way round because of the fencing. The principal benefit went to the *kamnan*, who came second in terms of the annual award of merit points, for which he received an undisclosed sum of money from the provincial administration. Had he come first, he would have received a gold medal and a revolver. Following this, however, his uncharacteristic burst of enthusiasm for village development, which had surprised many villagers who had grown accustomed to his concern for his own private business affairs, waned. By 1986, the fences had fallen into disrepair.

As a one-off event, the competition is symbolic rather than characteristic of the various aspects of exercise of state power through rural development outlined above. However, these can be expanded on with reference to the broader thrust of state-led rural development strategy in Ban Dong and Ban Mai. Standardization is a key element in this strategy and can be viewed in a number of ways. At an organizational level, standardization reflects the incorporation of village structures into the bureaucratic framework, which stresses uniformity. Thus committees, modes of operation, structures of authority, and even specific material aspects of development such as fence building are all determined by a set of rules imposed from outside and above. At a political level, standardization is part of the stress on the oneness of the Thai nation and metropolitan cultural domination. This hegemonic aspect can be seen materially in Ban Dong and Ban Mai in the awnings in front of each roadside house, many of which are painted in the red, white, and blue colours of the national flag, and some of which display pictures of the royal family and slogans extolling civic virtues that have been provided by the district office. More generally, the various *klum* and training sessions described in the previous chapter are each used as a forum for dissemination of official policy. Many of the schemes that are introduced reflect an urban orientation, both in the discourse of 'civilization' and in the material emphasis, such as construction of waste bins, imposition of fines for cattle dung on the village streets in Ban Mai, and grid pattern of roads.

The co-optation of village leaders is part of the process by which the State uses rural development as a means of gaining control within the village. The Ban Dong *kamnan* and the Ban Mai village head find it in their own economic interest as well as politically convenient to serve as the mouthpiece of the district office at the village level, even though in private conversation they attest to the superficiality of official programmes (in the words of the Ban Dong *kamnan*, such programmes 'scratch where it doesn't itch; don't scratch where it itches'). Not only do they gain the major benefits of rewards for performance in competitions, but they serve as the channels through which resources enter the village, and these resources are greater for villages which are seen as 'ready, together [for development]' than others. In this context, the advantage of the awnings described above is largely symbolic. In Yot's words, 'If they see that we're ready, together [to conform], they [district officials] will come and help in other matters.' This is confirmed in official discourse by the DAE officer's repeated analogy of district office and villages as mother and children: the child who cries the loudest (that is, the village which shows it is ready, together) gets fed (helped) first. Readiness becomes conformity, togetherness unanimity of response to superior authority.

The competitive ethos of rural development strategy is enhanced by village-level competitions. The emphasis is on doing better than one's neighbour or neighbouring village. This reinforces the consumerist ideology that affects village life to an increasing extent, as each tries to outdo or at least keep up with others in terms of gadgetry, size of ceremonial feasts, or simply in providing their children with packaged snacks at school. The feeling of not wanting to be 'ashamed before others' is exploited in exhortation of villagers by officials to join in official schemes so as not to lose individual or collective face.

The power of state officials is also enhanced by such schemes in that they serve as the effective instigators, arbiters, and beneficiaries of many programmes. The district office decides which village is to be given priority and what type of programmes are to be put into effect. Since the judges are all senior district or provincial officials, conformity with their criteria of development is the key to success. If success is achieved, the immediate reward goes to village and district-level functionaries in the form of merit points, which for village officials may mean a material reward, while salaried officials are rewarded by a double jump on the civil service promotions scale.

The power that the State achieves over organization of village society through competitions is akin to that referred to by Foucault (1977: 184–5) in his discussion of examinations:

> The examination combines the techniques of an observing hierarchy and those of a normalizing judgment. It is a normalizing gaze, a surveillance that makes it possible to qualify, to classify, and to punish. It establishes over individuals a visibility through which one differentiates them and judges them. That is why, in all the mechanisms of discipline, the examination is highly ritualized. In it are combined the ceremony of power and the form of the experiment, the deployment of force and the establishment of truth. At the heart of the procedures of discipline, it manifests the subjection of those who are perceived as objects and the objectification of those who are subjected. The superimposition of the power relations and knowledge relations assumes in the examination all its visible brilliance.

Competitions are the epitome, not the sum, of state power, just as they provide the symbol, not the substance, of its rural development strategy.

A final point to make about the rural development strategy epitomized by village competitions is the superficial and short-term orientation it gives to initiatives. It is a reflection of the power that state officials and their village representatives have over village activity that many of those involved in fence building, training programmes, and other initiatives see them as of marginal relevance to their needs, but they are unable to do other than comply, or they find compliance less costly than doing otherwise. Non-compliance does take place on occasion as in the case of Bung Khiew, and this depends in part on strong independent leadership, although Boi had no part in this particular initiative. More often, non-compliance is a fragmentary dragging of feet, which is interpreted as apathy and results in more forceful measures of compulsion, leading to the common complaint associated with development measures of feeling forced, particularly in Ban Mai. In addition, the short-term orientation leads to an association of development with superficial infrastructure, pre-emptively usurping the concept and preventing its association with more substantial structural change.

Power, Production, and Participation

It has often been noted that the powerlessness of the poor is compounded by their lack of voice (see, for example, Chambers, 1983: 131ff.). In fact, the Ban Mai villager's statement at the head of this chapter needs to be modified; what the rural poor lack is a *public* voice, but their 'hidden transcript'[16] expresses eloquently their position *vis-à-vis* various forms of power, the statement itself being one example.

In relation to the power of the State, specific rural development schemes are punned via their acronyms or other titles: *ro' pho' cho'* (Accelerated Rural Development) becomes *ruam phuak khon chua* (a gathering of the evil [corrupt]); *ko' so' cho'* (Rural Employment Generation Programme) becomes either *kin saam chan* (eat [that is, be on the take] at three levels [village head, *kamnan*, district official]) or *koong sin chaat* (cheat the life out of the nation); and *Phaen din tham Phaen din tho'ng* (land of Buddhist virtue, land of gold) becomes *Phaen din tho' Phaen din thae* (land of desperation).

The situation of the rural poor *vis-à-vis* power not directly associated with the State is expressed in statements such as (in a reference to corruption by village leaders and officials), 'Justice is at the whim of the "big boys"'. More direct statements are made with reference to specific instances of perceived injustice: '[One of the Ban Mai tractor owners] exploits the poor', in reference to the low wages he pays and the high prices he charges in his shop and for basic medical treatment, since he is also *tambon* doctor.

However, the power of the State and the power of certain individuals are not seen as entirely separate. The association between State and other local powers is captured in the following observation: 'The Government doesn't reach [us] farmers; it only gets as far as the merchants.' With reference to the police, it is often commented that they 'squeeze [literally, plough] the poor'. A vivid analogy in Ban Dong was to compare the poor with fish in a water jar, which could easily be caught; the rich are like fish in a stream, difficult to catch. Another was to liken poor villagers who use wood on their own land to 'chicks in their [officials'] hands' which (who) could be squeezed at any time, while timber contractors go scot-free if they offer bribes of the right amount.

This discourse of the poor is an articulation of the subjective reaction to exercise of power in a context of changing polity and production relations at the village level. Attempts to increase one form of control, over the vagaries of the natural environment, lead to a loss of other forms of control as a result of the change in production relations and the associated transformation of the village polity. However, this does not represent a neutral substitution of one type of control by another. The key difference is that between control, or lack of it, by people over their natural environment, and control by people over other people. The essential variable is the aspect of power.[17]

Returning to the theme of participation, the means by which control over production can be increased by the majority of rural producers becomes the key challenge, and this requires an understanding of the relationship between production and power in the two communities under study. This relationship is reviewed briefly in three main dimensions: the association of control over production in the context of changing production relations with positions of political power at the village level; the way in which exercise of power affects production; and the embryonic forms of countervailing power that show signs of emerging in indigenous attempts to retain or regain control over production.

Chapter 5 documented the coexistence of economic power and other types of power among key individuals at the village level. That this coexistence is more than coincidence is implied by the criteria for assumption of formal village leadership, and it has been shown that these positions are then reinforcing of economic status. The significance of this overlap is that decentralization of power in the name of participation, through institutions such as the TC, merely serves to decentralize inequality and reinforce or reshape, rather than replace, 'non-rational' aspects of power and economic relations.

Indirect expression of power affects production in a number of ways. The desire for control as expressed in the resettlement of Ban Mai villagers in the nucleated grid-plan settlement precludes a range of productive economic activity and makes field-cropping less convenient for those with fields at a distance from the village. Training sessions and village meetings are time-consuming, and during the agricultural season they are regarded as seriously disruptive by those with urgent tasks to attend to. Power exerted by feared individuals in several cases deprives producers temporarily or permanently of control over key means of production to which they are entitled.

Countervailing power is expressed quietly and, to most outsiders, almost invisibly. Scott emphasizes the importance of everyday resistance, as at once the 'unremitting warfare that [takes] place day in and day out' (1986: 5) and an effective if not revolutionary means of resisting demands of the State and dominant classes. Scott (1986: 22) defines everyday resistance among peasants as:

> . . . any act(s) by members of the [oppressed] class that is (are) intended either to mitigate or to deny claims (e.g. rents, taxes, deference) made on that class by superordinate classes (e.g. landlords, the state, owners of machinery, money-lenders) or to advance its own claims (work, land, charity, respect) *vis-à-vis* these superordinate classes.

Thus, although collective action is emphatically not a necessary part of resistance, intentions and symbolism or ideology are part of the act.

In Ban Mai, resistance to resettlement is justified first and foremost in terms of convenience for agricultural production, although there is also a subjective expression of the freedom from being 'forced' or 'pestered'. In the words of one who has resisted resettlement: 'Whose convenience is it [resettlement] for—ours or theirs? For them it's fine, they can keep control. Here [on the farmstead he has resisted leaving] we're out of sight and earshot, and that worries them. Yet here we can raise chickens and ducks, can get some work in before breakfast. . . .'

Although much everyday resistance is fragmentary, this particular case involves a number of homesteads in one of the older communities of Ban Mai. Other forms of resistance include the Bung Khiew refusal to build fences, and the rich discourse of everyday resistance is evident in the hidden transcript outlined above.

Participation and Rural Development in Perspective

This final section examines local rural development schemes in the revised perspective on participation discussed in this chapter. Questions considered concerning particular initiatives are listed as follows. How relevant is it to production? How does it affect relations of control and power? Whom in the community is it relevant to and in what way? The initiatives covered are those discussed in the previous chapter.

BAAC credit is clearly of immediate relevance to production. As we saw in Chapter 5, 30 per cent of credit for inputs to agriculture in Ban Dong and 18 per cent in Ban Mai come from this source. This form of credit is cheaper than non-institutional credit and, as such, it gives recipients control over inputs that would otherwise be difficult to attain. In this respect, BAAC credit as the State's principal financial commitment to agriculture in Lan Sak and elsewhere enhances participation in the high-input production regime that predominates. However, by promoting involvement in such a regime and by enforced continuation of involvement through the debt-cycle, credit on easy terms ironically serves to decrease control in the long run by those with insufficient means of production to keep their heads above water. This is manifested both directly in the credit in kind that BAAC clients are forced to take and indirectly in the loss of control over production decisions that are detailed in Chapter 5. It is ironic that many of the poorest farmers in Ban Dong and Ban Mai forego BAAC credit not only because they are excluded by virtue of their economic status from joining a BAAC group, but also sometimes because they prefer to borrow from fellow villagers over whom they feel they have some sanction and who can therefore be expected to show some flexibility and accept partial repayment in services other than cash. Since BAAC works more or less independently of the district administration and village polity, BAAC groups do not impinge on power relations within the village to any significant degree. Where BAAC does enhance the position of the better-off villagers is in giving long-term credit for purchase of machinery, in particular tractors and power tillers.

The CDD housewives' group only affects production marginally in its associated savings scheme. In Ban Dong, this scheme involves a larger number of women than in Ban Mai, but in neither case has the limited amount of savings been put to any productive use. Rather, such groups place individuals in positions of authority as minor state functionaries within the village and give state officials access to village institutions and village women's labour in support of the state's own programmes. Proposed training, which would follow CDD use of housewives' groups elsewhere in Thailand, involves handicraft production and cottage industry. These initiatives tend to impose urban standards on production by women, failing to take into account their role in agricultural production.

The Bung Khiew Rice Bank is relevant to production in as much as it provides a cheap means of credit for a subsistence crop and maintains resources within the community. It removes one of the main forms of dependence on external resources that existed in the marginal rice economy of Bung Khiew—that is, the need to borrow rice in deficit years. As such, it increases the control of the community as a whole over the basic item of subsistence, and since lending priority is based mainly on need, it benefits the least well-off most, although this will be less relevant by 1989 when the 60 *kwien* that have been accumulated are sufficient to fulfil most borrowing needs among the members. Control over the terms of lending and the direction of the initiative are in the hands of the members. The Rice Bank also serves as a forum for other community initiatives, and it has the potential (expressed by members) for communal marketing and purchase of inputs, increasing the bargaining power of Bung Khiew villagers *vis-à-vis* the market. Already, it has been used to negotiate external resources in the form of the rice barn, a stock of rice, and a concrete grain-drying yard. Thus it has moved beyond the retreatist self-help function criticized by Scott.

The Bung Khiew Buffalo Bank is also of direct relevance to production in that it gives farmers direct control over the means of tillage. It removes another main area of dependence on external resources for subsistence production in Bung Khiew agriculture. Control is collective, and leadership is representative of this relatively undifferentiated community. The initial beneficiaries have been the poorest members of the community. Control over the Buffalo Bank is less indigenous than in the case of the Rice Bank since the resources initially came from the outside in the form of donations. As a result, the Buffalo Bank members initially felt accountable to the NKYFRD, and in cases where there was a problem (for example, the death of several buffalo), these outsiders have been consulted. This has decreased as more of the Bank's buffalo are now offspring of the original herd and are thus seen as indigenous community resources.

The final scheme under consideration for its participatory content is the Bung Khiew Irrigation Channel. This was part of an effort to secure control over another factor necessary for subsistence production—water. Unlike the Rice Bank and Buffalo Bank, it was not inherently concerned with production relations but rather with mobilization of a resource for community use. This initiative had its roots in indigenous forms of co-operative development, and it was preceded by several attempts that relied solely on local resources. Through a local leader, Bung Khiew villagers called on and secured a commitment to provide external resources in their attempt to construct the channel in 1984–5, both from NGO sources and from the State. The participatory nature of this scheme was thus based on indigenous modes of mobilizing community resources, but it included an adaptation for incorporation into the wider community in its use of key link figures to secure assistance from further afield. Ironically, its ultimate demise resulted from frictions internal to the Ban Dong community.

Conclusion

If the tone of this chapter has been somewhat negative, it is because the emphasis has been on a fundamental contradiction concerning participation and the existing terms of incorporation faced by Ban Dong and Ban Mai villagers. Where possible, potentials have been identified and spaces for action pointed out. The concluding chapter that follows pursues some of these potentials and examines some of the wider implications of participatory rural development.

1. See Turton (1984b). The flexibility of interpretation of 'democracy' (*prachaathipatai*) in the Thai context opens it to manipulations in the constitutional field similar to those of participation in the field of development. Thai 'democracy' celebrated its fiftieth anniversary in 1982, the 1932 abolition of the absolute monarchy having marked the start of the 'democratic' era. However, most of this period has seen domination of the political arena by the military and several abrogations of the Constitution. Democracy is popularly used in contradistinction to communism and is thus associated with support for the national symbols of nation, religion, and monarchy. One Lan Sak village headman pointed out the newly installed public-address system in his village as evidence that democracy had arrived, since the national anthem could now be played for all to hear and stand at attention to each day at 8 a.m. and 6 p.m. On a more mocking note, the Thai political system is often referred to as 'Thai-style democracy' or 'half-baked democracy'.

2. See Goulet (1989) for a recent overview of the way in which participation is used in development and of how its meaning continues to change with changing political contexts.

3. The dilemma of participation through revolutionary action has been commented on in the context of the Bhoomi Sena movement in Maharashtra (Rahman, 1981: 20–1; original emphasis):

'Often in order to promote participation on a wide scale, macro-action will involve struggles with opposing macro-forces representing the status quo of the social structure and institutions, and the contingencies of such struggles may necessitate that the immediate issues and methods of action be determined centrally. The dilemma is that in thus seeking to "liberate", the very thing to be liberated—i.e. people's creativity—may fail to be *created*, and what has not been created cannot be *liberated*. In such a situation the most likely outcome of a successful macro-action would seem to be the domination of the new institutions by one or another of the forces that already exist (e.g. party or government bureaucracy), to promote *their* power rather than "people's power".'

The disillusionment that led to the decline in fortunes of the Communist Party of Thailand after 1979 was partly due to this high level of centralization.

4. Six dimensions are discussed overall, as follows. Participation is seen as *encounter* between the excluded and those who maintain exclusion. Such encounter may take many forms from bargaining to armed struggle, between groups, classes, organizations, and so on. *Movements and organizations* are of inherent interest, and the focus is on internal organization, interests, leadership, forms and tools of struggle, circulation of information, and education regarding the aims of the movement of organization. *Individual experience* is relevant to participation, since individual consciousness is 'the crucible in which social forces are put into human action'. This is termed the 'biographical approach'. *Programmes or projects* implemented from above are of interest, particularly regarding the motivation of their sponsors: are such programmes 'system maintaining' or 'system transforming'? More abstractly, *policy contributing to national development* is a determinant of participation: most systems espouse the ideals of democracy, but it is important to see in what form it is promoted. The space for increased participation exists as an 'open frontier in all societies and the main forces of most popular and emancipatory movements are deployed along it

[the frontier] or seeking it out'. Last, *anti-participatory structures and ideologies* need to be examined, in particular in the context of contemporary forms of modernization and nation building (Pearse and Stiefel, 1979).

5. See in particular Chenery *et al.* (1974). This study was itself sponsored by the World Bank. Its starting point was inequality associated with growth in LDCs, but it did not see the two as necessary correlates. The study examined the context and scope for intervention and identified target groups before going on to a technocratic analysis of policy options.

6. See Muecke (1980) on Village Scouts. The president of the Ban Dong Village Scouts, which is now more or less inactive, is a wealthy rice mill owner and buffalo *rentier*. Turton (1984b: 32) notes that the membership of Rotary and Lions Clubs consists of local élites, who often wield power in semi-legal or illegal and repressive ways.

7. On the dual role played by traditional village leadership, see Moerman (1969) on synaptic leaders. In 1960, the headman of Ban Ping, a relatively homogeneous and isolated community, was facing the difficulty of having to please two constituencies, namely officials and villagers; he was the 'door' of the village. Partly by comparison with villages that had been more fully integrated into the wider polity and economy, partly by far-sightedness, Moerman foresaw the decline of the synaptic role of the leader as he became more accountable to and dependent on officials and external resources.

8. The timing of meetings at various levels is a clear indication of the persistence of the top-downward orientation, despite rhetoric on participation that would suggest the contrary. Meetings at each level—village, district, provincial, regional, national—are timed to follow the meeting at the level immediately above, indicating the direction in which information and policy orders are designed to flow.

9. See James Scott and others on everyday forms of peasant resistance in the January 1986 issue of *Peasant Studies*; see also Scott (1985).

10. In his *Peasant Society and Culture*, Robert Redfield (1956) defines the peasantry in terms of its place as a 'part society', emphasizing not only its indigenous agrarian tradition but also its production relationship with the larger society (Redfield, 1956: 1–22; 23ff.).

11. Recently, the need for self-reliance has found its way into the discourse of state-led rural development. In part, this is a progressive step in the approach of state functionaries. However, sceptics see this emphasis as a means of cutting costs and reducing the burden on strained government budgets. Certainly at the local level, the frequent lambasting of villagers for sitting back and waiting for government assistance is evidence of this attitude among some officials. One criterion for selecting outstanding *kamnan* and village heads, as stated in the official local administrator's diary for 1984, is help organized by these leaders in construction of public infrastructure, without relying on public money, to the tune of at least 50,000 baht. This includes schools, health clinics, meeting halls, roads, bridges, irrigation channels, weirs, fire engines, wells, community ponds, district headquarters, police stations, and houses for government officials (Department of Local Administration, 1984: 73).

12. Compare *kodmaai paa* (law of the forest) with *kodmuu* (literally, group rules) of village leader Phra Pho Pan in Ban Mai Sawan (Tanabe, 1986). Many aspects of traditional leadership and changes therein following increased state attention to this previously isolated village are similar to the situation of the *khon to* and leaders who succeeded him in Ban Mai. See in particular pp. 37–41.

13. ALRO employs several labourers in Ban Mai. Because of the favourable rates of pay, there is heavy competition for such work and a certain amount of ill-feeling is generated through jealousies, including accusations of favouritism against influential villagers who hold sway with ALRO officials.

14. CDD was set up in the early 1960s with the explicit role of being the Government's eyes and ears at the village level, as well as fulfilling the hegemonic function of showing concern for village development. While collecting data at Lan Sak, the author overheard the district CDD officer giving his monthly briefings to the *tambon*-level workers, stressing above all the need to report immediately if there was any unusual gathering or stirring within their areas.

15. In particular, leaders of the Farmers' Federation of Thailand (FFT) were targets of assassination by right-wingers. In 1975, over thirty FFT leaders were killed in this way, without a single assassin being caught (Kanoksak and Kanchana, 1985: 22).

16. The 'hidden transcript' of the rural poor is a concept used by James Scott to refer to the discourse of the powerless in the absence of the powerful. Public discourse only provides a limited exposé of real attitudes, and the greater the disparities of power, the greater the extent of the 'hidden transcript'. Such a thesis conforms with the nature of public and private discourse in Ban Dong and Ban Mai, the more blatant power differences in the latter being reflected at once in a greater level of bitterness expressed in private, often-hushed conversation, and a smaller number of opportunities for public exchange (James Scott: public lecture at Thammasat University on 16 May 1985).

17. This is reflected in popular sentiment expressed in Seni Saowapong's novel *Pisat* (Devil) (1981: 283; author's translation), in which he follows Sai's thoughts after nearly getting shot:

'Back in the days of clearing the forest, humans only faced wild animals and nature; we could at least anticipate how and when the danger was going to come and take some steps to protect ourselves in advance. But in these days of exploitation, use of power, and competing interests, we can hardly tell when and in what form the danger will be upon us, when people are corrupted into despising each other with bribes and other forms of evil. . . .'

8
Dilemmas of Participatory Development

THE purpose of this study has been to identify and examine a contradiction inherent in participatory rural development, especially regarding production for the majority of rural producers. Briefly recapitulated, this is the loss of local control over resources necessary for production, entailed in an incorporative development strategy in which participation is invoked as a means of affording access to wider societal resources. The focus has been on processes of change, both directed change and spontaneous responses to a changing social and physical environment. There has been no attempt to propose alternative strategies for development, for in revised perspective, participation is seen as a dialectical process concerning power relations at the local level rather than an implementation of standardized prescriptions. This concluding chapter examines some of the wider implications of adopting such a participatory approach to development.

Since local context and aspects of power have been important in the preceding account, it is worthwhile reviewing some salient empirical findings. Lan Sak agriculture has seen a rapid set of material changes as a result of changing social and physical environments in the context of recent settlement of previously isolated communities. The changing material basis for production, new opportunities and constraints, and an increasing role of capital in production form the background to changing production relations within the communities under study. However, the nature of these changes differs between the communities as a result of various factors, such as: ecologically determined differences in production regime; patterns of settlement; the role of State and other developers; patterns of differentiation; and response to resource shortage. Changes in power relations create internal axes of tension, where previously the principal axis was between a relatively isolated community and the outside world. Not only are these internal manifestations of power intimately connected with changes in production relations; they are also important in determining control within nominally participatory institutions that are part of rural development strategy.

A Participatory Development Dilemma

In terms of the contradiction identified, the dilemma of participatory development becomes one of how to maintain control over production within the local community, while at the same time increasing community control over wider resources necessary for production. As we have seen, attempts to secure such wider control frequently lead to concentration of control and power within the community, and the objective of participation at a wider level is lost in the disintegration of control over local institutions. The dilemma can be viewed in two main dimensions: as a problem of organizational design and as a structural problem concerning the political economy of the village.

The organizational dimension of the dilemma is the problem of how to adapt existing institutions or establish new forums for action without bureaucratizing the process so that non-participatory structures become inherent. The problem is exacerbated by exclusive attention to organizational forms and consequent neglect of how these forms are established and of interaction within new structures and social processes, particularly *vis-à-vis* power relations. For some state developers, the primary objective may well be to establish such a bureaucratization of village process, and in this sense the contradiction is more apparent than real in the terms in which participation is conceived of by such developers. However, this is not true of all state developers and manifestly not so for NGO developers. The problem for the latter is, in the first instance, one of how to establish innovative forms of participation that do not conflict with indigenous modes of control over and through village leaders. Subsequently, the issue of spreading such forms to cover a wider area than the single community or subcommunity, both in terms of replicability and in widening solidarity networks, raises the problem of standardization and consequent lack of local involvement in shaping new institutions.

The structural dimension of the dilemma is concerned above all with differentiation within the village and the consequent divergence of interest between the majority of rural producers and those who secure control, not only over important areas of the village economy but also over supposedly participatory institutions. This poses a number of alternatives for participatory initiatives. On the one hand, initiatives can be exclusive in order to minimize internal power differences. On the other, they may work within the traditionally non-exclusive modes of village society and make use of the wider connections and larger resources that inclusion of wealthier villagers allows. Initiatives may address areas of major significance to distribution of resources within the community, or they may avoid conflict by concentration on peripheral areas of the village economy. Initiatives may be oriented to a particular group, such as by age, sex, or residence within the village, or they may be geared to a particular issue or activity.

Obstacles to Participation

In light of the above dilemma and in terms of its organizational and structural aspects, some of the more concrete obstacles to and spaces for participatory action need to be reiterated before a final discussion of the implications of a participatory approach. The obstacles to participation for the rural poor in Ban Mai and Ban Dong have been seen in terms of obstacles to control over production, in the face of a lack of political and economic power within the village. An important contributor to this powerlessness is the problem of fragmentation, a set of processes that alienate individuals in three important dimensions: spatially, consciously, and socially.

For individuals in Ban Dong and even more so in Ban Mai, lack of control over basic resources for production has meant having to seek opportunities external to the village, and this is an area where participatory initiatives have little potential for organizing the rural poor. Temporary or permanent migration beyond the village is one of the most fragmenting of all the consequences of inability to secure a livelihood locally, and this obstacle to participation is thus particularly relevant in the transitory situation of recently settled communities in Lan Sak.

Other fragmenting aspects of change that make it difficult for the poorer sections of the village to take part in co-operative initiatives designed to facilitate control include ambiguous class identification and intensification of work. The lack of clear class identification among the peasantry is enhanced by the ambivalent situation of rural producers who are at once wage labourers and employers of labour; concurrently tenants, landowners, and even landlords renting out (mortgaged) land; and simultaneously subsistence farmers and commercial croppers. Intensification of work among debt-ridden farmers is a result of the introduction of double-cropping, of off-season employment to pay off debt or accumulate the capital necessary for inputs in the increasingly capitalized production regime, or of intensive labour input in a deteriorating natural environment, in an attempt to avoid debt that results from capitalization.

The effects of such fragmentation for participatory initiatives are to reduce the time available for organizational aspects of participation and to undermine potential communality of interest. Many of the poorest families in Ban Mai find it difficult to attend monthly meetings despite the fine imposed for absence, since they may be away from the village for periods of labouring, involved in labour-intensive cultivation on their own fields due to lack of capital, or engaged in wage labouring on other people's land in a hand-to-mouth existence. For this group, any extra demands on their time beyond official meetings are difficult to justify. The corollary of this is the position of wealthier villagers who employ wage labourers on their fields and have a correspondingly greater amount of time for involvement in formal institutions such as the VC and the establishment of contacts with district officials. On the other hand, villagers in Bung Khiew still have periods of the year in which social activity is important, and this has been a vital element not only in maintaining the cohesion of the community but also in catering for the organizational demands of the Rice and Buffalo Banks. Indeed, poorer villagers working their own land in Ban Mai frequently identify lack of free time as being one of the hardships of being a *chaorai* as opposed to a *chaonaa*.

Since many aspects of development cater specifically to smallholders working their own land, the direct or indirect alienation of poorer farmers from control over production precludes successful participation in many types of initiative. Wealthier farmers and ALRO officials in Ban Mai claim that smaller farmers 'are not serious' about farming—for example, in not providing the proper inputs or in spending too much time away from the farm. However, smaller farmers themselves say that this is a consequence of 'being squeezed'. The result is a set of short-term strategies for survival and a failure to practise longer-term soil conservation, such as by participation in compost training programmes run by the Land Development Department. Meanwhile, wealthier farmers who rent debtors' land for cultivation have little incentive for long-term soil management, and a vicious circle is continued of declining yields and short-term response in which local orientation in the management of resources is steadily undermined.

Participation through co-operative institutions is difficult to establish in the face of increasingly dominant money-lenders. Som's daughter (Case 9, Chapter 5) was to have been sent for training to the NKYFRD co-operative training centre near Uthaithani, but the need for credit forced her to work as a housemaid for her mother's creditor. Co-operative marketing cannot be established so long as farmers are obliged to sell produce through their creditors and suppliers. Moreover, increasing institutional credit does not on its own solve the problem, since such credit is incremental and conditional to a particular (and unsustainable) production regime, rather than liberating from the constraints of the money-lenders. In the past, such control over production was limited to external money-lenders and its effects were minimized by a low-input production regime. However, as more control is assumed by key villagers, so it becomes interwoven with village-level production relations and community-based co-operative institutions, posing obstacles to participatory initiatives.

Another set of obstacles to participation is connected with subjective aspects of change. The traditional Thai social structure is one of masters and followers, and the assumption of power by individual villagers often does less to blur this difference or give the latter representation among the former than to transform such villagers into masters themselves. Not only does this have a divisive effect at the village level, it also reinforces the sense among the majority that certain domains remain the affairs of others. Thus institutions such as the VC, TC, and other development institutions become the preserve of these key individuals. Such lack of a sense of ownership of new institutions among the majority of villagers is also apparent even where power differences are minimized, such as in the case of Bung Khiew Buffalo Bank which villagers initially saw as the property of NKYFRD. This points to another principal obstacle—that of uncertainty—as discussed in the previous chapter. The absolutism of the Thai State and weak development of civil society (Turton, 1987) undermine confidence in the legitimacy of non-state institutions, and rhetorical statements by officials as to the rights and duties of villagers do little to offset the pervading climate of suspicion and fear that surrounds innovative and non-official action. Meanwhile, within the bureaucracy, the accountability to seniors and lack of accountability downward lead to a hierarchical and non-participatory mode of action that readily extends itself to the bureaucratization of village procedures. The frustration of some local officials with development initiatives that contravene such control from above can be detected in the district accountant's recommendation that the author study royal projects rather than development initiatives in Lan Sak, since the royal projects get things done by having someone to 'oversee, or point an accusing finger [that is, maintain control]'. He sees the failure of local state-led projects to do the same as a problem of inadequate resources rather than difference of approach.

Spaces for Action

Despite the considerable obstacles to participatory development resulting from concentration of control and power within the communities under study and despite the perpetuation of non-participatory attitudes, recent developments have opened up a certain amount of space for action. One such opening is the legitimation of NGO activity in rural areas. Partly as a result of liberalization of state development policy and partly due to an awareness of the constraints and openings among NGO workers themselves, the working atmosphere between the two sectors has eased. Each main region now has a Working Group responsible for co-ordination between NGOs and state developers. Although NGO workers were initially wary of the potential co-optive pitfalls of such co-operation, especially since non-governmental organizations were at first to include agribusiness (this sector was given its own co-ordinating group under the Sixth Plan), growing confidence among NGO workers has allowed them to take part at an equal level in such exchanges, and thus also to increase potential influence over development strategy at a wider level than is possible within the limited geographical scope afforded by NGO project areas. The prominence of individual NGO workers at a local level is exemplified by the head of NKYFRD, who uses to effect his position as president of the Agricultural University Alumni Association in Uthaithani in securing co-operation from irrigation officials, ALRO, DAE, and other organizations.

A second positive development regarding a more participatory strategy is an increasing awareness of the wider meaning of participation by certain officials and others such as doctors, monks, and teachers. This has been afforded in part by increased contact with the cadre-type of approach of NGO workers and the dissemination of ideas in magazines such as *Folk Doctor*, *Social Development*, and newsletters of various organizations. However, it is also partly a spontaneous response by individual officials committed to social development and presented with new opportunities as rural development becomes a major plank of state strategy in rural areas.

Among villagers, the potential for participatory action is enhanced by a slowly growing confidence in the legitimacy of independent action. Many local-level workers comment that villagers are becoming bolder or cleverer in dealing with authority. In part, these trends are due to integration into a national polity that plays at least lip service to principles of democracy. However, the most significant factor in enhancing participatory action by villagers within and beyond the village is the emergence of local leaders who at once differ from the unrepresentative formal leaders such as the Ban Dong and Ban Mai village heads, while managing to utilize new structures for the benefit of the community. An example of such a leader is Boi in Bung Khiew, who has been instrumental in involving villagers in the various programmes described in Chapter 6. An important aspect of Boi's leadership is his concern to involve other community members in assuming responsibility, in order to avoid the common phenomenon found at every level of Thai society of individuals who 'wear many hats', and who in such concentration of responsibility and power diminish both participation and efficiency within the organizations for which they are responsible.

Implications of Participatory Development

Since participation has become such a common element of development discourse, we might best be able to gain an understanding of its implications by reflecting briefly on its rationale: why participation? As we noted in the previous chapter, each actor on the development stage rationalizes participation in terms of a particular perspective on how people are to be involved in a wider polity and economy. Participation is to involve people in something from which they have hitherto been excluded, in order to spread the material and social benefits of inclusion. The implications of participatory development, then, are in two main areas: the reversals inherent in a strategy that starts with people making choices over wider strategies that affect the way in which their lives are run, rather than having such strategies determined by others; and the way in which incorporation itself affects the lives of those involved.

As villages such as Ban Dong and Ban Mai are integrated more fully into national structures of State and capital, the reversals implied by a participatory approach can be seen less and less as bound by local considerations. Significant areas of villagers' lives are affected by decisions taken at centres remote from Lan Sak, and control over such decisions can be established only by representation at a higher level or by increasing collective bargaining power. Existing means of non-local representation (notably, the national Parliament) are at present meaningless in terms of offering alternatives concerning issues affecting the lives of villagers. Organs for collective bargaining among farmers are still weakly developed in rural Thailand, but institutions such as Bung Khiew Rice Bank can be seen as embryonic forms of organization that may provide the base for an extended solidarity. It has been noted how leadership associated with this initiative has been instrumental in limited but significant ways in negotiating for external resources and in maintaining a stand against externally imposed programmes. However, the broader prospects for establishment of strong bargaining instruments in the hands of individually powerless sections of the rural community are still remote, and there is an ever present tension in the desire for state developers to maintain control over new groupings.

The implications for individuals of participation via incorporative rural development strategy are ambivalent. On the one hand, incorporation in principle involves people in the material benefits of the wider society and in deciding how those benefits are to be distributed. On the other hand, this study has shown how skewed such involvement is at the local level, and that this results from, and is not in spite of, the particular participatory approach of State-led rural development. Incorporation as it impinges on the life of the poorer rural producer takes the form of increasing demands on his or her time, rising levels of debt, higher levels of uncertainty regarding means of livelihood, and decreased sanction over local leaders.

An alternative approach to implications of participation, and one that perhaps transcends some of the rhetoric associated with the concept, is to consider in what areas participation is of relevance in improving the livelihood of the majority of rural producers. Clearly, certain aspects of rural development require technical and administrative expertise and therefore direction that are beyond the immediate capability of individual villagers. Thus the notion of maximizing direct participation in every aspect of rural development is neither realistic nor desirable from the point of view of most of those involved. Johnston and Clark's (1982) combination of 'cogitation' and 'acting out' is clearly a *sine qua non*, and the question becomes one of how the cogitation can best be oriented to the needs of less powerful sections of the community in such a way as to reduce uncertainty and increase control that people have over livelihood.

In the context of state-led rural development in Thailand, a key priority for increasing control in this sense is in clarifying the status and function of external developers *vis-à-vis* the local communities. The head of NKYFRD says that he would now prefer not to be known as a 'developer', for such a status has become ambiguous and tends to usurp moral responsibility that people have in deciding for themselves. He would rather be seen as an 'educator', leaving it up to people to apply his teaching or otherwise. From the point of view of villagers, such a clarification of status especially among the numerous state officials and their village-level proxies seems essential if state developers are to be seen as providing services to be called on by locally responsive and representative groups, rather than as dictators of change from above.

In the last instance, participation as increased control over livelihood cannot be divorced from the material realities of production in a local and wider context. The NGO worker referred to above does not see the difference betweeen Ban Mai and Bung Khiew as essentially one of attitude or social cohesion. In his words, 'the villagers are ready to exploit each other' in Bung Khiew, just as they are already doing in Ban Mai; the fundamental difference between the two communities is that in Bung Khiew they have not reached the same level or type of material development. On the one hand, this study has attempted to move beyond a purely materialist analysis of change and has used local discourses to assess its subjective meaning. On the other hand, the shaping of participatory initiatives in two recently settled and rapidly changing communities has been shown to depend largely on historically and locally specific material conditions and social relations of production. In practice, therefore, the research imperative as a basis for practical action is to gain an understanding of these realities, both through objective familiarity with local material conditions and through the subjective medium of discourse.

Bibliography

Akin Rabibhatana (1969), *The Organization of Thai Society in the Early Bangkok Era: 1782–1873*, Ithaca: Cornell University Southeast Asia Program (Data Paper No. 74).

——— (1980), *Problems in Rural Development Work: The Case of the Maeklong Integrated Rural Development Project*, Bangkok: Thai Khadi Research Institute.

ALRO (Agricultural Land Reform Office) (n.d.), *Landlessness in Upper Northern Thailand*, Bangkok: Asian Employment Programme.

Amin, Samir (1976), *Unequal Development*, New York: Monthly Review Press.

Anan Ganjanapan (1984), 'The Partial Commercialisation of Rice Production in Northern Thailand (1900–1981)', unpublished dissertation, Cornell University.

——— (1989), 'Conflicts Over the Deployment and Control of Labor in a Northern Thai Village', in Gillian Hart, Andrew Turton and Benjamin White (eds.), *Agrarian Transformations: Local Processes and the State in Southeast Asia*, Berkeley: University of California Press.

Ananya Bhuchongkul (1985), 'From *Chaonaa* to *Khonngaan*: The Growing Divide in a Central Thai Village', unpublished Ph.D. thesis, University of London.

Apichaat Thongyuu (1984), *Watthanatham kab Ngaan Phatthanaa* (*Culture and Development Work*), Bangkok: Saangsan Press.

Bamrung Bunpanya (1984), 'Thammai To'ng Phuud theung Kaanmiisuanruam kho'ng Prachaachon: Thatsana jaak Kaanphatanaa Eekachon' ('Why Speak of People's Participation: An NGO View'), in Thawithong Hongwiwat (ed.) (1984), *Kaanmiisuanruam kho'ng Prachaachon nai Kaanphatthanaa* (*People's Participation in Development*), proceedings of a seminar on 'Community Participation: Policies and Methods', held at the Public Health Policy Study Centre, Mahidol University, Bangkok.

Bharadwaj, Krishna (1985), 'A View on Commercialization in Indian Agriculture and the Development of Capitalism', *Peasant Studies*, Vol. 12.

Bloch, Maurice (ed.) (1975), *Political Language and Oratory in Traditional Societies*, London: Academic Press.

Boonchana Klankamsorn and Thongchai Charuppat (1983), *Sathaanakaan Paa Mai kho'ng Prathet Thai nai Chuang Raya Weelaa 21 Pii (Tangtae Phor Sor 2504–2525)* (*Forest Situation of Thailand in the Past Twenty-one Years (During 1961–1982)*), Bangkok: Royal Forestry Department.

Bottomore, Tom (ed.) (1983), *Dictionary of Marxist Thought*, Oxford: Basil Blackwell.

Buijs, D. (1982), 'On Admittance, Access, Cooperation, and Participation; the Basic Concepts of the "Access and Participation" Research', in B. Galjart and D. Buijs (eds.), *Participation of the Poor in Development*, Leiden: Institute of Cultural and Social Studies, University of Leiden, Leiden Development Studies No. 2.

Chai-anan Samudavanija (1984), 'Rabob Raachakaan kab Kaanmiisuanruam kho'ng Chumchon: Phijaranaa nai ngae Mahaaphaak' ('The Bureaucratic System and Community Participation: Macro-scale Considerations'), in Thawithong Hongwiwat (ed.) (1984), *Kaanmiisuanruam kho'ng Prachaachon nai Kaanphatthanaa* (*People's Participation in Development*), proceedings of a seminar on 'Community Participation: Policies and Methods', held at the Public Health Policy Study Centre, Mahidol University, Bangkok.

Chambers, Robert (1983), *Rural Development: Putting the Last First*, London: Longman.

Chatthip Nartsupha and Suthy Prasartset (1981), *The Political Economy of Thailand, 1851–1910*, Bangkok: Social Science Association of Thailand.

Chatthip Nartsupha *et al.* (1981), *The Political Economy of Thailand, 1910–1932*, Bangkok: Social Science Association of Thailand.

Chayan Vaddhanaphuti (1984), 'Cultural and Ideological Reproduction in Northern Thai Society', unpublished Ph.D. dissertation, Stanford University.

_____ (1990), 'In Search of the Village Community in the Context of Conflict and Change', paper presented at workshop on *The Village Revisited: Community and Locality in Southeast Asia*, Centre for Asian Studies (CASA), Amsterdam: published by CASA in *Proceedings*.

Chayanov, A. ([1926] 1966), *The Theory of Peasant Economy*, Homewood, Illinois: Richard D. Irwin.

Chenery, H. *et al.* (1974), *Redistribution with Growth*, Oxford: Oxford University Press.

Chin, S. C. (1977), 'Shifting Cultivation—A Need for Greater Understanding', *Sarawak Museum Journal*, Vol. XXV, No. 46.

Chit Nilaphanich (1984), 'Saphaa Tambon kab Kaanmiisuanruam kho'ng Prachaachon: Naioobaai lae Konlawithii' ('The Tambon Council and People's Participation: Policy and Methods'), in Thawithong Hongwiwat (ed.) (1984), *Kaanmiisuanruam kho'ng Prachaachon nai Kaanphatthanaa* (*People's Participation in Development*), proceedings of a seminar on 'Community Participation: Policies and Methods', held at the Public Health Policy Study Centre, Mahidol University, Bangkok.

Conklin, Harold C. (1957), *Hanunoo Agriculture: A Report on an Integral System of Shifting Cultivation in the Philippines*, FAO (Food and Agriculture Organization) Forestry Development Paper No. 12, Rome.

Demaine, Harvey (1984), *Self-help Land Settlement Schemes: Their Contribution to Thai Rural Development*, paper presented at the International Conference on Thai Studies, Bangkok, 22–24 August.

_____ (1986), 'Kanpatthana: Thai Views of Development', in M. Hobart and R. Taylor (eds.), *Context, Meaning, and Power in Southeast Asia*, Ithaca: Cornell Southeast Asia Program.

Department of Local Administration (1984), *Banteuk Nakpokkhrong Thongthii* (*Local Administrator's Diary*), Bangkok: Ministry of the Interior.

Donner, Wolf (1978), *The Five Faces of Thailand: An Economic Geography*, New York: St. Martins.

Douglass, Mike (1983), 'The Korean *Saemaul Undong*: Accelerated Rural Development in an Open Economy', in David Lea and D. P. Chaudhri (eds.), *Rural Development and the State: Contradictions and Dilemmas in Developing Countries*, London: Methuen.

_____ (1984), *Regional Integration on the Capitalist Periphery: The Central Plains of Thailand*, The Hague: Institute of Social Studies Research Report Series No. 15.

Eckholm, Erik P. (1977), *The Picture of Health: Environmental Sources of Disease*,

New York: Worldwatch Institute.

Embree, John (1950), 'Thailand: A Loosely Structured Social System', *American Anthropologist*, Vol. 52.

Evers, Hans-Dieter (ed.) (1969), *Loosely Structured Social Systems: Thailand in Comparative Perspective*, Yale University, Cultural Report Series No. 17.

FAO (1973), *People's Participation in Development*, Poona, Calcutta: Asian Regional Workshop, 2–12 September.

—— (1981), *Administering Agricultural Development for Small Farmers: Issues in Decentralization and People's Participation*, Rome.

FAO/UNEP (1981), *Forest Resources of Tropical Asia*, Tropical Forest Assessment Project, Rome.

Feder, Gershon (1987), 'Land Ownership Security and Farm Productivity: Evidence from Thailand', *Journal of Development Studies*, 24(1), pp. 16–30.

Feeny, David (1977), 'Induced Technical and Institutional Change: A Thai Case Study', in G. P. Means (ed.), *The Past in Southeast Asia's Present*, selections from the proceedings of the annual meetings of the Canadian Council for Southeast Asian Studies at McMaster University, 4–5 November.

—— (1982), *The Political Economy of Agricultural Productivity: Thai Agricultural Development 1880–1975*, Vancouver: University of British Columbia Press.

—— (1984), *Agricultural Expansion and Forest Depletion in Thailand, 1900–1975*, Yale University, Economic Growth Centre Discussion Paper No. 458.

Foster, George (1967), 'Introduction', in Jack Potter *et al.* (eds.), *Peasant Society: A Reader*, Berkeley: University of California Press.

Foucault, Michel (1977), *Discipline and Punish: The Birth of the Prison*, London: Allen Lane.

Frank, Andre Gunther (1967), *Capitalism and Underdevelopment in Latin America*, New York: Monthly Review Press.

Giddens, Anthony (1984), *The Constitution of Society: Outline of the Theory of Structuration*, Oxford: Polity.

Girling, John (1981), *Thailand: Society and Politics*, Ithaca: Cornell University Press.

Goldberg, Ray A. (1979), *Agribusiness Management for Developing Countries—Southeast Asian Corn System and American and Japanese Trends Affecting It*, Cambridge, Massachussetts: Ballinger.

Gould, Jeremy (ed.) (1981), *Needs, Participation, and Local Development*, Helsinki: Finnish National Commission for UNESCO Publications.

Goulet, Denis (1989), 'Participation in Development: New Avenues', *World Development*, 17(2), pp. 165–78.

Griffin, Keith (1979), *The Political Economy of Agrarian Change: An Essay on the Green Revolution*, London: Macmillan.

Hainsworth, Geoffrey B. (1982), 'Beyond Dualism: Village Level Modernization and the Process of Integration into National Economies in Southeast Asia', in Geoffrey B. Hainsworth (ed.), *Village Level Modernization in Southeast Asia: The Political Economy of Rice and Water*, Vancouver: University of British Columbia Press.

Hanks, Lucien (1972), *Rice and Man, Agricultural Ecology in Southeast Asia*, Chicago: Aldine Atherton.

Hardin, G. (1968), 'The Tragedy of the Commons', *Science*, Vol. 162.

Harrison, Mark (1982), 'Chayanov's Theory of Peasant Economy', in John Harriss (ed.), *Rural Development: Theories of Peasant Economy and Agrarian Change*, London: Hutchinson.

Harriss, John (ed.) (1982a), *Rural Development: Theories of Peasant Economy and Agrarian Change*, London: Hutchinson.

_____ (1982b), 'Social Organization and Irrigation: Ideology, Planning, and Practice in Sri Lanka's Settlement Schemes', in T. P. Bayliss-Smith and Sudhir Wanmali (eds.), *Understanding Green Revolutions: Agrarian Change and Development Planning in South Asia: Essays in Honour of B.H. Farmer*, Cambridge: Cambridge University Press.

Hart, Gillian; Turton, Andrew; and White, Benjamin (eds.) (1989), *Agrarian Transformations: Local Processes and the State in Southeast Asia*, Berkeley: University of California Press.

Heyer, Judith *et al.* (eds.) (1981), *Rural Development in Tropical Africa*, London: Macmillan.

Hindess, Barry and Hirst, P. Q. (1975), *Pre-capitalist Modes of Production*, London: Routledge and Kegan Paul.

Hirsch, P. (1987), 'Socialisation of the Military or Militarisation of the Society?', *Far Eastern Economic Review*, 10 September.

_____ (1989), 'Settlement and Resettlement on Marginal Land: A Case Study from Thailand', *Australian Geographer*, 20(1).

_____ (1990), 'Bounded Village and the State on the Thai Periphery', paper presented at workshop on *The Village Revisited: Community and Locality in Southeast Asia*, Centre for Asian Studies (CASA), Amsterdam: published by CASA in *Proceedings*.

_____ and Lohmann, L. (1989), 'The Contemporary Politics of Environment in Thailand', *Asian Survey*, 29(4).

IBRD (1959), *A Public Development Program for Thailand*, Baltimore: Johns Hopkins Press.

_____ (1980), *Thailand: Toward a Strategy of Full Participation*, Washington, DC: World Bank.

_____ (1983), *Rural Growth and Employment*, Washington, DC: World Bank.

Ingram, James (1971), *Economic Change in Thailand 1850–1970*, Palo Alto: Stanford University Press.

Irvine, Walter (1982), 'The Thai–Yuan "Madman" and the "Modernising Developing Thai Nation" as Bounded Entities Under Threat: A Study in the Replication of a Single Image', unpublished Ph.D. dissertation, University of London.

Ishii, Yoneo (1986), *Sangha, State, and Society*, Honolulu: University of Hawaii Press.

Johnston, B. F. and Clark, W. C. (1982), *Redesigning Rural Development: A Strategic Perspective*, Baltimore: Johns Hopkins University Press.

Johnston, David Bruce (1975), 'Rural Society and the Rice Economy in Thailand: 1880–1930', unpublished Ph.D. dissertation, Yale University.

Johnston, R. J. (ed.) (1981), *The Dictionary of Human Geography*, Oxford: Basil Blackwell.

Kanoksak Kaewthep and Kanchana Kaewthep (1985), 'The Political Economy of Thai Peasantry: A Case Study of the Farmers' Federation of Thailand, 1973–1976', paper presented at the Third Thai–European Seminar Hua Hin, 9–12 April.

Kemp, Jeremy (1987), *Seductive Mirage: The Search for the Village Community in Southeast Asia*, Amsterdam: Centre for Asian Studies.

Kent, G. (1981), 'Community Based Development Planning', *Third World Planning Review*, Vol. III.

Khan, Sadruddhin (1986), 'Foreword' in *The Vanishing Forest: The Human Consequences of Deforestation*, London: Zed Books.

Lan Sak DAE (Department of Agricultural Extension) (1985), *Khormoon Kaankaset Pii 2527/2528 Amphoe Lan Sak Changwad Uthaithani* (*Agricultural In-*

formation for Lan Sak District, Uthaithani Province 1984/1985).

Land Development Department (1984), *Raingaan Kaansamruat Din: Khroongkaan Padiruup Thiidin Tap Salao* (*Soil Survey Report: Tap Salao Land Reform Project*), Report No. 371, Soil Survey Division, Bangkok.

Lenin, V. I. ([1899] 1982), 'The Differentiation of the Peasantry', in John Harriss (ed.), *Rural Development: Theories of Peasant Economy and Agrarian Change*, London: Hutchinson.

_____ ([1902] 1973), *What Is to be Done?*, Peking: Foreign Language Press.

Lightfoot, Paul (1985), 'BAAC Lending to Small-scale Farmers', Bangkok, unpublished BAAC working paper.

_____ and Fox, Jacqueline (1983), *Institutional Credit and Small-scale Farmers in Northeastern Thailand*, University of Hull: Centre for Southeast Asian Studies, Occasional Paper No. 5.

Lipton, Michael (1977), *Why Poor People Stay Poor: Urban Bias in World Development*, London: Temple Smith.

Luxembourg, Rosa ([1913] 1963), *The Accumulation of Capital*, London: Routledge and Kegan Paul.

MacFarland, George (1944), *Thai–English Dictionary*, Stanford: Stanford University Press.

Marzouk, G. A. (1972), *Economic Development and Policies: Case Study of Thailand*, Rotterdam: Rotterdam University Press.

Mehta, Niranjan (1981), 'An Analysis of Some Asian Experiences in Alleviating the Disabilities of the Rural Poor and Improving the Accountability of Public Agencies—Implications for Policy', unpublished paper presented at ESCAP Regional Workshop on the Development of Low Income Groups and Improving Accountability of Public Agencies in Rural Areas, 27–30 October.

Ministry of the Interior (1982), *Population Characteristics, Number of Tambons, Mubans and Dwellings by Amphoe: 1981*, Bangkok: Department of Local Administration.

Moerman, Michael (1968), *Agricultural Change and Peasant Choice in a Thai Village*, Berkeley: University of California Press.

_____ (1969), 'A Thai Village Headman as a Synaptic Leader', *Journal of Asian Studies*, Vol. XXVIII.

Morell, David and Chai-anan Samudavanija (1981), *Political Conflict in Thailand: Reform, Reaction, Revolution*, Cambridge, Massachussetts: Oelgeschlager, Gunn & Hain.

Muecke, Marjorie (1980), 'The Village Scouts of Thailand', *Asian Survey*, Vol. 20.

Nart Tuntawiroon (1984), 'Public Perception of Rain Forest and its Perception in Thailand', in Sahabat Alam Malaysia, *Environment, Development, and Natural Resource Crisis in Asia and the Pacific*, Kuala Lumpur: SAM.

National Primary Education Office (n.d.), *Phleeng lae Khati Phot Khamkhwan pheua Kaanphathanaa* (*Songs and Slogans for Development*), Bangkok: Educational Project for Village Development in Poverty Concentration Districts, 1982–1986.

NESDB (National Economic and Social Development Board) (1977), *Fourth National Economic and Social Development Plan, 1977–1981*, Bangkok: Office of the Prime Minister.

_____ (1980), *Statistical Reports of Changwad: Uthaithani*, Bangkok: Office of the Prime Minister.

_____ (1981), *Fifth National Economic and Social Development Plan, 1982–1986*, Bangkok: Office of the Prime Minister.

New Internationalist (1989), 'Say, Write, Scream: Language Lives', January issue.

Ng, Ronald (1978), 'Man and Land in Northeast Thailand', in P. A. Stott (ed.), *Nature and Man in Southeast Asia*, London: School of Oriental and African Studies.

NSO (National Statistical Office), *Annual Statistical Yearbooks, 1981–4*.

Palmer, I. (1975), 'Problems of Access: Notes on Indonesian and Malaysian Cases', *Development and Change*, Vol. 6.

Panayotou, Theodor (1983), 'Renewable Resource Management for Agricultural and Rural Development in Southeast Asia: Research and Policy Issues', paper presented at the fifth National Biennial Meeting of the Agricultural Economics Society of Southeast Asia (ASSEA), Bangkok.

Parkin, David (ed.) (1982), *Semantic Anthropology*, London: Academic Press.

Pathaan Suwannamongkol (1984), 'Thatsana Baang Prakaan nai Reuang Saphaa Tambon kab Kaanmiisuanruam kho'ng Chumchon' ('Some Views on the Tambon Council and Community Participation'), in Thawithong Hongwiwat (ed.) (1984), *Kaanmiisuanruam kho'ng Prachaachon nai Kaanphatthanaa* (*People's Participation in Development*), proceedings of a seminar on 'Community Participation: Policies and Methods', held at the Public Health Policy Study Centre, Mahidol University, Bangkok.

Pearse, Andrew (1980), 'Launching the Debate', UNRISD Popular Participation Programme working seminar, Oxford, 23–26 September.

——— and Stiefel, Mathias (1979), *Inquiry into Participation—A Research Approach*, Geneva: UNRISD.

Pei Shang-ji (1985), 'Some Effects of the Dai People's Cultural Beliefs and Practices upon the Plant Environment of Xishuangbanna, Yunnan Province, Southwest China', in Karl Hutterer *et al.*, *Cultural Values and Human Ecology in Southeast Asia*, Ann Arbor: University of Michigan.

Pelzer, K. (1945), *Pioneer Land Settlement in the Asiatic Tropics*, New York: American Geographical Society.

Phairat Decharin (1984), 'Naioobaai lae Konlawithii Kaanmiisuanruam kho'ng Chumchon nai Yuthasaat Kaanphatthanaa patjuban' ('Policy and Methods for Community Participation in Current Development Strategy'), in Thawithong Hongwiwat (ed.) (1984), *Kaanmiisuanruam kho'ng Prachaachon nai Kaanphatthanaa* (*People's Participation in Development*), proceedings of a seminar on 'Community Participation: Policies and Methods', held at the Public Health Policy Study Centre, Mahidol University, Bangkok.

Popkin, Samuel (1979), *The Rational Peasant: The Political Economy of Rural Society in Vietnam*, Berkeley: University of California Press.

Potter, Jack M. (1976), *Thai Peasant Social Structure*, Chicago: University of Chicago Press.

Rahman, Md. Anisur (1981), 'Some Dimensions of People's Participation in the Bhoomi Sena Movement', occasional paper of UNRISD Popular Participation Programme, Geneva.

Redfield, Robert (1956), *Peasant Society and Culture*, Chicago: University of Chicago Press.

Reynolds, Craig and Hong Lysa (1983), 'Marxism in Thai Historical Studies', *Journal of Asian Studies*, 43(1), pp. 77–104.

RFD (Royal Forestry Department) (1987), *Forestry Statistics of Thailand*, Bangkok: RFD.

Rigg, Jonathan (1986), 'The Chinese Agricultural Middleman in Thailand: Efficient or Exploitative?', *Singapore Journal of Tropical Geography*, Vol. 7.

Riggs, Fred (1966), *Thailand: The Modernization of a Bureaucratic Polity*, Honolulu: East–West Centre Press.

Rogers, Barbara (1980), *The Domestication of Women: Discrimination in Developing*

Societies, London: Kagan Page.

Saneh Jamrik (1983), *Problems of Development in the Thai Political Setting*, Bangkok: Thai Khadi.

—— (1984), Comments on Phairat Decharin's article, in Thawithong Hongwiwat (ed.), *Kaanmiisuanruam kho'ng Prachaachon nai Kaanphatthanaa* (*People's Participation in Development*), proceedings of a seminar on 'Community Participation: Policies and Methods', held at the Public Health Policy Study Centre, Mahidol University, Bangkok.

Scarborough, Vanessa (1985), 'Indonesia: Peasant Resistance to Hegemonic Change', research report, Department of Anthropology, School of Oriental and African Studies, University of London.

Schumacher, E. (1973), *Small is Beautiful: A Study of Economics as if People Mattered*, London: Blond and Briggs.

Scott, James (1976), *The Moral Economy of the Peasant: Rebellion and Subsistence in Southeast Asia*, New Haven: Yale University Press.

—— (1984), 'History According to Winners and Losers', in Andrew Turton and Shigeharu Tanabe (eds.), *History and Peasant Consciousness in Southeast Asia*, Osaka: National Museum of Ethnography (Senri Ethnological Studies 13).

—— (1985), *Weapons of the Weak: Everyday Forms of Peasant Resistance*, New Haven: Yale University Press.

—— (1986), 'Everyday Forms of Peasant Resistance', *Peasant Studies*, Vol. 13.

Seni Saowaphong (1981), *Pisat* (*Devil*), Bangkok: Dokyaa.

Shaffer, B. (1975), 'Editorial', *Development and Change*, Vol. VI.

Sharp, Lauriston and Hanks, Lucien (1978), *Bang Chan: Social History of a Rural Community in Thailand*, Ithaca: Cornell University Press.

Silcock, Thomas (1970), *The Economic Development of Thai Agriculture*, Canberra: Australian National University.

Siwarak Siwarom (1985), 'Chaonaa kab khwaam taek taang thaang chonchan' ('Peasants and Class Differentiation'), paper presented to seminar of the Political Economy Group, 7 April 1985, at Kroek College, Bangkok.

Somboon Suksamran (1982), *Buddhism and Politics in Thailand: A Study of Socio-political Change and Political Activism of the Thai Sangha*, Singapore: Institute of Southeast Asian Studies.

Stiefel, Matthias and Wolfe, Marshall (1984), *The Quest for Participation: Social Movements, the State, and People's Participation in Latin America and Some Countries of Asia*, Geneva: UNRISD.

Stott, P. A. (ed.) (1978), *Nature and Man in Southeast Asia*, London: School of Oriental and African Studies.

Suchit Bunbongkan (1987), *The Military in Thai Politics 1981–86*, Singapore: Institute of Southeast Asian Studies.

Supot Thepawan (1982), *Pesticides in Thailand: Use and Hazards*, Bangkok: Chulalongkorn University Social Research Institute.

Suthiporn Chirapanda and Worawate Tanrontanyalak (1981), *Landlessness in Central Thailand*, Bangkok: ALRO.

Takaya, Yoshikazu (1987), *Agricultural Development of a Tropical Delta: A Study of the Chaophraya Delta*, Honolulu: University of Hawaii Press.

Tanabe, Shigeharu (1978), 'Land Reclamation in the Chaophraya Delta', in Yoneo Ishii (ed.), *Thailand: A Rice Growing Society*, Honolulu: University Press of Hawaii.

—— (1981), 'Peasant Farming Systems in Thailand: A Comparative Study of Rice Cultivation and Agricultural Technology in Chiangmai and Ayuthaya', unpublished Ph.D. dissertation, University of London.

—— (1986), *Nung Leuang Nung Dam: Tamnaan kho'ng Phuunam Chaonaa haeng*

Laannaa Thai (Dressed in Yellow, Dressed in Black: Chronicles of a Northern Thai Farmers' Leader), Bangkok: Sangsan.

Thai Volunteer Service (1987), *Thamniab Ongkaan Phatthanaa Ekachon nai Prathet Thai (Directory of Non-governmental Development Organizations in Thailand)*, Bangkok: Khor Or Sor (TVS).

Thawithong Hongwiwat (ed.) (1984), *Kaanmiisuanruam kho'ng Prachaachon nai Kaanphatthanaa (People's Participation in Development)*, proceedings of a seminar on 'Community Participation: Policies and Methods', held at the Public Health Policy Study Centre, Mahidol University, Bangkok.

Thongchai Winichakul (1988), 'Siam Mapped: A History of the Geobody of Siam', unpublished Ph.D. thesis, University of Sydney.

Turton, Andrew (1975), 'Northern Thai Peasant Society: A Case Study of Jural and Political Structures at the Village Level and their Twentieth Century Transformations', unpublished Ph.D. dissertation, University of London.

_____ (1984a), *Popular Participation in Rural Thailand: An Overview Report*, Geneva: UNRISD Popular Participation Programme.

_____ (1984b), 'Limits of Ideological Domination and the Formation of Social Consciousness', in Andrew Turton and Shigeharu Tanabe (eds.), *History and Peasant Consciousness in Southeast Asia*, Osaka: National Museum of Ethnography (Senri Ethnological Studies 13).

_____ (1989), 'Local Powers and Rural Differentiation', in Gillian Hart, Andrew Turton and Benjamin White (eds.), *Agrarian Transformations: Local Processes and the State in Southeast Asia*, Berkeley: University of California Press.

Uhlig, Harald (ed.) (1984), *Spontaneous and Planned Settlement in Southeast Asia*, Hamburg: Institute of Asian Affairs.

UNRISD (United Nations Research Institute for Social Development) (1978), *Proposed UNRISD Research Programme on Participation*, Geneva.

Uthaithani Provincial Administration (1977), *Phaen Phathanaa Changwad Uthaithani Phor Sor 2520–2524 (Uthaithani Provincial Development Plan 1977–1981)*.

Vanpen Surarerks (1986), *Historical Development and Management of Irrigation Systems in Northern Thailand*, Chiengmai: Department of Geography.

Wattana Wattanwijarn *et al.* (1985), 'Detection of Virus in the Snakehead Fish During a Disease Epizootic by Light and Electron Microscopy', *Natural History Bulletin of the Siam Society*, Vol. 33.

White, Ben (1989), 'Problems in the Empirical Analysis of Agrarian Differentiation', in Gillian Hart, Andrew Turton and Benjamin White (eds.), *Agrarian Transformations: Local Processes and the State in Southeast Asia*, Berkeley: University of California Press.

Wilson, David (1962), *Politics in Thailand*, Ithaca: Cornell University Press.

Witayakorn Chiangkul (1983), *The Effects of Capitalist Penetration on the Transformation of the Agrarian Structure in the Central Region of Thailand (1960–1980)*, The Hague: Institute of Social Studies.

Withaya Sucharithanarugse (1984), 'The Idea of Power in Thai Society', in B. J. Terwiel, *Development Issues in Thailand*, Gaya: Centre for Southeast Asian Studies.

Wolf, Eric (1966), *Peasants*, Englewood Cliffs: Prentice Hall.

Worsley, Peter (1984), *The Three Worlds: Culture and World Development*, London: Weidenfeld and Nicholson.

Young, Stephen (1968), 'The Northeastern Thai Village: A Non-participatory Democracy', *Asian Survey*, Vol. 8.

Zimmerman, Carl (1931), *Siam Rural Economic Survey*, Bangkok: Bangkok Times Press.

Index

ACCUMULATION, 138, 189
Agriculture, 2; capitalist development of, 6, 12, 38, 196, 202, 208; choice in, 92–4, 196; diversification of, 2, 41ff., 60, 65, 199; expansion of area, 33, 39ff., 42; extension work, 46, 81–2, 109; inputs, 12, 21, 41, 74, 77, 99, 105, 106–8, 117, 127, 134, 137, 201; intensification, 41, 157; investment, 45; productivity, 45; yields, 12, 44–5, 46, 60, 65, 74, 77
Akin Rabibhatana, 19, 23, 51
ALRO (Agricultural Land Reform Office), 21, 49, 62, 72–4, 76, 82–3, 94–7, 101, 122, 130–2, 137, 158, 160, 172, 200, 209, 227–8
Ambiguity, 184
Amin, Samir, 185
Anan Ganjanapan, 27–8, 32, 92, 157
Ananya Bhuchongkul, 34, 38, 111, 138, 157
Ao raeng see Labour, reciprocal
Apichaat Thongyuu, 29
Atavism, 86
Attitudes, of officials, 82–3
Ayuthaya, 19, 35, 50

BAAC (BANK FOR AGRICULTURE AND AGRICULTURAL CO-OPERATIVES), 21, 23, 81, 99–105, 123–5, 130, 131, 134, 145n., 178, 181n., 201–2, 219; access to credit, 27, 132; and inputs, 109, 200; groups, 161, 165–7
Bamrung Bunpanya, 192
Ban Dong, 69
Ban Mai, 72
Ban Rai, 3, 57, 142
Bangkok, 10, 19, 22, 34, 35, 40, 49, 71, 74, 111, 130, 131, 134, 143, 157, 198, 208
Banks, commercial, 99
Boonchana Klankamsorn, 10
Borrowing, 140, 141–2, 167
Buddhism, 12, 24, 31n., 47, 48, 52, 155, 160, 162
Buffalo, 64, 71, 109, 119, 121, 122, 132, 167; theft, 140
Buffalo bank, 81, 84, 85, 170–1, 194, 220, 227
Buijs, D., 185
Bung Khiew Irrigation Channel, 158, 172–6, 179, 220
Bureaucracy, 16, 19, 20, 21, 23, 24, 51, 55n., 82, 98, 181n., 186, 189, 202–3, 225, 228
Burma, 40, 54n., 149

CANALS, 40, 49
Capital, 98–110, 114, 137, 143–4
Capitalism, 6, 8, 11, 18, 20, 29, 90, 102, 149, 159, 188, 195
Cassava, 32, 41–3, 50, 66, 70, 73, 87n., 110, 127, 128
Central Plains, 2, 3, 25, 33, 35, 36, 38, 40, 43, 49, 60, 65, 111, 143
Chai-anan Samudavanija, 19, 23, 32, 51, 184
Chainat, 41, 69, 122, 133, 174
Chambers, Robert, 5, 185, 216
Chaonaa (rice farmer), 118, 227
Chaophraya Dam, 41, 46, 86n.
Chaophraya River, 3, 56
Chaorai (non-rice farmer), 126, 227
Charcoal, 77, 87n., 115–16, 121, 140
Chatthip Nartsupha, 32, 152
Chayan Vaddhanaphuti, 18, 35, 51
Chayanov, A., 91
Chin, S. C., 44
China, 23, 48
Chinese, ethnic, 19, 83, 156
Chit Nilaphanich, 190, 193
Chonburi, 39, 43, 48
Chulalongkorn, 19
Clark, W. C., 230
Class, 6, 19, 27–8, 83, 91, 178, 186, 196, 226
Commercialization *see* Agriculture, capitalist development of
Community, 5, 91, 212
Competitions, 159, 213–16

Conklin, Harold C., 44
Consumerism, 123, 141, 157, 159, 185, 199, 215
Control, 10, 92, 195; and participation, 201–12; by state, 14, 34, 48, 62, 97, 165, 200, 207, 212, 215–16; over labour, 110–15, 135, 199; over resources, 10, 30, 76, 77, 85–6, 90, 92ff., 117, 139, 144, 177, 224; over tillage, 137
Co-operation, 16, 148ff.; and change, 156–8; and participation, 197–8; traditional, 152–3
Co-operatives, 101, 149, 180n.
Cotton, 73, 109, 127
CPT (Communist Party of Thailand), 12, 21, 23, 50, 51, 54n., 151, 181 n., 221n.
Credit, 12, 21, 27, 74, 99, 100
Crop prices, 208
Cropping patterns, 118
Culture, and forest settlement, 47–8

DEBT, 27, 38, 66, 79, 95, 96, 110, 119, 121, 126, 131, 132, 137 142, 198, 199; cycle, 103, 219; repayment, 103–5
Deforestation, 10, 32, 41, 60, 72, 115; causes, 2, 33ff., 75; effects, 75; extent, 33ff.; in Lan Sak, 3, 56, 75
Demaine, Harvey, 8, 49
Democracy, 12, 15, 221n.
Developers, 20ff., 81–3
Development: and groups, 158ff., and moral values, 14, 160; and production, 89–90; dilemmas of, 1, 2, 3, 225; ecological aspects of, 2, 52–3; ideas about, 6, 8, 10ff.; incorporative, 3, 5, 10, 85; national, 2; participatory, 6, 28ff., 84–5; plans, 2, 10, 161; rural, 2, 4–6, 9ff., 16, 21–5, 30, 52–3, 67, 79, 81, 84–6, 90, 161, 200, 201, 206, 216; state-led, 12, 16, 18, 21, 86; structures, 16ff.; uneven, 2
Differentiation, social, 14, 25, 27, 78, 90–2, 95, 117ff., 144, 160, 177, 179, 199, 207, 212
Dilemmas of development, 1, 2, 3, 225
Discourse, 5, 8, 12ff., 19, 152, 160, 179, 182n., 194, 210, 217, 231
District administration, 16, 50, 81–2, 175, 203, 209–10, 213
Diversification of agriculture, 2, 41ff., 60, 65, 199
Douglass, Mike, 18
Drought, 60, 121–2, 124

ECONOMISM, 144n.
Education, 19, 20, 122
EEC (European Economic Community), 43
Electrification, 13, 70, 73, 127, 133, 159, 200
Embree, John, 151
Employment, 71
Environment, 2, 75–6; degradation, 44, 60, 63, 74, 90, 117, 145n., 207
Evers, Hans-Dieter, 151

FAO, 9
Farmers' Marketing Organization, 101
Farmers' associations, 101
Feder, Gershon, 49
Feeny, David, 33, 34, 39, 44, 45, 46, 51
Fences, 179, 213–14, 218
Fertilizer, 12, 41, 64, 74, 103, 105, 109
FFT (Farmers' Federation of Thailand), 181n., 222n.
Field crops, 65ff., 74, 77, 126; *see also* Upland crops
Floods, 60, 70, 73, 75, 121
Forest: as refuge, 51–2; encroachment, 33, 200; ideas about, 47–8
Foucault, Michel, 216
Fragmentation, 226
Fuel, 115–16

GIDDENS, ANTHONY, 117
Girling, John, 19, 41, 43, 111, 203
Goldberg, Ray A., 50
Goulet, Denis, 9
Groups, 99, 149; housewives', 81, 125, 161, 164–5, 202, 219; ideas about, 158ff.; indigenous, 163, 171–2; NGO, 162–3, 167–71; official, 161–2, 164–7, 189, 202, 213; permanent, 165
Growth, 8, 10, 11, 22, 28, 184, 188

HAINSWORTH, GEOFFREY B., 8, 207
Hanks, Lucien, 33, 36, 38, 49, 51
Hardin, G., 77
Harriss, John, 90
Hart, Gillian, 91, 92
Health, 110
Heyer, Judith, 18
Hire-purchase, 101
Hirsch, P., 48, 98
Hmong, 35
Hong Lysa, 18
Housewives' groups, 81, 125, 161, 164–5, 202, 219

IBRD (WORLD BANK), 2, 9, 22, 25, 41, 65, 188
Ideology, 11ff., 31n., 91–2, 178, 186
Imperata, 44, 105
Incomes, 11
India, 45
Individualism, 36, 146n., 150, 155–6, 157, 159–61, 201

Individualization, 148
Indonesia, 92
Industrialization, 8, 22, 184
Inequality, 10–11, 16, 25–7
'Influence', 77, 96, 211
Infrastructure, 33, 35, 49
Ingram, James, 10, 40, 41
Irrigation, 41, 45, 64, 70, 71, 98, 118–19, 154, 157, 163, 172ff.

JAPAN, 43
Johnston, David Bruce, 32, 34, 37, 40, 43, 46, 49, 152
Johnston, B. F., 230

KAMNAN, 16, 28, 172, 174, 176, 179, 181n., 182n., 192, 203ff., 211, 213–15
Kamphaengphet, 142
Kanchanaburi, 43, 48, 67
Karen, 35, 57, 71, 122
Kemp, Jeremy, 36
Kenaf, 43, 54n.
Khan, Sadruddhin, 3
Kinship, 129, 156, 201
Klum *see* Groups
Knowledge, 77, 109, 116–17, 209
Korat, 110

LABOUR: as commodity, 90, 115, 159, 207; control over, 110–15; household, 25, 38, 43, 74, 78, 91, 103, 110–11, 123, 132, 146n., 198–9; management, 114–15; reciprocal, 74, 78, 111–14, 119, 121, 122, 123, 126, 153–4, 156–8, 196, 198–9; slave, 34, 38, 198–9; status, 198–9; wage, 25, 27, 34, 71, 74, 112–14, 121, 122, 124, 125, 196, 198, 208
Lan Sak, 3ff.; cultivation in, 63–7, 90, 92, 224; development in, 81–5, 163ff.; participation in, 192–4, 195, 198–201; resource depletion, 139–43; settlement of, 56–63, 171; social structure, 117ff., 152–8; violence in, 211
Land: concentration, 79; disputes, 37, 56, 62; in Lan Sak, 94–7; inheritance, 95, 145n.; levelling, 98; ownership, 86n., 97, 118, 136–7, 143; preparation, 127; prices, 60, 62, 87n., 95, 198; reform, 10, 21, 72, 80, 129, 205; rental, 96–7, 121, 139; settlement, 3, 9, 32ff., 49–50; shortage, 32, 41, 60, 110; tenure, 25, 34, 70, 99; title, 34, 70, 76, 94; concentration, 26, 136
Landlessness, 25, 49, 52, 59, 70, 96–7, 120, 126, 129, 142
Lao, 57, 59, 60, 62, 67, 70, 122, 124, 136, 153, 155, 156, 204
Laos, 57
LDAP (Local Development Assistance Programme), 179, 182n.
Leadership, 67, 79–80, 85, 170, 183, 189, 203–7, 215, 222n., 230
Legitimacy, 14, 92, 163, 191, 201, 210, 228, 229
Lenin, V. I., 90–1
Lightfoot, Paul, 27, 99
Lipton, Michael, 185
Livestock rearing, 67, 71
Local administration, 17
Local powers, 92, 212, 217
Lohmann, L., 48
Lopburi, 102

MAIZE, 32, 35, 41–3, 50, 60, 66, 70, 73, 75, 87n., 110, 127, 128; harvesting, 115, 128; planting, 74
Malaria, 56, 59
Malaysia, 45, 136, 143
Marketing, 35
Marzouk, G. A., 33
Mechanization, 27, 46, 116, 119, 126
Mehta, Niranjan, 195
Middle East, employment, 74, 143, 147n., 155
Middlemen, 119, 101–4, 208
Migration, 36, 51, 60, 75, 90, 142–3, 155, 200, 226
Military, 23, 31n., 81, 82, 146–7n., 162
Moerman, Michael, 35, 92, 140
Monarchy, 19, 189, 215
Moral economy, 149–50
Morell, David, 19, 32, 51, 184
Muecke, Marjorie, 162
Mung beans, 65, 66, 70, 73, 109, 120, 127; harvesting, 115

NAKORN SAWAN, 120, 142, 168
Nart Tuntawiroon, 33, 48
National development, 2
National Development Plans, 2, 21, 24, 53
National security, 11, 14, 21, 52
NESDB (National Economic and Social Development Board), 10, 17, 20, 22, 53, 79, 189, 203
Ng, Ronald, 34–5, 36
NGOs (non-governmental organizations), 12, 15, 21, 23–5, 53, 67, 81, 130, 151, 161–3, 178–9, 196, 228; projects in Lan Sak, 167–71
NICs (newly industrialized countries), 2, 7n.
NKYFRD (Nong Kha Yang Foundation for Rural Development), 81, 167ff., 173–6, 220, 227–8, 230
Nong Chang, 59, 65, 69–70, 80, 102, 119, 120, 125, 129

Nong Kha Yang, 129
North Thailand, 25, 33, 34, 35, 49, 151
North-east Thailand, 10, 21, 25, 33, 34–5, 36, 41, 48, 151
NSO (National Statistical Office), 60

OFF-FARM EMPLOYMENT, 67, 74, 111

PAAK MEUANG, 62, 65, 70, 81, 102, 103, 125, 132, 154, 166
Paedriw (Chachoengsao), 38
Pakistan, 45
Palmer, I., 185
Panayotou, Theodor, 10, 25
Parkin, David, 13, 16
Participation, 3, 14, 24, 183ff.; and control, 201–12; and co-operation, 197–8; and development, 6, 28ff., 184–9, 219–20; and power, 186–7, 189, 191, 212–18; and production, 195–7; and the State, 188, 212–16; implications, 229–31; in Lan Sak 192–4, 198–201; in Thailand, 188–92; interpretations, 3, 9, 184–8, 194–201; obstacles, 226–8
Pathaan Suwannamongkol, 193
Patron–client relations *see* Patronage
Patronage, 39, 79, 92, 102, 103, 201
Pearse, Andrew, 9, 186–8
Peasant economy, 149–58
Peasantry, 19, 34, 150–1, 222n.; and production, 5, 147n.
Pei Shang-ji, 48
Pelzer, K., 45
Periphery, 2, 3, 9, 32, 46, 52
Pesticides, 12, 41, 46, 65, 74, 105, 120, 128, 146n.
Petchaboon, 142
Phaen din tham—Phaen din tho'ng programme, 14, 15, 83
Phairat Decharin, 190, 191
Philippines, 23, 45
Ploughing, 64, 71, 109–10, 111, 126, 128, 132, 135, 177
Police, 23, 37, 62, 77, 82, 211, 217
Popkin, Samuel, 149–51
Potter, Jack M., 151–2
Poverty, 25, 60
Power, 10, 15, 97, 129, 135, 186–7, 189, 191, 195; and participation, 186–7, 189, 212–18; and production, 217–18; bargaining, 161, 162, 183, 197, 211; decision making, 195
Power tillers, 109, 119, 123, 177
Production, 89ff.; and power, 217–18; and production, 5; relations of, 11, 18, 20, 88n., 94, 126, 139, 156, 159, 177, 188, 195, 204; and change, 78–9
Puey Ungpakorn, 23

RAILWAYS, 46, 49
Rainfall, 75, 87n.
Rangsit, 40, 45
REGP (Rural Employment Generation Programme), 181n., 209
Resistance, 6, 15, 194, 214, 217, 218, 222n.
Resources: and change, 76–8; control over, 10, 76, 85–6, 90, 94, 139, 144, 177, 224; external to village, 80, 207, 215; local, 139–41, 169, 204; management, 78; shortage, 139–43
Reynolds, Craig, 18
RFD (Royal Forestry Department), 48, 56
Rice bank, 81, 84, 85, 167–70, 178, 179, 194, 210, 220, 227, 229
Rice borrowing, 140; cultivation, 9, 44, 59, 63–5, 70, 77, 98, 109, 111, 118–19; expansion of economy, 32–4, 39ff.; harvesting, 153; marketing, 119; milling, 65, 77; planting, 75; premium, 41, 46, 54n.; price, 40, 46, 115; transplanting, 64
Rigg, Jonathan, 35
Roads, 13, 21, 34, 35, 37, 49–50, 57, 58, 62, 70, 73, 79, 82, 125, 143, 158, 171–2, 200
Rogers, Barbara, 165
Rural development, 2, 4, 5, 6, 9ff., 16, 21–5, 30, 52–3, 67, 79, 81, 84–6, 90, 161, 200, 201, 206, 216

SAKDINA, 19
Saneh Jamrik, 2, 191
Scott, James, 15, 143, 149–51, 194, 197, 218, 220
Seed, 105
Self-help, 14, 88n.
Self-reliance, 5, 12, 15, 24, 71, 141, 222n.
Seni Saowaphong, 148
Settlement: of Lan Sak, 56ff., 69–70; patterns, 38, 62, 70, 71, 155, 200
settlers, 35, 36
Shaffer, B., 185
Share-cropping, 79, 96, 120, 121, 145n.
Sharp, Lauriston, 33, 36, 38, 49, 51
Shifting cultivation, 35, 44, 54n.
Siwarak Siwarom, 27–8
Social differentiation *see* Differentiation
Soil erosion, 76
Soil fertility, 75–6, 135
Sorghum, 66, 70, 73, 121
South Korea, 45
South Thailand, 34
Soya beans, 66, 73
Sri Lanka, 45, 182n.
Standardization, 214–15, 225
State: and development, 12, 18, 21, 138,

161–2, 178, 230; and participation, 188, 212–16; control by, 14, 34, 48, 62, 97, 165, 200, 207, 212, 215–16; formation, 6, 8, 11; nature of the Thai, 18, 31n.
Stiefel, Matthias, 9, 184, 185, 186–8
Stott, P. A., 44, 48
Students, role of, 23
Subsistence agriculture, 38, 59, 62, 78, 116, 131–2, 138, 139, 195
Sugar-cane, 32, 33, 39, 41, 43, 50, 66–7, 73, 87n., 96
Suphanburi, 45
Surveillance, 21, 211
Suthiporn Chirapanda, 25

TAIWAN, 43, 45
Tak, 142, 143
Takaya, Yoshikazu, 34, 45
Tambon council, 16, 17, 28, 81, 172, 175, 179, 181n., 190, 192–3, 200, 203, 227
Tambon doctor, 84, 88n., 110, 192, 217
Tanabe, Shigeharu, 33, 40
Tap Salao Dam, 75, 87n., 98
Tap Salao River, 59, 63–4, 67–70, 154, 171–2
Technocracy, 6, 20
Tenancy, 25
Thai economy, 1–2
Thai Volunteer Service, 24
Thailand, 45
Thawithong Hongwiwat, 9, 190, 191
Thongchai Winichakul, 10, 48
Threat, 211–12
Thung Khaa, 59, 72, 80
Timber concessions, 56, 76, 80; illegal trade, 56, 73, 74, 77, 80, 142, 205; local use, 70
TPC (Thai Plywood Company), 56, 60, 62–3, 70, 78, 87n., 172, 205
Tractors, 27, 38, 74, 84, 109, 111, 121, 128, 134, 135, 139, 159
Traders, 38, 62, 102, 121, 125, 134, 138, 199
Training, 13, 81–2, 160, 194, 283
Turton, Andrew, 9, 11, 12, 20, 35, 86, 92, 189, 193, 198, 206, 211–12, 228

UHLIG, HARALD, 32, 33, 35, 36, 38, 39, 41, 43, 44, 49, 50, 53, 65, 94
Uncertainty, 77, 207–12, 228
UNRISD (United Nations Research Institute for Social Development), 184, 186–8, 189, 192, 212
Upland crops, 32, 41ff.; *see also* Field crops
Urbanization, 8, 13, 19
Uthaithani, 3, 4, 56, 57, 58, 60, 62, 63, 67, 70, 75, 76, 81, 82, 102, 119, 125, 130, 143, 158, 160, 167, 174, 205, 227

VAN DER HEIDE SCHEME, 45–6
Vanpen Surarerks, 154
Vietnam, 150, 162, 181n.
Village committee, 16, 17, 28, 125, 134, 136, 138, 179, 192–3, 200, 205–6, 226–7
Village élites, 20, 28, 30, 78, 79, 86, 91–2, 151, 164, 189; head, 16, 28, 131, 133, 192, 203ff.; meeting, 193, 222n.; size, 156, 179, 201; structure, 149
Villagization, 63, 72
Violence, 37, 56, 62, 96, 141, 211

WAGE LABOUR *see* Labour
Wages, 115
Water, control over, 97–8
White, Ben, 91
Wildlife, 62, 63, 69, 76, 140
Wilson, David, 32
Withaya Sucharithanarugse, 22, 48, 51
Wolfe, Marshall, 185
Women, 141, 155, 164–5
Worsley, Peter, 6

YAANG RESIN, 59, 72, 76–7, 86n., 116, 172
Yields *see* Agriculture, yields
Young, Stephen, 212

ZIMMERMAN, CARL, 32